SOCIAL INCLUSION AND HIGHER EDUCATION

Edited by Tehmina N. Basit and Sally Tomlinson

First published in Great Britain in 2012 by

The Policy Press
University of Bristol
Fourth Floor
Beacon House
Queen's Road
Bristol BS8 1QU
UK

Tel +44 (0)117 331 4054
Fax +44 (0)117 331 4093
e-mail tpp-info@bristol.ac.uk
www.policypress.co.uk

North American office:
The Policy Press
c/o The University of Chicago Press
1427 East 60th Street
Chicago, IL 60637, USA
t: +1 773 702 7700
f: +1 773-702-9756
e:sales@press.uchicago.edu
www.press.uchicago.edu

British Library Cataloguing in Publication Data
A catalogue record for this book is available from the British Library.

Library of Congress Cataloging-in-Publication Data
A catalog record for this book has been requested.

ISBN 978 1 84742 797 7 hardcover

Cover design by The Policy Press.
Front cover: image kindly supplied by istock.com
Printed and bound in Great Britain by TJ International,
Padstow
The Policy Press uses environmentally responsible print
partners

We dedicate this book to our children and grandchildren.

May you inherit a world that is truly socially inclusive.

Contents

Foreword by David Watson   vii

Notes on contributors   ix

Introduction   1
Sally Tomlinson and Tehmina N. Basit

Part One: Issues in social inclusion

one   Capitals, ethnicity and higher education   17
      Tariq Modood

two   Widening participation from an historical perspective: 41
      increasing our understanding of higher education and
      social justice
      David W. Thompson

three   Broadening participation among women and racial/ethnic   65
      minorities in science, technology, engineering and maths
      Terrell L. Strayhorn, James M. DeVita and Amanda M. Blakewood

four   Social inclusion in a globalised higher education   83
      environment: the issue of equitable access to university in
      Australia
      Richard James

five   From minority to majority: educating diverse students in   109
      the United States
      Yolanda T. Moses

six   Equity, diversity and feminist educational research: enhancing   129
      the emerging field of pedagogical studies in higher education
      for social inclusion
      Miriam E. David

seven   Social justice as a matter of policy: higher education for the   149
      masses
      Trevor Gale and Deborah Tranter

Part Two: Perspectives on widening participation

eight   'I've never known someone like me go to university': class,   173
      ethnicity and access to higher education
      Tehmina N. Basit

nine   Widening participation in the higher education   193
      quasi-market: diversity, learning, and literacy
      Rob Smith

ten	*Para crecer*: successful higher education strategies used by Latina students	215
	Pamela Hernandez and Diane M. Dunlap	
eleven	Empowering non-traditional students in the UK: feedback and the hidden curriculum	237
	Andy Cramp	
twelve	Teaching Indigenous teachers: valuing diverse perspectives	255
	Ninetta Santoro, Jo-Anne Reid, Laurie Crawford and Lee Simpson	
thirteen	Widening access to higher education through partnership working	273
	Jaswinder K. Dhillon	
fourteen	Higher education, human rights and inclusive citizenship	295
	Audrey H. Osler	
Index of authors		313
Index of subjects		317

Foreword

David Watson

The intertwined issues of access, widening participation, social justice and social mobility, as they affect and are affected by higher education, wax and wane in intensity and importance in differing national contexts and at different times. Currently they are often very 'hot', and nowhere more so than in the UK. Here, a Conservative–Liberal Democratic Coalition government has proved itself a global outlier in terms of positioning higher education as part of a response to the mix of economic downturn, international tensions and rapid development of information and communications technologies that characterises the second decade of the 21st century. The system is to be rationed, marketised (without in fact trusting the consumers to make the correct choice of institution, subject or mode of study) and significantly deregulated, with historical patterns of public investment replaced by a precarious formula for co-payment.

What this odd mixture of national priorities will produce in terms of who wants to and who does get in to higher education, what they receive, and what the effects will be on public and private returns across the spectrum of health, happiness and democratic tolerance, as well as economic prosperity, is deeply uncertain. Meanwhile, other richer and poorer countries are united in a sense that continuing to invest in higher education has to be part of the solution to the challenges of economic recovery and social cohesion rather than simply an obstacle in the path of rapidly fixing public expenditure.

Meanwhile, the educational research literature presents no clear-cut solutions to the problems of variable aspiration, of variable resources (financial and moral) and of varying levels of achievement and reward for groups across society seeking (or not seeking) and succeeding (or failing) to capitalise on the potential benefits of post-compulsory learning. This is apparently not for want of trying, and any new book on the issue has to offer more than simply a recapitulation of the perennial themes. The equation is highly complex, with variables including class, ethnicity, gender, age, subject of study and location. The policy options all present wicked issues of distribution and effect (eg how to advantage the disadvantaged without further advantaging the already advantaged). And the practice can be confused, as initiatives in admissions, in pedagogy and in assessment can confound the worthy intentions of their designers.

However, I do believe that this collection helps to significantly move us forward, not least because of its avowed focus on the 'voices of students and staff' in universities in the UK, the US and Australia. All too frequently, policy and practice in these contentious areas has been something done to and for, rather than with and by, the participants. Instead, the editors and authors of this work have taken a rigorously participative and bottom-up approach, to good effect. I commend their work to all serious and thoughtful students of the subject.

Sir David Watson
Principal of Green Templeton College, Oxford
1 June 2011

Notes on contributors

Professor Tehmina N. Basit

Tehmina Basit is Professor of Education and Director of the Institute for Education Policy Research at Staffordshire University. She has previously held posts at Keele University, Manchester Metropolitan University, University of Leicester, and University of Wolverhampton. Her PhD at the University of Cambridge examined the educational, social and career aspirations of teenage Muslim girls in Britain. Her research interests include: the education of minority ethnic groups; race and ethnicity; gender; social class; citizenship and young people; social justice; social inclusion; initial teacher training; the professional development of teachers; and qualitative research methodology. She has directed a number of externally funded regional and national research projects. Her latest book, *Conducting Research in Educational Contexts* (2010) was published by Continuum.

Amanda M. Blakewood

Amanda Blakewood is a PhD candidate in Higher Education Administration and Research Associate for the Center for Higher Education Research and Policy (CHERP) at the University of Tennessee in Knoxville. Her research interests include: identity development for college students; gender issues in science, technology, engineering and maths (STEM) education; and college student retention for targeted populations in higher education. Amanda received her BA degree from the University of Central Florida and her MS degree from the University of Tennessee in Knoxville in College Student Personnel.

Dr Andy Cramp

Andy Cramp is currently Head of MA Education Studies at the University of Wolverhampton. He has worked in a range of education settings across sectors. He started his teaching career as an English lecturer while working on a PhD. He then trained as a secondary school teacher and taught English to speakers of other languages (ESOL) in Tanzania as a volunteer. On his return to England, he taught ESOL and English Literature in colleges in London. After 15 years in further education, he moved back into the university sector. Andy has a lifelong commitment to outdoor learning and is passionate about encouraging learning informally and unconventionally. His research interests lie in these areas and in education for social justice and sustainability.

Laurie Crawford

Laurie Crawford is a Gamilaroi man from Western New South Wales. He trained as a teacher in the early 1980s and taught in rural primary schools before becoming a teacher educator at Charles Sturt University, Australia, where he has taught Indigenous Studies and Primary School curricula to pre-service teachers.

Professor Miriam E. David

Miriam David, PhD, AcSS, FRSA, is Professor Emerita of Education and was Professor (2005–10) and Associate Director (Higher Education) of the ESRC's Teaching & Learning Research Programme (2004–09) at the Institute of Education, University of London. She is a visiting professor in the Centre for Higher Education & Equity Research (CHEER), University of Sussex. She is a Fellow of the Royal Society of Arts, an Academician of the Academy of Social Sciences and was awarded an honorary degree of doctor of education by the University of Bedfordshire (2009). She was chair of the Council of the Academy of Social Sciences (AcSS) from 2005 to 2009 and is on the Governing Council of the Society for Research in Higher Education (SRHE). She is renowned for her feminist educational research on gender, social diversity and inequalities. She has published widely including an intellectual biography in 2003 *Personal and Political: Feminisms, Sociology and Family Lives* (Stoke-on-Trent: Trentham Books).

Assistant Professor James M. DeVita

James DeVita is a clinical Assistant Professor of Higher Education at Iowa State University and affiliate of the Center for Higher Education Research and Policy (CHERP) at the University of Tennessee in Knoxville. His research interests include: identity development for college students; research pedagogy in graduate preparation programmes; and issues of transition, access and retention for targeted populations in higher education. James received his BA degree in History and Sociology-Anthropology from Colgate University and both his MS and PhD degrees from the University of Tennessee in Knoxville in College Student Personnel/Higher Education.

Dr Jaswinder K. Dhillon

Jaswinder Dhillon has worked as a lecturer and teacher educator in adult, further and higher education. Her research interests include partnership working, social capital, social inclusion, social justice, teaching and learning and qualitative research methodology. Her PhD from the University of Warwick examined partnership working in post–16 learning. She is currently course leader for the MA in Higher Education at the University of Wolverhampton and contributes to teaching on the EdD in Educational Enquiry. She enjoys working in different countries and has experience of teaching in Holland, China and the Solomon Islands.

Professor Diane M. Dunlap

Diane Dunlap recently retired as Professor of Educational Leadership at the University of Oregon where she was professor and an academic administrator for more than 30 years. She specialises in the study and practice of mastery learning experiences and is particularly interested in extending such experiences to traditionally underserved or historically less successful populations in higher education. Her PhD in Educational Policy and Administration was from the University of Oregon in 1980. She is the author or co-author of four books, numerous book chapters, and more than 60 refereed articles and papers. She now makes her home in Maryland.

Professor Trevor Gale

Trevor Gale is Professor of Education Policy and Social Justice at Deakin University and the editor of *Critical Studies in Education* (founded in 2007). He was the founding Director of Australia's National Centre for Student Equity in Higher Education (2008–11) and is a past President of the Australian Association for Research in Education (2005). A policy sociologist with research interests in social justice in schooling and higher education, he is author and co-author of six books and over 150 chapters, journal articles and other research publications. His latest books are *Schooling in Disadvantaged Communities* (Springer, 2010) with Carmen Mills, and *Educational Research by Association* (Sense, 2010) with Bob Lingard. His views on student equity are regularly sought by government and the media, and he is a regular keynote speaker at national and international conferences.

Pamela Hernandez

Pamela Hernandez is a doctoral student in the University of Maryland, College Park Higher Education program, and received her MS in Educational Leadership and Policy Studies from the University of Oregon. She has experience in K-12 and higher education systems, having worked in the US private and public higher education institutions and local school districts. She was a University of Maryland, College Park, staff member for three years as the Coordinator for

Latino/a Student Involvement and Advocacy before deciding to pursue the doctoral degree full time. In this role, she advised multicultural and multi-ethnic students and organisations, managed large-scale event programmes, created a Latino-based community-service learning and leadership development programme, and initiated learning outcomes assessments and research for her unit. Her research interest is to explore Latina college women's strategies to access, and to successfully graduate from, a higher education institution.

Professor Richard James

Richard James is Pro Vice-Chancellor (Participation and Engagement), Professor of Higher Education and Director of the Centre for the Study of Higher Education at the University of Melbourne. His research interests include: access and participation; the quality of the student experience; and students' post-compulsory education choices. He has authored numerous research reports of national significance in Australian higher education as well as over 75 articles and chapters. His recent work has included: influential national studies of equity and university student finances; policy development work for the Indigenous Higher Education Advisory Council; and key advisory roles to government and universities on enhancing teaching and learning in higher education. Within the University of Melbourne, he has a leadership role in curriculum transformation and access programmes.

Professor Tariq Modood

Tariq Modood, MBE, AcSS, is Professor of Sociology, Politics and Public Policy and the founding Director of the Centre for the Study of Ethnicity and Citizenship at the University of Bristol. His recent publications include *Multiculturalism: A Civic Idea* (2007) and *Still Not Easy Being British: Struggles for a Multicultural Citizenship* (2010); and as co-editor, *Secularism, Religion and Multicultural Citizenship* (2009) and *Global Migration, Ethnicity and Britishness* (2011). He is a regular contributor to the media and policy debates in Britain, was awarded an MBE for services to social sciences and ethnic relations in 2001 and elected a member of the Academy of Social Sciences in 2004. He served on the Commission on the Future of Multi-Ethnic Britain, the Institute for Public Policy Research Commission on National Security and on the National Equality Panel, which reported to the UK Deputy Prime Minister in 2010.

Professor Yolanda T. Moses

Yolanda Moses is Professor at the Department of Anthropology, University of California, Riverside, and Associate Vice Chancellor for Diversity, Excellence and Equity. She is Chair of the National Advisory Board of the American Anthropological Association's project, 'Race: Are we so Different?'. This is a multi-faceted award-winning public education initiative that is changing the way Americans talk about and understand race in the United States. See www.understandingrace.org. She is a co-author of the book, *How Real is Race? A Sourcebook on Race, Culture and Biology* (2007), and in press, *Race: Are we so Different?* (2012). She is the former President of the American Association for Higher Education, President of the City University of New York: The City College and President of the American Anthropological Association (1995–97). In 2009 she was named a fellow of the American Association for the Advancement of Science. She was a member of the board of the Ford Foundation from 1996 to 2008. She is a regular faculty member in the Salzburg Global Seminar's ISP Global Citizen Program. She was presented with the Donna Shavlik Award for National Leadership for Women by the American Council on Education in 2007.

Professor Audrey H. Osler

Audrey Osler is Professor of Education and was founding Director of the Centre for Citizenship and Human Rights Education at the University of Leeds. She teaches on the interdisciplinary MSc Human Rights and Multiculturalism at Buskerud University College, Norway. In 2010, she was Visiting Professor at Utah State University and at Hong Kong Institute of Education. Her books include *Students' Perspectives on Schooling* (2010); *Teachers and Human Rights Education* (2010, with Hugh Starkey); *Changing Citizenship: Democracy and Inclusion in Education* (2005, with Hugh Starkey); *Teachers, Human Rights and Diversity: Educating Citizens in Multicultural Societies* (2005); and the prize-winning *Girls and Exclusion: Rethinking the Agenda* (2003, with Kerry Vincent). In 2011 she co-edited a special edition of *Education, Citizenship and Social Justice* on 'Education, human rights and social justice in East Asia' with Yan Wing Leung.

Professor Jo-Anne Reid

Jo-Anne Reid is Associate Dean of Education and Professor in the Faculty of Education at Charles Sturt University, Australia. She is interested in theories of social identity and subjectivity, and in the potential of post-structuralist theories of practice for rethinking schooling and difference. She has been continuously in receipt of research funding for the past 15 years, through University and National Competitive Grants and has published a wide range of articles and book chapters in the areas of teacher education, rural education, literacy education and research methodologies. Among her publications are: *100 Children Go to School* (1998) and *100 Children Turn 10* (2002), *Managing (Small Group) Learning* (2002) and *Literacies in Place* (2007).

Associate Professor Ninetta Santoro

Ninetta Santoro is Head of the School of Teacher Education at Charles Sturt University, Australia. Her research interests include how teacher identities are constructed and taken up within multi-ethnic educational milieus, the preparation of teachers for culturally diverse education contexts and issues of social inclusion, including Indigenous education and the education of refugees in rural Australia. She has published widely in the areas of difference and diversity within adult and secondary education, teacher education and qualitative research methodologies. She is currently a co-editor of the *Asia Pacific Journal of Teacher Education* and a member of the Research Institute for Professional Practice, Learning and Education at Charles Sturt University.

Lee Simpson

Lee Simpson is a Gureng woman from South East Queensland who graduated as a teacher in the late 1980s. She taught for five years in primary schools before becoming a teacher educator at Charles Sturt University and, more recently, at the University of Melbourne, Australia. She currently works as a senior administrator in Aboriginal Health and is completing a PhD in Education.

Dr Rob Smith

Rob Smith started his career teaching English in secondary schools in Birmingham, West Midlands. A decade of working in the further education sector involved him in the industrial relations issues of the time as a trade union (NATFHE) activist. His doctorate is based on what happened in the further education sector at that time. He is now a Senior Lecturer in Post Compulsory Education in the School of Education at the University of Wolverhampton. His current research interests centre on the tensions within higher and further education between educational and democratic values and the policy of marketisation, and the different identities that this tension gives rise to. Recent work through the Literacy Study Group has focused on the impact of market conditions on Literacy Education in further education settings.

Associate Professor Terrell L. Strayhorn

Terrell Strayhorn is Associate Professor of Higher Education, and African and African American Studies, at the Ohio State University, Director of the Center for Higher Education Research and Policy (CHERP), and Faculty Affiliate of the Kirwan Institute for the Study of Race and Ethnicity. Author/editor of five books, over 75 refereed journal articles and chapters, and over 125 (inter)national conference presentations, he is regarded as one of the most highly visible and productive new scholars in his field. Grants in excess of $700,000 from the National Science Foundation, US Department of Education, Tennessee Higher Education Commission, and American College Personnel Association, to name but a few, support his research on the retention and success of historically under-represented groups in higher education, graduate student persistence, transitions from high school to and through college, and broadening participation of women and minority ethnic groups in STEM fields. In 2011, *Diverse Issues* named him one of 12 leading scholars in the nation.

Dr David W. Thompson

David Thompson has worked within the UK higher education sector since 1998 in a variety of roles. These have included: managing lifelong learning and widening participation projects; promoting flexible study opportunities for part-time students; developing work-based learning programmes; researching the needs of students from low participation neighbourhoods; designing and piloting institutional personal development plans (PDPs); and developing international strategy and relations. He is currently Senior Lecturer at the School of Education, University of Wolverhampton. His primary fields of research are in adult learning, social inclusion, the history of education, education studies and lifelong learning. In all of these themes, the articulation between higher education practice, policy and theory is of particular interest. His experiences as a mature student through Access, a first degree in history and a PhD in Education inform his practice and research areas.

Professor Sally Tomlinson

Sally Tomlinson is a Senior Research Fellow in the Department of Education, University of Oxford, and an Emeritus Professor at Goldsmiths College, University of London. During the 1990s, she was Goldsmiths Professor of Education Policy, Dean of Education and a Pro-Warden (Vice Principal) of the College. She is currently a Visiting Professor at the University of Wolverhampton and held a Leverhulme

Professorial Emeritus Fellowship (2009–10). She has taught, researched and published for over 30 years in the areas of education policy, race, ethnicity and education, special education and 14–19 education. She has been a Trustee of the Africa Educational Trust for 20 years, which among other activities prepares students in areas of conflict for higher education. Her latest book, *Race and Education: Policy and Politics in Britain* (2008), examines the contradictions and challenges facing educators in a multicultural society over the past 50 years and sets educational issues and events within a wider social and political context, taking account of national and global influences and changing political beliefs over the years.

Dr Deborah Tranter

Deborah Tranter is Director of Student Equity at the Australian National University. She has had an extensive career in planning and managing equity and access programmes in Australian higher education. Her recently completed PhD focused on the influence of disadvantaged school culture on students' higher education aspirations. She was a co-investigator on federally funded research into intervention strategies in schools to widen higher education participation. She is an active member and current Co-convener (Student Equity) of the Australian national network of Higher Education equity practitioners (EOPHEA) and regularly presents at national conferences on her research on student equity in higher education.

Introduction

Sally Tomlinson and Tehmina N. Basit

The key issue this book addresses is that of the experiences of students from what has been termed 'non-traditional[1] backgrounds' in institutions of higher education. Over the past 30 years there has been a considerable expansion of higher education worldwide – in public and private universities, liberal arts colleges, community colleges and others – and a corresponding increase in the numbers attending. Who has access to higher education, and acquires qualifications that on the whole still guarantee lifetime higher incomes and status, has generated much debate and political intervention. While the politics of access has largely been framed in the language of social equity, encouraging the inclusion of women and men from lower socio-economic groups, those from minority ethnic groups, those with disabilities, and mature people (see Williams, 1997; Tapper and Palfreyman, 2005; Marginson, 2011), there has been minimal focus on what actually happens to the students once they are in the institutions.

Widening participation to include groups of people who do not have a tradition of higher education in their families has, over the past 30 years, become official policy in many countries. It reflects notions of equity and social justice, and the idea that if higher education is a public good, and mainly publicly-funded, then no group should be excluded. It also reflects governmental anxieties that 'knowledge economies' need more students educated to higher levels to keep national economies competitive, whatever their background. While there is a very large literature on the expansion of higher education, its causes and likely consequences, there has been less focus on the actual experiences of students from these diverse backgrounds, what teaching and learning is offered, and how they and the staff teaching them perceive their higher educational experiences.

Many new universities in the UK, including the University of Wolverhampton and Staffordshire University, subscribe to a widening participation agenda. At the University of Wolverhampton in England, a 'new university' created from existing institutions in 1992 and taking in large numbers of mature students, especially women, and students from racial and ethnic minority groups, academic researchers had begun to research the experiences of their students and those in other similar institutions. It seemed timely to build on this research and

1

engage with others researching and writing about the experiences of 'non-traditional' students in higher education, both in the UK and other countries. While many issues surrounding the inclusion of these groups in higher education are broadly similar, there were particular similarities in the UK, the US and Australia, and contributors were invited from these countries. The social exclusion of diverse groups from higher education in these countries has deep historical and structural roots, and the focus of this book is on previous exclusion by social class, ethnicity and gender and on the experiences of those now 'included'. The contributors themselves illustrate diversity with regard to gender, ethnicity, nationality and type of higher education institution. They are citizens of the UK, the US and Australia, half are female and half male, and their ethnicities include white, Indian, Pakistani and dual-heritage British; white, African-American and Latin-American; and white, dual-heritage and Indigenous Australian.[2] Marginson, himself Australian, has perceptively noted that an understanding of global, mass higher education needs a new imagining of equity issues (Marginson, 2011, p 3). The contributions in this book represent some attempts to understand how the recipients of 'equity' experience the widening participation agenda in these three countries.

The expansion of higher education

Public education systems, as Green noted, must be understood in relation to the historical development of nation states, which embodied a 'new universalism that education was applicable to all groups in society and could serve a variety of social needs', albeit serving the interests of the dominant classes in society (Green, 1990, p 79). In Europe, higher education in universities, despite their religious and charitable origins, long remained the preserve of small groups of upper-class males. In America and Australia, despite initially embracing the European idea of what constituted a university, more egalitarian philosophies appealed. The structural elaboration of higher education systems can be explained, as Archer (1982) suggested, by a variety of theoretical constructs, which may need modifications over time as the interplay between social conditions, political and cultural dominance, and assertive vested interests changes. Explanations for expansion might include, for example, modernisation theory, human capital theory, social justice and human rights theory, among others.

Current understandings of expanded higher education systems and their widening access programmes are probably best understood as closely related to the rise of competitive market ideologies, which place education change firmly under economic imperatives, and to ideologies of globalisation. Halsey pointed out that post-Second World War there had been a remarkable transformation of education related to political understandings of economic development, and that while more opportunities had been offered to women, working–class men and people from minority ethnic groups, the main thrust had been to enhance the 'quality of the workforce' (Halsey, 1997). Much of the current expansion is predicated on political claims that economic development and competition in a global economy require more people to be educated to higher levels, and that labour markets require enterprising workers fit for a globalising knowledge-based economy (Jessop, 2002, p 168).

However, there are also social justice and human rights claims that governments can no longer depend on a 'strategic management of ignorance among vast tracts of populations' (Archer, 1988, p 190). This is certainly illustrated by chapters in this volume, which show the assertion of women and people from minority ethnic groups, who no longer accept either their subordinate structural or cultural position. Allied to this are wider understandings that development of one's own individual human capital is a necessity for economic and social survival. A global consequence of expansion is that governments, having stressed the importance of higher education for all, now find that formerly excluded groups demand more of it. This results in vastly increased expenditure and, in the UK especially, much conflict is centred around who will fund higher education expansion, and whether a widening participation agenda will slow down if self-funded participation does not generate expected rates of return. Governments are finding considerable contradictions between assumptions that higher education can be expanded and the relative autonomy of institutions to deny access if not adequately funded. Barnett (2011) has cogently pointed out that while not all higher education takes place in universities, it is the universities, which are currently entrepreneurial, bureaucratic and managerial institutions, where money is a major consideration.

Social justice, cultural capital and the public good

A hundred years ago in most countries it was unthinkable that higher education institutions should include many of the groups in question and questions of equity and social justice were only beginning to be raised. In the UK in the early 20th century, women had only recently been permitted to enter universities. Cambridge University in England allowed women to study, but refused to give them degrees until

1948. An Association to Promote the Higher Education of Working Class Men was formed by Labour supporters in 1903 and a Workers Education Association was set up in 1909 with university extension courses opened. Oxford University supported the opening of Ruskin College for working-class men, although it was funded by an American philanthropist. The view that British imperial subjects, apart from a few rich or important men, should be offered higher education was unthinkable, although, a hundred years later, over a hundred nationalities are represented in British universities. In the US, equality had long been a central element in understandings of justice (Kirp, 1982), although, as chapters in this book illustrate, achieving justice in terms of racial and gender equity is still problematic. In historical terms, a social inclusion and widening participation agenda for higher education is relatively recent, and is part of wider struggles for social justice and equality.

In the UK, the US and Australia, the increase in absolute numbers in higher education and their origins by social class and ethnic groups has been a focus for research and for government policy (Bradley et al., 2008; Browne, 2010; Sullivan et al., 2011). The higher social classes continue to benefit most from university expansion, and although higher education is still largely a public good, substantially financed by the state through general taxation, 'it is disproportionally consumed by the children of the middle classes' (Tapper and Palfreyman, 2005, Preface). Previously excluded groups now apply and enter, but they largely attend the newer and less prestigious institutions rather than the old traditional ones, and the barriers facing students from working-class and minority ethnic group backgrounds are complex (Gorard et al., 2006). Major theoretical explanations for the difficulties facing access by 'non-traditional' students have been drawn from Bourdieu and Passeron's demonstration that education is underpinned by an arbitrary cultural scheme that is actually based on power relations – who has the power to determine what sort of education is distributed to which groups. The reproduction of a dominant culture through education plays a major part in the reproduction of whole social systems (Bourdieu and Passeron, 1977; Bourdieu, 1997). Economic capital is important, but social, cultural and linguistic capital determine access at all levels of education systems. Educational advancement or exclusion depends on ostensibly fair meritocratic testing, but the education system as a whole depends on a cultural competence that it does not itself provide. Families who possess social and cultural 'capitals' pass this on to their children and an ostensibly democratic system legitimates exclusion at higher levels. While Bourdieu's ideas have been subject to much elaboration and debate, the chapters in this book indicate that 'non-traditional' groups and their families are not 'cultural dopes', but find ways of acquiring or sustaining forms of capital that encourage and sustain their participation in higher education. Tariq Modood in particular develops the intriguing notion of 'ethnic capital' (Chapter One), and Tehmina Basit advances the concept of 'aspirational capital' (Chapter Eight).

A widening participation agenda has inevitably been bound up with what governments and other influential players consider to be the major purposes of higher education. The ideal, if not the practice, had been what Barnett described as 'the opening up of critical dialogue such that the knowledge structures on which it [the university] is engaged come under the severest assaults' (Barnett, 2011, p 27). But, by the 1990s, just as student populations had expanded, state requirements for new funding streams (especially from the students themselves), the control of numbers and research policies, accountability for teaching, and the need for institutions to be entrepreneurial and for research to demonstrate relevance and impact changed the idea of a 'university'. Universities as critical centres of knowledge and power were giving way to state-sponsored notions of impact and relevance. In addition, as Nixon has cogently demonstrated, notions of higher education as a public good have been eroded by commercialism and competition (Nixon, 2010). Students increasingly regard the goal of attending university in economic terms. In the UK, requirements to pay higher fees caused student street protests, although, in the US, the issue was regarded with some incredulity, as students there were accustomed to paying fees – extremely high in the case of the most prestigious universities.

Widening access in the globalised world

The expansion of higher education and the inclusion of former excluded groups worldwide has been accompanied by an intensification of a hierarchy of higher education institutions. This includes private institutions, which now offer around a third of all higher education globally. A rhetoric of national economic requirements, the creation of a knowledge economy and the need to sustain a position as a 'world-class' university has encouraged institutions to place themselves as far as possible at the higher end of this pillar of institutions. Globally, older, traditional universities, claiming a monopoly on the most valuable forms of knowledge, attempt to set themselves apart from newer institutions, which increasingly offer accreditation for new or different kinds of knowledge. Football-style league tables and research rankings encourage universities to compete in the marketplace rather than in a public service context. In the UK, post-1992, a group of 20 prestigious universities designated themselves as the Russell Group, meeting originally in the Russell Hotel in London. While there was no corresponding MacDonald's Group, whose meeting in MacDonald's restaurants might have been a suitable global antidote to claims of superiority, the newer UK universities created other groups, notably a Million+ group of post-92 universities. In the US, the hierarchy of institutions, from the exclusive Ivy League universities, through other private and state universities, to the four- and two-year community colleges, was already well known. In Australia, Marginson noted that the status hierarchy of universities creates profound obstacles to the achievement of equity policies overall. In terms of future jobs and life chances, 'Participation in a low-status institution is not the same as participation in a high-status institution' (Marginson, 2011, p 31). King (2009) has discussed this emerging global model of status hierarchies and competing world-class universities in the context of widening access and participation, and the goals of social inclusion. His view is that this global model does put these goals at risk as they are not issues that figure in league tables and rankings.

A major question worldwide is whether, in times of global economic recession, the expansion of higher education will slow down and whether students from both advantaged and less advantaged backgrounds will consider that a higher education is worthwhile. In all three countries studied here, it is the middle and upper social class groups who attend the more prestigious institutions, the most ambitious, as Ong put it, 'seeking to accumulate the world-class degrees and certificates that will open the door to a successful career in the international arena' (Ong, 2004, p 49). But the rates of return for having a higher education are complex for all social groups. In some cases, graduate unemployment is increasing and graduates are increasingly taking jobs for which degrees were not previously required, thus disadvantaging groups with lower qualification levels. If fees are raised and debt possibilities are higher, especially in times of economic recession, will non-traditional entry diminish and the widening participation agenda slow down? Or will there be, as the evidence so far indicates, more applications from potential students of all ages, if jobs are scarce or new skills are needed?

Higher education institutions are not only seen as an aid for disadvantaged individuals and groups, but also for whole regions. New universities and newer kinds of knowledge are increasingly regarded as crucial to the economic development of poorer regions (Charles, 2009). The Organisation for Economic Co-operation and Development

(OECD, 2007) has documented the dynamic effects expanding universities have on local and regional labour markets and the benefits to local civil society. While some courses may close and institutions may merge, there are no suggestions of lower student demand. It may be the case that a widening participation agenda will become part of a process of lifelong learning, as Schuller and Watson (2009) have suggested, in which institutions offering higher education, which include further education colleges and distance learning universities, become involved in national strategies for whole populations, rather than accepting the two-, three- or four-year course to be the start and end of higher education. This would help solve the 'fairness' issue of what happens to those who do not currently participate in higher levels of education. In the meantime, much will depend on what is actually offered to students from 'non-traditional' backgrounds and how they perceive and experience their higher education. The following chapters give some indication of what is happening in three different parts of the world.

The book

The book is divided into two sections. Although in the best academic traditions, theory and research can rarely be separated, some of the following chapters engage more with theoretical issues, while others detail empirical studies. Thus Part One discusses more theoretical issues of social inclusion, whereas Part Two considers empirical research on widening participation.

Tariq Modood introduces the theme of capital, ethnicity and higher education in Chapter One. He questions why some minority ethnic groups are over-represented in applications to higher education institutions and among higher education students in the UK, and others under-represented. Drawing on the concepts of cultural and social capital, he introduces the notion of 'ethnic capital'. He divides white cultural capital into two forms. The first is of working-class popular culture and the second is of middle-class culture. He argues that British parents of South Asian origin try to limit their children's exposure to the former and would like them to integrate into the latter, showing a determined effort to avoid one kind of dominant culture and embrace the other. He notes that minority ethnic groups in general, and South Asians in particular, appear to have a strong drive for qualifications, and considers why minority ethnic groups face an ethnic penalty regarding entry into prestigious universities and the subsequent financial gains expected by holders of degrees from such universities.

In Chapter Two, David Thompson discusses widening participation in higher education from an historical perspective. He argues that the marginalisation of activities to make university education more accessible, and the tensions between progressive and conservative opinion, have hindered widening participation and social justice for those at lower levels in the social class hierarchy. He highlights the differential participation between the middle and working classes, and the result of both discrimination and the hegemony of middle-class expectations. He offers readers the opportunity to understand the ways in which higher education developed and social exclusion was tackled in the UK, and the varying degrees of support or opposition from the educational, social and political establishments, and anticipates challenges in the future.

In Chapter Three, Terrell Strayhorn, James DeVita and Amanda Blakewood discuss the issue of broadening participation among women and minority ethnic groups in science, technology, engineering and maths (STEM)-related fields in the US. They observe that although the enrolment of women and minority ethnic groups on higher education courses has increased substantially over the last three decades, STEM degree completion rates show gender and ethnic disparities. They note that widening participation in STEM is viewed as a matter of accountability and global competitiveness, and STEM subjects enable women and under-represented groups to grow in ways that expand their pool of cultural and social capital, which can be turned into rewards and benefits for personal and national gain. Nevertheless, they point to the myriad barriers that women and minority ethnic groups encounter in STEM subjects, making it difficult to pursue diversity in these fields. They recommend the continuation of programmes to promote students' interest in STEM fields, early interventions to nurture students' interest in STEM subjects and information about STEM-related careers.

Richard James examines equitable access to higher education in Australia in Chapter Four. He demonstrates that, despite equity programmes, the same patterns of higher education expansion emerge worldwide, benefiting the higher socio-economic groups. He argues that an initial step towards more effective equity policies is to better theorise the precise nature of the problem. He identifies six myths that seem to permeate the views regarding equity in higher education, and which limit the capacity to consider more effective policies and initiatives. He points to the tension between equity and merit as they are currently conceived, yet notes that despite the apparently limited effects of the equity policy framework, it has persisted because it plays a symbolic role. He believes that the bold targets recommended by the Bradley review, which link expansion to equity following global patterns, especially in the UK, represent the first attempts towards the formulation of a policy framework to encourage universal participation in higher education in Australia.

Yolanda Moses considers the education of diverse students in the US in Chapter Five. She argues that although the US boasts a diverse range of higher education options such as community colleges, liberal arts colleges and public, comprehensive and for-profit institutions, many 'non-traditional' students do not, and cannot, take advantage of them. She presents a sobering picture of what the future may hold for first-generation minority ethnic and working-class students who may not be able to access higher education for financial reasons. Discussing the concepts of the engaged university and the engaged student, she calls for a holistic process of student engagement involving disciplinary, interdisciplinary and co-curricular studies, which should be part of the higher education experience to teach the students about themselves, their community and their world – knowledge that they should put to use as engaged citizens. She contends that higher education institutions have a moral imperative, and the talents, skills and resources, to provide the students with opportunities to achieve this.

Chapter Six by Miriam David is a memoir explaining how she became interested in gender issues, equality and higher education, and examines pedagogy in higher education in the UK context. She notes how feminist perspectives, along with other critical standpoints, have enhanced social and educational research, and argues that the increasing social diversity of undergraduate and postgraduate students globally, as well as in the UK, requires creative and innovative approaches to pedagogies and practices in higher education. She draws attention to the transformation of higher education in the last few decades in the UK and globally, but points out that these transformations have not necessarily been towards greater socio-economic equity and equality of opportunity for all disadvantaged groups. She, nevertheless, remains sanguine about the possibility of such transformations in the future involving creative pedagogies and inclusive practices.

In Chapter Seven, Trevor Gale and Deborah Tranter consider higher education for the masses in relation to social justice. They offer a historical policy analysis of higher education in Australia since its inception to determine how social justice is differently expressed at times of expansion and consolidation in the system. They draw on three perspectives of social justice, distributive, retributive and recognitive. They note that although expansion in Australian higher education has always been accompanied by distributive notions of social justice, economic justifications have dominated the arguments for expansion, with the result that social policy was subsumed by economic policy, and students from disadvantaged backgrounds largely enrolled on higher education courses to realise Australia's economic aspirations. They also argue that periods of consolidation in higher education provision tend to be accompanied by retributive concepts of social justice counter to the perceived excesses of distributive justice. Australian higher education policy and practice is still not fully informed by recognitive social justice.

In Part Two, Tehmina Basit examines class, ethnicity and access to higher education in Chapter Eight. Drawing on empirical research investigating the perceptions of 20 young people of minority ethnic origins in the UK, she explores the influence of class and ethnicity on their aspiration to and experience of higher education, or lack thereof. She argues that young people, who are brought up in an environment replete with cultural and social capital, effortlessly proceed to higher education and careers. Nevertheless, she also points to the verbal support and encouragement provided by uneducated working-class parents to their children to succeed in education followed by a career, and introduces the notion of 'aspirational capital'. She expresses concerns about the removal of the cap from university fees, the abolition of maintenance grants and the linkage of student funding with aptitude. She contends that those who are brought up in disadvantaged households, living in deprived neighbourhoods and attending underperforming schools will have their life chances drastically diminished by such policies.

In Chapter Nine, Pamela Hernandez and Diane Dunlap discuss the strategies used by Latina students to succeed in higher education in a predominantly white institution in the US. They highlight how successful Latina students deliberately use sorting and diagnostic strategies to balance between conflicting familial expectations, academic, religious and gender expectations, and personal and social relationships to create a space in which they can succeed academically. However, they are constantly redefining their roles, value systems and expectations of themselves and other Latinas. Success in higher education is achieved while managing their other roles such as women, daughters, mothers, role models, academics and so on. While they receive some support from their institution when they ask, they mainly rely on themselves and their friends to negotiate successful strategies. It is argued that each woman's understanding of her behaviour, skills, relational needs, expectations and sense of identity as Latina is influenced by personal choice behaviours and the reflection upon the consequences of such choices.

Using the concept of the hidden curriculum, Andy Cramp considers the significance of feedback to students in higher education in Chapter Ten. He draws on data collected at a post-1992 university in the UK, where half the young undergraduate student population is from the lowest social class and without the benefit of cultural capital. He shows how an intervention develops the students' understanding of feedback and enhances their confidence, self-esteem and academic development. He views feedback as a crucial part of the whole approach to learning and teaching, and highlights the value of dialogic feedback to support students who may be feeling vulnerable for various reasons. He argues that feedback on assessment is not simply a transmission process, but a complex act of social practice, which helps to extend students' understanding of unfamiliar assessment practices and facilitates their inclusion into the higher education community.

In Chapter Eleven, Ninetta Santoro, Jo-Anne Reid, Laurie Crawford and Lee Simpson consider diversity with regard to Indigenous teachers in Australia by looking at the experiences of current and former teachers in this group and the reasons for their under-representation in the teaching profession. The authors note, in particular, the positioning of such teachers as Indigenous by the teacher education curriculum and procedures, and suggest that such practices ignore the diverse nature of Indigenous identities and cultures and fail to value and utilise the diverse experiences that Indigenous people bring to enhance the teacher education curriculum. The identities of these teachers as understood by themselves in the home, family and community are often different from the way they are constructed through the discourse of teacher education. The authors fear that a teacher education curriculum that ignores the diverse nature of Indigenous cultures can alienate Indigenous pre-service teachers and lead to failure or withdrawal of these students.

Jaswinder Dhillon explores widening access to higher education through partnership working in Chapter Twelve. She draws on an empirical study that was undertaken at a time when both partnership working and social inclusion were key policy priorities. The research was conducted in an area of the UK with low levels of participation in higher education and involved senior managers from 17 organisations, who formed a sub-regional partnership as a strategy to raise aspirations, widen participation in higher education and promote social inclusion. She notes how the partnership, as an internally driven entity with a feeling of shared ownership and individual agency, created learning opportunities and progression routes into higher education for learners from disadvantaged areas, and capitalised on policy imperatives and targeted funding streams to progress projects. She further observes how the partnership was able to implement longer-term strategies to widen participation, rather than follow the government's focus on short-term projects.

In Chapter Thirteen, Rob Smith discusses participation in higher education in the quasi-market of education in the UK. He elucidates the difficulties of actual practice in taking forward a widening participation agenda, arguing that although the demands of global competition and a knowledge economy have encouraged mass higher education, the introduction of a competitive market notionally to encourage higher standards has created problems for teachers in higher education. He addresses the micro-politics of higher education classrooms, suggesting that 'community of practice' should be an organising principle. Trainee teachers, in particular, rather than being forced into prescribed roles, should find diversity at the centre of their educational experience, with classrooms becoming the meeting point for this diversity.

Finally, teaching for human rights and inclusion in higher education is examined by Audrey Osler in Chapter Fourteen. She focuses on the processes of teaching and learning about human rights and equality, and draws on her experience of teaching mature female students in a US university. She discusses how teachers and learners in higher education can deliberately or inadvertently facilitate student participation or cause exclusion, highlighting the complex ways in which students experience exclusion or discrimination. She explores the potential of human rights as procedural principles for debate and the degree to which contentious social, political and religious differences can be debated in an atmosphere of trust, and the possibility of human rights to provide a framework for enabling inclusion in diverse contexts.

Notes

[1] Although 'non-traditional' can include a number of groups, in the context of this book, the term means working-class, ethnic minority, or mature students who did not have a tradition of higher education in their family.

[2] Since labelling of groups by their race and ethnicity constitutes constantly changing social constructions, the contributors here use current descriptions. Thus, in the UK, black and minority ethnic (BME) and dual heritage is current terminology, although census returns demand more complex labelling. African- or Afro-Caribbean and labels by assumed nationality – Indian, Pakistani and so on – are also used. In the US, the contributors use a vocabulary of 'people

of colour', Latin-, African-American and so on; and in the Australian chapters, references are made to Indigenous Australians.

References

Archer, M.S. (1982) *The Sociology of Educational Expansion*, London: Sage.

Archer, M.S. (1988) *Culture and Agency*, Cambridge: Cambridge University Press.

Barnett, R. (2011) *Being a University*, London and New York: Routledge.

Bourdieu, P. (1997) 'The forms of capital', in A.H. Halsey, H. Lauder, P. Brown and A.S. Wells (eds) *Education, Culture, Economy, Society*, Oxford: Oxford University Press.

Bourdieu, P. and Passeron, J.C. (1977) *Reproduction in Education, Culture and Society*, London: Sage.

Bradley, D., Noonan, P., Nugent, H. and Scales, B. (2008) *Review of Australian Higher Education*, Canberra: Department of Education.

Browne, J. (2010) *Securing a Sustainable Future for Higher Education: an Independent Review of Higher Education Funding and Student Finance*, London: The Stationery Office.

Charles, D.R. (2009) 'Developing universities and research potential in peripheral regions', *Regions*, no 273, p 6.

Gorard, S., Smith, E., May, H., Thomas, L., Adnett, N. and Slack, K. (2006) *Review of Widening Participation Research: Addressing the Barriers to Participation in Higher Education*, York: University of York

Green, A. (1990) *Education and State Formation*, New York: St Martins Press.

Halsey, A.H. (1997) 'Preface', in A.H. Halsey, H. Lauder, P. Brown and A.S. Wells (eds) *Education, Culture, Economy, Society*, Oxford: Oxford University Press.

Jessop, B. (2002) *The Nature of the Capitalist State*, Cambridge: Polity Press.

King, R. (2009) *Governing Universities Globally; Organisations Regulation and Ranking*, London: Edward Elgar.

Kirp, D. (1982) *Just Schools: the Idea of Racial Equality in American Education*, Berkeley, CA: University of California Press.

Marginson, S. (2011) 'Equity, status and freedom; a note on higher education', *Cambridge Journal of Education*, vol 41, pp 23–36.

Nixon, J. (2010) *Higher Education as a Public Good*, London: Continuum.

OECD (Organisation for Economic Co-operation and Development) (2007) *Higher Education and Regions; Globally Competitive, Locally Engaged*, Paris: Organisation for Economic Cooperation and Development.

Ong, A. (2004) 'Higher learning, educational availability and flexible citizenship in a global space' in J.A. Banks (ed) *Diversity and Citizenship Education*, San Francisco, CA: Jossey Bass.

Schuller, T. and Watson, D. (2009) *Learning through Life; Inquiry into the Future of Lifelong Learning*, Leicester: National Institute of Adult Continuing Education.

Sullivan, A., Heath, A. and Rothon, C. (2011) 'Equalisation or inflation; social class and gender differences in England and Wales', *Oxford Review of Education*, vol 37, pp 195–214.

Tapper, T. and Palfreyman, D. (2005) *Understanding Mass Higher Education: Comparative Perspectives on Access*, London: Routledge Falmer.

Williams, J. (ed) (1997) *Negotiating Access to Higher Education*, London: Society for Research into Higher Education.

Part One
Issues in social inclusion

ONE

Capitals, ethnicity and higher education

Tariq Modood

Introduction

Savage, Warde and Devine (2004) argue that if we accept the shift in definition of class as macro-relationships such as exploitation to the possession of resources by individual actors – as many sociologists have done – then an argument can be made for the importance of concepts like cultural capital. They argue: 'If social class is a matter of categories of people accumulating similar volumes and types of resources, and investing them in promoting their own and their children's life chances, the metaphor of capital is helpful' (2004, p 7). I find this conception of social class as a likelihood of members achieving certain socio-economic goals (eg sustaining a position in or entering certain kinds of occupations) helpful. For the idea of class as life chances means that the definition of a class system depends not just on the existence of a hierarchy of classes, but on the probabilities of movement between classes. I also find the metaphorical extension of the idea of capital beyond the financial helpful. Yet, I want to argue here that both class and a Bourdieuian concept of cultural capital have certain important limitations in that neither of them is able to deal sociologically with some contemporary ethnic phenomena in relation to resources, capital and the likelihood of mobility.

This chapter arises in the context where, among sociologists, class is seen to be a much more substantial concept than ethnicity (see eg Fenton, 1999, 2003); where the influence of Bourdieu in the sociology of education is immense (Reay, 2004) and is believed to be transferable to ethnicity studies (May, 1999); and where the concept of cultural capital is enjoying a currency and an expectancy among those who believe that cultural pursuits have something to contribute to the amelioration of social exclusion. I want to challenge these positions by focusing on a major empirical question: why are non-white minority ethnic groups in Britain so over-represented in applications to and among students in higher education? The fact that they are is so counter-intuitive that while British sociologists have developed several lines of inquiry to explain the scholastic underachievement of non-whites (a phenomenon that has failed to occur, except in pockets), there are no theories to explain the phenomenon that *has* occurred. Initially, one might expect that this phenomenon might be most amenable to a cultural capital class analysis, given that it is about the acquisition of credentials for upward mobility in a stratified society and, after all, ethnicity is something to do with 'culture'. I shall show that this expectation cannot be fulfilled. Instead, I shall suggest, a version of or a derivation of the idea of social capital is more promising. The promise can be redeemed by studying some American sociology in which the Bourdieuian distinction between cultural capital, which is acquired through the family, and social capital as benefits mediated through social relations is not maintained; indeed, the former is swallowed up within the latter. An older influence on my thinking comes from an approach in British anthropology that was sometimes called 'ethnicity as a resource' (eg Wallman, 1979; Werbner, 1990a, 1990b; Ballard, 1996), although its interest was more in employment, especially self-employment.

In addition to the sociological puzzle, I am also motivated by a practical concern. Broadly put: how to achieve a society in Britain that is not racially stratified but in which recent non-white migrants and their progeny can come to have a genuine sense of belonging to Britain without having to disavow their 'ethnic' identities. My understanding of this is that it requires the possibility of significant intergenerational social mobility in which higher education has a critical role. A more specific concern (which informs the project mentioned in note 1) is about Pakistani young men. For, while Pakistani young men are not demographically under-represented in higher education and are more likely to go to university than their white peers, they are also over-represented among those with no or low qualifications and there are some indications that this latter group are not making, perhaps even not trying to make, the progress that their female peers exhibit.

The chapter is in three parts. First, I shall make the empirical case about the scale and character of minority ethnic representation in higher education. Second, I shall refer to some explanations for why this is the case. Here I will offer some answers that I believe to be true, some based on evidence and some speculative. Finally, I shall consider whether the concepts of cultural and social capital are of any assistance in organising and improving some aspects of what I believe are the answers. My interest is not in evaluating social capital theory per se, but in answering my earlier question.

Minority ethnic groups in higher education[1]

Contrary to the claims of most commentators at the time, when admissions to higher education began to be 'ethnically monitored' in 1990, they did not reveal an under-representation of minority ethnic groups (Modood, 1993). Moreover, all minority groups, with the possible exception of Caribbeans, have increased their share of admissions since then. Minority ethnic groups as a whole are much more successful in achieving university entry than their white peers. There are, however, important differences among and within groups.

Table 1.1: Higher education entrants (Home [UK] acceptances only), 2009

	%	Male–Female%
White	80.0	44–56
Black African	4.3	44–55
Black Caribbean	1.6	36–64
Black Other	0.3	39–61
Indian	3.6	49–51
Pakistani	2.7	49–51
Bangladeshi	1.0	49–51
Chinese	0.8	49–51
Asian Other	1.5	49–51
Mixed – White and Asian	1.0	47–53
Mixed – White and Black African	0.4	45–55
Mixed – White and Black Caribbean	0.9	38–62
Mixed Other	0.9	39–61
Other	1.0	45–55

Source: UCAS. Available at: http://www.ucas.com/figures/index.html

Note: Cases where ethnic origin was unknown are excluded.

Table 1.1 shows that by 2008, non-whites constituted 20% of higher education places offered to new students, this being almost double their share of the population. The national advantage established by women is also evident, although not all groups reflect it to the same degree. South Asian women are only slightly more likely to be offered a place. Older data show that while Indian women achieved parity with Indian men at the end of the 1990s, Pakistani women were eight percentage points behind male peers in 1997, and Bangladeshi women 12 percentage points behind (Modood, 2004, p 89), so the view that Asian Muslim girls are not allowed by their parents to be educated to the same level as boys is now quite outdated. The most significant gender gap is that Caribbean men continue to be a long way behind their female peers, and this gender gap is continuing; in 1997, the male–female ratio was 40–60 and had become in 36–64 in 2009. The 1990s was a period of considerable expansion in student places in higher education and much of it was accounted for by non-whites. While this partly reflected demographics, the trend analysis in Table 1.2 shows that between 1994 and 1999, at a time when the number of entrants to higher education rose by more than 20%, most minority groups increased by 40–85% (the Black Caribbean numbers, though, grew by just under 20%). At the end of the 1990s, the government set itself the target of getting 50% of young people into higher education by the age of 30. Table 1.3 shows the state of play by ethnicity. By the year 2001/02, the likelihood of white students entering higher education was only 38%, which was not only much lower than that of minority ethnic students taken together, but also lower than every single minority ethnic group. Sometimes it was not much lower (eg when compared with Bangladeshis and Black Caribbeans) and sometimes it was nearly half as low (eg when compared with Black Africans and Indians).[2] So we have the extraordinary situation in Britain where white people are far from achieving the government target, but all the minority groups except two have very nearly achieved it or greatly exceeded it (Connor et al., 2004, pp 43, 150). Later data for young people show that the minority advantage in participation is increasing (Broecke and Hamad, 2008).

There are also important differences within institutions and subjects. While some minority ethnic groups are very well represented in competitive subjects, they are (with the exception of the Chinese) still generally more likely to be in the less prestigious, less well-resourced post-1992 universities. This is especially true of Caribbeans, who are also more likely to be mature students (more than half of Caribbean women students are over 25 years old) and part-time students – all factors that have implications for career prospects. A level scores,[3] subject preferences, preference for local institutions and type of school or college attended are all factors that explain the concentration of minority ethnic groups (again with the exception of the Chinese) in the new universities. Nevertheless, one analysis shows that, even accounting for these factors, there is a clear institutional effect (Shiner

Table 1.2: Percentages of home-accepted applicants to degree courses

Ethnic origin	1994	1995	1996	1997	1998	1999	% change 1994–99
White	85.37	84.27	82.59	81.17	79.64	79.3	12.64
Black Caribbean	0.95	0.97	0.97	0.99	0.95	0.94	19.88
Black African	1.31	1.48	1.55	1.54	1.45	1.51	40.41
Indian	3.23	3.33	3.6	3.67	3.92	4.13	55.01
Pakistani	1.58	1.77	2	1.98	2.11	2.17	66.39
Bangladeshi	0.43	0.52	0.57	0.55	0.6	0.66	85.03
Chinese	0.76	0.81	0.88	0.88	0.9	0.94	50.89
Total (n)	228,685	240,710	246,503	276,503	272,340	277,340	

Source: UCAS Statistical Bulletin on Widening Participation (2000: 13, Table 5.2).

Table 1.3: Higher Education Initial Participation Rates (HEIPRs), England, full time and part time, 2001/02

Ethnic group	Male	Female	All
White	34	41	38
All minority ethnic groups	55	58	56
Black Caribbean	36	52	45
Black African	71	75	73
Black Other	56	72	64
Indian	70	72	71
Pakistani	54	44	49
Bangladeshi	43	33	39
Chinese	47	50	49
Asian Other	74	94	83
Mixed ethnic	35	44	40
All (known ethnicity)	37	43	40

Source: Connor et al. (2004).

and Modood, 2002). Comparing similarly qualified candidates and controlling for factors such as public schools, gender and so on, new (post-1992) universities respond more positively than old universities to non-white applicants and, within this sector, Chinese, Bangladeshi and Indian candidates appear to be favoured over whites. When applying to old universities, however, there is strong evidence that minority candidates face an ethnic penalty. Institutions within this sector are most likely to select white and, to a lesser extent, Chinese candidates from among a group of similarly qualified applicants.[4] Given the much larger proportion of applications from minority ethnic groups, although minority ethnic applicants may be admitted to old universities in reasonable numbers, they generally have to perform better than do their white peers in order to secure a place. As the type of institution from which you graduate can make a big difference to your career prospects, this bias makes older universities complicit in an institutional discrimination that hinders and slows down the dismantling of ethnic stratification.[5]

Some possible causes

Class

For most British sociologists, class is the best explanation of educational outcomes. For example, Goldthorpe's theory of social mobility holds that:

> individuals of differing class origins will differ in the use they make of available educational opportunities. Those from more advantaged class backgrounds, pursuing strategies from above, will exploit such opportunities more fully than will those from less advantaged backgrounds, pursuing strategies from below – and with the backing of superior resources. (Goldthorpe, 2003; see also Goldthorpe, 2000)

However one defines and operationalises it, class is important; but it may be far from the whole story. Some of the other factors may be to do with proximity to good schools or aspects of individual biographies, including the interests and efforts of one's parents. In the case of minority ethnic groups, there will be factors distinctive to particular groups or to the condition of belonging to a minority ethnic group in Britain today, such as racialised exclusion. Some of these distinctive factors will work to reinforce or deepen class effects; others to lessen them. Or, to put it another way, some of these factors will work to worsen the socio-economic position of a minority ethnic group relative to the rest of society; other factors may have the opposite effect. For example, a study of young people that systematically controlled for social class attributes found that the likelihood of achieving 5 GCSEs at A*–C for Pakistanis and Indians (analysed separately) was 10% higher than their white social class peers; for Black Caribbeans it was 8% less (Bradley and Taylor, 2004). Ethnic group membership, then, can mitigate or exacerbate class disadvantage; and this may, of course, change with the circumstances.

Again, while it is generally true that the minority ethnic groups with the largest proportions in higher education, especially in pre-1992 universities, have a more middle-class profile than other minority ethnic groups, it is not invariant; Pakistanis have a worse occupational, earnings and household profile than Caribbeans, but a larger proportion in higher education. Moreover, the undiluted class model is no help in explaining why minority ethnic groups (all of whom have or till recently had a [much] worse class profile than the white group) perform better than white students. This can be seen from Table 1.4, which shows university entrants of 2008 by ethnicity and parental social class.[6] It shows that class is a major factor: in nearly every group, the offspring of managers and professionals predominate but not in all cases, notably the Bangladeshis and Pakistanis. Indeed, in most minority ethnic groups, the university entrants are much more likely to be evenly spread across the occupational classes – including those in the 'Unknown' category, the majority of whom are likely to be unemployed or in casual work, the informal economy and hard to classify jobs, and not merely cases where the information is missing (Ballard, 1999). So, the significance that the conventional class analysis has in relation to the white group seems prima facie to at least need modifying in relation to some minority ethnic groups and does not hold at all for Bangladeshis, Pakistanis and Africans, among whom households headed by a routine, unemployed or occupation-unknown worker supply the majority of the entrants (nearly two thirds in the case of Bangladeshis).

To some extent, it can be countered that this was because the minority ethnic entrants' parental social class and educational capital was better than that suggested by their parents' occupations, for their occupational levels were depressed by migration effects and discrimination in the labour market. Due to this racial discrimination, migrants often suffered a downward social mobility on entry into Britain (Modood et al., 1997, pp 141–2). The only jobs open to them were often below their qualification levels and below the social class level they enjoyed before migration. This meant that not only did many value education more than their white workmates, but also saw it as part of the process of reversing their initial downward mobility, especially in the lives of their children. Certainly, if we look at the qualification levels of the migrants at the time of migration, this argument that migrants' occupational

Table 1.4: University entrants by ethnicity and parental social class, 2002 and 2008

	White	Black African	Black Caribbean	Indian	Pakistani	Bangladeshi	Chinese	Asian Other	Mixed White & Asian	Mixed White & African	Mixed White & Caribbean	Mixed other
Managerial and professional	41	29	29	34	21	17	28	32	46	33	32	38
Intermediate, supervisory, technical and self-employed	21	11	19	22	25	18	16	15	18	15	18	18
Semi-routine and routine	18	20	21	21	19	30	28	21	15	19	21	17
Unknown	20	40	31	24	35	35	27	32	21	33	29	27
Total	100	100	100	101	100	100	99	100	100	101	100	100

Source: UCAS online tabulation chosen by author.

class in Britain is not reflective of their true class and, hence, of their attitudes to education seems to have some plausibility (Modood et al., 1997, pp 68–9). It is particularly plausible in the case of the African Asians and perhaps also the Indians, but less so with other groups. In any case, class analysis by itself, even after taking initial downward mobility into account, is incomplete without acknowledging the economic motivation of migrants, the desire to better themselves and especially the prospects of their children.

Even more fundamentally, if we accept the definition of class in my opening quote – that social class is a matter of categories of people accumulating similar volumes and types of resources, and investing them in promoting their own and their children's life chances (Savage et al., 2004, p 7) – then, as I shall expand later, this categorisation of people by the possession of similar resources can be a characteristic of ethnicity. That is to say, it can vary across ethnic groups within the same occupational/income classes. Hence, ethnicity seems to cut across class here, possibly even to constitute class in some ways because ethnicity can mean resources.

Racism

Another line of explanation that has prominence in the literature points to the possible role of racism. This could, for example, consist of factors influencing how teachers treat different groups, policies that indirectly discriminate (eg by placing more pupils from certain ethnic groups in lower sets) and the general ways in which groups of people in British society are perceived and treated. Each of these can have an effect on the groups in question, who may then react in certain kinds of ways, most notably by being demotivated or confrontational. This may also lead to social stereotyping on the part of educators and university admissions tutors, creating a vicious cycle. This line of explanation seems to work better with black than South Asian people. For example, data from local education authorities suggest that at the beginning of schooling, and at the time of the first national tests at age 7, the difference between Caribbean and white students is relatively slight, and sometimes in favour of the Caribbeans. It is South Asian children, often coming from homes in which English, if spoken at home, is a second or third language, who begin their school careers with low averages (this was even more so when those who are in higher education today would have started schooling). However, South Asians slowly catch up while in secondary school and, in the case of some groups, overtake the white students, although the Caribbeans' average steadily drops behind that of the national average (Owen et al., 2000; NEP, 2010).

Perhaps, then, there is more racism against black than South Asian people, especially Indians. The evidence, however, points the other way. For example, the PSI Fourth Survey found that most people in 1994 believed that of all ethnic, racial and religious hostility, that against South Asians, especially Asian Muslims, is the greatest; this is likely to have increased post-9/11 (Modood et al., 1997). Indians, while clearly a successful group, are not immune from this hostility. The causes of the hostility may lie in perceptions of Pakistanis or (Asian) Muslims but the effects are visited on South Asians more generally, as turban-wearing Sikh men who have been abused as 'Islamic terrorists' could testify. Even within the specific context of schooling, South Asians experience more frequent and more violent racial harassment from other pupils than Caribbeans (Gillborn, 1998). So an appeal to racism by itself may have little explanatory value without considering how a target group reacts to exclusion. Bullying is supposed to put students off schools and academic work, but, as we have seen, South Asians make progress and they have very high staying-on rates beyond the period of compulsory schooling (Modood et al., 1997).

Ethnic strategies from below

Perceptions of racism and biases in the labour market may contribute to these high staying-on rates, but when Asians who stay on are questioned they give positive reasons (especially the desire to go to university) rather than negative reasons (such as the need to avoid unemployment) (Hagell and Shaw, 1996; Basit, 1997; Burgess et al., 2009). Even cultures that until recently might have been portrayed as opposed to the higher education and employment of women seem to be producing growing cohorts of highly motivated young women (Ahmad et al., 2003).

So minority ethnic groups in general and South Asians in particular seem to have a strong drive for qualifications. This 'motor' cannot be explained by short-term or Britain-only class analysis, although it is partly explained (more in the case of some groups than others) by long-term class analysis, which enquires into pre-migration class locations. It has to be noted, however, that this raises questions of commensurability and fit between what class means in contemporary Britain and what it means in radically different societies and economies. For example, how are Punjabi peasants who own very little individually but through an extended family own a small farm to be compared to hospital porters in London with higher levels of personal consumption and leisure time but little property?

Certainly, one will ultimately need a wider sociological framework, for it would not make sense to answer my question about minority ethnic entry into higher education in a way that did not connect with wider explanations. Racism, cultural adaptation and deprived neighbourhoods are among the features that one cannot ignore. Indeed, there are various sorts of disadvantages that one can stack up and they offer explanatory assistance if our need is to explain failure. But given that we are explaining success, all these factors serve only to compound the problem.

So, what is the source of this 'motor', this ability to drive through large-scale, sociologically corroborated disadvantages? Thinking particularly of the South Asians and Chinese, I speculate that the answer might lie in their families and communities. For instance, through the following causal sequence:

1. parents, other significant relatives and community members share some general but durable ambitions to achieve upward mobility for themselves and especially for their children and believe that (higher) education is important in achieving those ambitions, and so prioritise the acquisition of (higher) education;

2. they are successfully able to convey this view to their children who to a large degree internalise it and, even where they may not fully share it, develop ambitions and priorities that are consistent with those of their parents;

3. the parents have enough authority and power over their children, suitably reinforced by significant relatives and other community members, to ensure that the ambition is not ephemeral or fantastic but that the children do whatever is necessary at a particular stage for its progressive realisation.

Of course, not all South Asians (even in terms of groups, let alone within groups) are academically successful, but explaining success will be a major theoretical outcome – given the absence of suitable explanatory strategies – and perhaps, though, there are political pitfalls here, explaining the successful may help to throw scientific light on the cases of the unsuccessful. Moreover, that may be the basis for an understanding that could assist to reverse the circumstances of the unsuccessful.

My proposed triadic 'motor' is consistent with the data presented so far and hopefully can help to explain why socio-economic disadvantage and racism – indisputably real forces – do not have the effects that sociological research would have predicted. Let me offer a final piece of data that might support the line I am taking. Table 1.5 is from a survey of Year 13 students, in which respondents had to mark statements on

Table 1.5: Factors affecting decisions by potential HE entrants (Year 13) to go on to higher education by ethnic group (mean scores)

Scores range from one to five, where one represents 'Does not apply / no effect' and five represents 'Applies strongly/big effect'.

Issues affecting decision	Black African	Black Caribbean/other	Pakistani/ Bangladeshi	Indian	Chinese/Asian other	All minority groups	White
Few family been to university	2.8	2.9	2.8	3.1	3.0	3.0	2.5
Encouragement from family	4.0	4.0	4.0	4.0	3.8	4.0	3.4
Always assumed would go on to HE	4.0	3.2	4.0	4.1	3.9	3.9	3.1
Base N = 100% Min. respondents	94	68	117	166	68	567	217

Source: Connor et al. (2004).

a 1–5 scale (5 = strongly applies), and some answers are presented in aggregate form. Besides confirming that minority ethnic respondents in the sample, relative to white respondents, were more likely to have had few family members who had been to university, it reveals that they nevertheless had received more encouragement from family to go to university. Most counter-intuitive of all, they (except Black Caribbeans) were more likely to say that it had always been assumed they would go into higher education. As this counter-intuitive result neatly matches the counter-intuitive fact of minority ethnic over-representation, it is not unreasonable to suppose that the two are linked and that cultural and social capital might play a role.

Cultural and social capital

I shall review some contributions to these topics. I shall not try to offer a full picture of the views of any particular author or school, but shall state why I think a particular body of work may or may not be useful to me.

Bourdieu and cultural capital

Bourdieu's initial ideas about cultural capital seem to suit me very well: they were developed in relation to an inquiry about the non-random distribution of educational qualifications and he speaks about investment strategies employed by different kinds of families (Bourdieu, 1997). Moreover, a central point is that there are different forms of capital so that it is possible for a family to be poor in one form and rich in another, which fits my case of socio-economically disadvantaged Pakistani households having another kind of resource from which they can produce graduates. Highly relevant too is the view that familial norms are not irrelevant to the production of socio-economic advantages and disadvantages. Moreover, Bourdieu's work offers a theoretical framework for making the links to the wider social structure, power and ideology.

On the negative side, it has to be said that he has very little to say about ethnicity and indeed assumes a cultural homogeneity (at least within classes). His major limitation for me, however, is that he is asking about how the dominant class reproduces its domination, whereas I am asking how subordinate groups can achieve upward mobility. His interest is in how those with financial capital can convert it into educational qualifications and then back again. But my starting point are groups with little economic capital and Bourdieu's framework does not seem to be suitable for examining how such groups can generate social mobility for significant numbers of their members.

Bourdieu's work does, however, remind me of the American anthropologist, Ogbu, who has also tried to create a theoretical framework to connect society-wide socio-economic structures (what he calls 'the system') with the different trajectories and dynamics of various minority ethnic groups (what he calls 'community forces') (Ogbu and Simons, 1998). His fundamental distinctions revolve not around capital and class, but different kinds of minority ethnic groups. He distinguishes between voluntary or immigrant groups, such as, say, the Cubans or Koreans in the United States, and involuntary or non-migrant groups such as black people, indigenous people and Mexicans in that country. This is an extremely important and powerful distinction, although it ought not be treated too dichotomously, for most non-white groups in Britain are a legacy of empire and their movement to Britain needs to be dually characterised as a migration across countries and simultaneously as a movement internal to a political-economic system. Ogbu shows how the distinction of voluntary–involuntary arises from 'the system' (which conquers/enslaves or permits migrants to settle), but has profound consequences for 'community forces'. For example, it is argued that 'voluntary minorities are less conflicted about accommodating to white society, so their role models include people who fully adopt white ways and language', while of such persons among involuntary minorities, 'it is suspected that for them to have succeeded they probably have had to adopt white ways such as speaking standard English, which is seen as giving in to the white oppressor and abandoning their identity' (Ogbu and Simons, 1998, p 173). As Ogbu develops his theory with primary reference to school performance, it is clear that his cultural-ecological approach, in some ways resembling Bourdieu's ideas of cultural capital and *habitus*, has something relevant to offer to my concerns, as long as the voluntary–involuntary minority ethnic group distinction is not forcefully pressed.

Putnam and social capital

Robert Putnam is currently the name most associated with social capital (Putnam, 1995, 2000). His interest is in asking about the healthy functioning of contemporary liberal-democratic societies and so, no less than Bourdieu, is some distance from my question about how some specific groups are able to achieve social mobility by means of education. Nevertheless, I do think his work contains ideas useful to my inquiry, for example, his famous distinction between bonding, bridging and linking social capital. The first type of social capital is that which bonds a distinctive group together, but the other side of the coin is that it separates the group from others. This separation can be mitigated by members of the group at the same time developing bridges to members outside the group, which is the second type of bridging social capital. Finally, the form of social capital most relevant to mobility is linking capital, which links people across classes to those in positions of power or influence (Putnam, 1995, 2000). This distinction seems to be *prima facie* relevant in distinguishing between those South Asian communities who have achieved upward mobility, such as, say, the Gujaratis of Leicester, and those who have not, such as the Pakistanis of Bradford, perhaps because the latter, unlike the former, are strong in bonding capital but lack bridging and linking capital. Of course I do not mean to suggest – and one has to be careful not to suggest – that communities strong in bonding capital and weak in bridging capital are the sole cause of differential outcomes between the positions of different communities, for that would ignore how exclusion and segregation in the northern cities and elsewhere has been shaped by white people's preferences as individuals, and the decisions of local councillors, not least in relation to public housing. But nevertheless it seems to me to be possible to use Putnam's distinction between forms of social capital without 'blaming the victim'.

Another central contention of Putnam's is that participation in formal, voluntary organisations, regardless of the kind or quality of participation, is itself a decisive measure of all kinds of social goods from crime-free neighbourhoods to better personal health and higher personal incomes. I was at first sceptical about the utility of this proposition for my inquiry, but I note that at least one study has found that 'the organizational involvement of both parents and children promotes school achievement' (Bankston and Zhou, 2002, p 311; see also Zhou and Bankston, 1998).

'Ethnicity as social capital' studies in the United States

There are a number of American empirical analyses that apply a concept of social capital to the study of ethnic groups (for a list, see Bankston and Zhou, 2002, p 289). So far this body of work is not very well known in Britain, if citations are any indication. Broadly speaking, they seem to be in a stream, but correcting itself as it goes along by reference to findings. Derived from James Coleman (eg Coleman, 1988 and 1990; like Bourdieu, the interest was in explaining unequal scholastic outcomes), they were perhaps initially intimated by the economist Glenn Loury in relation to the labour market position of African

Americans (Loury, 1977). The empirical studies, while attempting to develop intermediate or grounded theory, do not slavishly follow any particular theorist or all aspects of the work of a useful theorist. For example, they assert the importance of the *social* in all kinds of ways, while Coleman attempted to explain the social in terms of an economic–psychological individualism. Again, Coleman believed that his work endorsed a certain moral conservatism on matters such as the importance of a non–working mother within a two-parent family for children's development, whereas the later studies on ethnicity give support to a broader range of positions. Moreover, Alejandro Portes, perhaps one of the first to use the ideas of social capital and network theory in relation to immigrant ethnicity, highlights negative as well as positive outcomes of social capital (Portes, 1998).

Bankston and Zhou (2002) are also critical of some of the ways that social capital has been used. They make some important and apposite philosophical points:

> social capital, a … metaphorical construction, does not consist of resources that are held by individuals or by groups but of processes of social interaction leading to constructive outcomes. Therefore, we argue that social capital is not located at any one level of analysis and that it emerges across different levels of analysis. The confusion over the meaning of this term, then, is a consequence of a metaphorical confusion of a substantive quantity (capital) and a process that takes place through stages (embedded, goal-directed relations). Locating and defining social capital is further complicated by the variability, contextuality, and conditionality of the process. Stages of social relations that lead to constructive outcomes for one group of people or in one situation may not lead to constructive outcomes for another group or in another situation. (Bankston and Zhou, 2002, p 286)

On their reading of the relevant literature, two particular dimensions of social capital seem to have emerged in research that are particularly relevant to the family: 'intergenerational closure' and 'norms enforcement' (Bankston and Zhou, 2002, p 287). The first is a specific case of the general interest, derived from Coleman, in 'dense associations' (Coleman, 1990), in the belief that the kind of relationships that lead to non-monetary exchanges and cooperative behaviour involve a high degree of trust, and this is likely to be fostered where individuals see themselves as similar, as sharing the same values, having frequent contact with each other and with each other's contacts and so on. In the case of families, 'intergenerational closure' is achieved where parents know the parents of their children's friends, so that the network of parents and the network of children involve many of the same families. Nevertheless, 'intergenerational closure' seems to set the bar too high; continuity of purpose and values across generations may be quite enough. We need to be careful of a general tendency to prefer dense and closed relationships in themselves, for, as early as the work of Granovetter (1973), it was clear that for many purposes, such as acquiring information about employment opportunities, positive outcomes are more likely to flow from a set of wide and loose relationships rather than 'dense' ones. This is one of the advantages of Putnam's concepts of bridging and linking capital, requiring the analyst to broaden the range of relationships that facilitate valuable social outcomes beyond the obvious ones of bonding. Indeed, in at least one empirical analysis, it has been found that the high academic scores of Asian Americans are not due to close parent–child ties, for those ties were absent (Bankston and Zhou, 2002, p 310). As for 'norms enforcement', it is of course critical that if certain goals are dependent on focused effort, then the norms that inform those goals must not only be shared, but also enforced, otherwise they would only be vague aspirations or good intentions.

The kind of ethnic capital I am interested in, then, seems to require three different stages or dimensions: relationships, norms and norms enforcement. However, the kind of relationships, norms and norms enforcement that will lead to university entry may vary across groups, time and place; indeed, an erstwhile successful strategy may need to be changed, as circumstances change. It is not, then, a competition between dense *versus* loose, but what might work for a particular group in specific circumstances. What kind of and how much of dense and what kind of and how much of loose? This of course would be highly relevant to current policy debates about segregation, disadvantage and social cohesion.

Focusing, however, on my own question, it does seem to be that this literature suggests an important triad: familial adult–child relationships, transmission of aspirations and attitudes, and norms enforcement. This triad seems to be highly pertinent to my suggestions as to where to find the 'motor' of South Asian academic success. This is not at all surprising for authors such as Zhou and Bankston, who have focused on groups, such as the Vietnamese, who arrived in the US poor, and without pre-existing ethnic community networks to assist them, and have achieved outstanding academic performance (Zhou, 1997; Zhou and Bankston,

1998). Moreover, it should, I believe, offer the opportunity to connect with other and wider social dimensions, for example, identity. People act (or try to act or fail to act) the way they do because it seems to them to be the behaviour of an identity that they believe they have or aspire to have; certain behaviours do or do not make sense, become possible or 'impossible', easy or difficult, are worth making sacrifices for, and so on, if certain identities – like minority ethnic identities – are strongly held. The triad may cluster with other beliefs and behaviours that give some South Asians a sense of who they are, their location in the world and what is expected of them. This can be a fruitful inquiry even if we reject ethnic essentialism (and are careful not to impose too restricted a purview of *which* adult–children relationships are important), for the self-concept that 'We as a group are striving and struggling to achieve higher status, prosperity and respectability in this land where the dice is loaded against us, but success is achievable, and you have to play your part' can be bound up with say, being Indian in Britain, even if it is only contingently and not essentially so. The transmission of a normative identity will, I believe, be more important than, say, parent–child 'quality-time', talking together about schoolwork or friendships, or any specific skills and knowledge transfer. Indeed, South Asian migrant parents may have little relevant economic/human capital to transmit, but subsequent human capital acquisition by their children may depend upon parent–child transmission of norms-laden and goals-directing identities. I believe the motivational power of identity does not necessarily need closed, dense communities and is more at the heart of minority ethnic social/cultural capital than, say, residential concentration, mutual self-help or community institutions.

If identity is too intangible an example, it is clear that the triad must connect with specific measurable behaviours, for example, making children do academic homework. Moreover, 'norms enforcement' cannot just mean discipline; it must also extend to include the provision of resources (like books and tutors) that enable children to proceed on the appropriate normative path. I believe this is an extremely fruitful line of inquiry, but the first step will have to be the creation of data, for at the moment (because researchers have not asked the appropriate questions) there is no data (by ethnicity) on what periods of academic work – not necessarily just set by the school – are done outside school hours, let alone what proportions of disposable income are spent by households on children's education.

Another way of going beyond the family is by looking at the locales in which the families under study are based and the ways in which the neighbourhoods contribute to or impede the realisation of the families' academic goals. Drawing on her study of Chinatown in New York and elaborating on the role that community organisations play there in assisting upward social mobility, Min Zhou makes a distinction between an ethnic/racial ghetto and enclave (Zhou, 1992, 2005). Both are typified by high levels of ethnic group segregation and an absence of highly paid jobs, but an enclave, unlike a ghetto, is likely to be economically dynamic and aspirant and allow cross-class relationships, thus enhancing information channels, job opportunities and models of academic and economic success, all of which reinforce the promise of upward mobility missing in a ghetto. This is a distinction that can be connected with Ogbu's approach described earlier, as well as Putnam's emphasis on the importance of bridging and linking, as well as bonding, capital. It is, therefore, another fruitful distinction to explore even though the levels of ethnic segregation in Britain are much lower than those in the US.

Conclusion

In the US literature I have been considering, the Bourdieuian distinction between cultural capital, which is acquired through the family, and social capital as benefits mediated through social relations is not maintained; the former is indistinguishably incorporated within the latter. This suits my purposes too, for if the question is what role ethnic background plays, the family is integral to that background, but clearly is not exhausted by it. Hence, perhaps the appropriate term should be 'cultural-social capital'; or perhaps, 'ethnic capital' (modified from 'ethnicity as social capital'; see Zhou, 2005). It perhaps runs the risk of reification and suggesting that a certain ethnic group (eg Pakistanis) are a static, homogeneous, neatly bounded group; features that I do not mean to imply but deny, if less radically than in the current social science orthodoxy, and which can be countered in analysis (Modood, 2007, pp 90–8). On the other hand, it has the advantage of flagging up diversity, namely that the capital in question will vary across ethnic groups, not just in degree, but also in kind; and also suggests a certain kind of marginality and exclusion that is not fully explicable in class terms. It has the further advantage that it limits the position that has to be defended: some or all of the uses of 'social capital' may be separated out from a particular use that relates to some ethnic groups.

I leave open for another discussion that the concept of cultural capital will resume relevance if we widen the picture and consider why minority ethnic groups experience an ethnic penalty in relation to entry into prestigious universities and the labour-market returns they receive for their university degrees – that is to say, to explain why these groups are not doing even better than they are (NEP, 2010, pp 224–31). Let me conclude by considering the suggestion that the reason that the power of established cultural capital does not seem to deter some minority ethnic groups from (higher) education is perhaps because they are outside the parameters of 'white' cultural capital in its entirety; that, unlike the white working class, they do not really pick up or understand the cues.[7] I think this is quite mistaken (although it might have been true at a very early point in the migration process). Leaving aside the perverse implication that minority ethnic groups will only start behaving in a disadvantaged way after they are socially included, I suggest that we need to divide 'white cultural capital' into at least two types. First, there is working-class, popular culture, often American-derived, especially in relation to youth culture, of Hollywood, soap operas, music, clothes/fashion, celebrities, football, pubs, clubs and bingeing. It is a dominant culture whose cues British African-Caribbeans have not only picked up, but in which they have come to be a leading-edge presence, quite remarkable for a group that is less than 2% of the population, stigmatised and economically disadvantaged (Hall, 1998; Modood, 1999). South Asian parents no doubt have little credibility in this domain and try to limit their children's exposure to it.

Second, there is a middle-class culture, meaning not just 'high culture' and leisure pursuits, but more importantly including high social status-conferring occupations and tending more towards respectability than celebrity and hedonistic consumption, and entry into which nearly always requires a good university degree. This is the dominant culture that non-white minority ethnic parents would like their children to integrate into, as so many other groups have done before, most conspicuously the Jews. So, it is not a question of missing cues, but of a determined effort to avoid one dominant culture and steer towards another. This of course still leaves open the question why in relation to universities many minority ethnic young people fail to think 'that's not meant for me' in the way that is supposed to be characteristic of many white working-class young people. I have offered a series of suggestions, ranging from my own speculations to critically and syncretically learning from the American literature, which, while in advance of its British counterpart, will certainly need to be appropriately reworked to answer British questions, including considering the interaction of ethno-religious factors with gender and class (Shah et al., 2010).

At the moment, South Asian university entrants are typically children of migrants; they are 'second generation' (Connor et al., 2004). In due course, however, this generation, having lifted itself into the middle class, will produce a generation that will benefit from some of the standard advantages of being born middle class, including the acquisition of cultural capital that assists entry into prestigious universities and professional and managerial jobs. We would then be studying a different phenomenon. My interest in this chapter has been in what kind of capital, if any, can explain the upward educational mobility of predominantly working-class, outsider, minority ethnic groups. The concept of ethnic capital might help us to understand the counter-intuitive findings of high success of members of underprivileged groups. I have shown that their educational progress creates a noteworthy anomaly for current cultural capital analysis.[8]

Acknowledgement

This is a revised and updated version of Modood (2004). I am grateful for the support of the Leverhulme Trust for its funding of the Migration and Citizenship Research Programme at the University of Bristol and University College London, of which this paper was a part; for its use in relation to the project findings see Shah, Dwyer and Modood (2010); and Modood and Salt (2011).

Notes

[1] For fuller evidential support for this section, see Modood et al. (1997, chs 3, 4) and Modood (2005, chs 3, 4).

[2] Not to mention the 'Asian Other' minority ethnic group, a term that includes disparate groups such as Sri Lankans, Vietnamese, Malaysians, but which are relatively small in absolute terms and so working out the proportion of the age group in higher education is less reliable. The same may apply to the Chinese in Table 1.1, for their representation is much lower than all other data has suggested so far (Modood, 2005).

[3] A levels are public examinations typically sat at the end of Year 13, and, while at the discretion of each individual university, the results of these examinations determine university entry. The higher the score, the greater the likelihood of entry into a prestigious university.

[4] The data set in question was reanalysed recently with results showing that 'bias' against ethnic minorities was confined to Law for all groups and against Pakistanis in most subjects (see Gittoes and Thompson, 2007; HEFCE, 2005). Why the HEFCE analysis differs from Shiner and Modood's (2002) has not

yet been established and is the subject of a Nuffield Foundation study at the LSE led by Michael Shiner.

[5] It ought to be borne in mind, however, that some ethnic minority groups have a disproportionately large proportion of their 18–24 year olds in higher education, and therefore are digging deeper into the natural talent available in that age group. Hence, it is not in itself surprising that a larger proportion of their applicants enter institutions that require lower A level entry scores. For, if we were to compare like with like, the peers of some who enter these universities are white people who are absent from higher education.

[6] This being the last year that data was collected using these socio-economic categories.

[7] I am grateful to Mike Savage for raising this point with me.

[8] After writing this chapter I discovered Laughlo (2000), which, while based on Norwegian data, is closely allied to the argument of this chapter (see also Storen and Helland, 2010; Fekjaer and Leirvik, 2011).

References

Ahmad, F., Modood, T. and Lissenburgh, S. (2003) *South Asian Women and Employment in Britain: the Interaction of Gender and Ethnicity*, London: Policy Studies Institute.

Ballard, R. (1996) 'The Pakistanis: stability and introspection', in C. Peach (ed) *Ethnicity in the 1991 Census. Volume 2. The Ethnic Minority Populations of Britain*, London: HMSO.

Ballard, R. (1999) 'Socio-economic and educational achievements of ethnic minorities', unpublished paper submitted to the Commission on the Future of Multi-Ethnic Britain, London: The Runnymede Trust.

Bankston, C.L. and Zhou, M. (2002) 'Social capital as process: the meaning and problems of a theoretical metaphor', *Sociological Inquiry*, vol 72, no 2, pp 285–317.

Basit, T.N. (1997) *Eastern Values; Western Milieu: Identities and Aspirations of Adolescent British Muslim Girls*, Ashgate.

Bourdieu, P. (1997) 'The forms of social capital', in A.H. Halsey, P. Brown and A.S. Wells (eds) *Education, Culture, Economy, Society.* Oxford, Oxford University Press, pp 46–58 (first published in Richardson, J.E. (ed) (1986) *Handbook of Theory for Research in the Sociology of Education*, Westport, CT: Greenwood Press).

Bradley, S. and Taylor, J. (2004) 'Ethnicity, educational attainment and the transition from school', *The Manchester School*, vol 72, no 3, pp 317–46.

Broecke, S. and Hamed, J. (2008) 'Gender gaps in higher education participation', DIUS Research Report 08 14, Department for Innovation, Universities and Skills.

Burgess, S., Wilson, D. and Piebalga, A. (2009) 'Land of hope and dreams: education aspirations and parental influence among England's ethnic minorities', Paper presented at SPA Conference, Edinburgh.

Coleman, J.S. (1988) 'Social capital in the creation of human capital', *American Journal of Sociology*, vol 94 Supplement: S95–S120.

Coleman, J.S. (1990) *Foundations of Social Theory*, Cambridge, MA: The Belknap Press.

Connor, H., Tyers, C., Modood, T. and Hillage, J. (2004) 'Why the difference? A closer look at higher education minority ethnic students and graduates', Research Report RR552, Department for Education. Available at: www.dfes.gov.uk/research/data/uploadfiles/RB552.pdf

Fekjaer, S. and Leirvik, M. (2011) 'Silent gratitude: education among second-generation Vietnamese in Norway', *Journal of Ethnic and Migration Studies*, vol 37, no 1, pp 117–34.

Fenton, S. (1999) *Ethnicity: Racism, Class and Culture*, Basingstoke and London: Macmillan.

Fenton, S. (2003) *Ethnicity*, Cambridge: Polity Press.

Gillborn, D. (1998) 'Race and ethnicity in compulsory schooling', in T. Modood and T. Acland (eds) *Race and Higher Education*, London: Policy Studies Institute.

Gittoes, M. and Thompson, J. (2007) 'Admissions to higher education: are there biases against or in favour of ethnic minorities?', *Teaching in Higher Education*, vol 12, no 3, pp 419–24.

Goldthorpe, J. (2000) *On Sociology*, Oxford: Oxford University Press.

Goldthorpe, J. (2003) '"Outline of a theory of social mobility" revisited: the increasingly problematic role of education', Conference in honour of Professor Tore Lindbekk, April, Trondheim.

Granovetter, M.S. (1973) 'The strength of weak ties', *American Journal of Sociology*, vol 78, pp 1360–80.

Hagell, A. and Shaw, C. (1996) *Opportunity and Disadvantage at Age 16*, London: Policy Studies Institute.

Hall, S. (1998) 'Aspiration and attitude … reflections on black Britain in the nineties', *New Formations*, Frontlines/Backyards Special Issue, vol 33, Spring.

HEFCE (Higher Education Funding Council for England) (2005) 'Higher education admissions: assessment of bias', HEFCE Research Paper 2005/47, December.

Laughlo, J. (2000) 'Social capital trumping class and cultural capital? Engagement with school among immigrant youth', in S. Baron, J. Field and T. Schuller (eds) *Social Capital: Critical Perspectives*, Oxford: Clarendon Press.

Loury, G. (1977) 'A dynamic theory of racial income differences', in P.A. Wallace and A. Le Mund (eds) *Women, Minorities, and Employment Discrimination*, Lexington, MA: Lexington Books.

May, S. (1999) 'Critical multiculturalism and cultural difference: avoiding essentialism', in S. May (ed) *Critical Multiculturalism: Rethinking Multicultural and Antiracist Education*, London: Falmer Press.

Modood, T. (1993) 'The number of ethnic minority students in British higher education', *Oxford Review of Education*, vol 19, no 2, June, pp 167–82.

Modood, T. (1999) 'New forms of Britishness: post-immigration ethnicity and hybridity in Britain', in R. Lentin (ed) *The Expanding Nation: Towards a Multi-Ethnic Ireland*, Dublin: Trinity College Dublin (reproduced in R. Sackmann, B. Peters and T. Faist [eds] [2003] *Identity and Integration: Migrants in Western Europe*, Aldershot: Ashgate).

Modood, T. (2004) 'Capitals, ethnic identity and educational qualifications', *Cultural Trends*, vol 13(2), no 50, June, pp 87–105.

Modood, T. (2005) *Multicultural Politics: Racism, Ethnicity and Muslims in Britain*, Minneapolis: University of Minnesota Press and Edinburgh: University of Edinburgh Press.

Modood, T. and Salt, J. (eds) (2011) *Global Migration, Ethnicity and Britishness*, Basingstoke: Palgrave.

Modood, T., Berthoud, R., Lakey, J., Nazroo, J., Smith, P., Virdee, S. and Beishon, S. (1997) *Ethnic Minorities in Britain: Diversity and Disadvantage*, London: Policy Studies Institute.

NEP (National Equality Panel) (2010) *An Anatomy of Economic Inequality in the UK*, London: HMSO.

Ogbu, J.U. and Simons, H.D. (1998) 'Voluntary and involuntary minorities: a cultural-ecological theory of school performance with some implications for education', *Anthropology and Education Quarterly*, vol 29, no 2, pp 155–88.

Owen, D., Green, A., Pitcher, I. and Maguire, M. (2000) *Minority Ethnic Participation and Achievements in Education, Training and the Labour Market*, London: Department for Education and Employment.

Portes, A. (1998) 'Social capital: its origins and applications in modern sociology', *Annual Review of Sociology*, vol 24, pp 1–12.

Putnam, R. (1995) 'Bowling alone: American's declining social capital', *Journal of Democracy*, vol 6, no 1, pp 64–78.

Putnam, R. (2000) *Bowling Alone: The Collapse and Revival of American Community*, New York: Simon and Schuster.

Reay, D. (2004) '"It's all becoming a habitus": beyond the habitual use of habitus in educational research', *British Journal of Sociology of Education*, Special Issue on Pierre Bourdieu's Sociology of Education, vol 25, no 4, September, pp 431–44.

Savage, M., Warde, A. and Devine, F. (2004) 'Capitals, assets and resources: some critical issues', Cultural Capital and Social Exclusion Workshop, January, Oxford.

Shah, B., Dwyer, C. and Modood, T. (2010) 'Explaining educational achievement and career aspirations among young British Pakistanis: mobilising "ethnic capital"?', *Sociology*, vol 44, no 6, pp 1109–27.

Shiner, M. and Modood, T. (2002) 'Help or hindrance? Higher education and the route to ethnic equality', *British Journal of Sociology of Education*, vol 23, no 2, pp 209–30.

Storen, L.A. and Helland, H. (2010) 'Ethnicity differences in the completion rates of upper secondary education: how do the effects of gender and social background variables interplay?', *European Sociological Review*, vol 26, no 5, pp 585–601.

Wallman, S. (1979) *Ethnicity at Work*, London: Macmillan.

Werbner, P. (1990a) *The Migration Process*, Oxford: Berg.

Werbner, P. (1990b) 'Renewing the industrial past: British Pakistani entrepreneurship in Manchester', *Migration*, vol 8, pp 7–39.

Zhou, M. (1992) *Chinatown: The Socioeconomic Potential of an Urban Enclave*, Philadelphia, PA: Temple University Press.

Zhou, M. (1997) 'Growing up American: the challenge confronting immigrant children and children of immigrants', *Annual Review of Sociology*, vol 23, pp 63–95.

Zhou, M. (2005) 'Ethnicity as social capital: community-based institutions and embedded networks of social relations', in G. Loury, T. Modood and S. Teles (eds) *Ethnicity, Social Mobility and Public Policy in the US and UK*, Cambridge: Cambridge University Press.

Zhou, M. and Bankston III, C.L. (1998) *Growing Up American: How Vietnamese Children Adapt to Life in the United States*, New York: Russell Sage Foundation.

TWO

Widening participation from a historical perspective: increasing our understanding of higher education and social justice

David W. Thompson

Introduction

It is tempting, when considering issues of access to education and social inclusion in the United Kingdom, to wholly root them in the contemporary discourse brought about by the post-1997 policies of the 'New Labour' government and the subsequent administrations. Equally, in the current climate, it would be understandable if policies such as widening participation to higher education were located within a postmodern construct: incorporating globalisation, post-Fordism, the skills agenda, meeting 21st-century challenges of rapid change and fragmentation, and so on. However, to do this, or any other research into social justice and education, without recourse to the wider historical perspective would be a mistake. Before entering into a study of contemporary aspects of creating greater access to higher education (also known as widening participation) and social inclusion generally, it is worth considering how in the past society responded to new initiatives in education provision. This tells us something about the ways in which the current climate, in which educationalists and practitioners currently operate, has developed. An investigation into the historical precedence is important if one is to fully understand the enormity of the task at hand today with respect to adult education and social justice. After all, how can the scale of the phenomenon be fully understood, or a prognosis made about the future, until one appreciates the influencing factors that have contributed to the conditions experienced today?

Too often, through no fault of their own, educators working on access and inclusion are locked into time-specific projects and initiatives, tied to demonstrable outcomes, and constrained by temporary contracts;

they are moulded and directed by the political dogma and expediency of the time. Potentially, this can stifle independent research that leads to a greater comprehension of the wider perspectives influencing their field. The aim of this chapter is to help the reader develop this wider context through an investigation, although by no means exhaustive, of certain discourses concerning universities, access, social justice and adult education. A key facet of this chapter will be a discussion of initiatives that have appeared episodically from the 19th century to the present day, revealing prevalent modes of thinking in the context of working-class education.

Just saying that this investigation is not exhaustive is doing a disservice to many who have contributed extensively to the debate on higher education and widening participation. But there is simply not enough room in this single chapter to do justice to such a wide-ranging and complex subject matter. Instead, it focuses upon exposing a narrower seam; its aim is to provide a slightly different angle to the general debate on widening participation in higher education. For the wider context within the United Kingdom, in terms of widening participation and higher education, it is only natural for me to direct the reader to the contributions of colleagues in this publication and to suggest further reading (eg McGivney, 1996, 2000; Reay, 1998a, 1998b; Preece, 1999a, 1999b; Thomas, 2001a, 2001b; Reay and Ball, 2005; Ball, 2006; see also the reports by Fryer, 1997; Kennedy, 1997; Dearing, 1999). Equally, for a more extensive discussion of higher education issues, the works of Archer (1979), Scott (1995), Coffield and Williamson (1997), Barnett (1997), Brown (1999, 2003a, 2003b), Watson (2002), Tight (2004), and Tight et al. (2009) would be appropriate.

Widening participation within a historical perspective has not been researched to any great extent, although more generally working-class adult education certainly has (see Simon, 1960, 1990, 1991, 1994; Lowe, 1989; Fryer, 1992; Fieldhouse and Associates, 1996). It should also be remembered that the working classes themselves often do not have their own interpretation to draw upon:

> The working classes rarely have their own authoritative history of working-class oppression, just fragments from the past. I suggest that this lack of any historical analysis of class processes, and concomitantly elite and middle-class domination and working-class resistance, contributes to a pervasive working class inability to construct an authentic working class identity in the 1990s. (Reay, 1998b, p 266)

More recently, however, there has been significant work produced in ways that do give a voice to the working classes and the great tradition of autodidacticism (see eg Rose, 2002). More research in this vein is needed if we are to better comprehend this field and strengthen the identity that Reay speaks of.

Widening participation provides a modern extension to tackling inequality and social exclusion through education-based initiatives, but measures designed to address social justice in this way have emerged over many decades. It can be defined as providing greater opportunities to those 'non-traditional' students who would not normally consider a university education as an option. Future historians will no doubt turn their attention to a fuller analysis of widening participation activity post-1997 and the watershed provided by the election of New Labour in the United Kingdom. This chapter marks the start of that process by considering an overview of historical research and mapping out some of the issues relating to the opening up and expansion of higher education.

Further, the way in which the chapter elaborates on the historical perspective, is through the identification of clear differences between middle-class and working-class ideologies and the resultant opportunities with respect to adult education. Class labels are of course constructed, deconstructed, generalised and interpreted in many different ways, but I believe they are still useful. Reay argues that class 'continues to be an important part of social identity into the millennium despite prevailing discourses which constitute it as irrelevant'; class still plays a major force in shaping identity, it 'tells us something very important about women's and men's lives' (1998b, p 260). Drawing upon Bourdieu to facilitate her interpretations; Reay is adamant that 'class just as much as gender, age, sexuality and ethnicity, infuses daily interactions; influencing to whom we talk and shaping what we say and how we say it'. Research has 'revealed an increasing middle-class policing of class boundaries' and the 'growth of educational segregation based on both class and ethnic divisions' (Reay, 1998b, pp 262–5). It is in this spirit of interpretation (and others such as Brian Simon) that this chapter is written.

Some early developments in widening access

The industrial revolutions of the late 18th and 19th centuries helped to provide an impetus for reform and change of the education system, as the emerging industrial and commercial entrepreneurs sought social change that reflected their new-found status and influence. During the 19th century, the development of widening access to education opportunities in England reflected fluctuating power struggles between institutions, governments and the burgeoning middle classes. The latter became increasingly confident in the importance of their role in society during the 19th century, which also witnessed early criticisms of the existing status quo that Oxford and Cambridge had maintained from medieval times. During this time, access to universities could be described in today's discourse as an attempt to 'widen participation', but only for the middle classes.

In the first decade of the 19th century, Sidney Smith and the Edinburgh Review attacked Oxford in particular as lacking in the provision of education that could be utilised to better 'man's estate'. At this time, hegemony or ownership of higher education was in the hands of the established Church, and the middle classes and non-conformists were in the position of 'assertion', as Archer (1979) referred to it in her analysis of the social origins of the education system. There was growing resentment of the religious bar that operated; while non-conformists could study, they could not claim a BA degree and were generally discouraged from study by being forced to attend the Church of England College Chapel. Resentment was combined with attacks on the two ancient institutions for not being, what one might call today, 'fit for purpose' in the modern age of the early 19th century. Dissenters and critics of what was seen as an institutional training ground for the orthodox clergy pointed to Oxbridge's preoccupation with the classics as anachronistic and inadequate for the modern-day demands of a growing, industrialised nation.

During the 1820s, James Mill attacked the universities for not being progressive. Simon suggested that Mill's 'primary concern at this period was to lead the non-conformist middle class in an assault on the clerical domination of education' (Simon, 1960, p 90). Bentham and his supporters, such as James Mill, Joseph Hume and Henry Brougham, also contributed their utilitarian views to the argument. During this period, the aristocracy still maintained hegemony in terms of politics, influence on education and social control. Waged against this were the flourishing middle classes; benefiting from industry and commerce, who at this time evidently held high opinions of themselves. They considered themselves to be 'this vast and unspeakably important portion of our population'. Research on *The Westminster Review* reveals James Mill's passionate clarion call at the time. Mill wrote:

> The value of the middle classes of this country and importance are recognised by all. These classes have long been spoken of, and not grudgingly by their superiors

themselves, as the glory of England.... The proper education of this portion of the people is therefore of the greatest possible importance to the well being of the state.... The people of the class below are the instruments with which they work. (Simon, 1960, p 78)

With these comments, we see an early intent to widen participation for the middle classes. From the final sentence, we also get a revealing insight into how some people viewed the lower stratification in society.

The University of London, established around 1826, became one of the first institutions that responded to this demand for education. It appealed to Jews, Catholics and non-conformists, all of whom were barred from Oxbridge, or at least not allowed to graduate. It marked the first real attempt to wrest the educational initiative and to widen participation for excluded middle-class citizens. Reaction from some quarters, especially the religious establishment, was hostile to this development; Thomas Arnold called it the 'Godless College', and it was thought a threat to both Church and state. It would not be the last time that moves to widen participation or challenge the convention of the day were met with hostility from conservative commentators, in the form of colourful hyperbole. In fact, as shall be seen, this emerged periodically and still surfaces today.

Tensions during this time surfaced between the commercial middle classes and the aristocracy, the disenfranchised and the enfranchised, the non-conformists and the established Church, the reform movement and the status quo. For a long period the 'squire and clergy' reigned over the 'entrepreneur and merchant'; privilege remained resolute to the tidal swell for reform. During this period, the working classes appeared to labour under the assumption that the middle classes might carry them along in the move towards political reform and better educational provision. Wanting universal education and wider suffrage, the middle classes had no intention of extending this to their 'instruments'. 'The workers had lent full support to the middle class in their struggle for Parliamentary reform but [were] strongly resentful of their exclusion from the franchise' (Simon, 1960, p 128). The middle classes therefore 'engaged in a fight on two fronts'. They attacked the aristocracy for their backwardness and resistance to reform, but also became increasingly involved in ensuring that the working class conformed as much as possible to what was perceived as the natural order.

Davies Giddy, MP for Helston, Higher Sheriff of Cornwall and later to be President of the Royal Society, wrote in 1807:

> [Education] would teach them to despise their lot in life, instead of making them good servants ... to which their rank in society had destined them. In fact, where education was promoted for the working classes it should be such that taught them their station in life. (Simon, 1960, p 132)

The radical Francis Place offered a different viewpoint. Place was an agitator, self-educated and a Chartist, wanting parliamentary reform and votes for working men. Writing in 1833, he observed: 'Nearly the whole body of those who are rich dread the consequences of teaching the people more than they dread the effects of their ignorance' (Simon, 1960, p 169).

In these two quotes we see a representation of a discourse repeated episodically throughout the history of education; the conservative, concerned about change and resorting to sermonising and haranguing, and the more liberal and measured call for reform. A social theory of discourse becomes evident in many of these dialectical exchanges:

> discourse as a political practice is not only a site of power struggle, but also a stake in power struggle: discursive practice draws upon conventions which naturalise particular power relations and ideologies ... the ways in which they are articulated are a focus of struggle. (Fairclough, 1992, p 67)

For much of the 19th century, adult education in Britain aimed at the working classes was actually directed in a way that often met the needs of 'bourgeois' society; for example, to produce more efficient workers, to reduce the alienating effects of industrialisation, as a response to the widening political franchise, or sometimes in an attempt at social justice. 'The middle classes became increasingly aware of the value of adult education as a means of moulding society in their image' (Fieldhouse and Associates, 1996, p 12). There were also concerns about too much education for the masses in a very practical sense. In 1870, the Reverend Nash Stephenson noted in Transactions of the National Association for the Promotion of Social Science that, in a now widely referenced quote:

> I have a misgiving as to the wisdom of opening up a scheme for the advancement of the working classes which might prove illusory, and of raising hopes which could never be realised. There must be hewers of wood and drawers of water. (Quoted in Lowe, 1989, p 167)

This ideology has a familiar ring today; consider how the concerns regarding the lack of hewers and drawers have been replaced by a 21st-century demand for more plumbers. While plumbing is of course a very skilled trade, the inference always appears to be that it is a trade only worthy of certain sectors of society.

Over time, and especially in the latter part of the 19th century, the middle classes gained more influence throughout politics and education. However, 'as the middle classes obtained gradually more control, the task of teaching the working class to recognise its own claims seemed much less urgent' (Simon, 1960, p 165). It has been argued (Anderson, 1992) that the middle classes were, in fact, assimilated into the ideology and culture of the aristocracy. The 'business' classes from the middle of the 19th century onwards were rapidly amalgamated into societal etiquette, and mirrored the outlook of the landed gentry and upper classes (Hobsbawm, 1999). A transition of emphasis took place from 'the shift of education of the sons of the well-born – the families of the aristocracy and gentry – to an education system that provides qualified and accredited labour power for the industrial and administrative bureaucracies of advanced capitalism', which reproduced the 'occupational and status advantages of its higher functionaries for a new generation' (Rustin, 1986, p 17).

From around 1850 onwards, increasing pressure developed for parliamentary action on education reform. Later in the century, this coincided with the second industrial revolution, from which the middle classes drew greater strength in terms of numbers and influence. For the first time, the government needed to pay serious attention to just what the universities were doing. Parliament began to reflect the rising middle classes and their intrusion placed the old educational order on the defence. This became the start of growing political involvement within the university system that continues to the present day.

The established Oxbridge elite opposed such intrusion into its affairs. At times, some dons resorted to a pejorative idiom as a defensive mechanism. Examples of this can be seen when the Government Commission of 1850 began to make inquiries regarding the way Oxbridge operated. An Oxford Professor of Divinity resorted to this hyperbolic tactic when protesting that the commission was 'fraught with immediate evil'; other colleagues called such intrusion 'dangerous ... ill-omened ... despotic' and even 'antiquated', also 'ungracious ... impolitic ... self-destructive' (quoted in Simon, 1960, p 293). The discourse here, to put it mildly, is alarmist and reveals a crude knee-jerk reaction from a selection of the elite holding privileged positions. This blunt approach hardly seems to change throughout time and is evident within the contemporary rhetoric surrounding access to higher education.

In the latter part of the 19th century, higher education began to evolve from a few 'ancient' universities servicing a very small elite, to a much wider system. There began a mushrooming of colleges and institutions, which were 'utilitarian' in nature; designed to train and educate and meet a new demand. During this time, the 'creation of a clearly defined and widely recognised hierarchical structure' emerged (Lowe, 1989). While those that formed the highest levels of such stratification, Oxford and Cambridge, gradually introduced new subjects, they nevertheless retained their indifference to the rest and often responded to proposals for reform with conservatism. The emerging civic universities catered specifically for the middle classes with science and engineering, but also aspired to the Oxbridge traditions. The prospectus of the University of Birmingham shortly after its charter in 1900 made it quite clear that the University 'is for training "captains of industry", not the rank and file, or even the non-commissioned officers'; revealing the mindset at that time (Lowe, 1989, pp 164–5).

The civic universities continued to draw upon the supply of people destined to be 'captains of industry', resulting in a consolidation of the stratification process that both reflected and served a differentiated society. This is an important point, this differentiation and stratification of institutions, and therefore opportunity, is still intact in the 21st century. While such a system may be almost impossible to deconstruct and has arguably served society well enough over the intervening years, it is also responsible for a lack of diversity, innovation and opportunity for large sections of society. Whether practitioner or theorist, one should consider this legacy when contemporary moves to open up elite systems to non-traditional students are attempted. To widen participation, practitioners need to allow for the tidal swell of conservative interests they are swimming against, with respect to some institutions at least:

> The swift growth and transition of the late 19th century had only briefly challenged these hierarchies: the adjustments of the early years of the new century served merely to confirm them ... it is possible to conclude that one important element in the dynamic of change was an acute awareness among the English upper and middle classes of the importance of social hierarchies. (Lowe, 1989, p 178)

It was not until the beginning of the 20th century, following a long gestation period, that attempts to (what we would call today) widen participation ultimately brought about university education for many of the middle classes. This occurred with the evolution of the civic universities born out of the Mechanics Institutes in towns and cities such as Manchester, Bristol, Leeds, Birmingham and Liverpool. These have been alluded to as middle-class or bourgeois universities that matured and ensured the interests of their own kind; 'a critical means of acquisition and transmission of cultural capital, vital if each new generation is to maintain and/or increase its advantages in competition with other social strata' (Rustin, 1986, pp 35–6).

The working classes continued to be granted few favours in this emerging and transforming higher education. Industrialists were wary of outlaying provision for educating working-class offspring for fear of interfering with time that should be spent labouring in factories. Writing in 1903, Robert Halstead, a Co-operative Society member and co-founder of the Workers Education Association (WEA), observed: 'if higher education of working men is to make desired progress, it will have to consolidate itself into a special movement' (WEA, 2004).

The one way in which Oxbridge did ultimately reach out, in terms of adult education, was through the extension movement, initiated around 1867 at Cambridge. Although the aim was to retain the core activity that strengthened the existing system, a contemporary letter stated 'the object of the 'extension' movement has been to see whether we could not open the gates of the university wider without injury to its proper functions and character' (Lowe, 1989, p 168). While hardly a ringing endorsement, it is at least a move in the direction of greater access and a certain acknowledgement of need. The initiative expanded towards the end of the 19th century and in the 20th century paved the way for organisations such as the WEA. The movement was peripheral, always at the edge of institutional activities, similar in some ways to widening participation today. During the heyday of the extension movement, the extent to which these activities were marginalised was colourfully described by Margaret Cole when writing about the tutorial classes taken by G.D.H. Cole and others. The classes:

> Often involved the tutor in dark journeys in crammed local
> trains or tubes at rush hour. They were apt to take place not
> in purpose-built accommodation – or anything of the kind
> – but in something like a council schoolroom with desks
> made to fit infants, not grown men, hired for the evening
> from the local trades council, or in other places intended
> for other uses. (Simon, 1990, p 52)

While WEA activists and educationalists such as Mansbridge and Tawney emphasised the extension movement as an opening up of university provision, in reality it seems that the initiatives allowed Oxbridge to steer clear of widespread internal reform (Lowe, 1989, p 169). The extension movement did, however, enable Oxbridge to be seen as encompassing and appealing to a wider social range. That said, Mansbridge, who had both learnt and taught within the extension movement, was forced to conclude that it had become 'mainly a middle-class movement' and ultimately realised that 'the consumers of the education must themselves take an effective part in its provision' (Marsh, 2002, p 4). The dominant and conservative ideology prevailed; the experiences of the University Extension College at Reading revealed, ironically, that in fact sometimes initiatives gravitated in the opposite direction. In its early days, the College reflected the philosophy of the extension movement, but this became a lesser part of the College's activities, until eventually its patrons renamed it University College. Reading shifted towards what became a more conventional and conservative concept of what a university should typically represent: 'in many respects the experience of Reading can be seen as representative of the failure of the whole university extension movement. Exeter University Extension College underwent a similar development' (Fieldhouse and Associates, 1996, pp 200–1). This is symptomatic of how new opportunities in education are sometimes assimilated by those who know how to work the system to their own advantage. Another example was the system of scholarships. Barnes (1996), in her study of English civic universities and their affinity to Oxbridge ideals, observed that post-First World War scholarships 'contrary to intentions' did not result in any great increase in attendance of those from less wealthy homes. Instead, most grants were awarded to those who held the advantage of a public school education. Further, she argues that in fact the vast majority of people living in provincial cities where civic universities were located never crossed the boundaries into the campus and were ignorant of the activities that were conducted within (Barnes, 1996, pp 285, 304).

The pattern of development between aristocracy and the bourgeoisie was a compromise of principles that has other parallels in the British class system (Rustin, 1986, p 31). However, it appeared that no such compromise trickled down to the working class. Indeed, much of the middle classes continued to fight hard in order to maintain their hard-earned status and avoid compromise. R.H. Tawney, writing in 1922, observed:

There is a general belief among thoughtful working people that higher education in general, and Oxford and Cambridge in particular, had been organised in the past too largely for the convenience of the well-to-do classes, and that, though a certain number of able boys pass to them, no very persistent and strenuous efforts have been made to remove financial obstacles. The workman in a mining village or cotton town sees his clever boy prevented from going to university by lack of means, while the son of his employer, even if not conspicuously intelligent, appears to be admitted without difficulty. The ill-will which results is not negligible. (Lowe, 1989, p 174)

This aversion to satisfy working-class educational needs was challenged in part, particularly during the 1920s, with a mushrooming and development of organisations aimed at providing for working people. Simon (1990) has synthesised this into what he called the 'struggle for hegemony' during the period 1920–26. The organisations in question included the WEA, the Communist Party, the Workers Educational Trade Union Committee (WETUC) and the National Council of Labour Colleges (NCLC). However, the established authority was suspicious of lending any aid to organisations that potentially, in their view, encouraged actions that might be subversive, revolutionary or lead to independent thought to any great extent (Fieldhouse and Associates, 1996). Again, authority figures resorted to inflammatory language in a riposte that exposed their anxieties. For example, J.P.M. Millar of the NCLC felt obliged to respond to the criticism of Conservative politician Lord Eustace Percy; writing to Percy in 1926 he noted: 'My Lord, a short time ago in a speech delivered at Newcastle, you made a violent attack on this organisation (the NCLC) and upon myself. In this attack you described our educational policy as poisonous and pestilential' (Simon, 1990, p 53).

Such discourse masked different ideological standpoints; 'where contrasting discursive practices are in use in a particular domain or institution, the likelihood is that part of that contrast is ideological' (Fairclough, 1992, p 88). Fairclough, for example, discusses the use of the AIDS disease as an unfortunate metaphor for plague in ways that reconstruct social reality as a disease of 'the other' (1992, pp 197–8). Organisations such as the NCLC were regarded by some conservative commentators of the day as the 'other'; they were under constant scrutiny. The then Board of Education issued a 'Responsible Body' status to the WEA for the provision of adult education. Percy,

President of the Board, revealed his concerns when he commented on the granting of the status to the WEA as 'about the best police expenditure we could indulge in' (WEA, 2004). By 'police expenditure', Percy appears to be referring to the state funding allocated to those organisations responsible enough to provide learning that was not in any way radical, subversive or revolutionary, and did not lead to insurrection. Funding and provision was strictly controlled and if individuals wanted to enter mainstream university education they had to do so through traditional avenues.

Expansion and contradiction?

The expansion of students in higher education between 1957 and 1963 led to an increase of almost 50%, from 148,000 to 217,000 and prompted the Robbins Report (Simon, 1991, p 223). This constituted a major investigation into the pattern of provision and how future higher education might develop. A major conclusion was that the system should expand to meet the demands of many more students and with a wider range of provision. The 'Robbins principle' was established: that is, 'courses of higher education should be available for all those who are qualified by ability and attainment to pursue them and who wish to do so' (Allen, 1988, p 43). The Robbins Report appeared as demand governed supply and successive governments were attracted to the idea of the need for a modern, educated Britain to meet the aspirations of increased economic growth and prosperity. However, others describe the Robbins Report as 'the definitive charter of the bourgeois university'; while the recommendation appeared to make entitlement universal, 'in fact it was still highly partial and selective' (Rustin, 1986, p 39).

Contemporary attitudes and contributions to the Robbins Report reveal the difference between progressive and conservative outlooks, with the latter intent on maintaining the status quo. Simon summarises the different camps:

> The most 'progressive' standpoints were expressed by organisations connected with the labour movement; the TUC [Trades Union Congress], the Communist Party and possibly the Fabians, and from the teachers … though not from the grammar school and public school headmasters … this indicated a line up that had achieved considerable educational advantages in the past. The most conservative evidence came from the vice chancellors and, regrettably,

from the AUT [Association of University Teachers]. (Simon, 1991, p 228)

The hierarchical structure was reinforced post-Robbins; the emergent binary system (despite Robbins' call for a unitary system) spawned the polytechnics, which had less appeal to the middle classes. Statistics (Anderson, 1992, p 62) point to a much higher ratio of working-class students in the polytechnics and concludes that they did more for the unskilled working class in particular. Meanwhile, it 'protected the status of the universities' and their elite practices; while the polytechnics encouraged part-time study, promoted vocational courses and maintained links with their localities (Anderson, 1992, p 27). Depending upon one's point of view, this could either be seen as a natural response to market-led demands or a form of informal educational apartheid that has perpetuated ever since. Today, it could be argued that stratification is even more pronounced; represented by the 'elite' Russell Group, the pre-1992 institutions and the post-1992 former polytechnics. Ironically, the attempt to widen participation through the recently introduced Foundation Degree programme and new programmes of study has only served to differentiate the structure of higher education in the UK.

During the 1970s, more courses were developed that were oriented towards women and, by the late 1980s, there was a growing importance of gender studies and the role of women in society (Westwood and Thomas, 1991, p 15), although these remained a small proportion of courses in higher education. In addition, radical and neo-Marxist critiques were developed, and the work of Freire was drawn upon in the case of adult education (Field, 2002, p 129). Taylor and Ward conclude that in fact a wide variety of institutions, voluntary and statutory, were involved in education and training, particularly with the unemployed. This included churches, charities, voluntary organisations, the TUC and local government (Taylor and Ward, in Lovett, 1988, p 243). An area that attracted much interest in the 1960s and 1970s, in terms of adult education, was that of community development (Westwood and Thomas, 1991, p 12). Such initiatives with the unemployed, through trade unionists and through the access 'movement', gave mature students a much higher profile in higher education (Yarnit, quoted in Mayo and Thompson, 1995, p 72). However, the election of the Thatcher government in 1979 witnessed 'great trauma to the stability and promise of adult education in the 1970s', and 'The disturbance to the equilibrium of British Society was profound' (Westwood and Thomas, 1991, p 15). The emphasis on radical or innovative education drew criticism. The Thatcher government acted as an antidote to radical approaches within the system and forced innovation out into community education and local education authorities. Thomas noted that the attacks on the education system and adult education were both demoralising and destructive. During the 1980s, financial and organisational change instigated by the Thatcher government 'considerably affected' university adult education provision and had an extremely negative impact. Funding cuts of 14% in 1981 resulted in the loss of academic staff, increased workloads and increased staff–student ratios. The combination of financial cuts and new working practices undermined the capacity to become involved in working-class adult education. The policies of Thatcher and the 'New Right' facilitated the 'apparent need for change' and turned the education system:

> into one more outpost of the enterprise culture, operating according to business principles and driven by the so-called logic of the market ... they also acted as a way of re-inventing education as a means of people-processing and control, rather than as a potential tool for liberation. (Mayo and Thompson, 1995, p 1)

The great irony, of course, is that in 1993 the Conservative government opened up the university system and enabled the old polytechnics to become new universities in their own right. In one legislative swoop many more people came to experience higher education; however, this did not appear to open up the pre-1992 system to any extent and the social mix of students remained relatively unscathed.

What emerged in the 1990s, at least, was the 'Access' to higher education initiative and a move to encourage opportunities for progression. Changes in central government policies and the commitment of local education authorities to equal opportunity resulted in strategies 'to open up the whole of post-compulsory education to adult learners' (Tuckett, quoted in Westwood and Thomas, 1991, p 27). During the 1980s, there was a stronger move towards progression and the role of adult learners in higher and further education. Higher education institutions, faced with declining numbers of younger students, linked up with the further education sector to develop 'Access' courses to attract mature students:

> The most significant developments of the decade in higher education have been led by polytechnics in the expansion of Access course provision.... Courses linking higher education institutions to colleges and more unusually adult

education institutes, sought to target student groups under-represented in the higher education student body. (Tuckett, quoted in Westwood and Thomas, 1991, pp 31–2)

By 1989, there were approximately 400 Access courses in 50 local education authorities, with 600 students in further education colleges (Reay et al., 2005, p 6). However, this was tempered at the same time because 'access to elite establishments remains restricted' (Reay, 1998a, p 520).

Despite education initiatives such as Access, community education and more 'radical' provision, the educational elite appeared to change little. There were 'ideological and structural problems ... these institutions are concerned only marginally with working-class adult education ... they are all, in different ways, linked both structurally and ideologically to existing patterns of provision and to the dominant culture and its assumptions' (Lovett, 1988, pp 258–9). Others argued 'that alongside the academic and social selectivity of higher education institutions, the relative status and social exclusivity of choice-making are key factors in generating and reproducing patterns of internal differentiation' (Reay et al., 2005, p 29). That is to say, cultural and social capital, material constraints, social perceptions and distinctions, and forms of self-exclusion are all at work in the process of choice. Universities still played a key role in the reproduction of class inequalities (Leathwood, 2004, p 34); 'the picture that emerges is of a socially differentiated higher education sector, with elite institutions tending to be dominated by [the] middle class' (Leathwood, 2004, p 38). Research commissioned by the then government also revealed 'middle-class resistance to widening participation' (Leathwood, 2004, p 42). Thus, despite some advances in exposing higher education to a more diverse student population, the structure and culture of the system remained conservative. This is the legacy that current initiatives to widen participation have inherited.

A review of two documents separated by nearly 100 years, reminds us of this legacy and that there are many parallels between situations at the beginning of the 20th and 21st centuries. The 2003 White Paper was compared to the *Oxford and Working-Class Education Report* of 1908. Parallels include foundation degrees, the need for flexible approaches to learning and matters of finance; combined with themes relating to 'attainment', 'aspirational', 'admissions' and 'logistical' barriers (McNicol, 2004).

Inheriting the discursive legacy: barricades, Faust and a moral panic

We witness similar conservative attitudes replicated in the 21st century, in terms of moves to open up the higher education system to students less fortunate and unable to benefit from employing the right kinds of cultural and social capital. Discourse is used again with pejorative tendencies; language and rhetoric designed to deflect New Labour from its social inclusion policies with respect to higher education.

'The middle classes are fighting back. Some of Britain's top schools are going to "black" Bristol University for [its] "pernicious social engineering policies"' (Heffer, 2003). So cried Simon Heffer as he too worried about the assertion to open up the system. Deborah Orr responded to these verbose headlines with a much-needed sense of equilibrium:

> Middle England critics like to call this messing around with admission criteria 'social engineering'. But the truth is that it is they who have forever been indulging in social engineering, by purchasing their children's futures. Now they are incandescent with rage that the task of gaining unassailable advantage for their offspring is no longer going to be quite so foolproof as it has always been. (Orr, 2003)

Heffer's rhetoric had been picked up before by the Select Committee on Education and Skills, with respect to higher education funding. The Chair asked the Higher Education Funding Council for England Chief Executive Howard Newby:

> We have this scurrilous campaign from the *Daily Mail* and elsewhere, and we know why there is a scurrilous campaign, because it will impinge on what is seen as a right to get their children into the best higher education institutions in the country through a preferred route. Now is that not what the fuss is all about? They have had an easy ride for a long time, have they not? (*Hansard*, 2003)

Newby was forced to admit that there was 'something of a moral panic taking place' (*Hansard*, 2003).

A further pejorative example, this time through a metaphorical and literary reference, came from an Oxbridge Vice-Chancellor in a 2003 speech. It was insisted that 'the University would not enter into a Faustian bargain with the government on widening access in return for higher fees' if it compromised admissions policy (Baty, 2003). The Faustian reference implies of course some kind of pact made with the Devil. It is possible that the Vice-Chancellor sympathised with the need for wider access; but again the language and unfortunate choice of metaphor exposes the conservative and reactionary mindset through power and discourse.

It is reasonable to assume, of course, that there is no distinct ideological dividing line or dichotomy between those who resolutely maintain and defend the traditional approach to higher education, and an opposition or working-class movement intent on reform. Many from middle-class backgrounds support meritocratic and inclusive principles of wider access and social policies enabling access for anyone who wishes to enter academic study, irrespective of upbringing. There is no clear united movement presenting a consistent opposition to such policies. Few are prepared to oppose outright or openly criticise; the former Chief Inspector to Schools (1994–2000) Chris Woodhead is an exception, however. Woodhead admits he is one of the 'elitist whingers'. Liking castle or war-like metaphors, he sent out a rallying cry to man the 'barricades'. In light of a national shortage of tradespeople, he suggested that what was really needed was more men and women with practical skills. The inference, it seemed, is that these tasks should be left for the working class or 'not so bright', who need not be encouraged into higher education. He quoted dropout rates in new universities that attract greater proportions of working-class people as an excuse to encourage the take-up of other types of education (*THES*, 2002). One is left with an inference that professions such as teaching, medicine and law are reserved for one particular social set; cementing social, economic and education hierarchies. The metaphor of war (in this instance manning the barricades) in social discourses has been recognised with numerous examples acknowledging the 'effectiveness of metaphors in structuring reality in a particular way' (Fairclough, 1992, pp 195–6). In 2009, Woodhead returned to the headlines, this time with a religious broadside. He noted that 'not very bright' children should be taken out of the classroom to undertake practical courses and concludes 'why do we think we can make him brighter than God made him' (*Guardian On-line*, 2009).

Discourses can quickly take on the vernacular of the *zeitgeist*. The economic downturn and banking crisis of 2009, connected to 'toxic mortgages' and sub-prime lending in the US, is an example. With respect to access to higher education, we witness a corresponding discourse that suggests 'toxic talk poisons admissions debate' (*THES*,

2009). Note how in 1926 the discourse of Lord Eustace Percy, discussed earlier, regarding 'poison' and 'pestilence' coincided with the worldwide epidemic of Encephalitis Lethargica in the 1920s and shortly after the 1918–20 'Spanish Flu' pandemic. Readers might like to look out for new discourses appearing around higher education and social justice in the future, and what 'social engineering' is taking place (as critics of initiatives such as access to higher education pejoratively label it).

In the meantime, let us remind ourselves of some of the language waged against much of the work to innovate and open up access to universities; it is Faustian, despotic, Godless, a threat, evil, dangerous, ungracious, impolitic, ill-omened, fraught, poisonous, pernicious and pestilential. We are told to 'man the barricades', that a 'moral panic' is taking place, universities will be 'blacked', 'do battle against the enemies' and the 'Trojan horse', that the 'citadel' is at risk, not to 'open the gates' too wide as it might cause 'injury', that we must make sure we have 'hewers' and 'drawers', that people's 'station in life' should be clear, and many are just 'instruments' with which to work. More recently, we are told that we must also take care not to become embroiled in 'toxic talk' on admissions. The friction between the dissenting middle classes and the Anglican Church and governments of the 19th century have been replaced in the 21st century with tensions between the professional middle classes and any government attempting to open up the education system. It is exactly this sector (those with dominance) that carefully control the educational reins and who, ultimately, have a far greater voting influence.

Conclusion

This chapter advances the proposition that the marginalisation of activities to open up university education, and the dichotomous tension between progressives and conservatives, has hindered the development of widening participation and social justice for those at the lower levels of the social strata. This has been compounded by what could be called reactionary rhetoric.

In many respects, widening participation placed within a historical perspective follows Archer's (1979) comparative analysis of the origins of educational systems. That is to say, it follows a trend where assertion is pitted against dominance; however, 'working class assertion came from a group which had neither political influence nor economic surplus' (Archer, 1979, p 124). Three factors in the maintenance of domination have been emphasised; monopoly of ownership of educational facilities, protective constraints and legitimatory ideology (Archer, 1979). Such strong forces can lead to the marginalisation of innovation and widening access; they provide a construct for the continued social and institutional stratification we see today.

The New Labour White Paper of 2003 reminded us that 'the social class gap in entry to higher education remains unacceptably wide. While many more people from all backgrounds benefit from higher education, the proportion coming from lower-income families has not substantially increased' (Department for Education and Skills, 2003). Within this context, one is constantly reminded of many of the challenges to participation in practitioner accounts of contemporary projects to widen access (Thompson, 2008, 2009):

> Education remains an important factor for creating social justice and opportunity for all social classes; but those that maintain control, and who are aware of these potential opportunities, jealously guard their prized possession.
>
> It is evident that 'professional' or 'expert' opinion is emphasised at the expense of other forms of evidence ... in this sense the least powerful are 'silenced' ... or when such evidence is heard, it is mediated through the voices of middle-class academics. (Greenbank, 2006, p 160)

Education, however, remains an essential element for increasing life chances and banishing exclusion and oppression; thus, the International Federation of Workers' Educational Associations issued the following statement: 'Education is of great importance to people in their struggle to overcome deprivation, exploitation and oppression. In leading to a better understanding of human problems, and assisting the search for possible solutions, education can be a liberating factor' (Fryer, 1992, p 313).

People in power 'will strive to reduce and maintain at a low level the ambition of those personnel who fill essentially subordinate positions' (Blackledge and Hunt, 1985, p 83). 'Social closure and sponsored mobility imply the existence of an elite more or less conspicuously manipulating the system to suit its interests' (Anderson, 1992, p 65). In such an environment, working-class interests easily lose out to those who have ownership (dominance) of the education system and are much better protected through a closer interaction with their political masters:

> Parents who are themselves of middle class status expect
> their children to enjoy the same advantages, and will use
> their knowledge of the system and their financial power
> to secure whatever education is necessary to ensure this
> ... self reinforcing [and] inheriting. (Anderson, 1992, p 66)

This overview of the education system mirrors Weber's notion of 'social closure' as an apt description of elite control over an education system that reflects and sustains society's hierarchies. 'In England we are led to suggest that education is much more concerned with the maintenance of social stratification then the improvement in mobility, no-matter what the policy makers wish' (Blackledge and Hunt, 1985, p 88); this situation has barely changed in the intervening years.

The brief discussions here partly represent the wax and wane of conflicting influences over the university system episodically since the 19th century. Throughout, adult education of the working classes remained a peripheral issue until such times that it imposed itself on the consciousness of those maintaining hegemony. What we also see is irrational and pejorative language revealing deep-seated prejudice and bias interwoven throughout the last two centuries. This language and discourse can still be detected in modern times in the widening access debate.

This chapter has provided an important exercise. The reader should understand the precedents that have been set in the development of higher education and the tackling of social exclusion, and the attitudes shaped by stakeholders and guardians of the system. By considering these developments, the reader will achieve a greater understanding of the landscape in which projects to widen participation and initiatives to reduce social exclusion operate. In addition, one can relate and appreciate the varying degrees of support or opposition from the education, political and social establishments. In doing so, one can gauge the strength of the tide that projects and practitioners might be swimming against. This study informs the theorist and practitioner, who always need to be mindful of the wider context. It creates an opportunity to compare the past and apply it to the present, as well as anticipate the potential challenges presented in the future, in any form and at any level of education. The historical dimension relating to social justice can provide a solid grounding for further analysis and represents a process that readers may wish to apply when engaging with other important themes covered throughout this book.

References

Allen, M. (1988) *The Development of the British University System. The Goals of Universities*, Maidenhead: The Society for Research into Higher Education and the Open University Press.

Anderson, R.D. (1992) *Universities and Elites in Britain since 1800*, Basingstoke: Macmillan.

Archer, S. (1979) *Social Origins of Educational Systems*, London/Beverley Hills, CA: Sage.

Ball, S.J. (2006) *Education Policy and Social Class. The Selected Works of Stephen J. Ball*, Abingdon: Routledge.

Barnes, S.V. (1996) 'England's civic universities and the triumph of the Oxbridge ideal', *History of Education Quarterly*, vol 36, no 3, pp 271–305.

Barnett, R. (1997) *Towards a Higher Education for a New Century*, Institute of Education, University of London.

Baty, P. (2003) *Times Higher Education Supplement*, 17 October.

Blackledge, D. and Hunt, B. (1985) *Sociological Interpretations of Education*, London: Croom Helm.

Brown, R. (1999) 'Diversity in higher education: has it been and gone?', *Higher Education Review*, vol 31, no 3, pp 3–16.

Brown, R. (2003a) 'What future for higher education?', *Higher Education Review*, vol 35, no 3, pp 3–22.

Brown, R. (2003b) 'New Labour and higher education: dilemmas and paradoxes', *Higher Education Quarterly*, vol 57, no 3, pp 239–48.

Coffield, F. and Williamson, B. (1997) *Repositioning Higher Education*, Buckingham: The Society for Research into Higher Education and Open University Press.

Dearing, R. (1997) *The National Committee of Enquiry into Higher Education Report*, London: HMSO Crown Copyright.

Department for Education and Skills (2003) *The Future of Higher Education*, London: Crown Copyright.

Fairclough, N. (1992) *Discourse and Social Change*, Cambridge: Polity Press.

Field, J. (2002) 'Educational studies beyond school', *British Journal of Educational Studies*, vol 50, no 1, pp 120–43.

Fieldhouse, R. and Associates (1996) *A History of Modern British Adult Education*, Leicester: NIACE.

Fryer, B. (1992) 'The challenge to working-class adult education', in B. Simon (ed) *The Search for Enlightenment: The Working Class and Adult Education in the Twentieth Century*, Leicester: NIACE.

Fryer, R.H. (1997) *Learning for the Twenty-First Century*, First report of the National Advisory Group for Continuing Education and Lifelong Learning, www.lifelonglearning.co.uk/nagcell/index.htm.

Greenbank, P. (2006) 'The evolution of government policy on widening participation', *Higher Education Quarterly*, vol 60, no 2, pp 141–66.

Guardian On-line (2009) 'Middle-class pupils have better genes, says Chris Woodhead'. Available at: www.guardian.co.uk (accessed 11 May 2009).

Hansard (2003) 5 March.

Heffer, S. (2003) 'Why we middle classes have had enough', *Daily Mail*, 5 March.

Hobsbawm, E. (1999) *Industry and Empire: The Birth of the Industrial Revolution*, New York, NY: New Press.

Kennedy, H. (1997) *The Kennedy Report. Widening Participation in Further Education*, The Further Education Funding Council.

Leathwood, C. (2004) 'A critique of institutional inequalities in higher education (or an alternative to hypocrisy for higher education policy)', *Theory and Research in Education*, vol 2, no 1, pp 31–48.

Lovett, T. (ed) (1988) *Radical Approaches to Adult Education: A Reader*, London: Routledge.

Lowe, R. (1989) 'Structural change in English higher education 1870–1920', in D. Muller, F. Ringer and B. Simon (eds) *The Rise of the Modern Educational System: Structural Change and Social Reproduction 1870–1920*, Cambridge: Cambridge University Press.

Marsh, G. (2002) *Mansbridge: A Life. A Biographical Note to Celebrate the Centenary of the WEA*, Workers Education Association.

Mayo, M. and Thompson, J. (eds) (1995) *Adult Learning: Critical Intelligence and Social Change*, Leicester: NIACE.

McGivney, V. (1996) *Staying or Leaving the Course: Non-Completion and Retention of Mature Students in Further and Higher Education*, Leicester: NIACE.

McGivney, V. (2000) *Working with Excluded Groups*, Leicester: NIACE.

McNicol, S. (2004) 'Access to higher education among lower socio-economic groups: a historical perspective', *Journal of Access Policy and Practice*, vol 1, no 2, pp 162–70.

Orr, D. (2003) 'Middle England reveals a terrible insecurity', *The Independent*, 7 March.

Preece, J. (1999a) 'Difference and the discourse of inclusion', *Widening Participation and Lifelong Learning*, vol 1, no 2, pp 16–23.

Preece, J. (1999b) *Combating Social Exclusion in University Adult Education*, Aldershot: Ashgate.

Reay, D. (1998a) '"Always knowing" and "never being sure": familial and institutional habituses and higher education choice', *Journal of Education Policy*, vol 13, no 4, pp 519–29.

Reay, D. (1998b) 'Rethinking social class: qualitative perspectives on class and gender', *Sociology*, vol 32, no 2, pp 249–75.

Reay, D., David, M.E. and Ball, S. (2005) *Degrees of Choice: Social Class, Race and Gender in Higher Education*, Stoke-on-Trent: Trentham Books.

Rose, J. (2002) *The Intellectual Life of the British Working Classes*, London: Yale University Press.

Rustin, M. (1986) 'The idea of the popular university', in J. Finch and R. Rustin (eds) *A Degree of Choice? Higher Education and the Right to Learn*, London: Penguin.

Scott, P. (1995) *The Meanings of Mass Higher Education*, Buckingham: The Society for Research into Higher Education and the Open University Press.

Simon, B. (1960) *Studies in the History of Education, 1780–1870*, London: Lawrence and Wishart.

Simon, B. (ed) (1990) *The Search for Enlightenment. The Working Class and Adult Education in the Twentieth Century*, Leicester: NIACE.

Simon, B. (1991) *Education and the Social Order, 1940–1990*, London: Lawrence and Wishart.

Simon, B. (1994) *The State and Educational Change*, London: Lawrence and Wishart.

THES (*Times Higher Education Supplement*) (2002) 'Trouble in the Trades', 29 March.

THES (2009) '"Toxic" talk poisons admissions debate, V-C says', 29 January.

Thomas, E.A.M. (2001a) *Widening Participation in Post-Compulsory Education*, Stoke-on-Trent: Staffordshire University Press.

Thomas, E.A.M. (2001b) 'Power, assumptions and prescriptions: a critique of widening participation policy-making', *Higher Education Policy*, vol 14, no 4, pp 361–76.

Thompson, D.W. (2008) 'Widening participation and higher education. Students, systems and other paradoxes', *London Review of Education*, vol 6, pp 137–47.

Thompson, D.W. (2009) *Articulating Widening Participation Policy, Practice and Theory*, Saarbrucken: VDM Verlag.

Tight, M. (ed) (2004) *The Routledge Falmer Reader in Higher Education*, London: RoutledgeFalmer.

Tight, M., Mok, K.H., Huisman, J. and Morphew, C (eds) (2009) *The Routledge International Handbook of Higher Education*, London: Routledge.

Watson, D. (2002) 'Can we do it all? Tensions in the mission and structure of UK higher education', *Higher Education Quarterly*, vol 56, no 2, pp 143–55.

WEA (Workers Education Association) (2004) Workers Education Association online resources. Available at: http://www.wea.org.uk/Centenary/timeline/1920.htm (accessed 5 May 2004).

Westwood, S. and Thomas, J.E. (eds) (1991) *The Politics of Adult Education*, Leicester: NIACE.

THREE

Broadening participation among women and racial/ethnic minorities in science, technology, engineering and maths

Terrell L. Strayhorn, James M. DeVita and Amanda M. Blakewood

Introduction

Increasing the number of women and members of minority racial/ ethnic groups in science, technology, engineering and maths (STEM)- related fields in higher education, and in the STEM workforce, is a compelling national interest in the US. Although college enrolment rates among undergraduates, including women and racially diverse students, have increased significantly over the last 30 years – from 11 million in 1976 to over 18 million in 2006 – STEM degree completion rates are marked by large, persistent gender and racialised disparities. For instance, women earn 75% of all bachelor's degrees in psychology, yet only 21% of those in engineering and computer science (US Department of Education, 2007). Similarly, only 24% of under-represented minority ethnic groups earn a degree in STEM fields within six years of initial enrolment compared to 40% of white students. Gender and racial gaps may be the consequence of barriers students face in the educational or STEM pipeline, which has also been referred to as 'pathways' to and through college.

In this chapter, we discuss the importance of diversity and inclusion in STEM, identify challenges that women and minority ethnic groups face in these fields, and outline several strategies that prove effective in broadening participation among women and minority ethnic groups in STEM. Recommendations for conducting future research, improving practice and formulating higher education policy are provided.

Barriers to women students' participation in STEM

Despite several decades of research devoted to increasing women's participation in STEM fields, sizeable gaps between the sexes remain. Statistics obtained from the National Science Foundation (NSF) paint an alarming portrait of a leaky pipeline for women in STEM. While 51% of all bachelor's degrees in science and engineering are earned by women, they comprise only 45% of master's degrees and 39% of doctorates in STEM fields. In contrast, women earn 61% of bachelor's degrees, 63% of master's degrees and 58% of doctorates in non–STEM fields such as the humanities and social sciences (NSF et al., 2006). The next section identifies three barriers that have been shown to limit the number of women in STEM fields: lack of interest in and exposure to technical careers, stereotypical gender roles, and the limited number of women role models and mentors.

One barrier that is related to the low representation of women in STEM fields is lack of interest in and exposure to scientific and technical careers. For example, some scholars have suggested that women are less confident in their abilities to perform quantitative cognitive tasks, thereby reducing their interest in STEM fields and related careers (Betz and Hackett, 1981). In recent years, however, studies have shown that women possess equal talent and interest in STEM fields, especially if their interests are nurtured in ways similar to men (Spelke, 2005). The problem is that women are not encouraged to pursue STEM-related work, on average, based on stereotypical beliefs about what constitutes 'women's work' (Bergeron et al., 2006). This addresses another barrier faced by women who aspire to STEM careers.

Indeed, a second barrier that may reduce, if not eliminate, women's participation in STEM fields is stereotypical beliefs about gender roles. Specifically, some parents, teachers, educators and policymakers subscribe to a set of perceived behavioural norms associated with one's sex or biological assignment as 'male' or 'female'. Gender roles, then, can serve as a division of labour by sex or gender. And some individuals assume stereotypical or traditional beliefs about the attitudes and behaviours that characterise one's identity. Therefore, to some, a woman is *supposed to be* warm, inviting, nurturing and passive. A man, on the other hand, is *supposed to be* active, strong, commanding and aggressive. Extrapolating this further, stereotypical gender roles might also suggest that men are supposed to pursue scientific and technical careers, while jobs in social work, nursing and teaching are seen as 'women's work' (Bergeron et al., 2006). Stereotypical gender roles limit parents' and teachers' ability to see women as future scientists and can, thereby, significantly affect child-rearing practices, early exposure to such fields and the messages that people send to women about working in STEM.

Lastly, scholars have pointed to the lack of a critical mass of women in STEM, which, in turn, affects the pool of women available from which students might choose role models and mentors, and it may also lead to feelings of isolation and chilly climates in STEM disciplines (Hall and Sandler, 1982; Clark and Corcoran, 1986). For instance, men outnumber women by approximately three to one in physical and computer sciences and nearly four to one in engineering at the junior faculty ranks (ie instructor, assistant professor). At the senior faculty level (ie associate or full), sex disparities are even more pronounced with men outnumbering women 4:1 in computer science, 7:1 in maths and physical sciences, and 13:1 in engineering (National Science Board, 2006). This significantly limits the number of women available to serve as advisors, role models and mentors to all students, but especially women pursuing a STEM degree. Also, despite strategic efforts to change the nature of traditionally male-dominated STEM fields, studies suggest that sex discrimination persists (American Council on Education, 2005). Discriminatory actions range from being ignored by male professors and overtly discriminating statements to sexual harassment. Unfortunately, women represent only one group whose participation in STEM fields is fraught with seemingly intractable barriers. Students from minority racial/ethnic groups also remain under-represented in STEM fields.

Barriers to participation in STEM by students from minority racial/ethnic groups

Research has examined the academic and social experiences of minority racial/ethnic groups in STEM fields. Three major barriers to their STEM participation are: lack of pre-college preparation for STEM; negative perceptions of STEM careers in general and scientists in particular; as well as unwelcoming, unsupportive environments in STEM majors and classrooms. Each of these is discussed in the context of prior research findings.

Minority ethnic groups, on average, are less well prepared than their white and Asian counterparts to major in a STEM field based on limited access to and low achievement in science and maths courses. Researchers have shown that students from different racial groups are provided with different opportunities to learn (OTL), particularly in the areas of maths and science (Oakes, 1983, 1990b; Stevens, 1993; Winfeld, 1993; Kim and Hocevar, 1998; Darity et al., 2001; Tate, 2001), with historically under-represented minority racial/ethnic groups suffering the most limited OTL. Oakes pointed out that 'unequal learning opportunities provide some specific clues to how *educational practices* may help create and perpetuate differences in achievement and participation' (1990a, p iv, emphasis added), as unequal opportunities of this kind cascade over time into intractable inequities that significantly reduce students' chances for upward social mobility and academic success. One such educational practice is tracking where students are assigned to lower-ability groupings in college preparatory classes such as maths and science. As a result, tracked students, who are disproportionately students from minority ethnic groups, are exposed to less rigorous courses and marginally qualified teachers (Carroll, 1989; Oakes, 1990a; Winfeld, 1993; Tate, 2001). Consequently, they have 'considerably less access to knowledge that is considered necessary either for science and mathematics careers or for becoming scientifically literate, critically thinking citizens, and productive members of an increasingly technological workforce' (Oakes, 1990a, p 45). Without the requisite knowledge and skills, students from minority racial/ethnic groups are less likely to express an early interest in STEM, pursue an academic major in STEM or persist through college to earn a bachelor's degree in a STEM field.

A troubling outcome of these inequalities is reflected in the performance of students from minority racial/ethnic groups on standardised tests, which are required by many institutions of higher education for admission. One national report conducted by the American College Test (ACT, 2000) found a significant relationship between ACT maths and science performance and two additional factors: (a) the rigour of coursework in maths and science; and (b) the likelihood to major in maths and science during college (Harmston and Pliska, 2001). Since it has well been established that disproportionate numbers of students from minority ethnic groups attend high schools that offer limited opportunities to learn college preparatory maths and science, it is not surprising to find these students among the lowest-performing groups on both the ACT and SAT maths and science sections (Stanley and Porter, 1967; Lubinski and Benbow, 1992; Tate, 1997; Harmston and Pliska, 2001; Supiano, 2008). Given the significance placed on test scores by colleges and universities, OTL disparities can have long-term and cascading effects on students' social mobility and access to higher education.

Despite sizeable investments in pre-college outreach and student support services by federal agencies, attrition rates for African-American and Hispanic students recruited to STEM fields remained at over 50%, well above their Caucasian and Asian American peers (Seymour and Hewitt, 1997). While some research points to the poor preparation students from minority ethnic groups receive prior to college, coupled with the intense demands of maths and science courses during the first semester of college, as main causes (Maton et al., 2000; Daempfle, 2003), other studies show that students from minority ethnic groups leave STEM, and engineering specifically, for non-academic reasons. These include negative racial stereotypes and a lack of positive roles models from minority ethnic groups in STEM fields, which contribute to a chilly climate for students from minority ethnic groups that also inhibits success (Seymour and Hewitt, 1997). Indeed, the chilly climate experienced by students from minority ethnic groups in higher education as a whole has been well established (eg Watson et al., 2002; Swail et al., 2003), particularly at predominantly white institutions (PWIs) where minority racial/ethnic groups encounter 'obstacles to persistence [such] as racism, hostility, prejudice, discrimination, a "chilly" climate, instructional bias, negative stereotypes, self-doubt, alienation, isolation, and cultural insensitivity' (Swail et al., 2003, p 20).

These obstacles are amplified in STEM fields where students from minority ethnic groups are disproportionately under-represented and lack positive roles models among both their peers and faculty members (Grandy, 1998; Leslie et al., 1998; Byars-Winston et al., 2007; Johnson, 2007; Cole and Espinosa, 2008). Grandy, for example, found that students who were more supported by individuals of similar racial/ethnic backgrounds were more likely to exhibit higher levels of ambition and commitment to STEM fields than their peers who received little or no support from similar individuals. Additionally, students' perceptions of scientists further complicates the barriers to minority ethnic group achievement in STEM fields as 50 years of research confirms that, after controlling for differences in gender, national origin, age (or grade level) and racial identity, students perceive science to be a field for old, white males (Finson, 2002). These perceptions, when considered with the absence of positive role models, portend significant social barriers to enhancing minority ethnic group participation and success in STEM fields. Taken together, these three barriers significantly limit the participation of 'under-represented minorities' (URMs) in STEM fields. In fact, in 2004, the Sullivan Commission announced URMs are 'missing persons' in science fields.

To reduce, if not eliminate, the gaps discussed above, US colleges and universities have taken several steps to broaden the participation among women and members of minority racial/ethnic groups in STEM.

Strategies to broaden the participation of women in STEM

Based on an empirically derived understanding of barriers that limit or restrict women's participation in STEM fields, government organisations and institutions of higher education alike have established programmes and services that are designed to encourage the participation of women in STEM fields. Three such programmes are discussed.

First, programmes have been established to nurture women's interest in science and maths courses, as well as STEM and STEM-related careers. For instance, The Laser Academy at Queensborough Community College in the City University of New York system was created to introduce women to high-tech careers. Students participate in a range of activities including guest speaker series, career and personality assessments, as well as field experiences to expose them to the myriad jobs within STEM and related fields. Similarly, the STEM Lecture Series at the University of California, Riverside was designed to accentuate the teaching, research and careers of women (and men) in STEM fields. Topics, in the past, ranged from women in medicine to statistics, from domestic violence to women's lives in STEM. Anecdotal and evaluation evidence suggest that the programmes hold promise for addressing the barriers identified earlier in the chapter.

Second, research on women's entry and retention in STEM fields emphasises the importance of social integration – students forming meaningful interpersonal relationships with peers and faculty members (Sax, 1994). Scholars have pointed out that this can be difficult when one is in the minority, such as women in male-dominated fields like engineering and computer science (Sax, 1994). Thus, some programmes, such as the Women in Science and Engineering (WISE) programme at the University of Wisconsin-Madison, offers formal peer mentoring from upperclassmen to freshmen women. As another example, the Department of Computer Science and Software Engineering (CSSE) at Rose-Hulman Institute of Technology has developed an online social network for women in CSSE and those aspiring to careers in science and technology. The online social network has two major objectives: (a) to facilitate women students' interaction with alumnae; and (b) to serve as a platform for high school students to interact with women students and alumnae. The online network is mutually beneficial – students should receive helpful advice and feedback about gender-related issues in STEM, whereas alumnae benefit from interactions with students and the sense of generativity that mentoring affords. Initial list of programme features included a forum where members can post questions/concerns and links to information on how to prepare: (a) as a high school student aspiring to major in CSSE as an undergraduate; and (b) as an undergraduate student interested in graduate study. While preliminary, evaluation data (eg enrolment, participation rates, usage) suggest the effectiveness of the online social network (Mohan and Chidanandan, 2008).

There are other programmes that emphasise academic and social integration. For instance, to provide a more supportive environment for women and to facilitate women's interest and success in STEM fields, the Faculty of Engineering, Computing and Creative Industries at Napier University established a student support forum for females (SSF4F). The programme was designed to reduce feelings of isolation, facilitate interaction among women students in STEM and expose women students to female professionals who could help them anticipate what to expect as a woman working in a male-dominated industry. SSF4F comprises two main components: online resources (ie social networking, information dissemination) and events aimed to support one's transition from student to professional. Findings, to date, suggest that the programme is effective in four major areas: the majority of respondents report gains in terms of receiving valuable career- or industry-related information, networking with practitioners, learning new skills (eg communication), and socialising with other women students in STEM (Cairncross et al., 2008).

Strategies to broaden participation of under-represented minority ethnic groups in STEM

While barriers to participation by minority racial/ethnic groups and success in STEM fields seem daunting, there is hope. Various interventions have been described in the recent literature, all noting some success. For instance, Tate (1997) found that educational reforms aimed at minimising the inequalities between minority ethnic groups and white students have succeeded in narrowing the gap in basic skills acquisition in maths. His analysis supports the conclusion that changes in fiscal policy, such as expenditures on instructional materials, and cultural policy, such as pedagogy and curriculum, can positively affect the participation and achievement of students from minority ethnic groups in academic experiences that hold the strongest association with achievement in STEM fields.

Collaborative efforts between institutions of higher education and national organisations provide additional justification for optimism. The Meyerhoff Scholars Program at the University of Maryland, Baltimore

County (UMBC) has been successful at enhancing achievement, graduation rates and acceptance to graduate programmes in science and engineering for students from minority ethnic groups (Maton et al., 2000). The programme is comprehensive and includes financial support, a summer bridge component, personal advising and counselling, tutoring, and summer research opportunities; the programme also engages faculty members, members of the local community and parents in supporting the education of students from minority ethnic groups in STEM fields. As the authors aptly conclude, Meyerhoff is a 'well-designed university-based intervention [that] can increase the numbers of [minority ethnic group] undergraduate college students who succeed in science, mathematics, and engineering' (Maton et al., 2000, p 648). While successful, the financial support required to maintain such a programme is sizable, demanding resources that some institutions cannot sustain without external support.

There are other examples of collaborative programmes. For instance, the Alliance for Graduate Education and the Professoriate (AGEP) Program is a collaborative initiative between Howard University, the University of Texas at El Paso (UTEP) and the NSF. In addition to broadening minority ethnic group participation in graduate programmes, AGEP prepares students from minority ethnic groups for the unique challenges they will encounter as URM graduate students, faculty members and role models in STEM fields. While the weight of assessment data suggests the programme's effectiveness in terms of increasing the number of undergraduates who consider graduate school, a substantial contribution – approximately $5 million in 10 years from the NSF – was needed to effectively support the programme. Thus, like the Meyerhoff Scholars Program, readers are cautioned to realise the human and fiscal cost associated with establishing and maintaining such programmes. Still, given their record of success, they represent promising practices for broadening participation among minority racial/ethnic groups in STEM. And cost alone – in dollars and cents – is insufficient cause for retreat.

Prior research has stressed the role that academic and social integration play in the persistence of URMs in STEM fields. Chubin et al. (2008) reported that fewer than two in five (40%) URM first-year students who enter engineering actually graduate with an engineering degree within six years; most leave for non-academic reasons. To provide students from minority ethnic groups with the academic and social support needed for success in STEM, some colleges have established formal interventions ranging from living-learning communities and summer bridge programmes to coordinated programmes (Strayhorn and DeVita, 2009). For instance, Lafayette College offers a POSSE programme. POSSE consists of several components: (a) 10-student cohorts per participating College; (b) extensive eight-month, pre-college training on leadership, college culture, time/financial management, team-building, cross-cultural communication and academic excellence; (c) campus visits from POSSE staff each semester; (d) an on-campus mentor; and (e) an annual spring retreat where POSSE students and their mentors meet to discuss issues chosen by students. By focusing on inner-city schools, POSSE cohorts recruit large numbers of economically disadvantaged students and/or students from minority racial/ethnic groups. Preliminary evaluation data suggest that the programme is effective, especially in terms of helping POSSE students navigate the academic integration process (eg being involved in class, meeting professors) (Jones and Were, 2008).

Feeling a sense of belonging or 'community' is also critically important to the retention and success of students from minority racial/ethnic groups, particularly in STEM fields (Hurtado and Carter, 1997; Strayhorn, 2008), although many report feelings of isolation, unwelcoming and alienation. A number of interventions have been directed towards addressing this very issue. For instance, Dartmouth College has established 'Engineering Workshops', which is a peer mentoring programme that aims to improve retention of first-year students by 'drawing them into the engineering school community while they are still taking prerequisite calculus and physics courses' (Hansen et al., 2008, p T4D-19). The goals of the workshops are: (a) to facilitate engagement among engineering students; (b) to initiate students to the engineering school and its culture of teamwork and collaboration (eg design projects, problem sets); and (c) to nurture their interest in STEM by providing 'real-world' applications of maths and physics – the course in which they are currently enrolled. Workshops meet weekly for approximately two hours in the engineering school; two upper-class engineering majors facilitate each workshop. Preliminary evaluation data suggest effectiveness in three areas: (a) after four academic terms, attendance was high, particularly among women and students from minority racial/ethnic groups; (b) nearly all respondents reported attending to get help with their homework, work in groups or receive advice from upper-class students; and (c) several data points suggest that the workshops were very effective at providing a positive, supportive environment for doing homework. By exposing first-year students to the school's culture and more advanced students in the major, and meeting on a consistent basis to talk about issues raised by the students, Engineering Workshops seem to effectively raise or sustain students' interest in STEM, increase their knowledge and understanding of the school, and facilitate a sense of belonging, thereby reducing feelings of isolation, loneliness and motivational uncertainty (ie 'Why am I doing this?') (Hansen et al., 2008).

Conclusion

Recall that the purpose of this chapter was to discuss the importance of diversity and inclusion in STEM, identify challenges that women and people from minority racial/ethnic groups face in these fields, and outline several strategies that prove effective in broadening participation among these groups. Here we recap a few of the points raised in the chapter and identify limitations to what we know about participation in STEM among women and URMs. Drawing upon information highlighted in the chapter, we close by offering a set of empirically derived recommendations for educational policy and practice that hold promise for broadening participation among women and URMs in STEM.

Indeed, increasing diversity in higher education by broadening participation among women and people from minority racial/ethnic groups in STEM is a compelling national interest in the US as it is often posited as an issue of accountability and global competitiveness. The defence of diversity in STEM fields might also turn on a 'value added' argument as well – that is, that STEM majors learn and grow in ways that expand the social and cultural capital reservoirs of women and URMs, which, in turn, can be used or exchanged for monetary and non-monetary rewards or benefits. For instance, STEM majors tend to develop stronger critical thinking, scientific writing and analytical skills than their non-STEM counterparts (Pascarella and Terenzini, 2005). Critical thinking, writing and analytical skills have been correlated with higher annual earning, occupational status and job satisfaction upon college graduation (Pascarella and Terenzini, 2005), although findings are a bit uneven across studies.

The myriad barriers that women and URMs face in STEM fields complicate pursuing diversity in such fields. For instance, women report a lack of female mentors and role models, similar to URMs who struggle to find same-race mentors upon whom they can rely for academic and social support. Perhaps uniquely, women often have to confront stereotypical gender roles that describe them as nurturers, carers and mothers, thereby 'unfit' for scientific and technical work in STEM, but perfectly suited for 'women's work' in fields such as social work and nursing. URMs, on the other hand, encounter racial stereotypes and discrimination in STEM classrooms and professional fields; for instance, some faculty may assume that African-Americans and Latinos are unlikely to succeed in STEM because 'minorities just don't do well in science and maths', as if the 'problem' is an innate, and incorrigible, learning deficiency.

In response, federal agencies, as well as colleges and universities, have invested considerable time and resources into establishing new or revising existing programmes that are designed to mitigate these problems or compensate for deficiencies produced by inequities in the educational pipeline. Programmes vary in purpose and structure. For instance, the Laser Academy is designed to expose women to high-tech careers through speaker series and related activities, while online social networks (eg CSSE) serve as support mechanisms for women in computer science. Comparatively, URM students have benefited from the Meyerhoff Scholars Program, which offers invaluable support in multiple forms: a summer bridge component, mentoring and tutoring. Similarly, POSSE facilitates URM students' engagement in activities that improve their time-management skills, as well as enlarges students' knowledge of post-secondary options through campus visits. This is important as students cannot attain what they do not 'see' or think possible; simply visiting a campus can increase a student's interest in higher education and bring the impossible dream to feasible reality.

Limitations of prior research and implications for the future

Although collectively the studies reviewed in this chapter provide persuasive evidence supporting the effectiveness of support programmes for women and URMs in STEM, there are several limitations to the research. First, most studies examine the effects of a single practice on entry into or retention in STEM, and that single practice is studied in isolation. Yet, broadening participation among women and people from minority racial/ethnic groups in STEM is an ill-structured problem (Kitchener, 1986), one whose complexity defies solutions of a singular nature. Future researchers might address this limitation by conducting longitudinal studies that aim to measure the time-varying effects of multiple interventions on STEM outcomes.

A second limitation is that a vast majority of studies are limited to a single institution or small institutional sample, with few exceptions (Sax, 1994; Cole and Espinosa, 2008). It is possible that STEM majors at University A are different from STEM majors at University B, thereby reducing the generalisability of findings from a study of students at University A only. It is also true that students who choose to participate in programmes such as WISE, POSSE or AGEP are qualitatively different from students who opt not to participate in such programmes. Without sufficient controls on background traits or appropriate experimental designs, research findings may have limited applicability to students in general. Therefore, any assertions made should not be overstated.

Third, the weight of empirical evidence is based on self-reported data, self-reported gains and studies that lack statistical controls for pre-college achievement and experiences. Self-reports are open to challenges to criterion and construct validity, but growing evidence suggests that self-reported outcomes are reasonable proxies for objective, standardised measures (Anaya, 1999). To complement this line of inquiry, future researchers should employ standardised measures of learning and development such as standardised test scores, critical learning inventories (Kolb, 1985) or psychosocial development questionnaires. While these limitations merit attention, they do not reduce the importance of previous studies that contribute to our understanding of women's and URMs' experiences in STEM and related fields.

Recommendations for policy and practice

Information presented in this chapter suggests a number of recommendations for future education policy and practice. First, policymakers should continue to advocate for the formulation and implementation of policies that establish new or improve existing programmes that promote students' interest in STEM fields. Such programmes include WISE, Meyerhoff Scholars and AGEP, to name but a few. Given the increasing number of women and URMs expected to enter STEM over the next few decades, additional programmes are likely to be needed.

Not only should policymakers continue to present legislation that ensures continued provision of these types of programmes, but they should also make decisions that provide continued financial support at the federal level. Recall that programmes such as AGEP, McNair Scholars and WISE require sizable financial investments to cover costs associated with programme management (ie staff, facilities) and programme content (eg stipends, materials, trips). Continuing to direct money to programmes that effectively broaden participation among women and people from minority racial/ethnic groups is essential as 'unfunded mandates' rarely reap noticeable gains.

Clearly, interventions aimed at nurturing students' interest in STEM, increasing their understanding of STEM careers and demonstrating the relevance of STEM to solving 'real-world' problems are helpful. Thus, programme directors should consider this information when making decisions about programme objectives and curricula. Exposing women and URMs to professionals working in engineering or computer science, providing information about the nature of faculty work or engaging students in design activities that encourage them to apply STEM concepts to solving real-life problems (eg deciding water quality treatment, building erosion scaffolding, writing a programme to build web pages) can stimulate students' interest in STEM, increase their odds of choosing a STEM major in college and increase or sustain their interest in graduate study.

Some engineering students fail to see the potential and practical benefits of engineering and the important role that engineering plays in the 'real world', which leads some students to choose majors and careers in disciplines that have obvious value to society. To ameliorate this problem, professional associations might launch marketing initiatives that highlight the nature of STEM work, identify career options within STEM and underscore the salaries and benefits afforded to those who enter the profession. Similarly, K–12 teachers might consider the use of collaborative and/or service-learning activities to influence students' perceptions of and career interests in STEM.

Clearly, interventions should begin early and engage multiple agents (eg teachers, peers, parents) in socialising students to STEM fields and related career options. Parents and guardians play a significant role in shaping students' initial perceptions about STEM, the viability of STEM as a career option and its relevance to one's community of origin or larger society. Thus, what parents think about STEM affects the perceptions of their offspring, even though national data suggest that few parents have accurate information about STEM fields and ways to rear women and people from minority racial/ethnic groups for such careers. It seems imperative, then, for programmes to engage parents in educationally meaningful ways; for instance, parents might attend workshops that offer practical strategies for nurturing students' interest (eg field trips, conversations) and achievement (eg study tips, homework time) in scientific and technical subjects.

To extend what is known about programmes and services that hold promise for broadening participation among women and URMs in STEM, policymakers should link funding streams (eg grants, awards) to assessment/evaluation efforts. In other words, federal, state and even institutional grants to establish new or improve existing programmes should require programme directors to collect, analyse and report findings that demonstrate the programme's efficacy. The evidence presented in this chapter should be a part of the discussion when developing such grants and/or reports. Using information from this chapter and others included in this volume can help policymakers, educators and parents work more effectively with students early in their educational trajectories and, in that way, provide hope for broadening participation among women and URMs in STEM fields.

References

American College Testing Program (2000) *ACT Institutional Data File, 2000,* Iowa City: Author.

American Council on Education (2005) *An Agenda for Excellence: Creating Flexibility in Tenure-track Faculty Careers,* Washington, DC: American Council on Education, Office of Women in Higher Education.

Anaya, G. (1999) 'College impact on student learning: comparing the use of self-reported gains, standardized test scores, and college grades', *Research in Higher Education,* vol 40, pp 449–526.

Bergeron, D.M., Block, C.J. and Echtenkamp, B.A. (2006) 'Disabling the able: stereotype threat and women's work performance', *Human Performance,* vol 19, no 2, pp 133–58.

Betz, N.E. and Hackett, G. (1981) 'The relationship of career-related self-efficacy expectations to perceived career options in college women and men', *Journal of Counseling Psychology,* vol 28, pp 399–410.

Byars-Winston, A., Estrada, Y., Howard, C., Zalapa, J. and Davis, D. (2007) 'Empirical insights into STEM retention of targeted students: a social cognitive approach. Available at: www.cew.wisc.edu/sloan (accessed 12 November 2009).

Cairncross, S., Gordon, K., Ratcliffe, D., Tizard, J. and Turnball, C. (2008) 'Valuing diversity: development of a student support forum for females', *Proceedings of the Frontiers in Education (FIE) Conference,* F4B-14-19.

Carroll, J.B. (1989) The Carroll model: a 25-year retrospective and prospective view', *Educational Researcher,* vol 18, no 1, pp 26–31.

Chubin, D.E., Donaldson, K., Olds, B. and Fleming, L. (2008) 'Educating generation net – can US engineering woo and win the competition for talent?', *Journal of Engineering Education,* vol 97, no 3, pp 245–57.

Clark, S.M. and Corcoran, M. (1986) 'Perspectives of the professional socialization of women faculty', *The Journal of Higher Education,* vol 57, pp 21–43.

Cole, D. and Espinosa, A. (2008) 'Examining the academic success of Latino students in science technology engineering and mathematics (STEM) majors', *Journal of College Student Development*, vol 49, no 4, pp 285–300.

Daempfle, P.A. (2003) 'An analysis of the high attrition rates among first year college students in science, math, and engineering majors', *Journal of College Student Retention: Research, Theory, and Practice*, vol 5, no 1, pp 37–52.

Darity, W., Jr., Castellino, D., Tyson, K., Cobb, C. and McMillan, B. (2001) 'Increasing opportunity to learn via access to rigorous courses and programs: one strategy for closing the achievement gap for at-risk and ethnic minority students', *North Carolina State Department of Public Instruction*.

Finson, K.D. (2002) 'Drawing a scientist: what we do and do not know after fifty years of drawings', *School Science and Mathematics*, vol 102, no 7, pp 335–45.

Grandy, J. (1998) 'Persistence in science of high-ability minority students: results of a longitudinal study', *The Journal of Higher Education*, vol 69, no 6, pp 589–620.

Hall, R.M. and Sandler, B.R. (1982) *The Classroom Climate: A Chilly One for Women?*, Washington, DC: Project on the Status and Education of Women, Association for American Colleges.

Hansen, E., Stein, E. M. and May, V.V. (2008) *Work in Progress: Building Community among First-Year Engineering Students*, ASEE/IEEE Frontiers in Education Annual Conference Proceedings, T4D, 19-20.

Harmston, M.T. and Pliska, A. (2001) *Trends in ACT Mathematics and Science Reasoning. Achievement, Curricular Choice, and Intent for College Major: 1995–2000*, Iowa City, IA: ACT, Inc.

Hurtado, S. and Carter, D.F. (1997) 'Effects of college transition and perceptions of campus racial climate on Latino college students' sense of belonging', *Sociology of Education*, vol 70, no 4, pp 324–45.

Johnson, D. (2007) 'Sense of belonging among women of color in science, technology, engineering, and math majors: investigating the contributions of campus racial climate perceptions and other college environments', unpublished dissertation at the University of Maryland. Available at: http://www.lib.umd.edu/drum/bitstream/1903/7723/1/umi-umd-5000.pdf (accessed 12 November 2009).

Jones, S.A. and Were, M. (2008) 'Impact of the POSSE program on the academic integration of minority engineering students', *Proceedings of the Frontiers in Education (FIE) Conference*, S4F-7-11.

Kim, S. and Hocevar, D. (1998) 'Racial differences in eighth-grade mathematics: achievement and opportunity to learn', *The Clearinghouse*, pp 175–8.

Kitchener, K. (1986) 'The reflective judgment model: characteristics, evidence, and measurement', in R. Mines and K. Kitchener (eds) *Adult Cognitive Development*, New York, NY: Praeger.

Kolb, D.A. (1985) *Learning Style Inventory*, Boston, MA: McBer and Company.

Leslie, L.L., McClure, G.T. and Oaxaca, R.L. (1998) 'Women and minorities in science and engineering: a life sequence analysis', *The Journal of Higher Education*, vol 69, no 3, pp 239–76.

Lubinski, D. and Benbow, C.P. (1992) 'Gender differences in abilities and preferences among the gifted: implications for the math–science pipeline', *Current Directions in Psychological Science*, vol 1, no 2, pp 61–6.

Maton, K.I., Hrabowski III, F.A. and Schmitt, C.L. (2000) 'African American college students excelling in the sciences: college and postcollege outcomes in the Meyerhoff Scholars Program', *Journal of Research in Science Teaching*, vol 37, no 7, pp 629–54.

Mohan, S. and Chidanandan, A. (2008) 'Work in progress: an online support system for women in computer science', *Proceedings of the Frontiers in Education (FIE) Conference*, S4F-13-14.

National Science Board (2006) *Science and Engineering Indicators 2006* (2 vols), Arlington, VA: National Science Foundation.

National Science Foundation, National Institutes of Health, US Department of Education, NEH, USDA, and NASA (2006) *Baccalaureate-Origins of US Research Doctorate Recipients, 1995–2004*, Chicago, IL: National Opinion Research Center.

Oakes, J. (1983) 'Limiting opportunity: student race and curricular differences in secondary vocational education', *American Journal of Education*, vol 91, no 3, pp 328–55.

Oakes, J. (1990a) *Multiplying Inequalities: The Effects of Race, Social Class, and Tracking on Opportunities to Learn Mathematics and Science*, Manchester, IN: The Heckman Bindery, Inc.

Oakes, J. (1990b) 'Opportunities, achievement and choice: women and minority students in science and mathematics', *Review of Research in Education*, vol 16, pp 153–222.

Pascarella, E.T. and Terenzini, P.T. (2005) *How College Affects Students: A Third Decade of Research*, vol 2, San Francisco, CA: Jossey-Bass.

Sax, L. (1994) 'Retaining tomorrow's scientists: exploring the factors that keep male and female college students interested in science careers', *Journal of Women and Minorities in Science and Engineering*, vol 1, pp 45–61.

Seymour, E. and Hewitt, N.H. (1997) *Talking about Leaving: Why Undergraduates Leave the Sciences*, Boulder, CO: Westview Press.

Spelke, E.S. (2005) 'Sex differences in intrinsic aptitude for mathematics and science? A critical review', *American Psychologist*, vol 60, no 9, pp 950–58.

Stanley, J.C. and Porter, A.C. (1967) 'Correlation of scholastic aptitude test score with college grades for negroes versus whites', *Journal of Educational Measurement*, vol 4, no 4, pp 199–218.

Stevens, F.I. (1993) 'Applying an opportunity-to-learn conceptual framework to the investigation of the effects of teaching practices via secondary analyses of multiple-case-study summary data', *Journal of Negro Education*, vol 62, no 3, pp 232–48.

Strayhorn, T.L. (2008) 'Fittin' in: do diverse interactions with peers affect sense of belonging for black men at predominantly white institutions?', *The NASPA Journal*, vol 45, no 4, pp 501–27.

Strayhorn, T.L. and DeVita, J.M. (2009) 'Measuring the impact of a summer bridge program on underrepresented minorities' academic skill development', *NetResults*. Available at: http://www.naspa.org/membership/mem/pubs/nr/default.cfm?id=1703 (accessed 14 October 2009).

Supiano, B. (2008) 'Number of AP test takers and scores are up, but racial gap persists', *The Chronicle of Higher Education*. Available at: http://chronicle.com/daily/2008/02/1656n.htm (accessed 14 February 2008).

Swail, W.S., Redd, K.E. and Perna, L.W. (2003) 'Retaining minority students in higher education: a framework for success', in A.J. Kezar (ed) *ASHE-ERIC Higher Education Report: Volume 30, Number 2*, San Francisco: Jossey-Bass. Available at: http://www.studentretention.org/pdf/Swail_Retention_Book.pdf (accessed 12 November 2009).

Tate, W.F. (1997) 'Race-ethnicity, SES, gender, and language proficiency trends in mathematics achievement: an update', *Journal for Research in Mathematics Education*, vol 28, no 6, pp 652–79.

Tate, W.F. (2001) 'Science education as a civil right: urban schools and opportunity to learn considerations', *Journal for Research in Science Teaching*, vol 38, pp 1015–28.

US Department of Education, National Center for Education Statistics. (2007) *The Condition of Education 2007 (NCES 2007)*, Washington, DC: U.S. Government Printing Office.

Watson, L.W., Terrell, M.C., Wright, D.J. and Associates (2002) *How Minority Students Experience College: Implications for Planning and Policy*, Sterling, VA: Stylus Publishing.

Winfeld, L.F. (1993) 'Investigating test content and curriculum content overlap to assess opportunity to learn', *The Journal of Negro Education*, vol 62, no 3, pp 288–310.

FOUR

Social inclusion in a globalised higher education environment: the issue of equitable access to university in Australia[1]

Richard James

Introduction

Internationally, equity is usually considered to be one of the three fundamental measures of the effectiveness of a higher education system, alongside quality and efficiency. Equity is therefore one of the enduring issues for higher education policymakers, to be ignored at their peril. The importance attached to equity in higher education is unsurprising. It touches our beliefs about justice and our hopes for a fairer society, for social change and for national development. It also touches our hopes for our own families. For these reasons, equity is an issue on which many people have strong opinions and it is frequently the source of superficial newspaper headlines and cheap political point-scoring. From a public policy perspective, equity is a fine example of the limits of policy in creating social change, for equity in higher education is undoubtedly one of the 'wicked problems' for policymakers.

This chapter draws on a number of studies conducted by the Centre for the Study of Higher Education (James et al., 1999; James, 2001; James, 2002). The chapter is broad-ranging rather than narrowly focused. It would be possible, of course, to devote the entire chapter to the equity issues around gender, disability, rurality or Indigenous people's participation. But the chapter's focus in the main part is on the challenge of widening access for people from low socio-economic status backgrounds, for this is one of the persistent and seemingly intractable equity issues in Australia.

For a concept that is so widely discussed, and which has such intuitive appeal, equity is surprisingly difficult to define with precision. The various implicit and explicit conceptions of equity in higher education include the following:

- those who have the ability to go on to university are able to do so;
- there are no barriers to access to university;
- the selection for university places is on academic merit;
- the selection for university places is without discrimination on the basis of social class, gender, religion or ethnicity; and
- all people have the same opportunity to develop their talents.

The differences in these conceptions are subtle, but they are far from trivial. They lead to differing sets of assumptions regarding policy strategies and alternative ways of assessing the effectiveness of interventions.

The formal definition of equity in Australian higher education derives from the landmark discussion paper *A Fair Chance for All* (NBEET, 1990, p 8):[2]

> The overall objective for equity in higher education is to ensure that Australians from all groups in society have the opportunity to participate successfully in higher education. This will be achieved by changing the balance of the student population to reflect more closely the composition of the society as a whole.

Internationally, the goal of achieving more parity between the composition of university populations and national populations is one of the more widespread conceptions of equity, for it helps establish aspirational targets. Beyond this, the idea of equity usually involves sometimes vague notions of merit, fairness and equality of opportunity. It must be said that none of these concepts is straightforward, for each involves complex and problematic notions of justice and choice (see eg Rawls, 1973; Sen, 1995). Academic merit is perhaps the most enduring idea associated with equity, although it is increasingly troublesome in mass or universal higher education systems – in which over 50% of people go to university – to sort the people who are more deserving of higher education from those who are less deserving.

Equity in higher education *is* worth worrying about. Higher education confers significant individual benefits in terms of personal development, social status, career possibilities and, of course, lifetime earnings. But, while individual social justice has been the major imperative behind many equity initiatives, there has long been an argument, especially in the US, that improving the higher education participation of people from disadvantaged groups is essential for their long-term social and economic integration, and that widening participation and intergenerational social mobility might lead to a more cohesive and economically successful society.

The broad international patterns of participation in higher education

Worldwide, there has been massive, sometimes staggering, growth in higher education participation in the last 50 years, including in most developing nations. Despite the expansion in participation, demographic imbalances in the people going to university continue to be striking in most nations. In some countries, women are still very under-represented, while, in others, they are clearly in the majority, although not necessarily in all fields of study or at all levels of awards. Minority ethnic groups are highly under-represented generally, although this is not always the case. But the most widespread and persistent source of disadvantage in access to higher education is associated with low social class or low socio-economic status (SES). This is not just narrow economic disadvantage, but also involves the absence of Bourdieu's broader concept of social and cultural capital. In most nations, even in developed nations with strong egalitarian traditions, social class is the single most reliable predictor of the likelihood that individuals will participate in higher education at some stage in their lives. This is particularly true in developing countries, where poorer students have little chance of gaining entry into higher education, but it is also true in the most developed countries, where the people from low SES backgrounds who do reach higher education are less likely to find places in the most prestigious institutions and fields of study.

Low rates of higher education participation often reflect endemic educational disadvantage that may begin in the earliest years of schooling. Internationally, the under-representation of people from low SES backgrounds is a result of the combined effects of: lower school completion rates; lower levels of educational attainment in schools, thus limiting opportunities in the circumstances of competitive entry based on academic achievement; lower levels of educational aspiration; lower perceptions of the personal and career relevance of higher education; and perhaps alienation from the culture of universities in some cases. There is also a range of interrelated financial factors of course.

It is extremely difficult to make direct quantitative comparisons of national patterns of access to tertiary education on the basis of socio-economic status. First, the idea of social class is highly intangible and firmly grounded in national social, cultural and economic systems. Thus, when SES is measured it is done so on quite different indicators and scales. Second, higher education systems also differ significantly and what is classified as higher education differs between countries. As a result of these two factors, little comparative data is available. The Organisation for Economic Co-operation and Development (OECD), for example, in the otherwise excellent *Education at a Glance* (2006a) dataset, reports higher education participation only in aggregate figures, by gender and for people with disabilities.

Despite these problems with comparison, the broad international situation, at least in developed nations, is illustrated by the following national vignettes. Germany is renowned for its highly stratified secondary school system, one outcome of which is sizable imbalances in higher education participation. One study in the late 1990s (Schnitzer et al., 1999) reported that only 33% of lower social background children reached upper secondary school and only 8% entered higher education. In comparison, 84% of upper social background children reached upper secondary and 72% entered higher education – a ninefold difference.

The dubious achievement of the most socially polarised higher education system of the EU appears to go to Portugal. The Portuguese higher education system expanded after the revolution in 1974, but a firm binary divide was maintained between universities and polytechnics. The equity performance of Portuguese higher education is possibly the worst among EU nations, with people in the lowest social grouping being *10 times* less likely to attend university than people in the highest social grouping.

In the UK and US, access to higher education for low socio-economic background people appears to be diminishing in relative terms due to the combined effects of standardised entrance testing and higher tuition costs (Layer, 2005). It is of course impossible to summarise fairly the diverse US system of public and private universities, for the institutions run the full spectrum from highly inclusive to highly socially elitist. There are many universities with aggressive and effective equity programmes, sometimes enshrined in state legislation that specifies admissions targets. But there are also some of the most socially privileged institutions in the world in which family influence and 'cheque-book' admissions prevail. A powerful account of this phenomenon has been provided by Daniel Golden in *The Price of Admission* (2006). Overall, however, the US has a fine tradition of open access and equity that has focused on the participation of minority groups, particularly after President Lyndon Johnson's legislation for affirmative action to redress the legacy of racial discrimination, which opened the doors of universities to African-Americans. Significantly, though, affirmative action is still under sustained attack and, in the past decade, affirmative action programmes in the US have been successfully challenged in legal cases (ironically on moral grounds) with significant ramifications for public and institutional policies for staff and student recruitment alike (Allen, 2005; Douglass, 2007).

Astin and Oseguera (2004) have provided a damning account of growing inequality in US higher education (see Figure 4.1) following an analysis of three decades of data. They concluded that the data reveal:

> substantial socio-economic inequities in who gains access to the most selective colleges and universities in the United States. Further, these inequities have increased during recent decades, despite the expansion of remedial efforts such as student financial aid, affirmative action, and outreach programs. American higher education, in other words, is more socioeconomically stratified today than at any time during the past three decades. Although the underlying reasons for these trends are not clear, it may well be that they are at least partially attributable to the increasing

Figure 4.1: Trends in the parental income distributions of freshman entering the most selective (top 10%) institutions, 1985–2000

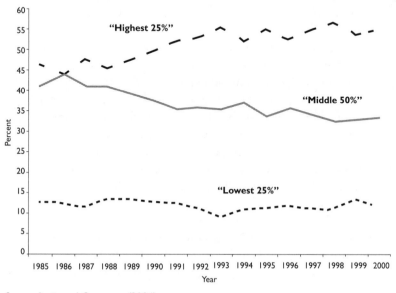

Source: Astin and Oseguera (2004).

> competitiveness among prospective college students for admission to the country's most selective colleges and universities. (Astin and Oseguera, 2004, p 338)

The UK has adopted an ambitious equity agenda under the rubric of 'widening participation' with strategies that include the removal of upfront fees, funding incentives to universities and the encouragement of part-time attendance. The widely touted goal of Tony Blair is for 50% of 18–30 year olds to participate in higher education by 2010, to be achieved from the present base of 43%. The present social imbalances in UK higher education participation are sizable. Around half of the population in England is defined as belonging to lower socio-economic groups, but these people represent only 28% of young, full-time entrants to first degree courses. The Higher Education Funding Council for England (HEFCE) (2006, 2007) has reported that young people from the most prosperous areas are *five to six times* more likely to go to university than young working-class people in particular areas of disadvantage. In Ireland, the tertiary education system has expanded greatly, however the students who have benefited have been drawn disproportionately from managerial and professional classes (OECD, 2006b).

Finland is an important example because, despite being renowned for its egalitarian public school system, its higher education participation is heavily skewed according to parental educational backgrounds. The *OECD Thematic Review of Tertiary Education* reported that large inequalities in access persist in Finnish tertiary education:

> Participation rates in university education among young students (aged 20–24) differ considerably according to the educational background of their parents. The relative chance of entering university education has remained at least ten times higher during the last decades for those coming from academic home backgrounds compared to students from less educated families. The expansion of the tertiary system appears to have narrowed the relative advantage of an academic home background to seven-fold. (Davies et al., 2006, p 21)

Many nations have introduced equity policies. These have taken a number of forms, including: the removal or reduction of perceived barriers, through avenues such as scholarships to help meet the cost of fees or living costs; compensatory admission for students with lower levels of school achievement; and programmes described as affirmative action that focus on minority group membership as the basis for admission. Policies for affirmative action or positive discrimination have been highly contentious, for they have conflicted with conceptions of merit. The admission of people with lower levels of educational attainment has been seen by some to lower academic standards and to take places away from those who deserve them.

In many nations, the ongoing policy issue of equity of access is interwoven with speculation about a desirable *overall* participation rate in higher education. National targets for unrelenting expansion have been driven by the idea of the knowledge society and the perhaps simplistic assumption that higher and higher rates of university participation will automatically lead to enhanced national economic performance. However, as yet, there is no sound way of estimating the overall higher education participation rate needed for optimum national economic performance. Blair's UK target of 50% participation has been the subject of withering criticism by Alison Wolf of the Institute of Education (Wolf, 2002), who argued that the target has no empirical basis and was established in ignorance of the complex relationship between education and labour markets. Further, Wolf proposed that the target might lead to the coercive participation of students who do not really wish to be at university.

So how does Australia fare?

Australia has been a leader in establishing a national equity policy framework, for which it has an international reputation. In addition to the equity framework, the Higher Education Contribution Scheme (HECS) has been a powerful equity device. The effect of HECS has been twofold: as an income contingent loan, it has removed the obstacle of upfront fees, while the revenue from HECS has funded expansion in the number of places available.

The equity policy framework has generated useful time-series data on domestic students, an excellent data set compared with the data available in other nations, allowing for detailed analyses (see eg Dobson, 2003; James et al., 2004; Coates and Krause, 2005). In terms of subgroup participation, Australia does not fare too badly, certainly better than some EU nations. However, the participation patterns are far from satisfactory for a nation that takes pride in its egalitarianism.

The Australian data set shows that good progress has been made in improving the participation of people with disabilities, people from non-English-speaking backgrounds and women – women are now over-represented in most fields, but not all and certainly not at higher degree level. Arguably, the group that has benefited the most from the expansion of higher education in Australia is middle-class females – at least in access to university, although perhaps not in subsequent careers. The situation with Indigenous people's participation is mixed and far from satisfactory. For a period, there was growth in access, although this has stalled in recent years and appears to be dropping. A proportion of the access to higher education for Indigenous people has been provided by sub-degree and enabling programmes. Higher degree enrolments and completions are modest. The principal challenges here are in recruiting Indigenous students who are prepared for university – given that school completion rates for Indigenous people are about half of those for other Australians – and in retaining students once enrolled, for the university completion rate for Indigenous enrollees remains well below 50%. There is much to be proud about in Australian higher education, but it is impossible to be fully proud until we do better for Indigenous Australians. More Indigenous Australians are desperately needed in the professions and with PhDs to set up a positive cycle of aspiration in Indigenous communities.

There are two other groups for which little progress has been made: people living in rural or remote areas, and people from low SES backgrounds. Both groups are highly under-represented and for both the participation shares have not budged despite 15 years of equity policy. The policy framework uses three SES groupings (the other countries that have substantial data tend to use more categories) measured using a postcode index calculated on census data: low SES students are defined as those whose permanent home is in the bottom 25% of postcodes (with medium SES and high SES people defined as representing 50% and 25% of postcodes, respectively).

Table 4.1 shows the typical national participation shares of the three SES groups during the past two decades. To put these figures into concrete terms, people from high or medium SES backgrounds are twice as likely to go to university as those from low SES backgrounds. People from high SES backgrounds are close to *three times* as likely to go to university as those from low SES backgrounds. Though this is rarely mentioned, people from medium SES backgrounds are proportionally under-represented in higher education, albeit only modestly. It is worth nothing that the likelihood of medium SES Australians attending university is only 56% of the likelihood of high SES Australians doing so.

That these imbalances have remained virtually unchanged (see Figure 4.2) – with typical variations of only tenths of percentage points annually, and no discernible overall trend – during a period of

Table 4.1: University participation share by socio-economic status for domestic students and national reference points (%)

	Low SES	Medium SES	High SES
Reference point based on postcode distribution	25.0%	50.0%	25.0%
Share of university places[a]	14.5%	44.5%	39.0%

Note: [a] Typical figures for the entire 1991–2005 period, although some students are not classified.

Figure 4.2: Participation share by socio-economic group, 1991–2002 (%)

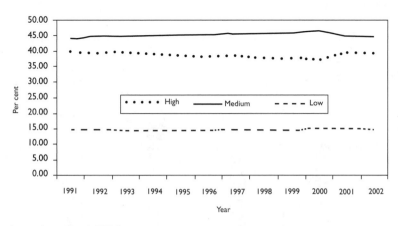

Source: James et al. (2004).

significant expansion in the number of domestic students in Australian higher education is amazing. It is tempting to conclude that university admission and selection processes are quite rigid in reproducing a certain social order.

The contrasts between group participation shares are even more extreme if the leading universities and the courses for which there is the most competitive entry are considered. People from lower socio-economic backgrounds are less successful in gaining access to the high-demand universities and courses. In parallel with international patterns, people from low SES backgrounds are particularly under-represented in medicine, law and architecture, but less under-represented in teacher education and agriculture. Students from high SES backgrounds comprise over half of all the students in master's degrees and doctorates.

The Group of Eight (Go8) research-led universities fall well below the national mean for participation shares of people from low SES backgrounds (Figure 4.3). In total, lower SES students have only about 11% of the share of places. But it should be noted that even the institutions among the most effective in enrolling students from lower socio-economic backgrounds just reach or barely exceed the notional 25% reference point. For example, in the 2005 figures (see Table 4.2): Newcastle reached 27.4%, Victoria University 23.8% and the University of South Australia 24.1%. Newcastle does exceptionally well, in part because of its geographical location, but also due to a thriving foundation programme that is without parallel in Australian higher education.

Figure 4.3: Participation share of SES groups by broad university type, 2002

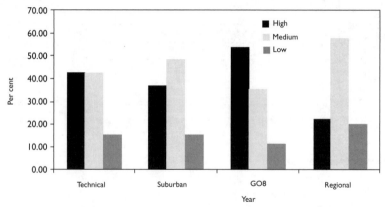

Source: James et al. (2004).

Importantly, there is now evidence of an *increasing* social polarisation between universities. Between 2001 and 2005, the proportion of low SES students dropped in all of the research-led universities that form the Go8 (see Table 4.3) with the exception of the University of New South Wales (which began that period with the lowest proportion for its state). One factor in this trend appears to be the intensification of competition for university places in the most highly selective universities and the continuing high level of social stratification of secondary school achievement. The differences between the universities in Table 4.3 are largely due to locational effects and the geographical regions from which the universities draw high proportions of their students rather than university policies.

Table 4.2: Participation share for students from low SES backgrounds (all ages) for selected universities, 2005 (%)

	Low SES (%)	State total
Victoria University	23.8	13.5
RMIT University	13.3	13.5
Deakin University	13.2	13.5
Swinburne University of Technology	10.2	13.5
The University of Melbourne	8.0	13.5
University of South Australia	24.1	20.5
Flinders University	20.6	20.5
The University of Adelaide	15.0	20.5
Griffith University	14.5	17.6
University of Queensland	14.5	17.6
The University of Newcastle	27.4	12.9
The University of Sydney	6.4	12.9
The University of New South Wales	5.5	12.9

Source: DEST (2006).

Table 4.3: Participation share for low SES students (all ages) in the Go8 universities, 2001 and 2005 (%)

	2001	2005	State/Territory total, 2005
Australian National University	4.6	3.5	3.5
University of New South Wales	5.1	5.5	12.9
University of Sydney	7.4	6.4	12.9
University of Western Australia	7.7	7.5	12.9
University of Melbourne	8.4	8.0	13.5
Monash University	13.9	13.0	13.5
University of Queensland	15.5	14.5	17.6
University of Adelaide	16.0	15.0	20.5

Source: DEST (2006).

It can be concluded from the Australian data that higher education disproportionately serves high SES people in Australia, as it does elsewhere in the world. The imbalances do not seem as extreme as in some other developed nations, although this may be an artefact of a classification that uses only three categories of social class and the use of a geographical postcode index rather than, say, parental occupation or educational attainment on which other national data are based.

The most prestigious universities are in a challenging position. Typically they have an informal, unwritten social contract because of their histories and, awkwardly, communities expect them to stand for academic excellence and equality of opportunity in equal measure. The tensions between these two values are profound in a society in which senior school completion rates and achievement levels are strongly correlated with socio-economic status. The bind for these institutions is that they are open to criticism of either elitism *or* declining standards if any changes are made to policies for student selection, access and equity.

Dispelling the myths surrounding equity of access in Australian higher education

The argument thus far can be summarised as follows. Worldwide, people from low SES backgrounds are highly under-represented in higher education, partly because school completion rates and school achievement levels are closely correlated with social class. Many nations have had equity policies to address this problem, but the effects of these are not at all clear. Certainly, at an aggregate level, these policies appear to have done little to reduce the persistent, proportional under-representation of low SES people. In fact, within the most expanded higher education systems, there is evidence of a polarisation of the socio-economic profile of the student body across different universities. Competition is heightened for the places in the most prestigious universities: students compete for entry to what are perceived to be the best universities, while, in turn, the more prestigious universities compete for the students with the highest level of school achievement.

Thus, growth in overall participation in higher education almost invariably leads to institutional stratification. There are strong social forces for this. Part of the private benefit of higher education is in the social differentiation it provides. This hinges on exclusiveness: the value of higher education as a private good is relative to the 'other'; that is, the people without higher education. The more people who have higher education, the less positional value it has. As overall access to higher education expands, the desire for social differentiation is therefore increasingly sought in choice of institution, course and higher degree studies. The expansion of participation leads to overtly tiered systems and elite universities can be expected to do very well in mass higher education systems, which they do, but equally they tend to become highly socially polarised.

So, do we give up on the problem of equity or should we aim to do better? People can live rewarding, happy lives without going to university, of course, and few would argue that it is socially or economically desirable for everyone to undertake higher education. But the unacceptable problem, in my view, is the extent of the social stratification of university participation in Australia, particularly in some institutions and courses, given the benefits that higher education confers on individuals and their communities. This stratification is easily overlooked on a day-to-day basis as, but for the more overt manifestations of social class, it is largely invisible on campus. The social stratification of university participation is partially because Australia's education systems fail to serve some Australians well rather than because of differences in intelligence or in the potential to benefit from higher education. To argue that the present participation imbalances are acceptable or inevitable would be to concede defeat on the capacity to improve our school systems unless it is assumed that intelligence is unequally dispersed across the social strata.

How much better do we need to do? This is a very difficult question to which there are no definitive answers. What is needed to do better? This is perhaps an easier question. An initial step towards more effective equity policies is better theorising on the precise character of the problem. Arguably there are six myths or misconceptions that appear to permeate thinking around equity in higher education and that limit the capacity to imagine more effective policies and initiatives. The first two to follow are the most prevalent of these myths.

Myth 1: 'Expanding participation will improve equity'

Whether or not this assertion is a myth is admittedly the subject of some debate. A common international strategy to advance equity has simply been to fund the expansion of access. While it is true that expansion can allow more people from lower socio-economic backgrounds to attend university, it is also the case that the benefits of higher rates of participation in higher education are spread roughly equally across social strata – this effect appears universally true in developed nations. So expansion alone does not improve the participation share of people from lower socio-economic backgrounds – thus, whether there are social equity gains is debatable. Almost paradoxically, expansion can lead to greater social inequality. As has been argued, mass or universal higher education systems invariably become highly stratified and access to the elite universities and most highly sought-after courses becomes heavily skewed towards the higher social classes.

Myth 2: 'Free or low-cost higher education will improve equity'

This is the second most prevalent myth. 'Free higher education' is the mantra in protests about the rising costs of higher education. But there is no evidence at all that free or low-cost higher education widens participation on a grand scale. In fact, during the initial era of free higher education in Australia, the social composition of the university student population was largely the same as it is today.

This myth is based on the assumption that cost is the principal barrier to access. Cost is a factor, but it is not the only factor. All the evidence points to lower levels of school achievement, lower aspirations and lack of perceived personal relevance being far more potent factors. In any case, it is probably a 'pie in the sky' hope to argue for free higher education. Governments seem unwilling or unable to provide the resources to fund appropriate quality higher education in an era of mass or universal participation. Free higher education is likely to lead to far fewer people going to university or very low-quality provision, or both. In the current context, free higher education would create a regressive tax situation in most nations for the middle and upper classes are over-represented compared with the lower classes. However, targeted reductions in the cost of higher education is definitely essential for the successful participation of some people, as the recent Centre for the Study of Higher Education (CSHE) study of student finances for Universities Australia has shown. Everything possible must be done to achieve minimal costs for students who otherwise would not be able to participate or whose quality of study would be seriously compromised by their financial circumstances.

Myth 3: 'Improving equity involves the removal of barriers to access'

The third myth involves an important conceptual shift. It is closely related to Myth 2. It is naive to think only in terms of removing barriers, or even to think in terms of the popular rhetoric of 'expanding choices'. The challenge is not only to remove or reduce barriers, where they exist, but also to *build* possibilities and choices: to raise aspirations, to raise perceptions of relevance and to boost personal educational achievement. Many young people do not even get to the point of confronting barriers or having 'choices' – education is a *precursor* to informed choice. So here is the rub: building possibilities is far more costly and needs far more imagination than removing barriers and it needs a long-term commitment. It requires improvements within all education sectors and a coordinated policy approach.

Myth 4: 'The onus is with universities to resolve equity problems'

No, not entirely. The die has been cast for many students well before the point of transition to higher education at which universities have the most influence. Differential school completion rates are a significant factor in the differential rate of transfer to higher education, as are differential levels of school achievement. Putting aside mature-age entry, universities in the main part play out their low SES recruitment initiatives around a relatively small, though nonetheless very important, target group of prospective students – those who have stayed at school and successfully completed secondary schooling, whose academic attainment is at a suitable level, and who see relevance in higher education and have confidence in their ability to succeed at university. For these students, much of the equity concerns are quite reasonably focused on financial issues. But these students represent a narrow slice of the participation imbalances. Focusing solely on these 'survivors' is to work on the margins of the equity problem. Again, the improvement of equity in higher education requires improvements within all education sectors.

Myth 5: 'Widening participation will lower standards or lower retention and completion rates'

The belief that widening participation will lower university standards is one of the most pernicious myths, reflecting a deeply pessimistic view of human potential and the capacity of education to develop people. The idea of standards in higher education is too conceptually complex to be examined properly here, but it is sufficient to say that using student achievement on entry as a measure of standards or a safeguard of standards is shallow thinking in a mass higher education system. The notion that 'inputs' safeguard academic standards is a relic of elite-era thinking, but it will persist until there are better ways of measuring 'outputs', that is, graduate capabilities. There is some truth in the assertion that widening participation will lower retention and completion rates, but the drop is unlikely to be dramatic. The current data show that there are few significant problems with retention rates, success rates and completion rates for people in the designated equity groups once they enrol in higher education, with the significant exception of Indigenous people (DEST, 2002).

Myth 6: 'Students can be selected for higher education on academic merit'

Well, yes, but only to a point. In mass or universal higher education systems in which perhaps half the population will undertake higher education, the idea of merit has less salience than it did in the elite era. Yet our hopes for meritocratic entry to university are still largely pinned on the ranking of school achievement. The Equivalent National Tertiary Entrance Rank (ENTER until 2009, later the Australian Tertiary Admissions Rank [ATAR]) ranks student achievement on a 0–100 scale and is the predominant selection device, certainly for school-leavers and the Go8 institutions in particular. Clearly, ENTER is not a measure of intrinsic individual intellectual ability. ENTER partly measures the cumulative advantage or disadvantage of family, school and community circumstances. ENTER measures preparedness, perhaps, and certainly not ideally, but it is a less than perfect proxy for the potential of individuals to thrive in and benefit from university study. Investing too much trust in ENTER as a fair and just indicator of merit for higher education is a mistake in a mass system.

The point here is that equity and merit, as they are currently conceived, are in significant tension. The concept of equity in elite systems of higher education was partly based on the meritocratic principle that certain people were deserving of higher education on the basis of 'untapped' intellectual potential and these people needed compensatory access. Equity was simply an appendage to merit. Martin Trow (1973, 2006) speculated that as systems moved from mass to universal participation, access would move from being a right to an obligation, and that meritocratic admissions coupled with compensatory programmes for equity purposes would be replaced by more open access. Internationally, there is little evidence of this occurring on a large scale, even in the most expanded systems.

Taking bold steps: some ideas on advancing equity in Australian higher education

This section offers a set of interrelated ideas that might allow the problem of the under-representation of people from low SES backgrounds to be tackled in a more active way and on a larger scale. It illustrates the major change in thinking and policy that would be needed. However, if new approaches are not adopted we must reconcile ourselves to continuing with well-meaning initiatives that have limited impact and periodic hand-wringing over the seemingly intractable nature of the problem.

Frame policy around a multi-causal understanding of the factors underlying under-representation

The problem of educational disadvantage will be addressed in only a piecemeal fashion while it continues to be depicted almost solely in terms of financial disadvantage and financial barriers. The limited and simplistic theorising that narrowly equates socio-economic educational disadvantage with financial hardship needs to be eliminated. Similarly, the persistent concepts of external 'barriers to access' and the 'deserving poor', despite the appeal of the latter, need to be downplayed. The cost of higher education (real or perceived) is only one inhibiting factor. Boosting the encouraging or enabling factors is as necessary as removing barriers, including the barrier of cost. Scholarships and other forms of financial incentive and support are essential for removing financial deterrents and hardship, but are only part of the solution – these are a necessary but not sufficient condition.

Improve the definition and measurement of socio-economic status

Ironically, while SES is perhaps the most important demographic characteristic for equity purposes, its measurement is the most fraught. Considerable work needs to be done to improve the way in which socio-economic status is defined and measured. The present postcode index has been a useful and inexpensive way of estimating aggregate participation shares and trends, but it is not an appropriate way to identify individual socio-economic status or educational disadvantage. It is likely that the use of the postcode index underestimates the social stratification in Australian higher education.

The idea of social classes or social strata is relatively unproblematic, but the identification of individuals with particular social classes is highly problematic. By and large, people do not self-identify with social classes and there may be some stigma in doing so. Thus, one of the main problems for universities in implementing access programmes is in targeting prospective students and in distinguishing between individual educational disadvantage and the patterns of disadvantage experienced by particular groups. Here the postcode index fails us almost totally. The postcode index is rarely, if ever, used by universities to explicitly target postcode regions. This non-alignment of monitoring measures with intervention strategies is an obvious shortcoming of the equity policy framework. Measurement alternatives need to be considered, including parental occupations, educational levels and income levels. Of course, these alternatives are not without limitations of their own and to collect data on any of them would be intrusive and more costly than the present approach. But advancing an evidence-based approach to policy certainly requires improvement in the measurement of individual socio-economic status.

Set targets and provide more incentives for universities

The Higher Education Equity Program (HEEP) has provided modest financial incentives in return for what has become a ritualised annual reporting of institutional equity plans. The government might employ new policy devices that establish incremental targets and financial incentives. These might have a particular focus on the Go8 universities where there is a pressing need to more effectively recruit low SES students, especially from the most under-represented schools. The measurement dimension of equity policy is critical. In modern higher education, what is measured counts, thus what is measured and the way in which it is measured can drive university behaviours in powerful ways.

Reach back into schools, well before the school–university transition

As has been argued, equity initiatives will have limited impact if they operate only at the point of transition to university. Yet there is a tendency within universities for equity of access to be perceived primarily as a student *selection* issue. The present participation inequities might be reduced if there was a commitment to focusing more energy on the early stages of the creation of educational ambition. This would require programmes in under-represented schools and communities to build aspirations, raise confidence in the relevance of higher education and contribute to higher levels of academic achievement early in students' secondary schooling. This would require universities to establish stronger partnerships with disadvantaged schools, districts, regions and communities to build aspirations among students in middle secondary school, or earlier. In some cases, this may mean establishing preferential pathways into university.

Select students more flexibly by being less reliant on school achievement ranking, and encourage and support mature-age entry

Continuing improvement in the pathways into higher education that bypass competitive selection procedures is essential, and this includes through mature-age entry. Competitive entry based on school achievement is a major stumbling block for young people from low SES backgrounds: in their personal assessment of their possibilities; in their actual chances; and in their assessment of the labour-market value of courses to which they might realistically gain access.

As has been argued, there is a gridlock, of sorts, at the point of selection for entry to university. Admission is conceived largely in meritocratic terms to which is coupled a suite of special admissions or compensatory mechanisms for equity purposes. Typically, equity policy initiatives attempt to influence the compensation side of this equation. The merit–compensation monolith might equally be softened if the present belief in merit, narrowly construed around senior secondary achievement, is confronted.

The challenge of loosening the alignment of ideas about merit with school achievement rank is greatest for the Go8 universities of course. These universities might, for example, preserve a higher proportion of higher education places and create alternative entry schemes for prospective students who are unlikely due to their circumstances to be successful in securing the high grades needed for competitive entry. However, any programmes of this kind will likely elicit concern about 'falling standards'. Rarely is school achievement not the 'bottom line' for admissions and the litmus test of standards – a rise in the overall school achievement ranks for courses appears to be celebrated in most universities.

Renew first-year curricula

Equity policies and programmes are closely related to choices about the curriculum and approaches to teaching and learning, although this is rarely recognised. The student selection and recruitment stance adopted by institutions influences first-year curriculum decisions, for universities are required to teach students who are more diverse and perhaps less well prepared in conventional terms. So the widening of participation, especially in the Go8 universities, invites a reconceptualisation of first year curricula to accommodate students from different backgrounds with different types of preparedness. While school achievement is not an ideal measure of individual ability, it is probably a reasonable indicator of the immediate preparedness for higher education, albeit for some fields of study more so than others.

Develop better ways of measuring graduate outcomes

This final suggestion might look odd at first. However, a value-added measure of the outcomes of university education might help break down the vertical stratification of Australian universities. Without better information on what graduates have learned and what they are capable of doing, institutional positional status based on reputational effects will prevail. In turn, the competition for places in the institutions offering the highest positional status will continue to be fierce, and so the cycle will go on.

This suite of suggestions demonstrates that widening participation in a major way would be costly and there are no 'quick fixes'. Non-traditional students are more costly to attract to university and require more academic support and other forms of support once enrolled. But this is what is required if serious inroads are to be made into the present participation imbalances.

Global student flow: can a new conception of equity be developed?

There is a one major and striking gap in the analysis thus far. About one quarter of students in Australian universities are international students and Australian universities intensively recruit students throughout South-East and East Asia, including more recently through the establishment of offshore campuses in a number of countries. Yet, with regard to this large group of students, there has been no discussion of equity of access and of what this might mean in the international context. Much of the analysis of internationalisation and student mobility has focused on standards and the quality of provision, competition between countries, and university rankings. There has been some research into the student experience and some discussion on the effects on curricula, but little detailed research on this. But there has been virtually no examination of the composition of the student body participating in international higher education. Here the data available to us are very poor. Most nations do not have reliable data on the numbers of students travelling overseas for higher education purposes, let alone data on their demography. In Australia, we have no data on the socio-economic composition of international students and it is difficult to imagine how we might collect such data given that the present measures of socio-economic status do not translate across borders.

Equity policy and the thinking around equity is embedded within national policy frameworks. International student mobility confounds assumptions about merit and equity, for the conceptualisation of social class and indeed the measurement of school achievement are relative and firmly grounded in particular national social, economic and educational frameworks. There are presently no studies that explore equity across national borders. An international project is needed to consider the equity issues in international higher education, in particular, to examine how more comprehensive and more refined databases might be collected to monitor student demography in the context of global cross-border student flows. There are indications that the EU might take steps in this direction.

With the cross-border flow of students and the personal, social and economic benefits inherent in achieving a university education, equity in higher education should be a significant international issue, particularly for developing nations (Naidoo, 2007). A scenario can be imagined in which international social elites are increasingly mobile for higher education, especially graduate education, and a wealthy group of people will have access to highly prestigious institutions and premium-quality education. Issues of access and equity in higher education will surely need to be addressed globally as well as nationally.

Concluding comments

The recent history of equity in Australian higher education highlights the triumph of social complexity over policy aspirations. Despite the apparently limited effects of the equity policy framework, it has been persisted with largely unchanged. Partly, this is because equity policy simply plays a symbolic role; that is, it is important to maintain an espoused commitment to equity even if the policy is achieving seemingly modest gains.

Overall, the equity discourse in Australia needs reinvigoration. In 2008, Universities Australia commissioned the CSHE to undertake a national scoping study on equity of access, with a focus on people from low SES backgrounds in rural and metropolitan areas and Indigenous people (CSHE, 2008). This study preceded the Review of Australian Higher Education, a sweeping review led by Professor Denise Bradley. The subsequent review recommendations set bold targets for the expansion of access to Australian higher education and the achievement of equitable participation (DEEWR, 2008).Among 46 recommendations, the review proposed that the Australian government set a national target of at least 40% of 25–34 year olds attaining a qualification at bachelor level or above by 2020.This recommendation was a direct response to Australia's slipping performance against OECD nations in extent of degree attainment and the growing prevalence of 50% attainment targets among OECD nations. The proposed target represents an increase in degree completion from the base in 2008 of around 30%.

The Bradley recommendations also addressed social inclusion. The review proposed that the Australian government establish a national goal of 20% of higher education enrolments at undergraduate level being people from low socio-economic status backgrounds by 2020. Again, this was a bold target, against the present participation share for low SES Australians that hovers at around 15%.

The targets for expansion and equity were quickly endorsed by the government.The panel proposed that to support the achievement of the social inclusion target, performance incentives be put in place:

> 4 per cent of all funds for teaching will be directed to outreach and retention initiatives.All institutions in receipt of Commonwealth funds for teaching will be expected to establish initiatives to increase both the enrolment of, and success of, students from disadvantaged backgrounds. Part of this allocation will be directed to the support of outreach activities in communities with poor higher education participation rates. In partnership with schools and other education providers, higher education institutions will work to raise aspirations as well as provide academic mentoring and support. The bulk of the allocation will be distributed to institutions on the basis of their success in enrolling and graduating students from low socio-economic backgrounds. (DEEWR, 2008, p xiv)

The Bradley review represents the first attempt to formulate a policy framework to encourage and enable universal participation in higher education in Australia.The recommendations link expansion tightly to equity and in doing so follow familiar international patterns, especially the widening participation policies of the UK.The challenges for policy and practice are immense.

As higher education systems have massified the focus of concern for equity is changing. Whereas the interest was once primarily on aggregate patterns of access to higher education, more attention is now being given to the nature of the particular universities and courses to which people gain access, and indeed more interest in the nature of outcomes too. Clearly, all higher education is not equal, and as the differences in purposes, quality and outcomes become sharper, the implications for equity will need renewed examination.

Notes

[1] An earlier version of this chapter was presented at the University of Melbourne, Faculty of Education, Dean's Lecture Series, 18 September 2007.

[2] *A Fair Chance for All* (NBEET, 1990) also established a 'data-driven' policy framework structured around six designated equity groups and five performance indicators:

- Equity groups: people from low socio-economic backgrounds, people in rural or isolated areas, people with disabilities, Indigenous people and people from non-English-speaking backgrounds, and women, especially in non-traditional fields of study and higher degrees.

- Performance indicators: access, participation, success, retention and completion.

See also Martin (1994).

References

Allen, W.R. (2005) 'A forward glance in the mirror: diversity challenged – access, equity and success in higher education', *Educational Researcher*, vol 34, pp 18–23.

Astin, A.W. and Oseguera, L. (2004) 'The declining "equity" of American higher education', *Review of Higher Education* vol 27, pp 321–41.

Coates, H. and Krause, K. (2005) 'Investigating ten years of equity policy in Australian higher education', *Journal of Higher Education Policy and Management*, vol 27, pp 35–47.

CSHE (Centre for the Study of Higher Education) (2008) *Participation and Equity*, Canberra: Universities Australia.

Davies, J., Weko, T., Kim, L. and Thulstrup, E. (2006) *OECD Thematic Review of Tertiary Education. Finland Country Note*, Paris: OECD.

DEEWR (Department of Education, Employment and Workplace Relations) (2008). *Review of Australian Higher Education: Final Report*, Canberra: Australian Government Publishing Service.

DEST (Department of Education, Science and Training) (2002) *Achieving Equitable and Appropriate Outcomes: Indigenous Australians in Higher Education*, Canberra: Australian Government Publishing Service.

DEST (2006) 'Students 2005: selected higher education statistics'. Available at: www.dest.gov.au

Dobson, I. (2003) 'Access to university in Australia: who misses out?', in M. Tight (ed) *Access and Exclusion*, London: JAI Elsevier Science.

Douglass, J. (2007) *The Conditions for Admission: Access, Equity and the Social Contract of Public Universities*, California: Stanford University Press.

Golden, D. (2006) *The Price of Admission: How America's Ruling Class Buys Its Way into Elite Colleges – and Who Gets Left Outside the Gates*, Virginia: University of Virginia Press.

HEFCE (Higher Education Funding Council for England) (2006) 'Widening participation: a review', report to the Minister of State for Higher Education and Lifelong Learning by the Higher Education Funding Council for England.

HEFCE (2007) *Strategic Plan 2006–2011*, London: Higher Education Funding Council for England.

James, R. (2001) 'Participation disadvantage in Australian higher education: an analysis of some effects of geographical location and socio-economic status', *Higher Education*, vol 42, pp 455–72.

James, R. (2002) *Socio-economic Background and Higher Education Participation: An Analysis of School Students' Aspirations and Expectations*, Canberra: Australian Government Publishing Service.

James, R., Wyn, J., Baldwin, G., Hepworth, G., McInnis, C. and Stephanou, A. (1999) *Rural and Isolated Students and Their Higher Education Choices: A Re-Examination of Student Location, Socio-economic Background, and Educational Advantage and Disadvantage*, Canberra: Australian Government Publishing Service.

James, R., Baldwin, G., Coates, H., Krause, K. and McInnis, C. (2004) *Analysis of Equity Groups in Higher Education 1991–2002*, Canberra: Department of Education, Science and Training.

Layer, G. (ed) (2005) *Closing the Equity Gap: The Impact of Widening Participation Strategies in the UK and the USA*, Leicester: National Institute of Adult Continuing Education.

Martin, L. (1994) *Equity and General Performance Indicators in Higher Education. Vol 1: Equity Indicators*, Canberra: Australian Government Publishing Service.

Naidoo, R. (2007) *Higher Education as a Global Commodity: the Perils and Promises for Developing Countries*, London: The Observatory on Borderless Higher Education.

NBEET (National Board of Employment, Education and Training) (1990) *A Fair Chance for All: National and Institutional Planning for Equity in Higher Education, a Discussion Paper*, Canberra: Australian Government Publishing Service.

OECD (Organisation for Economic Co-operation and Development) (2006a) *Education at a Glance*, Paris: OECD.

OECD (2006b) *Higher Education in Ireland (Reviews of National Policies for Higher Education)*, Paris: OECD.

Rawls, J. (1973) *A Theory of Justice*, Oxford: Oxford University Press.

Schnitzer, K., Isserstedt, W., Mussig-Trapp, P. and Schriebe, J. (1999) *Student Life in Germany; The Socio-economic Picture, Summary of the 15th Social Survey of the Deutsches Studentenwerk (DSW)*, Bonn: Bundesministerium fur Bildung und Forschung.

Sen, A. (1995) 'Gender inequality', in M. Nussbaum and A. Sen *The Quality of Life*, Oxford: The Clarendon Press.

Trow, M. (1973) *Problems in the Transition from Elite to Mass Higher Education*, Berkley, CA: Carnegie Commission on Higher Education.

Trow, M. (2006) 'Reflections on the transition from elite to mass to universal access: forms and phases of higher education in modern societies since WWII', in J. Forest and P. Altbach (2006) *International Handbook of Higher Education*, Netherlands: Springer, pp 243–80.

Wolf, A. (2002) 'Too many students?', *Prospect*, July, no 76, www.prospectmagazine.co.uk/2002/07/toomanystudents/

FIVE

From minority to majority: educating diverse students in the United States

Yolanda T. Moses

Introduction

Not since the G.I. Bill in the late 1940s has there been more national focus on the importance of post-secondary education for all Americans in the US. But as America goes to college, issues of cost, preparation, access, articulation (from kindergarten through an undergraduate degree) and retention continue to loom large. Access for all Americans as a concept is more important now than ever before. But achieving that access is often very problematic. While the US boasts an array of diverse higher education options, from community colleges to liberal arts colleges, public comprehensive and for-profit institutions, many non-traditional students do not and cannot take advantage of them. These students are plagued by such challenges and barriers as: (1) failure to get through the secondary education pipeline; (2) lack of or poor counselling in secondary school; (3) lack of funds and, just as important, the perception of lack of funds; and (4) lack of strong retention programmes at most post-secondary institutions. This chapter makes the case that every sector of higher education and every institution type have an important role to play in the success of non-traditional students in higher education in the US. To do anything less will put the lofty ideal of the US as an educated pluralistic democracy for all in jeopardy. This means that there is an urgent national need for a shift in thinking, policy and action in US higher education, around how it engages students, especially under-represented students, in the pipeline from secondary schools. That shift needs to put more onus for the access and success of students on institutions rather than only on the shoulders of those same students.

Higher education for all? Setting the stage

This chapter starts from the position that higher education in the US should be a right for all qualified citizens (and increasingly non-citizens as well), as long as they are making satisfactory progress towards getting their degrees from high school as well as from college/university; especially at the BA level or the BS level. As a matter of fact, President Obama has recently become one of the national champions of universal higher education in the US. But that has not always been the case in the country.

Not since the Second World War and the passage of the G.I. Bill of Rights for US veterans has there been more unprecedented access to higher education than there has been in the last 25 years. This federal Bill, called the Servicemen's Readjustment Act of 1944, almost did not become law because there were elitist politicians who believed that higher education in the US would be watered down and that college and university degrees would become less prestigious because, for the first time in American history, working-class people of all colours, ethnicities and backgrounds could attain post-secondary education. Passage and implementation of this law prompted major shifts in the national vision of higher education. One was the creation of the community college system in California to serve the thousands of veterans wanting to attend college. This novel idea allowed working adults to go to their first two years of post-secondary education in their own communities and neighbourhoods, thus keeping families intact (American Association of Community Colleges, 2000; Bowen et al., 2005). A second effect of the Bill was the new concept that a student could attend a four-year institution and receive a bachelor's degree while still working. This is best exemplified by the City College of the City University of New York, the first four-year institution in the US to establish an evening BS/BA programme (Metzger, 1977). A third effect of the G.I. Bill was that it offered many under-represented veterans from minority racial/ethnic groups the opportunity to attend post-secondary educational institutions in unprecedented numbers as well. To summarise, the major outcome of the federal G.I. Bill that changed US society as a whole was that it provided for the very first time access to knowledge for people who had previously been denied that access due to their class, race/ethnicity and geographical location, among other factors (Bowen et al., 2005).

America's college population has grown substantially since the Second World War. Before that, college graduates were not a common phenomenon. Many states enlarged their university systems, and enrolments at private colleges and universities also grew (Carnevale and Fry, 2000, p 15). By 1963, enrolment had risen to 4.3 million students. Over the next two decades, US college enrolments tripled to more than 12 million students, largely due to the entry of the baby-boomer generation. Higher college enrolment also prompted a gradual shift in the US economy from blue-collar to white-collar jobs, especially for white males (Carnevale and Fry, 2000, p 13; Bowen et al., 2005).

Between 1982 and 1995, college growth continued, but at a slower pace. Non-traditional students aged 25 and older – including children of the baby-boomer generation known as Generation Y – increased the enrolment numbers in higher education again. Those 18–24 year olds will account for roughly two thirds of the increase in the number of undergraduates by 2015, or 1.7 million out of the 2.6 million additional students.

A dramatic rise in immigration continues to increase campus growth. Between 1960 and 1980, about 450,000 immigrants legally came to the US each year. By 1980, that number had soared to 800,000 annually. Four of the five states projected to have the largest increases in undergraduates by 2015 – California, Texas, Florida and New York – also top the list of states with the highest number of immigrants since 1980 (Carnevale and Fry, 2000, p 15).

Older students were predicted to again flock to higher education in the 21st century. This population will include baby boomers on sabbaticals, retiring and pursuing lifelong learning courses, and career-switchers. This number will also include mature workers returning to school for more mid-career education. Older students may account for a full 31% – or about 800,000 students – of the projected 2.6 million rise in undergraduate enrolment between 1995 and 2015 (Carnevale and Fry, 2000, p 15).

An analysis of the ethnic/racial mix of this diverse population illuminates the shifting trends. White non–Hispanic students will continue to be the largest group on college campuses overall. The numbers will rise from 9.5 million in 1995 to 10 million in 2015. But Euro-American students as a percentage of all undergraduates will decline from 70.6% in 1995 to 62.8% by 2015. On the other hand, African-American, Hispanic and Asian/Pacific Islander students will account for 80% of the increase in undergraduates by 2015, or 2 million of the 2.6 million new students. Minority racial/ethnic groups will together increase their percentage of the undergraduate population from 29.4% to 37.2% and will actually outnumber Euro-American students on campuses in the District of Columbia, as well as in the states of California, Hawaii and New Mexico. Texas will be evenly split between Euro-Americans and minority racial/ethnic students by 2015 (Carnevale and Fry, 2000, p 21). The University of California Riverside already has a majority of its undergraduate student population from minority racial/ethnic groups as of 2009 (University of California Riverside, 2009).

Despite the good news that a growing number of students from minority racial/ethnic groups are projected to attend college by 2015, the playing field is still not level. Despite steady gains, the proportion of black and Hispanic students who attend college still lags behind the attendance of white students and Asian-Pacific American students. By 2015, African-Americans are projected to make up 19.5% of all 18–24 year olds in the population, but they are projected to account for only 11.9% of the 18- to 24-year-old undergraduates. Hispanics will be 18.9% of all youth in the college-aged bracket, but will account for only 13.1% of the 18- to 24-year-old undergraduates. There are at least three major reasons for the gap. First, it appears from the research that both groups choose not to attend college or university due to the perceived high cost of a college education. Second, when they do attend, they tend to go to community college; the literature is very clear that the transfer rates from community college to a four-year institution are low for all students, but even lower for students from minority racial/ethnic groups. Third, when students from minority racial/ethnic groups enter four-year colleges and universities, they tend not to graduate (Carnevale and Fry, 2000, p 31).

It is clear that most colleges and universities want to maximise their enrolments with the new students of the 21st century. It is also clear that most colleges and universities have embraced, at least at the mission level, the value of diversity in the student body. It is not clear, however, that colleges and universities are developing the strategies needed to reach out to those diverse populations (on all measures of diversity, but especially race/ethnicity), recruit them and provide them with the collegial environment in which they can succeed. Success is defined as achieving the higher educational goals that the students set out to achieve. Whether it is a BS/BA degree, two years at one institution and then transfer to another institution, US institutions need to be better in tune to the needs of their students, but especially under-represented students from minority racial/ethnic groups.

Where we are in the 21st century: differentiation in higher education – maximising post-secondary opportunities

As we end the first decade of the 21st century, educational institutions in the US are continually trying to get data to better understand the complexity of the lives that college and university students lead. One thing we know is that in terms of the college experience, there is no 'one size fits all' model for the American college-going student. Students in the 21st century are highly mobile and are looking for flexible, just-in-time education. Often, students may not begin and receive their bachelor's degrees from the same institutions. How will students get the coherence and quality in their curriculum that they need and pay for? How do we guarantee the integrity of the courses and curriculum we offer across institutions and institutional types? These are some of the major challenges we face.

The new, for-profit and proprietary institutions have begun to offer the mobile and part-time student the modularised, high-quality courses, certificates and programmes that they cannot receive from more traditional institutions. Technology-based instruction is increasingly used to offer students programmes at times and places suitable to their needs. Even on traditional university campuses, it is often the professional schools and colleges such as health, medicine and education that offer the cutting-edge models of flexibility for the delivery of education (Wilson, 2010).

Students are also forcing better articulation among institutions of higher education. Often, students can be discouraged from transferring credits earned in community college to local universities. The rationale that universities often give is that they cannot be sure of the quality of instruction or whether the learning outcomes are comparable. Students, especially older students, are beginning to vote with their feet, seeking out those institutions, whether traditional or non-traditional, that will fulfil their needs (American Association of Community Colleges, 2000; Wilson, 2010).

In the coming years, colleges and universities must do a better job of fulfilling their own mission niche, rather than trying to imitate elite private or large public research universities. There are over 5,000 colleges and universities in the US. From exclusive Ivy League universities, to mostly private small liberal arts colleges, large public land grant universities, comprehensive state universities and private proprietary colleges and universities, there is something for everyone. There is just as much a need for excellent student-centred community colleges and regional comprehensive universities as there is for private liberal arts colleges and elite research universities.

Higher education and the science, engineering, technology and mathematics fields: a national imperative

There is a perfect storm brewing in the US around the production of the next generation of science professionals being trained in the science, engineering, technology and mathematics (STEM) fields. More women and under-represented students from minority racial/ethnic groups are going to colleges and universities than ever before, but women tend to enter the STEM fields in lower numbers than males (especially white and Asian-Pacific American males). Under-represented high school students from minority racial/ethnic groups are often not encouraged to pursue college and, when they do pursue higher education, they are not encouraged to enter STEM fields, or stay in them (National Science Foundation, 2002).

As of 2004, 42% of college students were enrolled in community colleges with 51% of them indicating an intention to pursue a four-year degree (Hoachlander et al., 2003). The reality is that only 30% of these students actually transfer to four-year institutions. Only about 10–15% of students who start their study at two-year colleges successfully complete a four-year degree (Snyder and Hoffman, 2001). Students from minority racial/ethnic groups comprise 28% of college students today and are estimated to represent approximately 50% of new students that will enrol in college by 2014 (Snyder and Hoffman, 2001). In addition, as of 2002, 73% of the students enrolled in US colleges and universities were non-traditional (US Department of Education, 2002). Higher education faces a question of readiness for both non-traditional students and students from minority racial/ethnic groups. Most of these students, both older and from minority racial/ethnic groups, are underprepared, with only 47% having completed a college preparatory curriculum. Of new students, 53% must take remedial coursework upon entering college (US Department of Education, 2002, p 125, Table 29-3).

The norm is no longer attendance at one institution for an entire education. There is a growth in the number of two-year colleges, comprehensive universities and for-profit institutions. Today, 28% of undergraduates attend college part-time (Adelman, 1991). In addition, more students than ever before must work to finance their higher education. King and Bannon (2002) found that, in 1999, 74%

of full-time undergraduate students worked; of these, 46% worked at least 25 hours per week; 20% worked at least 35 hours per week; and community college numbers look very similar.

Diversity of modes of learning in the STEM fields is changing as well. For the past decade at least, the focus of undergraduate education, especially in the STEM fields, has been on trying to document the learning process. In this rapidly changing environment of diverse modes of learning, we know that students are much less likely to be proficient at learning from a textbook. They are also less likely to sit passively and listen to a lecture or in a lab. They are more likely to learn by finding information on the web and from interactive computer-based experiences and experimenting on their own in the laboratory when they have the opportunity. Developments in technology and the explosion of electronic information such as the use of technology for entertainment (from computer games to animated entertainment, digital movies and music) have had a profound impact on students' perception of the undergraduate science experience as well. As a result, they are more disengaged, and more easily bored in the classroom with traditional ways of learning.

These demographic changes, combined with the lack of preparation in secondary schools, and in some of the community colleges, are seriously affecting the ability of higher education to produce bachelor's degrees in the sciences in general, and especially in the mathematical and physical sciences. While the percentage of freshmen who say they are interested in all STEM programmes remains at 25–30%, the percentage is lower for those interested in either mathematics or physical science. As a matter of fact, data from the National Centre for Education Statistics show that in degrees awarded between 1970 and 2001, degrees in mathematics have a three-decade decline. As the student demographic becomes increasingly diverse, the importance of undergraduate degree production in these STEM disciplines is more important than ever.

Why is this the case? The reality is that, in a number of ways, undergraduate education (especially the role of the community colleges) plays a critical role in the STEM activities of the nation. The undergraduate degree drives the graduate education efforts in STEM disciplines. Graduate programmes in turn support research and technological innovations that ultimately support the basis of US economic competitiveness on a global scale (Friedman, 2005, 2008). The need for this scientific know-how includes the ever-growing areas of national defence and homeland security in the US. The graduate STEM enterprise also produces the next generation of faculty for our colleges and universities. By 2015, half of the faculty in these institutions will be eligible for retirement (Finkelstein and Schuster, 2001), and faculty in four-year institutions, in community colleges and in K–12[1] education come from the pool of students who are in our institutions of higher education today. We also need the US STEM pipeline full and healthy to produce the entry-level (associate and bachelor's degree) technical workforce that is essential to US industries maintaining market share. A later section of this chapter will examine the state of that education in the STEM fields and what is being done to change it.

Challenges to achieving our goal of educating the majority

In the US, higher education is often described by educators and political leaders as the cornerstone of a thriving democracy. Opportunities to pursue higher education are available to millions of people in the country, who just 50 years ago would not have even had the option of attending a college or university. That is the picture of the glass half full. For over a decade, a debate has been raging about the goals of higher education in US society because some are concerned that higher education is increasingly becoming more of a private than a public good. Should every citizen in the US who qualifies be able to achieve his or her goal of higher education? Or should higher education just be the province of those who have the economic means to acquire that educational experience (Bowen et al., 2005)? There are over 5,000 colleges and universities in the US with varying missions of service, but there is one system that is truly unique – the California public higher education system. Based on what is called the 'The Master Plan for Higher Education', the California system was designed to provide every resident of the state who qualified for admissions an opportunity to attend a higher education institution. This Plan technically gives every resident access to higher education instruction from the first year of undergraduate education through to the doctoral level. This Plan is 50 years old and still evolving. One of the economic problems being faced by the largest public higher education system in the world is the fact that what used to be free education at the local community college level may be pricing poor and working-class Californians of all ancestries out of higher education (Thelin, 2004).

On a national level, in 1862 the federal government of the US passed the Morrill Land Grant Act. The lofty notion of higher education for the public good has at least part of its roots in that law. In the 19th Century, this Act provided for the establishment of institutions of higher education (primarily for white male students, because a separate system was formed for black students and for women) that focus on agriculture and engineering, but also languages, arts and history. In 1862, the US had over 80% of its economy in agriculture. Today land grant universities continue in every state, in these familiar roles, but also in new ones such as serving a major stimulus to state and regional economies, generating $5 on average for every state dollar invested. They bring in research grants and contracts as well as new businesses; and nearly two thirds of them sponsor research parks or business incubators (Bowen et al., 2005).

The land grant model suggests a great opportunity to revisit the mission of higher education at the dawn of the 21st century around the question of defining the role of higher education in promoting the public good in a much more pluralistic America. Conferences and gatherings of educators in the latter part of the 20th and the beginning of the 21st century spoke to this theme. The resounding outcomes of these conferences, symposia and forums was a recommitment to an affirmation of the ideal, if not the reality, of the continuing role of higher education as a public good in a democratic society and as a core value. This has the moral authority and obligation to provide access and excellence in education at all levels for the range of needs of the pluralistic citizens of the US.

How do institutions commit and recommit themselves to do this work on the ground? In the US, this work has been increasingly done over the past decade through such programmes as service learning, community-based research and campus–community partnerships, among others. This activity is a 21st-century model of the 19th-century Agricultural Extension Office. The US has seen the growth on campuses of centres devoted to community and public service ventures at colleges and universities across the nation, including land grant colleges. Some national higher education organisations such as the American Association for Higher Education (now defunct), the American Association of Colleges and Universities, the American Association of State Colleges and Universities, the National Association of Independent Colleges and Universities, and Campus Compact have mounted major initiatives to harness and leverage up this work on behalf of the whole of higher education (Ehrlich, 2000; Sirianni and Friedland, 2001; Tonkin et al., 2004). The movement has been called in some circles, 'The Engaged Campus' movement. This movement sprang out of the critique of higher education levied by the Kellogg Commission in its 1999 report, *Returning to Our Roots: The Engaged Institution*. This movement looks at the issues of engagement from three levels within the institution: from the students' level, through faculty/ programmes and to institutional and community partnerships (Ehrlich, 2000; Sirianni and Friedland, 2001). Let us explore this model a bit further to see how it has been, and can continue to be, used to help enhance the learning experiences of marginalised students in higher education.

It is increasingly clear that some colleges and universities are doing a good job to promote the social and civic engagement of their students, their faculty and administrators with each other, and with the communities that they serve. Yet there is still no comprehensive model that integrates all of these best practices of engagement into one whole. That is what is needed! We need institutions that incorporate a research, teaching and service paradigm into one whole. We need the 'engaged campus model'.

The engaged campus

The phrase 'engaged campus' encompasses a number of overlapping issues and activities that link individuals and institutions of higher education with their communities. The concept rejects the ivory tower image of campus life, promotes curricular changes and pushes for changing the research culture that dominates late 20th-century and 21st-century higher education. Various national meetings and manifestos of the past few years have identified a need to clarify the language for a national agenda of democratic engagement, while recognising that such terms as civic, democratic and community are themselves contested. The specific categories vary, but the components of the engaged campus movement generally include the following concerns.

Student learning based on service to community

This movement is built primarily on an interest in effective learning. It connects theory to practice, extends the classroom into the community (service-learning), encourages problem-based and interdisciplinary learning, and fosters collaborative and democratic pedagogies. At its best, service-learning is not the application of classroom learning; rather, it is the solving of complex social and civic problems in partnership with a community.

The decline of student engagement in civic life of the community and nation

For at least a decade *before* the election of Barack Obama in 2008, there was a lack of student engagement in political activity, especially voting and participation in traditional social organisations (Jones, 2008). Many observers still see student disengagement as a serious threat to a vibrant democracy and look to higher education to reverse the trend. They are particularly troubled by the juncture of a decline in student interest in politics with a rise in volunteerism. How is that explained? Research shows that although young people have a very strong distrust of formal politics and politicians, they are inclined to volunteer to help their communities through service projects (Ehrlich, 2000). Others counter that the forms of engagement have simply changed for the current student generation or should be addressed as part of the call for civic renewal by all members of society – especially those members who have been historically marginalised and left out of the power process (Jones, 2008).

A reward structure in higher education to honour the renewed interest in faculties' public role through action research, professional community service and community-based teaching and research

This interest is also part of the larger movement to redefine faculty work as discovery, learning and engagement and to adopt the criteria offered in *Scholarship Reconsidered* by Ernest Boyer (1990) as a blueprint for action. Interest in civic engagement has spawned a number of publications, meetings and a national review board for the scholarship of engagement. One challenge has been to define this work as an integral part of the faculty role rather than an additional work burden. In addition, a new reward system is necessary for faculty to want to be involved in the scholarship of engagement rather than in traditional research. Research has also shown that students from minority racial/ethnic groups tend to be interested in classes, research and projects that focus on social, political, economic, health and cultural issues that interest them and are relevant to their home communities (Washington, 2007; Young, 2007; Smith, 2009).

Diversity programmes that create inclusive, multicultural learning environments

The goal of these programmes is to further students' intellectual and moral development and support democratic pluralism at the same time. The programmes frequently challenge the traditional structures of classroom authority and notions of democratic rights and responsibilities built upon dominant cultural norms. They assert that democracy needs to be built on striking a balance between valuing differences and promoting inclusive excellence based on identity and culture. These initiatives often bring together academic and student affairs areas and integrate academic theory and practice from both areas. These programmes often speak to what we call in US institutions of higher education the 'climate' of an institution. Climate may seem intangible, only a concept. But students – especially marginalised students – can perceive it in how they are treated with regard to their race/ethnicity, gender, class, sexual orientation or values and beliefs (Johns and Sipps, 2007; Harper and Quaye, 2009).

Community-building partnerships

Built upon mutual interest and trust, partnerships between higher education and local communities may focus on economic and physical infrastructure, improving public schools and health care, and the efficient use of limited resources. These partnerships share a commitment to a broadly inclusive and democratic engagement of the campus with the community. This is reflected in shared authority, rather than expert–client or researcher–subject relationships. These partnerships have the potential for encouraging lifelong learning among traditional and non-traditional students and helping communities to shape a more just society. They also offer solutions to the increasing fragmentation and isolation of work in the academy by promoting cross- and interdisciplinary work. However, there need to be more effective linkages among this cluster of interests so that they reinforce rather than duplicate each other and allow those who are working for democratic engagement to compound rather than dilute resources. Campuses have the capacity to do this work, to support the holistic success of their under-represented students around integrating issues of social and civic responsibilities into their education (Tierney, 1993; Mukhopadhyay and Moses, 1997; Torres et al., 2003).

How does it happen? First, it takes visionary leadership from the top of the institution, from the President or Chancellor. These leaders must promote leadership for community-building partnerships from all areas of the campus, including but not limited to student affairs, faculty and staff, and the student body. Together these groups should ask and answer questions that lead to a shared vision of a truly engaged campus, such as: how would academic affairs and student affairs collaborate? And how can campus leaders encourage faculty to participate in research and teaching initiatives that enhance institutional knowledge both inside and outside of the university or college around issues of inclusion and engagement?

Student resources

One of the major barriers to students from minority racial/ethnic groups attending post-secondary education institutions in the US is financial. Community colleges are less expensive, and elite private universities pay full tuition and room and board for poor, bright students, but the majority of students pay for their own education from their own savings, work or from public grant or loan programmes. The most popular national grants programme is the Pell Grant, which is targeted at low-income students, but does not cover all the costs of attending most institutions. President Obama has made a commitment to the opportunity to attain a higher education for all US citizens as the way to end poverty. But, with the rising cost of tuition, books and daily living expenses, it will be difficult to make that a reality for all students, especially, black, Hispanic and Native American students.

Lack of communication

Public higher education institutions fall far short of making an effective case to external stakeholders (parents, taxpayers, legislators, potential donors and foundations) about the value of what they do on a daily basis for society. Researchers, scholars and educators need to do a more effective job of telling the important story of the role the institutions play in creating professionals for an educated workforce; conducting crucial research that improves people's lives; assisting students to develop critical thinking, computational and writing skills; and a host of intangible experiences inside and outside of the classroom that prepare students to be leaders in their communities, both local and global.

In addition to providing a service and a learning experience for students, one of the most important potential effects of engaged campus projects is engagement in public dialogue that informs the community about what higher education does, and how this ultimately benefits local communities, states and the country as a whole (Sirianni and Friedland, 2001; Marginson, 2010).

Accountability: defining learning outcomes

Since the early 1990s, institutions of higher education in the US have been grappling with the question of how to define learning outcomes. In that period, a virtual cottage industry sprang up to take on the challenge of articulating clear and concise measures of success (Maki, 2004; Bok, 2006). However, assessment really came of age in the last decade of the 20th century when it moved from the 'margins' of faculty consciousness to the 'centre' of campus life because of the imperative for institutions, often imposed by outside agencies and stakeholders such as accrediting agencies and disciplinary associations, to document the learning success of their students (Maki, 2004; Bok, 2006; Smith, 2009).

In this period, a new series of assessment tools surfaced. These included: electronic portfolios to measure individual learning as well as institutional accountability; the National Survey of Student Engagement (including an initiative to encourage its use at more than 100 institutions serving marginalised students); and the seven-step student learning assessment process developed by Linda Suskie and Andrea Leske (Suskie, 2009). In the last few years, additional tools such as rubrics and computer simulations provided alternatives to the traditional pen and paper tests. In addition, some campuses have begun to develop, test and use individually customised assessment tests (Maki, 2004).

There are even a few institutions that have revolutionised their whole system for measuring quality. One example is Alverno College, a small, private Catholic college located in inner-city Milwaukee, Wisconsin. Thirty years ago, with a growing student population of first-time college-goers, lower socio-economic students, non-traditional students, older women students and students from minority racial/ethnic groups, the leadership of Alverno decided to redefine its mission to provide a changing student body with the specific skills and abilities they needed to be successful learners. To do this they developed a set of eight explicit abilities each student would have to master in order to graduate, and implemented two main strategies for meeting them: (1) developing a pedagogy and process capable of continuous improvement; and (2) investing in programmes to encourage collaborative faculty work to develop an academic curriculum that also integrated student development. This interactive student–faculty process replaced the traditional grade system. By all accounts, the institution has been hugely successful (Diez, 1990, 1998; Diez et al., 1994; Diez and Hass, 1997; Mullen, 2001, pp 55–6).

Installing a holistic system such as the one at Alverno requires enlightened and dedicated leadership on the part of the faculty, administrators and trustees. Alverno could have continued to engage students in the way that it had since it opened in 1887. But instead it chose bold, transformational change, rather than slower incremental change with no guarantee that those incremental steps would ever have resulted in the outcome that produced the institution that is now considered a national leader. Most institutions, however, have taken an incremental approach in building what Peggy Maki (Maki, 2004) calls 'a culture of inquiry' that comprises a commitment to ongoing institutional learning as well as to student learning. This work of assessment at all institutional levels is by no means finished. If anything, being able to articulate the value-added experiences that are provided to diverse students is becoming one of the primary ways of demonstrating institutional effectiveness overall.

Conclusion

This chapter has presented an overview of the demographic, pedagogical and structural realities that marginalised and poor working-class students face as they negotiate the challenges of higher education in the US. It includes a sobering picture of the perfect storm that is brewing among unprepared and underprepared students in the high school pipeline. Many of these first-generation college-going students lack economic resources, creating the possibility that the largest group of marginalised and working-class students in our history may be denied access for financial reasons. The financial crisis is occurring just as the current generation of professionals will be ready to retire, by 2015, at a time when the nation needs their talent the most, especially in the STEM fields.

Difficult as this situation is, higher education does have the potential to surmount these obstacles. So, this section will present some reasons for hope: some promising practices, designed to increase the access and success of marginalised, poor and first-generation college-going students in a variety of types of institutions.

Develop effective K-16 pipelines

Filling the K-16 pipeline, especially in the STEM fields, is a national problem. The K-12 educational system, higher education, foundations and communities all share the responsibility for working together to create and maintain a K–20 pipeline. The community college is the engine that can drive this initiative because it has the flexibility and the capacity that K–12 and four-year degree and research institutions lack. It is also the sector of education that contains the largest number of under-represented students from minority racial/ethnic groups, poor students and non-traditional students.

Connect the engaged student to the engaged university

Students in the US increasingly are expected to log in many hours of community service before they graduate from high school. It is important that faculty, staff and administrators in both the academic and student affairs side of the institution recognise that it takes 'a whole campus' to graduate a student. Co-curricular, interdisciplinary and disciplinary studies are all a part of the holistic process of engagement that students should experience as they are learning about themselves, their community and their world.

This engagement, far from being on the margins of a liberal arts or technical education, should, in fact, be the core purpose of that education. If our institutions of higher education are not providing the opportunities for our students to take the knowledge they gain and put it to use as engaged citizens, then who will be the engaged citizens of the future? Higher education institutions have both a moral imperative and the unique set of talents, skills and resources to do it.

Build the culture of inquiry

Establishing a 'culture of inquiry' on campus requires establishing a learning outcomes culture. A learning outcomes culture is one in which everyone knows and is committed to organising for learning and producing explicit outcomes. This will take time, but this process should not be left to chance. Learning outcomes for both students and the institution should be developed as deliberately as the institutional strategic plan is. Part of that plan should include a way to follow and track students until they are successful (at least five years after graduation at the bachelor's level). Campus stakeholders should understand the value of the culture of inquiry for everyone, as well as what the learning outcomes will be for all students in all classes.

Promote enlightened leadership within and external to the institution

Through the process of shared governance, campus leadership should be reflected at all levels of the institution. Institutional transformation around diversity, excellence and inclusion is the responsibility and opportunity for all internal stakeholders including students, staff, faculty and administrators. The transformation process will also require collaboration for mutual gain with external stakeholders such as: accreditation agencies, disciplinary associations, professional associations, government offices, the policy community, the general public and the media.

This list of promising practices is still visionary on most campuses. The goals of marginalised student recruitment and retention on the majority of higher education campuses remain to be attained. To truly focus on the civic and social responsibility of higher education in service to society requires a deep understanding of what diverse students need to become engaged citizens and decision-makers in 21st-century America. It also requires focusing on how to make the vision a reality. Some things are already apparent: Higher education will need to do this work in a spirit of cooperation, thinking across borders and boundaries, and engaging other sectors and leaders of society as a whole. There is no more appropriate group to take on this task than the leaders that are already involved in or would like to be involved in the work of college and university transformation. Transformational change starts with taking the first steps. That first step has far been surpassed in the US, but so many more people must become involved before we will, in reality, have a movement for that change.

Note
[1] K-12 refers to kindergarten through 12th grade; K-16 is kindergarten through four years of higher education; and K-20 is kindergarten through eight years of higher education.

References
Adelman, C. (1991) *Answers in the Toolbox: Academic Integrity, Attendance Patterns, and Bachelor's Degree Attainment*, Washington, DC: US Government Printing Office.

American Association of Community Colleges (2000) *1901–2001: Celebrating a Century of Innovation in Higher Education*, Washington, DC: American Association of Community Colleges.

Bok, D. (2006) *Our Underachieving Colleges: A Candid Look at How Much Students Learn and Why They Should Be Learning More*, Princeton, NJ: Princeton University Press.

Bowen, W.G., Kurzweil, M.A. and Tobin, E.M. (2005) *Equity and Excellence in American Higher Education*, Charlottesville, VA: University of Virginia Press.

Boyer, E. (1990) *Scholarship Reconsidered: Priorities of the Professoriate*, Princeton, NJ: Carnegie Foundation for the Advancement of Teaching.

Carnevale, A.P. and Fry, R.A. (2000) *Crossing the Great Divide*, Princeton, NJ: Educational Testing Service.

Diez, M.E. (1990) 'A thrust from within: reconceptualizing teacher education at Alverno College', *Peabody Journal of Education*, vol 65, no 2, pp 4–18.

Diez, M.E. (ed) (1998) *Changing the Practice of Teacher Education: Standards and Assessment as a Lever for Change*, Washington, DC: American Association of Colleges for Teacher Education.

Diez, M.E. (2001) 'Assessment's future in teacher education: an assessment scenario from the future', in R. Lissitz and W.D. Schafer (eds) *Assessments in Educational Reform*, Needham Heights, MA: Allyn and Bacon.

Diez, M.E. and Hass, J. (1997) 'No more piecemeal reform: using performance-based approaches to rethink teacher education', *Action in Teacher Education*, vol XIX, no 2, pp 17–26.

Diez, M.E., Rickards, W. and Lake, K. (1994) 'Performance assessment in teacher education at Alverno College', in W. Thomas (ed) *Promising Practices*, Washington D.C.: Association of Independent Liberal Arts Colleges for Teacher Education.

Ehrlich, T. (2000) *Civic Responsibility and Higher Education*, Phoenix, AZ: The Oryx Press.

Finkelstein, M.J. and Schuster, J. (2001) 'How changing demographics are reshaping the academic profession', *AAHE Bulletin*, vol 54, no 2, pp 3–7.

Friedman, T.L. (2005) *The World is Flat*, New York, NY: Farrar, Straus and Giroux.

Friedman, T.L. (2008) *Hot, Flat and Crowded*, New York, NY: Farrar, Straus and Giroux.

Harper, S.R. and Quaye, S.J. (eds) (2009) *Student Engagement in Higher Education*, New York, NY: Routledge.

Hoachlander, G., Sikora, A.C. and Horn, L. (2003) *Community College Students: Goals, Academic Preparation, and Outcomes*, Washington, DC: US Department of Education, National Center for Education Statistics.

Johns, A.M. and Sipp, M.K. (eds) (2007) *Diversity in College Classrooms. Practices for Today's Campuses*, Ann Arbor, MA: University of Michigan Press.

Jones, V. (2008) *The Green Collar Economy*, New York, NY: HarperCollins Publishers.

Kellogg Commission (1999) *Returning to Our Roots: The Engaged Institution*, Washington, DC: Kellogg Commission.

King, T. and Bannon, E. (2002) *At What Cost?*, Washington, DC: The State PIRG, Higher Education Project.

Maki, P.L. (2004) *Assessing for Learning: Building a Sustainable Commitment across the Institution*, Sterling, VA: Stylus Publishing.

Marginson, S. (2010) 'The rise of the global university: 5 new tensions', *The Chronicle of Higher Education*, 30 May. Available at: http://chronicle.com

Metzger, W.P. (ed) (1977) *The College of the City of New York: A History*, New York, NY: Arno Press.

Mukhopadhyay, C. and Moses, Y.T. (1997) 'Re-establishing "race" in the anthropological discourse', *American Anthropologist*, vol 99, no 3, pp 517–33.

Mullen, R. (2001) 'The undergraduate revolution: change the system or give instrumentalism another 30 years?', *Change*, vol 33, no 5, pp 54–8.

National Science Foundation (2002) *Division of Science Resources Statistics, Science and Engineering Doctorate Awards: 2001, NSF 03-300, Table 4*, Arlington, VA: National Science Foundation.

Sirianni, C. and Friedland, L. (2001) *Civic Innovation in America. Community Empowerment, Public Policy, and the Movement for Civic Renewal*, Berkeley and Los Angeles, CA: University of California Press.

Smith, D.G. (2009) *Diversity's Promise for Higher Education: Making It Work*. Baltimore, MD: Johns Hopkins University Press.

Snyder, T.D. and Hoffman, C.M. (2001) *Digest of Education Statistics 2000*, Washington, DC: US Department of Education, National Center for Education Statistics.

Suskie, L. (2009) 'Is it possible to assess fairly?', *AAHE Bulletin*, vol 52, no 9, pp 7–9.

Thelin, J.R. (2004) *A History of American Higher Education*, Baltimore, MD: Johns Hopkins University Press.

Tierney, W.G. (1993) *Building Communities of Difference*, Westport, CT: Bergin and Garvey.

Tonkin, H., Deeley, S.J., Pusch, M., Quiroga, D., Siegel, M.J., Whiteley, J. and Bringle, R.G. (2004) *Service-Learning across Cultures: Promise and Achievement*, New York, NY: The International Partnership for Service-Learning and Leadership.

Torres, V., Howard–Hamilton, M.F. and Cooper, D.L. (2003) *Identity Development of Diverse Populations*, San Francisco, CA: Jossey-Bass.

University of California Riverside (2009) *2009 UCR Facts and Impacts*, Riverside, CA: University of California Riverside.

US Department of Education (2002) *The Condition of Education 2002*, Washington, DC: National Center for Education Statistics.

Washington, P. (2007) 'Community based service learning: actively engaging the Other', in A.M. Johns and M.K. Sipp (eds) *Diversity in College Classrooms: Practices for Today's Campuses*, Ann Arbor, MA: University of Michigan Press.

Wilson, R. (2010) 'For-profit colleges change higher education's landscape. Nimble companies gain a fast-growing share of enrollments', *Chronicle of Higher Education*, 7 February.

Young, R.L. (2007) 'Cross-cultural experiential learning', in A.M. Johns and M.K. Sipp (eds) *Diversity in College Classrooms. Practices for Today's Campuses*, Ann Arbor, MA: University of Michigan Press.

SIX

Equity, diversity and feminist educational research: enhancing the emerging field of pedagogical studies in higher education for social inclusion

Miriam E. David

Introduction

The aim of this chapter is to consider educational research on social and gender equity from a feminist perspective and to question the recent debates about diverse forms of social inclusion or exclusion. In other words, my definition of social inclusion is about how to include disadvantaged and previously excluded social groups, such as women and those from working–class family backgrounds, in higher education policies, pedagogies and practices. My interest in the challenging debates about different forms of social equity or the broader notion of equality of educational opportunity in terms of family social class backgrounds and/or gender is long-standing, as I will show later.

My recent concern has been twofold: first, to stimulate interest in innovative approaches to education, through pedagogical research, to contribute to debates within higher education about developing teaching and learning methods to enhance social and gender equity and forms of social inclusion in terms of class, gender, family and ethnicity. This stands in contrast to social exclusivity linked to increasing forms of social stratification, and the lack of social mobility through and in higher education.

Second, David Willetts, Minister for Higher Education in the Coalition government reignited debate about these very issues of social inclusion or exclusion in a talk discussed in the media (GEA, 2011). It is claimed that he argued that 'Feminism trumps egalitarianism' (GEA, 2011). The core of his argument was about social mobility and the effects that feminism was having: namely, that social mobility had stalled and that jobs for working-class men had been stymied through feminism. Given that middle-class women now attended universities and, through forms of assortative mating, married middle-class men who also had well-paying jobs, they had taken jobs such that they were denying opportunities for working-class men to participate in the labour market. In other words, Willetts launched an attack on feminist research and practices around innovative forms of social inclusion through higher education.

A personal approach to social inclusion from a feminist perspective

As a feminist social scientist, I have been involved in university education throughout my career and I wish to offer some thoughts about what I have learned about policies for equity and social inclusion, and pedagogical practices, based upon my own experiences through social and educational research and also feminist activism. Hopefully, I may be able to provoke debate based upon my broad understanding of the changing field of global higher education. This understanding has been developed through my personal involvement in the changing practices of higher education, and attempts to transform policies and pedagogies in the direction of greater social and educational equality or inclusion. I have long been involved in social and educational research, especially on public policy questions on gender, family and socio-economic disadvantage (David, 1980, 2003).

I entered the academy back in the 1970s from a period as a social researcher in both the UK and US. I was involved in teaching and researching social and educational policies, through developing critical perspectives on family and gender. The subject of social welfare, family and educational policies lent itself to critiques and attempts to transform political and social life. Indeed, the post-war development of the social sciences was oriented towards social change and greater social equality. A gender or feminist perspective developed from a broader movement for social and political change, both nationally and internationally. Indeed, the feminist perspectives developed in the academy in the 1970s and 1980s drew largely upon work in the US and parts of Europe, most especially France. These later became known as 'second-wave feminism' to contrast with the work of suffragettes and others in the late 19th and early 20th century arguing for political inclusion and involvement internationally (see eg David, 2009c).

As feminist social scientists, we began to develop social research and appropriate methods to understand the complexities of developing and advanced industrial societies. Our methods drew upon the social sciences and at the same time challenged some of the assumptions and contested some of the approaches. Overall, we wanted to transform social life in the direction of social equality and women's involvement in work and public life on an equal basis with men. Inevitably, this raised questions about childcare, education, employment, family lives, health, paid and unpaid work, and caring in old age (see eg Smith, 1987, 2005; Oakley, 2000, 2002, 2005; David, 2003). How was the social inclusion of previously excluded groups such as women and socially disadvantaged classes to be achieved?

As part of this process, I was involved in teaching undergraduate students in social policy and sociology concerned about family poverty and socio-economic or social class disadvantage, especially in education. My students were also concerned about women's role in the family and wider society, and at that time we began to develop feminist critiques of the patriarchal relations within advanced capitalist societies. Quite clearly, there have been several successive generations or groups of students (and their teachers) through higher education since the 1970s, and the curriculum and pedagogies of the social sciences have been transformed. These changes have been part and parcel of the overall expansion of higher education linked to socio-economic and political transformations globally and locally, what Slaughter and Rhoades (2004) as American scholars have called 'academic capitalism', the entwined nature of the knowledge economy. These generational changes have been linked to the wider socio-political global transformations from the social democracy and social liberalism of the 1960s–early 1980s, to the economic and neo-liberalism of the 1980s, 1990s and into the 21st century.

Expansions of higher education: for the knowledge economy and/or social inclusion?

These simple typifications of global and national moves from social democracy to neo-liberalism and the knowledge economy typified by forms of information technology stand as ways of still distinguishing between types of students, academic staff and researchers, linked to changing and developing subjects or disciplines within higher education. These have been part of a massive expansion of global higher education. Indeed, together with Delia Langa Rosado, I argued that this expansion could be questioned as to whether it created merely massive universities or universities for the masses, or the working classes, given that social equity was supposedly embedded within policies for higher education (Langa Rosado and David, 2006).

In the very recent policies on British higher education, there have been serious attempts to increase differentiation between the arts and social sciences and science, technology, engineering and medicine, including mathematics (STEM) subjects in terms of resources (Browne Report, 2010). The question of the subjects or disciplines taught in expanding systems of higher education has been the subject of much controversy since the 1960s and 1970s. The origins of the modern university have their roots in the medieval university and the teaching of law, medicine and theology (see eg David, 1980). Before the massive expansion of higher education, university education was for a narrow social elite rather than for the masses or to achieve social inclusion. In other words, it was socially exclusive and did not incorporate the meritorious necessarily within its practices. Officially, university education was seen as about what was called the 'liberal arts', which might have included natural science and medicine, and a commitment to 'knowledge for its own sake' or critical thinking, although also preparing for graduate professions. For example, undergraduate education at both Oxford and Cambridge led to the award of a Bachelor of Arts degree, whatever the subject studied, until the late 20th century.

As higher education has been expanded in relation to the changing global and knowledge economy there have been various attempts to link subjects or disciplines to new professions, and new forms of graduate employment and skills. Given increasing global economic competition, the question of the balances between broad groups of subjects such as the arts/humanities and the physical/natural sciences has become a key issue. Internationally, there has been pressure to distinguish between STEM and arts/humanities and the social sciences. There is also the question of the growth of new subjects and interdisciplinarity across and within broad groupings. For instance, the growth of the social sciences, and its links with health and medicine, has become an issue, as has the methodological approaches to study. The question of the role of mathematics, and statistics, across the sciences has been disputed.

There have also been major developments in research in and on higher education, including critical approaches to educational research and feminist theories and perspectives, over the last two decades (David, 2011). I now consider how these different perspectives are used in higher education research, and work-based learning, drawing on the research evidence from the UK government's Teaching and Learning Research Programme (TLRP). In drawing the threads together from these various theories and perspectives on educational research, my conclusions centre on feminist pedagogies and practices that also bear on inclusive pedagogies. I want to argue that this kind of critical and feminist research on teaching and learning is of relevance to developing perspectives in STEM, situated as it is within varying forms of global higher education today. Understanding our own social position and those of our students is extremely helpful to developing inclusive pedagogies and these in turn facilitate student learning and contribute to greater social equity and wider social inclusion and transformations.

Feminist theories and perspectives in the social sciences and educational research

As feminist theories and perspectives were taken up in universities, they tended to be influential in the development of social research, including education, at the same time as higher education expanded in relation to knowledge economies. Since the 1970s, there has developed a vast array of research and scholarship under the broad umbrella of feminist perspectives and theories, and yet the definition of women's or female roles is heavily debated. More women have entered the academy as students and subsequently as teachers and researchers, although their positioning has remained relatively circumscribed. Yet generations of feminist scholars and researchers have adopted and adapted approaches in their specific and substantive fields of endeavour.

At the turn of the 21st century, much of the debate turns upon methodological approaches to understanding women's complex positioning and cultural and social identities. These also concern central questions about perspectives on qualitative studies rather than the more traditional social scientific quantitative approaches. It could be argued that the social sciences have also been transformed by the various social and political changes towards marketisation and neo-liberalism and that, nowadays, social theories and methodologies themselves centre on in-depth qualitative analyses and personal and narrative approaches. On the other hand, it has also been argued that the socio-economic transformations have been such that feminist perspectives have been incorporated into higher education pedagogies and practices such that they are no longer distinctive.

While there has been massive social and economic change, it has not all been in the direction of greater social or gender equity or inclusion. Neo-liberalism has led to expanding educational markets and greater involvement of diverse groups, including women, in diverse forms of higher education, yet power differentials remain. I want to provide an illustration from an international symposium 'to address the meaning and impact of second-wave feminism on educational research' (Weiler and David, 2008, p 433) to flesh out these ideas about changing feminist perspectives in the context of neo-liberalism. This symposium was held at the American Educational Research Association (AERA) annual meeting in San Francisco in 2006 and papers were subsequently published as a special issue of the journal *Discourse: Studies in the Cultural Politics of Education* in 2008, where we 'struggle with how we have tried to develop and reflect upon our feminist ideas and ideals within the changing contexts of global higher education' (Weiler and David, 2008, p 433).

We argued that

> second wave feminism … challenged the prevailing androcentric assumptions then dominant in all of the metropolitan countries. While feminism took different trajectories depending upon local histories and politics, in each of the countries represented [Australia, Britain, Canada and the USA] … it had a profound impact on society and in academia. (Weiler and David, 2008, p 433)

In other words, second-wave feminist ideas were extremely influential in developing social and educational research in universities, but despite women academics' increasing involvement in the academy, in the context of neo-liberalism and individualism, research and scholarly endeavours are now more constrained.

The international scholars (from Australia, Canada, the UK and US) who presented papers in the special issue used feminist approaches to address:

> the impact of second-wave feminism in their own scholarship, tracing their own intellectual histories and discussing the continuing impact of second-wave feminism and the ways early feminist conceptions of the situated subject differ so profoundly from current conceptions of the ahistorical, decontextualized subject of neoliberal theory and policy. (Weiler and David, 2008, p 433)

For example, Lyn Yates (2008), an Australian academic and Pro Vice Chancellor (Research) at the University of Melbourne:

considers the influence of both the second wave and its difference from the dominant research and policy concerns of today. Yates recalls the intellectual excitement of feminist theory in the 1970s and 1980s and the sense that a major intellectual and political turn was in process. She also shows the shift to the individualized and market-oriented ideas dominating educational policy today and considers the parallel development of poststructural ideas of subjectivity and performance. She notes the significance of class location of Australian feminist educational scholars of the 1970s and 1980s, many of whom came from working class or rural families and who ended up in educational research because their university education was supported by full scholarships and fellowships, which would not have been the case in other fields. Their working class identities made them aware of class issues and drew them to movements seeking social justice; and of course their lived experience as women made them well aware of patriarchal privilege and open to the power of feminist critique. (Weiler and David, 2008, p 433)

Similarly, Kathleen Weiler (2008), an American educational historian:

discusses the strengths and weaknesses of second wave feminism, particularly around relationships between white women and women of colour. She argues that the women's movement affected all women in the USA, but that the political organizing and contributions of women of colour were not integrated into the dominant narrative of second wave feminism. These tensions were replicated as feminism as a political movement moved into the academy and as feminist scholarship developed within education. Despite the growing complexity of and conflicts within education feminism, Weiler argues that the basic political insight about the relationship between individual lives and broader cultural, political and economic forces that was the hallmark of the early women's movement continues to characterize feminist educational scholarship. (Weiler and David, 2008, p 435)

Kathleen Weiler and I conclude that feminist ideas remain vital for researching and understanding individuals' social and cultural identities despite the more constrained and individualised approaches to teaching in global higher education in the 21st century. We insist on maintaining a commitment to social and political equality in our teaching practices with a more socially diverse student population. We wrote that:

> there have been major transformations in higher education as individualized and market-oriented ideas have come to dominate educational policy. Given the growing social diversity among students in terms of social class, ethnicity, race and gender, *feminist ideas challenge us to think more deeply about pedagogies and practices and to develop new theories which critique essentialist notions of classed, racialized and gendered subjectivities and at the same time retain the original political vision of the women's movement.* (Weiler and David, 2008, p 435, emphasis added)

We continue to use feminist theories to provide critiques of transformations in global higher education in relation to both students and their teachers, the academic scholars, and to develop feminist pedagogies that put personal experiences of socio-economic diversity at the heart of socially inclusive teaching practices within the global academy.

Feminist perspectives on equity and social inclusion in higher education research

Taking forward the feminist ideal of developing inclusive practices in the 21st century academy that centre upon inclusive pedagogies and personally inclusive experiences, Louise Morley and I organised a symposium on 'The challenges for democracy and fairness in higher education'. We invited a number of feminist and gender scholars to consider questions of the implications of the expansions of global higher education for its organisation and transparent or inclusive processes for women as students and scholars. The symposium was subsequently published in the journal *Higher Education Policy* in 2009. In our editorial for the special issue we wrote that we wanted to:

> celebrate the gains and identify the challenges for gender equity in higher education in the 21st century ... [and] to consider and deconstruct different aspects of higher education *habitus* through a gender-sensitive lens using feminist methodologies developed from second-wave

feminism in the twentieth century. (Morley and David, 2009, p 1)

We too insisted on retaining a political vision of the feminist movement to challenge current higher education policies and practices in the broader context of the massive expansion of higher education today. These included scholars in the field of medical education and social and educational researchers critiquing the development of practices for a more socially diverse global higher education and challenging forms of social and gender equity or inclusion.

We argued that:

> it would be easy to rehearse yet another pessimistic repertoire of challenges for gender equity in the academy, especially given its diluted version from the stronger notions of gender equality as developed in the previous century. Gender and melancholy are often deeply connected (Butler, 2002), with a sense of loss, hurt and grief underpinning studies of gender and power in higher education. Desire, as well as loss, needs to be considered ... there are ... some possibilities for the future of higher education. A major cause for celebration is the way in which women have become highly visible as students, or consumers of higher education. Globally, there are now more women than men in undergraduate higher education. A challenge that remains, as Rosemary Deem indicates ... is [women's] representation in academic leadership. (Morley and David, 2009, p 1)

The international scholars addressed an array of challenges for gender inequalities in higher education using diverse feminist perspectives, but mostly with respect to students in a range of international contexts. Two central concerns were about policies on equity or widening participation in higher education from a diversity of social and gendered groups, since policies on 'fair access' and increasing participation from socio-economically diverse groups in higher education is now an international priority. In developed or metropolitan countries, there has been a shift in emphasis from gender equity for women, since more women now participate as students than men (Shavit et al., 2007), to access for working-class or poor young men:

> [Both] Louise Morley and Rosemary Lugg demonstrate how, when poverty is intersected with gender in sub-Saharan

Africa, participation rates of poor women are extremely low. [My own] … critical account of widening participation discourses and recent research also demonstrates how there are multiple and diverse higher educations, with social class or disadvantage still a central indicator for opportunity structures. There has been considerable concern about the under-achievement of working class boys in schools and this is slowly filtering into higher education, with fears that whole sectors of young men are becoming disaffected and marginalized from higher education opportunities. (Morley and David, 2009, p 2; see also David, 2009a; Morley and Lugg, 2009)

Given these global transformations, we concluded that:

gender in higher education is often encoded in a range of formal and informal signs, practices and networks. The gender debates are full of contradictions. Quantitative targets to let more women into higher education can fail, or be meaningless, while femaleness continues to be socially constructed as second class citizenship. However, gains have been made, and it is important to keep auditing the successes while creatively envisioning the changes that are still required. We hope … to imagine a future of higher education that is creative, challenging and exciting for subsequent generations of women as both academics and students. (Morley and David, 2009, p 2)

We had invited two scholars in medical education – Dr Kathy Boursicot of St George's Medical School, University of London, and Professor Trudie Roberts of Leeds University Medical School – to contribute and consider developing medical practices and education (Boursicot and Roberts, 2009). We were particularly interested in including a very traditional university subject to consider how the wider socio-political changes were influencing its pedagogies and practices. As we wrote:

Kathy Boursicot and Trudie Roberts are both qualified doctors now working in medical education. They have interrogated how the culture of a high status discipline, such as medicine, is still highly gendered even though quantitative representation of women is increasing at undergraduate level in the UK. (Morley and David, 2009, p 2)

In their review of the changing field and culture of medicine, Boursicot and Roberts did not find any evidence of the adoption of new practices based around feminist or inclusive pedagogies. What, then, might these entail? What is the recent evidence about teaching and learning from broader forms of educational research and how might these contribute to increasing social inclusion and inclusive pedagogies?

I turn now to discuss research evidence about how to engage and include socially diverse students in a range of subjects in higher education, including STEM, drawing on the evidence from the TLRP on widening participation in higher education. Two projects in particular offer evidence that can contribute to our understandings of changing subjects and new pedagogies and practices for the 21st century. I will focus most especially on mathematics as it has been seen both as a key requirement for higher education study and also as a particularly demanding subject for STEM. STEM has, as already noted, become an increasingly esteemed and prestigious set of disciplines for study at university. More intriguingly, the M in STEM is challenging and controversial. In the UK, M refers to mathematics for teaching subjects at university, whereas it refers to medicine as regards research funding criteria.

Social diversity, inclusion and critical perspectives in educational research

As noted in the introduction, there has been growing public debate about questions of social mobility and the extent to which modern societies and nation states, both locally and globally, are contributing to social change, linked with gender, ethnicity or race. David Willetts' comments cited in the introduction are just the latest instance of this increasingly public debate about equity and social inclusion (GEA, 2011). Education and policies for schools and post-compulsory and especially higher education or universities play an essential part in the growing global as well as national economies. Governments have increasingly argued for evidence or 'research' to inform public policies, including the relationship between economic and skill developments and educational systems. The critique of educational policies and the evidence base, however, are heavily challenged and contested. Gender, however, is often nowadays occluded in these perspectives.

Educational research has become highly contested as part of the growing debates about quality assurance and research funding through various different government bodies. The UK has been in the vanguard of developing measures to ensure quality in higher education research and teaching and has become a model for other metropolitan countries. An example of the entwined nature of higher education and the knowledge economy or 'academic capitalism' (Slaughter and Rhodes, 2004) can be found in developments in the UK, where the government decided to concentrate some of its research funding for education through the research council responsible, namely, the Economic and Social Research Council (ESRC). This targeted funding was for research on what became known not simply as education, but more specifically as teaching and learning at all levels and stages of education, or learning across the life course. Thus, the ESRC's TLRP was born in 1999 (see www.tlrp.org).

Over a 10-year period, 70 projects were conducted in about 60 different higher education institutions in the UK, largely but not solely within their schools or departments of education and including some specialist colleges for music and education (David, 2009b). The programme was managed collaboratively and collectively by a team of education and social researchers, for the last five years based at the Institute of Education, University of London. The overall directorship was by Professor Andrew Pollard, a distinguished sociologist of education, with myself directing the work on higher education and lifelong learning, including responsibility for social diversity and inclusion.

The research evidence from the post-compulsory and higher education projects has been drawn together in a series of commentaries that make available and summarise complex findings for a public and non-specialist audience, part of a new strategy of public engagement, knowledge transfer or impact. Two particular commentaries, which draw upon the production of evidence-informed principles for teaching and learning from the schools' projects, deserve mention. One addressed the question of *Effective Learning and Teaching in UK Higher Education* by summarising the findings from across 20 higher education projects, covering an array of subjects/disciplines and adapting the evidence-based principles for higher education (David, 2009b). The other commentary, equally imaginatively, used the findings from the post-compulsory and work-based learning projects (including examples from medical and postgraduate education) to draw up evidence-informed principles for *Higher Skills Development at Work* (Brown, 2009). A crucial issue from our principles is how to engage, include and ensure effective student involvement in their learning, which is necessary for educational and social success and the processes for accomplishing such social inclusion.

Equity and diversity in access to and widening participation in higher education

Within the higher education suite of projects, there were seven projects that were commissioned together to consider fair access and widening participation in higher education as a means to social inclusion. Given that this was a major global higher education policy initiative, the UK New Labour government was eager to gather evidence of its impact on policies, practices and pedagogies. It therefore commissioned projects through the ESRC's TLRP to study various facets of the implementation of widening participation in higher education as a strategy for social inclusion and equity (David, 2009d). The definition of widening participation, and, in particular, the social groups to be considered in a range of types of higher education systems and structures, was itself problematic. In the TLRP book that was published reporting on these collective findings, we wrote that 'specifically our concern is with widening participation to a diversity of individuals comprising the economically, educationally and socially disadvantaged, in terms of poverty or social class, and also age, ethnicity or race and by gender' (David, 2009d, p 3). We were however concerned with issues of 'fair access and participation' and the overriding issue of equity or equality for diverse groups. These had become public policy mantras about social inclusion as opposed to social exclusivity.

More importantly, given the socio-economic changes and expansion of higher education over the previous two or so decades, inevitably these issues were the concern of social and educational scholars. Nevertheless, given the fact that the government was funding the projects through the ESRC, it was inappropriate for these scholars to define themselves solely as feminist scholars. While 'the usual ESRC peer review process' (David, 2009d, p 16) was used, an explicit acknowledgement of a feminist perspective might have militated against success:

> However, it should also be noted how these seven diverse teams also included a diversity of researchers. Interestingly, the research teams comprised a significant number of equity, feminist and critical researchers, with four of the main grant-holders being senior women researchers, and each of the teams including several well-known women as diversity, equity, gender and feminist researchers. This represents a significant shift in the demography of social science research grant-holders in the UK over the past decade. It also provides an example of how transformations in the

demography of social science research have been occurring with changes in higher education. (David, 2009d, p 22)

The theoretical and methodological approaches taken by the seven projects therefore reflected these nuanced perspectives. For example:

> four of the teams (Crozier, Fuller, Hockings and Williams) drew on social or sociological and cultural theories to frame their research questions and approaches. Whilst they all tend towards social rather than economic theories to underpin their research, there are differences in their particular frameworks. Crozier's team has extended and developed earlier work, using Bourdieu's sociological theories. Fuller's and Hockings' teams have similarly been interested in how these theories have provided a framework for study. However, Fuller's team has foregrounded qualitative social network analysis and the role of social capital within networks. Hockings' team has drawn on social as well as psychological theories of learning, teaching and ways of knowing in their attempt to understand how students from diverse backgrounds engage and participate in different subjects. Williams' team has incorporated actor network theories, namely cultural, historical activity theories (CHAT) as a basis for their interpretations. (David, 2009d, p 21)

The findings and conclusions from the seven projects, however, also address questions of equity from a diverse range of perspectives, including gender as well as social disadvantage. We looked at both public policies and practices as ways to enhance and increase participation across a diverse range of systems and institutions (David, 2009d, ch 6). From a feminist and critical perspective, however, our findings centred upon improving institutional practices and developing new pedagogies to engage and include a diversity of students in new forms of learning (David, 2009d, ch 7). Both Williams' team and Hockings' team addressed pedagogies appropriate for socially diverse students in a range of different subjects and contexts and are particularly relevant to considering the STEM–non-STEM interface.

Hockings' team was keen to develop ways of enabling more socially inclusive learning environments using two very different universities and a range of subjects (communication and information technology

[CIT], science, health and social policy, and business) as the evidence base:

> To enable teachers to work in ways which acknowledge their students' strengths, experiences and abilities, teachers need the opportunity to consider issues of cultural, social and educational diversity and difference among students, and to be aware of their impact on the learning and teaching environment. This may require that they reflect on and reconceptualise their notions of student diversity. *They may also need to consider how they might redesign curricula and pedagogy to allow for greater student involvement.* To facilitate this, teachers need institutional policies which allow them adequate time and space for reflection and pedagogical development. (David, 2009d, p 197, emphasis added)

From the point of view of STEM, Williams' team provides the most interesting pedagogical evidence. They focused upon how students learn mathematics in order to participate in STEM subjects at university, although mathematics at A level is not necessarily a critical requirement for all STEM subjects (but a good GCSE pass is). They contrasted two approaches to teaching maths as a prelude to university and found that an approach that connects with student social and cultural identities is far more engaging than traditional 'testing to the test' methods, or what they call 'transmissionist' pedagogies. From their study they argued that:

> we are confident in offering 'connectionism' as a pedagogy that contrasts with 'transmissionism' as a cultural model of teaching practice that offers more opportunities for learners to engage deeply with mathematics.... 'Getting connectionist', however, might come to command some priority if it comes to be seen as essential to understanding and hence making mathematics count. (David, 2009d, p 184)

The study by Williams and his team (David, 2009d, ch 4, s 2; ch 7) focused precisely upon learning mathematics for participation in STEM subjects at university. While Williams would not be considered, nor consider himself, a feminist, in the emerging theories and perspectives of the 21st century, the notion of 'connectionist' pedagogies drawn from socio-cultural theories aligns quite easily with the feminist studies of personal, inclusive and feminist pedagogies. From this study, and his continuing work in higher education, his team is finding that pedagogies that connect with students' socio-cultural identities and experiences, what in other contexts are called personal or feminist pedagogies, are critical for enhancing teaching and learning in 'difficult' subjects for and at university. And, of course, mathematics is one of those 'difficult' subjects that contribute to studying medicine. Arguably, therefore, it is essential for innovative approaches to STEM, including for medical education, to consider developing 'connectionist' inclusive or feminist pedagogies.

Overall, in addressing the question of how to improve learning by widening participation in higher education, we concluded that it was essential:

> to develop pedagogies that are more inclusive given the increased diversity of the higher education population, with increasing numbers of students entering the system without an expectation of having a traditional academic engagement with their studies, and a consideration of pedagogical approaches in which learners teach each other and explore why deep-level learning results often seems to point to an interesting possible educational future for the twenty-first century. (David, 2009d, p 200)

Conclusions about social equity and inclusion from a feminist perspective

I hope that I have raised questions about how feminist perspectives have enhanced social and educational research around notions of social equity and inclusion. With the increasing participation of diverse groups in global higher education, and the rise of individualised and essentialised notions of individual subjects as part of the marketisation of higher education, feminist perspectives alone are simply no longer *de rigeur*. Instead, they contribute to and enhance other critical perspectives as is clear from the TLRP studies on widening participation. Such critical and feminist perspectives could also contribute to and enhance studies in STEM, including maths and medical education.

There is now a wealth of research evidence that the increasing social diversity of both undergraduate and postgraduate students in UK and global higher education requires creative and innovative approaches to pedagogies and practices in higher education. Many educational and social researchers have drawn on feminist perspectives to elaborate these pedagogical messages and hope to ensure greater social equity. In particular, Carole Leathwood and Barbara Read (2009) in their path-breaking study about the changing role of gender in higher education show that although on average there are now more women than men as students across an array of higher education institutions, this does not mean that they are included in privileged or high-status universities. They address the question raised by many key policy advisors and policymakers about a 'feminised future' given these shifts and argue that, given women's subordinate positioning in higher education, these concerns represent a 'fear of a feminised future' rather than its likelihood. However, they also illustrate the continuing efforts by feminist educational and social researchers to transform higher education practices and pedagogies in the direction of greater social inclusiveness.

Similarly, Louise Morley and colleagues (Morley and Lugg, 2009; Morley and Lussier, 2009; Morley et al., 2009) have argued imaginatively about the university of the future, and how to transform pedagogies and practices despite the forbidding global and local socio-political environment of fiscal austerity and economic retrenchment. She has both shown the constraints on developing equal educational opportunity structures for socially disadvantaged and poor students in African countries by comparison with the UK and also argued about the possibilities for feminist and critical academics (Morley, 2010a). In her recent professorial lecture, she raised innovative questions about how to develop critical and feminist pedagogies and perspectives for the rapidly changing global academy (Morley, 2010b).

While UK and global higher education has been transformed over the last few decades, in changing socio-economic and political contexts, because of the dominance of neo-liberalism and 'academic capitalism', these transformations have not necessarily been in the direction of greater socio-economic equity, inclusion and opportunity for all disadvantaged social groups. Nevertheless, the possibilities for further, and more equitable, social inclusion and transformations, in the direction of equity rather than exclusivity, in the universities of the future remain. These may, hopefully, both transform the array of subjects taught across STEM/non-STEM (and including both maths and medicine) and their pedagogies and practices, and allow for more creative opportunities for critical and feminist academics. Imagining an exciting and innovative future for global higher education remains more than just a dream and may excite new strategies for interdisciplinarity in pedagogies and practices. Many of the studies referred to from the TLRP and elsewhere offer hope for a more imaginative and liberal global university of the future with creative pedagogies and inclusive practices.

References

Boursicot, K. and Roberts, T. (2009) 'Widening participation in medical education: challenging elitism and exclusion', *Higher Education Policy*, vol 22, no 1, pp 19–37

Brown, A. (2009) *Higher Skills Development at Work*, London: Institute of Education. Available at: www.tlrp.org

Browne Report (2010) 'Securing a sustainable future for higher education', 12 October. Available at: www.independent.gov.uk/browne-report

Butler, J. (2002) 'Melancholy gender–refused identification', in M. Dimen and V. Goldner (eds) *Gender in Psychoanalytic Space: Between Clinic and Culture*, New York, NY: Other Press, pp 3–19.

David, M. (1980) *The State, the Family and Education*, London: Routledge.

David, M. (2003) *Personal and Political: Feminisms, Sociology and Family Lives*, Stoke-on-Trent: Trentham Books.

David, M. (2009a) 'Social diversity and democracy in higher education in the 21st century: towards a feminist critique', *Higher Education Policy*, vol 22, no 1, pp 61–81.

David, M. (2009b) *Effective Learning and Teaching in UK Higher Education*, London: Institute of Education. Available at: www.tlrp.org

David, M. (2009c) *Transforming Global Higher Education: A Feminist Perspective, an Inaugural Professorial Lecture*, London: Institute of Education.

David, M., with A.-M. Bathmaker, G. Crozier, P. Davis, H. Ertl, A. Fuller, G. Hayward, S. Heath, C. Hockings, G. Parry, D. Reay, A. Vignoles and J. Williams (ed) (2009d) *Improving Learning by Widening Participation in Higher Education*, London: Routledge Education Books.

David, M. (2011) 'Overview of researching global higher education: challenge, change or crisis?', *Contemporary Social Science*, vol 6, no 2, pp 147–65.

GEA (Gender and Education Association) (2011) 'Feminism trumps egalitarianism: the twisted logic of David Willetts'. Available at: www.gea.com

Langa Rosado, D. and David, M. (2006) 'A massive university or a university for the masses? continuity and change in higher education in Spain and England', *Journal of Education Policy*, vol 3, no 3, pp 343–64.

Leathwood, C. and Read, B. (2009) *Gender and the Changing Face of Higher Education: A Feminized Future?* Maidenhead, Berkshire: McGraw Hill/Open University Press with the Society for Research into Higher Education.

Morley, L. (2010a) 'Gender mainstreaming: myths and measurement in higher education in Ghana and Tanzania', *Compare: a Journal of Comparative Education*, vol 40, no 4, pp 533–50.

Morley, L. (2010b) 'Imagining the University of the Future', Professorial Lecture, University of Sussex, May 2010.

Morley, L. and David, M. (2009) 'Celebrations and challenges: gender in higher education', *Higher Education Policy*, vol 22, no 1, pp 1–2.

Morley, L. and Lugg, R. (2009) 'Mapping meritocracy: intersecting gender, poverty and higher educational opportunity structures', *Higher Education Policy*, vol 22, no 1, pp 37–61.

Morley, L. and Lussier, K. (2009) 'Intersecting poverty and participation in higher education in Ghana and Tanzania', *International Studies in Sociology of Education*, vol 19, no 2, pp 71–85.

Morley, L., Leach, F. and Lugg, R. (2009) 'Democratising higher education in Ghana and Tanzania: opportunity structures and social inequalities', *International Journal of Educational Development*, vol 29, pp 56–64.

Oakley, A. (2000) *Experiments in Knowing: Gender and Method in the Social Sciences*, Cambridge: Polity Press.

Oakley, A. (2002) *Gender on Planet Earth*, Cambridge: Polity Press.

Oakley, A. (2005) *The Ann Oakley Reader: Gender, Women and Social Science*, Bristol: The Policy Press.

Shavit, Y., Arum, R. and Gamoran, A. (2007) *Stratification in Higher Education: A comparative Study*, Stanford, CA: Stanford University Press.

Slaughter, S. and Rhoades, G. (2004) *Academic Capitalism and the New Economy: Markets, State and Higher Education*, Baltimore, MA: John Hopkins University Press.

Smith, D.E (1987) *The Everyday World as Problematic*, Milton Keynes: Open University Press.

Smith, D.E. (2005) *Institutional Ethnography: A Sociology for People*, Milton Keynes: Open University Press.

Weiler, K. (2008) 'The feminist imagination and educational research', *Discourse: Studies in the Cultural Politics of Education*, vol 29, no 4, pp 499–509.

Weiler, K. and David, M. (2008) 'The personal and the political: second wave feminism and educational research guest editors', *Discourse: Studies in the Cultural Politics of Education*, vol 29, no 4, pp 433–7.

Yates, L, (2008) 'Revisiting feminism and Australian education: who speaks? What questions? What contexts? What impact?', *Discourse: Studies in the Cultural Politics of Education*, vol 29, no 4, pp 471–83.

SEVEN

Social justice as a matter of policy: higher education for the masses[1]

Trevor Gale and Deborah Tranter

Introduction

This chapter provides a partial and historical policy analysis of Australian higher education (HE) since its inception in the mid–19th century. The chapter's interests are explored on three levels. In the background, there is an analysis of the relationship between social and economic policy, particularly the extent to which economic concerns dominate government policy agendas. Second, there is an interest in illustrating the extent to which HE policy is variously subsumed by the social and/or the economic. Third, and most explicitly, the chapter examines the social justice intent of Australian HE policy and how this is differently expressed at times of expansion and consolidation in the system.

In making assessments about the latter, we are informed by Gale and Densmore's (2000) three perspectives on social justice: *distributive*, *retributive* and *recognitive*. Distributive justice[2] can be defined in terms of 'freedom, social cooperation and compensation for those who lack the basics ... [achieved] through proportional distributions to individuals and groups' (Gale and Densmore, 2000, p 27). Retributive justice is concerned with 'liberty and the protection of rights ... [and] open competition and protection of life and property ... [including] punishment for those who infringe these rights' (Gale and Densmore, 2000, p 27). Recognitive justice involves the 'provision of the means for all people to exercise their capabilities and determine their actions ... [through] processes that generalise the interests of the least advantaged' (Gale and Densmore, 2000, p 27).

Drawing on these perspectives, we characterise the social justice inflection of expansionist HE policy in Australia since the Second World War in terms of 'compensation', 'equal opportunity' and 'equity'. In our assessment, each of these is a form of distributive justice. We also note periods of HE policy that are informed by retributive justice, although they are not periods with an explicit expansionist agenda. To date, recognitive justice has been largely absent from Australian HE policy.

The structure of the chapter is primarily chronological. We begin with an overview of the shifts in Australia from elite to mass to near-universal HE and note that increasing access to HE has not been of equal benefit to all Australians. We then canvass how successive Australian governments have sought to address this problem. We conclude that to be socially just in recognitive terms, HE policy must recognise the interests of the least advantaged by developing a deeper understanding of the knowledges, values and understandings of those who are under-represented and excluded from HE, especially people from lower socio-economic status (SES) backgrounds.

From elite to mass to near-universal higher education

The history of HE in Australia commenced in 1850 with the establishment of the University of Sydney (University of Sydney, 2010). Prior to this, the sons of Australia's privileged elite were sent to England to attend university, and often for their secondary education. The scarcity of secondary education opportunities in Australia meant that it took 30 years before the University's annual enrolment reached 100 students. In the meantime, universities were established in Melbourne (1853), Adelaide (1874) and Hobart (1890).[3] These early Australian universities were largely about the social reproduction of the elite (University of Melbourne, 2007). They initially taught a classical education of Greek, Latin, mathematics and science to a privileged few; extending in the 1860s at Melbourne, and 1890s at Sydney, 'to provide professional training for young men and women of the affluent classes … occasionally offering the chance for poor but brilliant scholarship students to rise professionally and socially' (University of Melbourne, 2007).

Women were admitted early to Australian universities (Adelaide and Melbourne in 1881) well ahead of Oxford (1920) and Cambridge (1948), but 'little importance was attached to issues relating to the social origins of students…. The status quo of the distribution of goods and privileges in society were simply accepted' (Anderson and Vervoorn, 1983, p 5). It was not until after the Second World War that Australians in general began to perceive education as a means to improving the life chances of individuals, no matter their social origins (Anderson and Vervoorn, 1983).

The last 50 years of the 20th century saw a remarkable transformation of HE in Australia, moving from an elite system catering to less than 4% of 17–22 year olds in the 1950s, to a mass system (Trow, 2006) with 32% of that age group participating by 2002 (Martin and Karmel, 2002). By 2002, Martin and Karmel estimated that the lifetime probability of attending university in Australia was nearly 50%. The Organisation for Economic Co-operation and Development (OECD) estimated that by 2006, Australia's graduation rate for first degrees reached 59% of the 'typical age cohort for tertiary education' (OECD, 2008, p 72), although this number includes Australia's relatively high percentage of international students.

From seven universities catering to 15,600 students in 1945, enrolments had increased by more than 17 times by 1975, to 273,000 students in 17 universities and over 70 advanced education institutions (Marginson, 1997). By 2007, the sector had expanded further to 39 public universities and a proliferation of mostly small, private, HE institutions, together catering to 772,000 Australian students and 294,000 fee-paying overseas students (DEEWR, 2009).

Alongside this massive growth in numbers has been the desire to widen participation to render it more representative of all Australians. Yet, despite long-standing policy initiatives introduced by governments since the 1960s, Australia's universities have remained dominated by the more affluent. For at least the last 20 years, people from low SES backgrounds have been around three times less likely to go to university than those from backgrounds of high SES (Bradley et al., 2008).

While some of the expansion in HE participation can be attributed to population growth, this only accounts for around a quarter of the expansion. The increase in expectations generated by secondary school completion rates and HE participation has been largely economically driven, reflecting the needs of a changing workforce and escalating demand for highly skilled labour. The demand for HE expansion is part of an international trend, driven by the human capital needs of a globally competitive and increasingly knowledge-based economy (Marginson, 2006; OECD, 2008). A well-educated population is now considered 'essential for the social and economic well-being of countries and individuals' (OECD, 2008, p 30). In most OECD nations, this requirement is exacerbated by an ageing population, falling birth rates and a decline in the school-leaver age group.

The international trend towards mass HE has meant that nations can no longer rely only on the middle-class school leavers who have traditionally populated universities. In countries with near-universal participation rates, students from high-income families are at 'saturation point' (HEFCE, 2006; Berger, 2008), adding impetus to broaden participation to students from 'non-traditional' backgrounds in order to 'produce the type of educated and skilled workforce needed to remain competitive and prosperous' (Berger, 2008, p 3). In Australia, Wells (2008) notes how a continuing decline in the school-leaver population, an ageing workforce and an increasingly knowledge-based economy mean Australia is rapidly moving towards a major skills crisis, particularly in relation to graduates.

Wells (2008) suggests that the economic imperative to widen HE participation is stark, providing powerful reinforcement for the social and moral imperatives to increase the participation of under-represented groups, including older workers who may have missed out on educational opportunities when they were younger. Equity in HE is now as much a matter of economic necessity as of social justice.

Compensation: higher education in terms of fairness

Australia thinks of itself as an egalitarian society (Greig et al., 2003), free of the class divides of the UK and where 'a fair go' means that everyone has the right to a quality education, a good job and a comfortable income. However, this view is becoming increasingly distant from the lives of many. Recent research points to an increasing divide in Australia between the rich and the poor, including the work rich and the work poor (Wicks, 2005; Vinson, 2007). In 2004, the first official government inquiry into poverty in Australia for 30 years found that 'at the end of the twentieth century, between 2 and 3.5 million Australians had incomes below the poverty line' (Saunders, 2005, p 2). A year later, the St Vincent de Paul Society reported that 4.5 million Australians (23% of the population) were living in households with a combined income of less than A$400 per week – with over 800,000 children growing up in jobless households (Wicks, 2005).

Socio-economic disadvantage in Australia is multidimensional and cumulative, incorporating far more than low income, and tends to be concentrated in particular locations. In a recent analysis of the distribution of disadvantage in Australia, Vinson (2007, p xi) describes 'a marked degree of geographic concentration of disadvantage' with just 1.7% of communities accounting for 'seven times their share of the top ranking positions' on the factors that contribute to entrenched poverty, including unemployment, inadequate education, physical and mental disabilities, limited access to information and communication technology, imprisonment and confirmed child maltreatment, and low income.

In Australia today, we see a substantial inequality in HE participation, determined very much by where one lives and where one goes to school. Table 7.1 illustrates that in 1999, for example, young people from the affluent eastern suburbs of Adelaide (Burnside) were up to seven times more likely to attend university than those from the outer northern suburbs (Elizabeth), the region with the third-lowest university participation rate in Australia (Stevenson et al., 1999).

Table 7.1: Regional participation in university for 19–21 year olds

Region	University	
	Rate (%)	**Rank (out of 290 regions)**
Burnside	53.4	11
Salisbury	14.3	254
Munno Para and Gawler	12.5	269
Elizabeth	7.6	288
South Australia	22.4	–
Australia	24.2	–

Source: Stevenson et al. (1999, Appendix B3).

Note: Although this data is now 10 years old and based on the 1996 Census, analysis of the 2006 census data points to even greater differences in university participation rates.

Successive Australian governments have attempted to address the issue of the under-representation of some groups in HE, culminating with the 2008 *Review of Australian Higher Education* (Bradley et al., 2008). The review found that despite Australia's rapid growth in HE participation overall, this expansion has not been accompanied by increases in social equity. Indeed, Figure 7.1 illustrates that the proportion of students from the lowest quartile of SES has remained remarkably stable over the last two decades at around 14.5% (compared to a population reference value of 25%), despite a wide range of policy initiatives across the sector.

Equal(ising) opportunity: higher education for all who are good enough

Concern about who gained access to HE, and education in general, grew out of the post-war nation-building and Keynesian principles of universal employment and equitable distribution of wealth stimulated

Figure 7.1: Low socio-economic status participation rate in higher education (%), 1989–2006

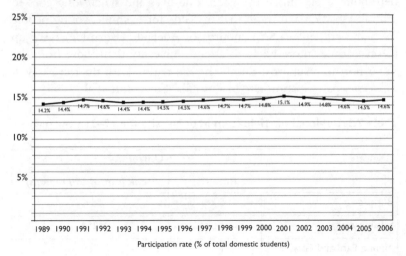

1989 1990 1991 1992 1993 1994 1995 1996 1997 1998 1999 2000 2001 2002 2003 2004 2005 2006

Participation rate (% of total domestic students)

Source: Bradley et al. (2008, p 29).

by government intervention. Education was to be the foundation for a new future for all Australians:

> A tremendous confidence in government was developing, and education was becoming a primary governmental instrument for solving problems.... Poverty would be overcome not by income redistribution, entailing a zero sum confrontation between the powerful classes and the state, but through the positive–sum instrument of education. When the educational standards of the poor were raised, poverty would disappear, amid general economic growth. (Marginson, 1997, p 14)

Community expectations for education attainment increased in response to the growing need for educated labour to serve the rapidly expanding government and services sectors (including education) and in response to government rhetoric that 'deliberately fostered ... a revolution in rising expectations' (Marginson, 1997, p 33). This popular demand was shaped by the two dominant policy discourses of human capital investment and equality of educational opportunity, and rapidly expanded to include HE as demand for university-educated workers extended to groups who had not considered this level of education prior to the war (Trow, 2006). Educational equality was about providing or distributing opportunities to all who could benefit from them, as articulated in the Martin report on the *Future of Tertiary Education in Australia*: 'In Australia it is widely accepted that higher education should be available to all citizens according to their inclination and capacity' (Martin, 1964, p i).

In response to the rapid expansion in enrolments following the war, the Menzies government commissioned reports from Mills (1950), Murray (1957) and then Martin (1964). These supported further significant expansion of HE in order to 'yield direct and significant economic benefits through increasing the skill of the population' (Martin, 1964, p 1) and led to major increases in Commonwealth funding of HE – from 20% of university income in 1951 to 43% of income by 1971 (Marginson, 1997).

As the Chairman of the Committee on the Future Development of Tertiary Education in Australia, Martin paved the way for the creation of a binary system of HE comprising the more prestigious research and teaching universities, and other more vocationally oriented teaching institutions, mostly colleges of advanced education (CAEs) and institutes of technology. Much of the growth in HE following this report was channelled into the latter, less costly institutions, including large numbers of students who were the first in their family to enter HE. In the 10 years following the Martin report, the number of students in HE more than tripled to 273,000 with students from CAEs and institutes of technology making up nearly 100,000 of the total by 1973 (Marginson, 1997).

The Whitlam Labor government was elected in 1972 on a strong education platform, with Whitlam asserting in his *Labor Policy Speech* that 'education is the key to equality of opportunity' (quoted in Marginson, 1997, p 17). Education was essential for the development of Labor's 'three great aims': to enhance equality, to involve all citizens in political decisions and 'to liberate the talents and uplift the horizons of the Australian people' (Australian Labor Party, 1972, quoted in Marginson, 1997, p 16). By 1974, the government had abolished tuition fees and introduced a universal (though means-tested) living allowance for HE students, with the aim of equalising access to HE for students from all SES backgrounds.

Under Whitlam, the federal government assumed full responsibility for HE funding and increased its funding threefold. Notwithstanding this substantial commitment, the socio-economic composition of the student population remained unchanged. The number of people from lower SES backgrounds attending HE increased, but so did those from higher SES backgrounds. Inequalities persisted as the binary system saw low SES students clustered in the CAEs, newer universities and in less prestigious disciplines such as teaching and business, while students from high SES backgrounds dominated the established universities and professional disciplines such as medicine and law (Anderson et al., 1980; Marginson, 1997). Any increase in equity that might have occurred had been effectively diluted within a stratified HE system.

Anderson's investigation of the impact of the Whitlam government's abolition of university tuition fees on the social composition of university students established that 'higher status social groups ... are consistently over represented', especially in the more prestigious universities and disciplines (Anderson et al., 1980, p 197). Anderson et al. (1980) determined that cost was not a significant disincentive on its own. They also demonstrated the complex interrelationship of four necessary conditions for entry to HE: *availability* of places, *accessibility* for qualified applicants, the *aspirations* of students to seek a place and *achievement* to qualify for entry. Anderson et al. concluded that financial assistance is insufficient if there is no aspiration and if universities maintain inflexible admissions procedures and conditions of entry. They recommended that policy to extend participation should focus on both the 'talented individual whose circumstances limit accessibility' (Anderson et al., 1980, p 201) and on the inflexibility of universities' admissions policies.

Developing this work further, Anderson and Vervoorn confirmed that despite the 'mushrooming growth of higher education' there had been 'little effect on the social composition of the student body' (1983, p 2). The HE population remained strongly skewed towards those from privileged backgrounds, with the patterns of participation revealing the same social inequalities as in the pre-war years. In accepting that 'basic scholastic ability of the sort demanded for higher study is evenly distributed throughout society' (Anderson and Vervoorn, 1983, p 2), Anderson and Vervoorn argued that the Australian HE population should be far more representative of the population as a whole.

Rationalisation: higher education is not for everyone

Macintyre (2008, p 3) observes that 'the Whitlam government marked the apogee of public investment in education and the end of two decades of uninterrupted economic growth'. Towards the end of the Whitlam government, economic recession was threatening and the prevailing view of political economics began to shift from the post-war Keynesian approach of funding demand from future income, to economic rationalism or market liberalism – responding to public demand with a more efficient supply (funded from current income) and/or redirecting demand into other less costly areas. This shift had a significant effect on equity in education, in particular on how equity and HE were conceived in new social and economic times.

Following 30 years of growth, the incoming conservative Fraser government faced rising unemployment and an increasing disillusion with the human capital arguments for HE expansion. Retention to Year 12 (the final year of schooling) slowed and even fell between 1975 and 1980, and school-leaver demand for HE decreased. Education policy turned to meeting the more immediate needs of industry and federal government effort was transferred to Technical and Further Education (TAFE) where the costs per student were roughly one third of those in HE. During these years, federal funding of TAFE increased by 80% and enrolments by a third (Marginson, 1997).

Whereas the creation of a binary system of HE had the effect of diluting social justice, the redirection of demand for HE into TAFE had the effect of displacing it from the HE policy agenda. An Australian government inquiry at the time (Williams, 1979) expressed the view that the structural causes of under-representation of particular groups in HE were more appropriately dealt with outside the sector, before students were admitted.

Equity: higher education in proportion

The Australian Labor Party was returned to government in 1983 with a commitment to enhancing participation in education, particularly for disadvantaged youth. The Youth Affairs portfolio was moved from the Department of Employment and Industrial Relations to the Department of Education and Training and a new Participation and Equity Program was introduced with a priority to address the interrelated problems of youth unemployment and low participation in post-compulsory education and training. A submission-based Higher Education Equity Program (HEEP) and the Aboriginal Participation Initiative (API) were introduced to fund equality of opportunity projects in HE.

During the latter half of the 1980s, retention to Year 12 and demand for university entry began to build again and 'the need for a better educated and more highly skilled population [was] clearly recognised and widely accepted' (Dawkins, 1988, p 4). Still informed by an economic rationalist disposition for lessening the cost of further expansion, the Minister for Education, John Dawkins, responded by introducing a user-pays Higher Education Contribution Scheme

(HECS), administered through the taxation system with university fees able to be deferred until a student earned a threshold income level. While 15 years of free tuition had come to an end, the introduction of HECS was promoted as an equity measure because of the deferred nature of repayments. The justification for its introduction included the favourable income expectations of graduates and the substantial taxpayer-funded subsidy to the more economically advantaged student body that still dominated HE. The private gains of HE became paramount in policy discourse, replacing the previous emphasis on the overall public good.

In addition to HECS, Dawkins' (1988) White Paper on the restructuring of Australian HE had a profound impact on the sector's structure, effectively abolishing the previous binary system of universities and CAEs, encouraging the merger of many smaller institutions, and creating a Unified National System of around 37 mostly large and diverse universities, with a significant net gain in university places. The White Paper also imposed widespread accountability measures on the sector, heralding an escalation of corporate approaches to university management and a new focus on entrepreneurial and marketisation activities (Marginson, 1997).

Based on a resurgence in human capital theory, one of the key principles behind the Dawkins reforms was that universities should not be the preserve of an elite, but should be accessible to all:

> In the past, the benefits of higher education have been enjoyed disproportionately by the more privileged members of our community. Those benefits need to be shared more widely and more equitably in the future.... The Government is committed to improving access to and success in the higher education system. This goal is critical to our ability to realise the potential of all Australians and to produce the highest quality graduates. (Dawkins, 1988, pp 6, 20)

Dawkins argued that people must not be excluded from university study on the basis of their disadvantage not only as a matter of social justice, but also as an economic imperative (Ramsay et al., 1998). Improving access to HE was an avenue for maintaining both international economic competitiveness and social cohesion:

> The current barriers to the participation of financially and other disadvantaged groups limit our capacity to develop

the highest skilled workforce possible and are a source of economic inefficiency.... [Higher education] promotes greater understanding of culture, often at odds with majority attitudes and, in doing so, supports the development of a more just and tolerant society. (Dawkins, 1988, p 7)

Dawkins conceded that growth of the system alone would not be sufficient and that 'more direct and specific strategies' (1988, p 21) were needed, including the development of 'a statement of national equity objectives [to] form the basis for further negotiations between the Commonwealth and institutions on the development and funding of their equity proposals' (1988, p 55). *A Fair Chance for All* (DEET, 1990) placed responsibility for improving student equity largely in the hands of the universities themselves: 'Higher education institutions ... have a clear responsibility to ... [change] the balance of the student population to reflect more closely the composition of society as a whole' (DEET, 1990, p 2).

Equity in HE became a matter of equal representation. Six groups of students were identified as under-represented in HE: people from socio-economically disadvantaged backgrounds; Aboriginal and Torres Strait Islander people; people from non-English-speaking backgrounds; people with disabilities; people from rural and isolated areas; and women in non-traditional studies. Universities were urged to set and report against targets that reflected the representation of these groups in the wider community. The ability of the sector to meet these new equity responsibilities was enhanced by the development of a set of equity indicators and accompanying definitions to measure performance against institutional targets and those of the sector as a whole (Martin, 1994).

A Fair Chance for All (DEET, 1990) has continued to provide the foundation for student equity in Australian HE. A comprehensive review was commissioned by the Australian Labor government in 1995 to assess progress towards meeting its equity objectives and to provide advice on future policy directions (NBEET and HEC, 1996). The review noted pleasing progress for most equity groups, but highlighted the very poor progress of both low SES and isolated target groups, particularly in relation to access and participation rates. It was an assessment echoed more than a decade later in the Bradley Review (Bradley et al., 2008).

The emphasis on government and institutional responsibility enunciated in the 1996 report reveals a shift in equity policy from a focus on under-representation and the deficits of equity group students to an acknowledgement of the complexity of educational disadvantage, in part arising from the education system itself. It recognised the role of the academic and administrative culture of the universities themselves in contributing to inequalities in access and success and reinforced the emphasis on institutional responsibility introduced by Dawkins' White Paper and *A Fair Chance for All*, extending accountability to all staff and 'the mainstream of higher education planning, governance, management and academic practice' (NBEET and HEC, 1996, p 76).

The review was finalised following the 1996 federal election and a change of government, and so never received formal policy status. However, its findings and recommendations have contributed to equity policy and planning at institutional levels with continuing emphasis on embedding equity in mainstream planning, policy and management, and on investigating and addressing the causes of inequity in HE (Ramsay, 1999).

Privatisation: higher education as individual choice

While the incoming Howard Coalition government continued to give nominal support to the equity framework established in *A Fair Chance for All*, it did so while adopting a more neo-liberal understanding of equity and HE. For example, its first budget in 1996 made major cuts to HE funding, increased HECS levels and significantly lowered the income threshold for their repayment. These changes were justified on the basis that the individual student rather than the general public was the primary beneficiary of HE. Informed by the same logic, discipline-based and differentiated HECS charges were also introduced; determined partly on the basis of teaching costs, but also justified on the expected financial return to students.

In her analysis of the change in policy direction, Ramsay commented that:

> Since the benefits of higher education are a matter of individual competitive advantage ... then the fate of those for whom this is not a realistic or available option is presumably to be viewed as an outcome of the market, and as such not to be tampered with. (1999, p 185)

In terms of social justice, this was a time where retributive justice was in the ascendancy: an individual gained the benefits of HE if they deserved to win a place within a competitive market through individual talent and hard work. Nevertheless, Ramsay acknowledged the continuing 'strength and significance of what remain[ed] of the Australian national equity framework' (1999, p 185), and also the apparent commitment of the sector to the strategic importance of the equity agenda. Certainly, institutional equity plans, including reporting against Martin's (1994) equity performance indicators and separate Indigenous education strategies, were maintained as part of national annual reporting requirements.

Concern about the impact on student equity of the increases to HECS and the lowering of the repayment threshold initiated a number of studies, some commissioned by the government (Andrews, 1999; Aungles et al., 2002) and others initiated independently (Chapman and Ryan, 2005). These suggest that while there may have been some initial fall in demand following the 1996 changes, particularly for mature-aged students, the overall impact had been insignificant and that 'the introduction of HECS and its variants since that time, have not discouraged overall participation in higher education among persons from a low SES background' (Aungles et al., 2002, p 3). Indeed, many concluded that HECS 'played a major role in facilitating greater access to higher education' (Aungles et al., 2002, p 30) and that 'it is the income-contingent repayment characteristic of HECS that protects the access of the relatively poor' (Chapman and Ryan, 2005, p 507). Certainly, the UK government modelled the introduction of their income-contingent, variable tuition fees in 2006 on Australia's HECS (Foskett et al., 2006). The impact of cost on the accessibility of HE for students from low SES backgrounds has remained a matter of considerable debate among researchers, particularly in relation to the significant additional expenses incurred by students from rural and isolated areas (Cardak and Ryan, 2006; Godden, 2007). Similar concerns are echoed in research overseas (Foskett et al., 2006; Finnie and Mueller, 2008).

The increased emphasis on a user-pays ideology was central to the Howard government's 1998 review of HE (West, 1998), which 'placed economic choice at the centre of decision-making' with only 'residual regulation to maintain access by some disadvantaged students' (Marginson and Considine, 2000, p 36). West sought to move HE from a supply-driven to a demand-driven model, including extension to the full fee-paying, domestic undergraduate market and the introduction of a voucher system of student entitlement. While most of the recommendations of this report were considered to be too politically hazardous at the time and were not adopted, they reappeared four years later in Brendan Nelson's *Crossroads* review (Nelson, 2002) and *Backing Australia's Future* (Nelson, 2003). Nelson, the Australian Minister for

Education at the time, introduced fee-paying undergraduate places for domestic students who could afford to pay their way into prestigious courses. He also permitted institutions to increase students' HECS contributions by up to 25%.[4]

To counter the increased cost of tuition, Nelson introduced the Commonwealth Learning Scholarships (to assist with education and accommodation costs), to be allocated to students on the basis of individual financial need. Increased funding was made available through a performance-based model to finance outreach and student support activities for low SES students, with a particular emphasis on the Coalition's strong rural and regional constituency.

Ironically, the same government that significantly increased HE costs, arguing that cost is not a major deterrent for people from low SES backgrounds, also chose to allocate substantial funds to provide scholarships as a key equity intervention to improve participation. The emphasis on scholarships reflected neo-liberal individualist or 'retributive' notions of social justice. Equity was targeted at the 'deserving individual'. This preference for a model targeting worthy individuals was in opposition to the more general adjustment to student finances required, and was argued for strongly by the sector (James et al., 2007).

Nelson also commissioned a review of equity groups and performance (James et al., 2004). The review noted that women, people from non-English backgrounds and people with disabilities had improved their participation significantly while there had been little progress for people from low SES, rural, isolated and Indigenous backgrounds. The report's emphasis on quantitative representation raised, for the first time, the question of men's under-representation, particularly in the disciplines of education and nursing, and suggested that men should be considered an additional equity group. Following significant debate across the sector concerning the question of disadvantage versus representation, gender was removed from the equity framework altogether, although universities were asked to continue to monitor gender across all fields of study. Recommendations for more comprehensive measures of educational disadvantage, including SES, were not adopted. However, reporting on the remaining equity performance indicators continued as a requirement within the national policy framework.

Widening participation: higher education as social inclusion

Despite these regulatory measures, equity continued to operate at the margins of most university activity. The election of the Rudd Labor government in 2007 on an 'education revolution' platform and its creation of a new Ministry of Social Inclusion, co-located with the Department of Education, Employment and Workplace Relations, provided an early indication that equity was to be more central to education policy. The adoption of the term 'social inclusion' suggested a 'Third Way' approach to social justice (Giddens, 2001), echoing the policy approach of the Blair government, which combined the economic and the social through a focus on inclusion in society, primarily through participation in the labour force.

The appointment of Denise Bradley – former Vice Chancellor and renowned advocate for educational equity – to chair the *Review of Australian Higher Education* (Bradley et al., 2008), and the emphasis on social inclusion and the transformative role of HE in that review's report, confirmed equity as central to policy development in Australian HE. The government's initial response to the Bradley report further confirmed this commitment, although it was somewhat circumscribed due to the global financial crisis. In particular, the government established targets to increase the proportion of Australian 25–34 year olds with a bachelor's degree to 40% by 2025 and the proportion of undergraduate enrolments from low SES backgrounds to 20% by 2020 (Gillard, 2009). While these targets are softer than those recommended by Bradley[5] and will not see Australia keep up with leading OECD countries such as Ireland, Sweden or even the UK, they began to create some unease among Australian universities, especially as they were to be accompanied by a more demand-driven model of student funding. Importantly, the then Minister for Education, Julia Gillard (2009), stipulated that 'every higher education institution must play its part … social inclusion must be a core responsibility of all institutions that accept public funding'.

Following this increased emphasis on widening participation in HE, many universities took up the government's challenge and embarked on reinvigorating and extending existing programmes and/or establishing new programmes aimed at encouraging and enabling more and different kinds of students to access and participate in HE. Increasing numbers of universities developed partnerships with schools in their catchment areas, while others developed partnership arrangements with other universities and/or TAFE institutions. In large measure, the significant boost in funding to universities provided under the Higher Education Participation and Partnership Program provided the stimulus for this increased level of activity.

Conclusion

There are at least three conclusions that can be drawn from this account of social justice in Australian HE policy. First, periods of expansion in the Australian HE system have always been accompanied by distributive notions of social justice: in this case, equal opportunity to access and participate in HE. To some extent, the need to redress the disadvantages experienced by some Australians has provided a rationale for expansionary periods. As Julia Gillard (Minister for Education from 2007 to 2010) has explained: 'A nation that thinks of itself as essentially egalitarian can't sit by idly while those from disadvantaged backgrounds are denied the life opportunities that come from higher education – things like higher incomes, career progression, intellectual fulfilment and self-knowledge' (Gillard, 2008).

However, it is important to note that historically the fair distribution of opportunities and outcomes has never been enough (in a policy sense) to justify HE's expansion. Economic justifications have also been required and, for the most part, have been the dominant element of any argument for expansion. Social policy has tended to be subsumed by economic policy.

In more recent times, the economic rationale for HE has been even more central, particularly in terms of justifying expansion. While earlier expansions to Australian HE were undertaken in response to high levels of unmet student demand (greater numbers of eligible applicants to university than places available), the current expansion to the system is being contemplated for very different reasons: the perceived need for more knowledge workers in order to increase the nation's competitiveness in a global knowledge economy.

In this context, students from disadvantaged backgrounds are being enlisted into university in order to achieve the nation's economic aspirations. Principles of social justice are involved to the extent that these aspirations require that the disadvantaged are not left behind in the nation's economic development. 'Widening participation' in HE and 'social inclusion' more generally are seen as possible only in periods of expansion; that is, the vision of social justice has tended to be distributive rather than redistributive. Equalising opportunities for social groups to participate in HE by redistributing existing opportunities (from the advantaged to the less advantaged) has not been a palatable option, whereas expanding the system has enabled the creation and distribution of new opportunities without old ones being lost, even though the evidence to date is that this has not led to greater representation in university of people from disadvantaged groups.

A second conclusion that can be drawn from the preceding analysis is that periods of 'consolidation' in HE provision (eg during the Howard government), tend to be accompanied by retributive notions of social justice (Gale and Densmore, 2000). Indeed, it can be argued that these periods are conceived as counter to the perceived excesses of distributive justice. The justification tends to be that access to HE by greater numbers of people undermines the benefits of HE (Gillard, 2008). In particular, the inclusion of more people from low SES backgrounds may be seen to undermine the talent and hard work of 'deserving individuals' and traditional notions of merit. In this sense, retributive justice calls into question the 'social' in social justice by emphasising and protecting the rights of individuals. It also emphasises the stratification of HE to facilitate the differentiation of opportunities according to 'merit'.

A third conclusion is that Australian HE policy and practice is yet to be fully informed by a recognitive social justice. Yet, as more and diverse groups of people gain access to HE, the silence with respect to who these students are and what they have to contribute cannot be justified in social justice terms. Specifically, 'the fetish with access to the curriculum, without considering the curriculum itself, is symptomatic of a central weakness in mainstream equality discourse' (Marginson, 1993, p 244). More qualitative concerns about the existing curricula, pedagogy and relations of power and governance within universities, have been generally ignored or 'only considered worth addressing to the extent that they inhibit throughput and output' (Fitzclarence and Kenway, 1993, p 93). It is no longer sufficient to think about equity in terms of proportional representation. Social justice in HE must also include a sense of 'epistemological equity'. As Sefa Dei explains:

> The question of how to create spaces where multiple knowledges can co-exist in the Western academy is central; especially so, since Eurocentric knowledge subsumes and appropriates other knowledges without crediting sources. At issue is the search for epistemological equity. (Sefa Dei, 2008, p 8)

In a context of HE for the masses, recognitive justice requires a deeper understanding of the knowledges, values and understandings that all students bring to university. And this necessarily implies creating spaces for them, not simply creating more places.

Notes

[1] This chapter is a reworked version of an article published in *Critical Studies in Education*, vol 52, no 1, pp 29–46.

[2] 'Distributive justice' is now a common theorisation of social justice, in particular in the work of Rawls (1971).

[3] It was not until the 20th century that universities were established in Queensland and Western Australia, and later still in regional centres and the national capital.

[4] During the Howard government, federal funding of universities declined in relation to the number of students enrolled by 4%, the only OECD nation to experience a decrease, compared to an OECD average increase of 49% (Marginson, 2007).

[5] Bradley et al. (2008) recommended a target of 40% participation of 25–34 year olds by 2020 and 20% low SES participation for all students, not only undergraduates.

References

Anderson, D.S. and Vervoorn, A.E. (1983) *Access to Privilege: Patterns of Participation in Australian Post-Secondary Education*, Canberra: ANU Press.

Anderson, D.S., Boven, R., Fensham, P.J. and Powell, J.P. (1980) *Students in Australian Higher Education: A Study of Their Social Composition since the Abolition of Fees*, Canberra: AGPS.

Andrews, L. (1999) *Does HECS Deter? Factors Affecting University Participation by Low SES Groups*, Canberra: DETYA.

Aungles, P., Buchanan, I., Karmel, T. and MacLachlan, M. (2002) *HECS and Opportunities in Higher Education: a Paper Investigating the Impact of the Higher Education Contributions Scheme (HECS) on the Higher Education System*, Canberra: DEST.

Berger, J. (2008) *'Why Access Matters' Revisited: A Review of the Latest Research*, Toronto: Millennium Scholarships.

Bradley, D., Noonan, P., Nugent, H. and Scales, B. (2008) *Review of Australian Higher Education: Final Report*, Canberra: Department of Education, Employment and Workplace Relations.

Cardak, B.A. and Ryan, C. (2006) *Why Are High Ability Individuals from Poor Backgrounds Under-Represented at University?*, Melbourne: LaTrobe University.

Chapman, B. and Ryan, C. (2005) 'The access implications of income-contingent charges for higher education: lessons from Australia', *Economics of Education Review,* vol 24, no 5, pp 491–512.

Dawkins, J.S. (1988) *Higher Education: A Policy Statement*, Canberra: AGPS.

DEEWR (Department of Education, Employment and Workplace Relations) (2009) *Students 2008 [Full Year] Selected Higher Education Statistics*, Canberra: DEEWR. Available at: www.dest.gov.au/sectors/higher_education/publications_resources/profiles/Students/2008_full_year.htm (accessed 2 September 2010).

DEET (Department of Employment, Education and Training) (1990) *A Fair Chance for All: Higher Education That's within Everyone's Reach*, Canberra: AGPS.

Finnie, R. and Mueller, R.E. (2008) *The Effects of Family Income, Parental Education and Other Background Factors on Access to Post-Secondary Education in Canada*, Toronto, ON: Education Policy Institute.

Fitzclarence, L. and Kenway, J. (1993) 'Education and social justice in the postmodern age', in R. Lingard, J. Knight and P. Porter (eds) *Schooling Reform in Hard Times*, London: Falmer Press, pp 90–105.

Foskett, N., Roberts, D. and Maringe, F. (2006) *Changing Fee Regimes and Their Impact on Student Attitudes to Higher Education*, Higher Education Academy funded research project 2005–06, University of Southampton, Southampton, UK.

Gale, T. and Densmore, K. (2000) *Just Schooling: Exploration in the Cultural Politics of Teaching*, Buckingham: Open University Press.

Giddens, A. (ed) (2001) *The Global Third Way Debate*, Cambridge: Polity Press.

Gillard, J. (2008) 'Equity in the education revolution', Paper presented at the 6th Annual Higher Education Summit, Star City, Sydney, 3 April.

Gillard, J. (2009) 'Ministerial keynote address', Paper presented at the Australian Financial Review Higher Education Conference, Sydney, 9 March.

Godden, N. (2007) *Regional Young People and Youth Allowance: Access to Tertiary Education*, Wagga Wagga: The Centre for Rural Social Research, Charles Sturt University.

Greig, A., Lewins, F. and White, K. (2003) *Inequality in Australia*, Cambridge and Port Melbourne: Cambridge University Press.

HEFCE (Higher Education Funding Council for England) (2006) *Widening Participation: a Review. Report to the Minister of State for Higher Education and Lifelong Learning*, London: Higher Education Funding Council for England.

James, R., Baldwin, G., Coates, H., Krause, K.-L. and McInnis, C. (2004) *Analysis Of Equity Groups in Higher Education 1991–2002*, Melbourne: Centre for the Study of Higher Education, University of Melbourne.

James, R., Bexley, E., Devlin, M. and Marginson, S. (2007) *Australian University Student Finances 2006: Final Report of a National Survey of Students in Public Universities*, Canberra: Universities Australia.

Macintyre, S. (2008) *Participation in the Classroom, Productivity in the Workforce – Unfulfilled Expectations*, Brisbane: ACER.

Marginson, S. (1993) *Education and Public Policy in Australia*, Cambridge: Cambridge University Press.

Marginson, S. (1997) *Educating Australia: Government, Economy and Citizen since 1960*, Cambridge: Cambridge University Press.

Marginson, S. (2006) 'Dynamics of national and global competition in higher education', *Higher Education*, vol 52, no 1, pp 1–39.

Marginson, S. (2007) *Education: Australia and the OECD*, Melbourne: Australian Policy Online. Retrieved 6 December 2010, from www.sisr.net/apo/election_education.pdf

Marginson, S. and Considine, M. (2000) *The Enterprise University: Power, Governance and Reinvention in Australia*, New York: Cambridge University Press.

Martin, L. (1964) *Tertiary Education in Australia: Report of the Committee on the Future of Tertiary Education in Australia*, Melbourne: Australian Universities Commission.

Martin, L.M. (1994) *Equity and General Performance Indicators in Higher Education: Volume 1 Equity Indicators*, Canberra: DETYA.

Martin, Y.M. and Karmel, T. (2002) *Expansion in Higher Education during the 1990s: Effects on Access and Student Quality*, Canberra: DEST.

Mills, R. (1950) *Interim Report by the Commonwealth Committee on the Needs of Universities*, Canberra: CTEC.

Murray, K. (1957) *Report of the Committee on Australian Universities*, Retrieved 6 December 2010, from www.go8.edu.au/index.php?option=com_content&task=view&id=249&Itemid=164

NBEET (National Board of Employment, Education and Training) and HEC (Higher Education Council) (1996) *Equality, Diversity and Excellence: Advancing the National Equity Framework*, Canberra: NBEET.

Nelson, B. (2002) *Higher Education at the Crossroads: an Overview Paper*, Canberra: DEST.

Nelson, B. (2003) *Our Universities: Backing Australia's Future*, Canberra: Commonwealth of Australia.

OECD (Organisation for Economic Co-operation and Development) (2008) *Education at a Glance 2008: OECD Indicators*, Paris: OECD.

Ramsay, E. (1999) 'The national framework for Australian higher education equity: its origins, evolution and current status', *Higher Education Quarterly*, vol 53, no 2, pp 173–89.

Ramsay, E., Tranter, D., Charlton, S. and Sumner, R. (1998) *Higher Education Access and Equity for Low SES School Leavers: a Case Study*, Canberra: AGPS.

Rawls, J. (1971) *A Theory of Justice*, Oxford: Oxford University Press.

Saunders, P. (2005) *The Poverty Wars*, Sydney: UNSW Press.

Sefa Dei, G.J. (2008) 'Indigenous knowledge studies and the next generation: pedagogical possibilities for anti-colonial education', *The Australian Journal of Indigenous Education*, vol 37S, pp 5–13.

Stevenson, S., Maclachlan, M. and Karmel, T. (1999) *Regional Participation in Higher Education and the Distribution of Higher Education Resources across Regions*, Canberra: Higher Education Division, DETYA.

Trow, M. (2006) 'Reflections on the transition from elite to mass to universal access: forms and phases of higher education in modern societies since WWII', in J. Forest and P. Altbach (eds) *International Handbook of Higher Education*, Netherlands: Springer, pp 243–80.

University of Melbourne (2007) 'History: about the university'. Available at: www.unimelb.edu.au/about/history/index.html (accessed 27 August 2010).

University of Sydney (2010) 'Understanding regional history'. Available at: www.usyd.edu.au/about/profile/history.shtml (accessed 27 August 2010).

Vinson, T. (2007) *Dropping Off the Edge: The Distribution of Disadvantage in Australia*, Richmond: Jesuit Social Services and Catholic Social Services Australia.

Wells, J. (2008) 'Trends in enrolments', Paper presented at the 10th Annual ATN Conference, Perth, January.

West, R. (1998) *Learning for Life: Review of Higher Education Financing and Policy*, Canberra: Australian Government.

Wicks, J. (2005) *The Reality of Income Inequality in Australia*, Melbourne: St Vincent de Paul Society.

Williams, B. (1979) *Education, Training and Employment: Report of the Committee of Inquiry into Education and Training*, Canberra: Commonwealth of Australia.

Part Two
Perspectives on widening participation

'I've never known someone like me go to university': class, ethnicity and access to higher education[1]

Tehmina N. Basit

Introduction

Britain is a country with a highly diverse population originating from various parts of the world. A large proportion of the minority ethnic people who have made Britain home for themselves and their future generations belong to the working class. Like most immigrants, these people are constantly striving for upward social mobility. Education is perceived as the most significant avenue through which these minority ethnic groups can improve the life chances of their children. Their aspirations for their children are sometimes viewed by educationalists and educators as unrealistic. However, the government's widening participation and social inclusion agenda has enabled many young people from working-class, minority ethnic backgrounds to enter higher education; something that they could not previously contemplate. Drawing on the theses of Bourdieu, Coleman and Putnam, and on data from an empirical study, this chapter examines the perceptions of minority ethnic young people in higher education. It investigates the role of cultural and social capitals in young people's desire for and success in higher education, and in improving their life chances. While young minority ethnic people belonging to educated middle-class families receive support and guidance from their parents, those from working-class backgrounds are disadvantaged by their social class as well as ethnicity. Beck (2000) contends that ethnicity and membership of the 'underclass' reinforce each other. He gives less importance to the fact that society is divided by various ethnic and religious identities, but is more concerned that the ethnic feature of skin colour determines an individual's inclusion in, or exclusion from, society.

Diversity in higher education

The education and training of minority ethnic groups has been a cause for concern in Britain for some time now. This is true of higher education as well as compulsory and tertiary education. A Department for Education and Skills (DfES) topic paper (Bhattachariya et al., 2003) states that the proportion of ethnic minorities participating in higher education is 13%. They are more likely to enter higher education through non-traditional routes rather than after A levels, and are concentrated in a relatively small number of mainly post-1992[2] universities. While they are more likely to have degrees as compared with their majority ethnic[3] counterparts, they are less likely to have a first- or upper second-class degree. This situation does not seem to have improved in almost a decade.

Very few studies (eg Osler, 1999) have examined the experiences of minority ethnic undergraduates in higher education. Research shows that ethnicity can be a reason for racism and discrimination in entry to, and experience of, higher education (see Modood, 1998; Shiner and Modood, 2002; Basit et al., 2007). While minority ethnic groups are over-represented in higher education in relation to their respective population sizes, applicants to old universities have a significantly lower success rate (Modood and Shiner, 1994). Consequently, many cannot get on to courses that lead to some of the professions. Additionally, many minority ethnic people enter higher education as mature students. For example, it was reported in 2000 that only 20% of African-Caribbean undergraduate students were under 21 (Pathak, 2000). When minority ethnic students' achievement is comparable to, or even exceeds that of, other groups they can still face discrimination in gaining access to higher education (TTA, 2000). This portrays a bleak picture of higher education for minority ethnic groups. However, a different scenario has emerged now, and Modood (2006) notes in a later chapter that higher education has been a major success story for non-white minority ethnic groups, something which became apparent since university entry data started recording ethnicity. Tomlinson (2008) observes that applications from minority ethnic groups to higher education institutions have confounded social class expectations as a much higher proportion from working-class backgrounds enter universities as compared with the majority ethnic group. This is also pointed out in a recent DIUS report which maintains that young people from minority ethnic backgrounds are overwhelmingly more likely to enter higher education as compared with their majority ethnic peers with the same prior attainment, indicating that factors other than past attainment affect the likelihood of participation in higher education (Broecke and Hamed, 2008).

Family attitudes and expectations have a substantial influence on young people's entry into higher education. Studies on parental and peer involvement in the higher educational choices that young people make points to the role of family and friends (Brookes, 2003; David et al., 2003). Research on young people in Scotland in their early twenties shows that familial educational and labour-market disadvantage is reproduced across the generations, and low attainment affects men and women differently across all ethnic groups (Howieson and Iannelli, 2008). It is argued that parental education and social class are just as important as the quality of primary or preparatory schools that children attend, particularly with regard to access to higher education, and this applies to both majority ethnic and minority ethnic people (Abbas, 2007). Research also indicates that minority ethnic groups view education as a means of upward social mobility (Mirza, 1992; Basit, 1997), and working-class parents have middle-class aspirations and attitudes to education resulting in tremendous support for their children's education, despite possessing minimal knowledge about it (Basit, 1997; Abbas, 2007). Ahmad (2001) highlights the way in which success in higher education is seen by young British Muslim women and their parents as conferring personal and social advantages, and notes that the pursuit of university education resulting in status, career and social mobility is not viewed as contrary to cultural and religious mores, as long as certain codes of behaviour are followed. Similarly, Ijaz and Abbas (2010) in their study on intergenerational change among British Pakistanis observe the stress placed by both first-generation and second-generation parents on the need to educate women, and their apprehension towards the impact of Western values on their children.

In some ways, then, minority ethnic groups have diverse expectations of and for their young people. While they want their children to succeed in education in the same way as any other aspiring parent would wish, they also expect their young people to conduct themselves in a certain way. However, few higher education institutions take diversity into account when devising curricula and policies. Two research projects, carried out at a post-1992 university, examined equality and diversity in the institution at undergraduate level. The first (Ahmad et al., 2006) reports variance across and within schools in the university in terms of the approaches, resources and barriers to embedding equality and diversity in the curriculum. It identifies a range of strategies including the adoption of certain policies, the establishment of specific posts, the setting up of particular committees and the development of specific teaching and learning methods. A number of barriers to equality and diversity are also identified in the curriculum. The study, however, found pockets of good practice in the curriculum, as did the subsequent project. This second study (Pinnock et al., 2008) aimed to explore effective practice in embedding equality and diversity in the undergraduate curriculum within the university's 10 schools in more depth. It notes that barriers to equality and diversity are more consistent across the subject areas and can be identified at university, school and staff levels. A key finding is the need to enhance current staff development, specifically in relation to the topic of equality and diversity in the curriculum. It points to the potential for shared ideas and peer learning within and between schools, and the need for senior management to explicitly encourage, and advise about, good practice in this area. A number of concerns are, nevertheless, raised about lack of support from lecturers regarding special needs, in particular disability.

A DfES project (Broecke and Nicholls, 2007) reports that while the participation of minority ethnic students in higher education is higher than majority ethnic students, the attainment of the former group is lower in terms of the class of the degree attained at undergraduate level (see also Connor et al., 2004). After controlling for a number of factors, Broecke and Nicholls (2007) still find an unexplained gap between the two groups. Although their findings do not automatically point to an ethnic bias in higher education, they believe that a number of variables that could not be included would have decreased the attainment gap. These include term-time working, parental income and education, English as an additional language, and previous institution attended. Lower attainment of minority ethnic students is also reported by Richardson (2008) who notes that the trend is greater in students who are older, or female, or part time or who are studying at post-1992 universities. He maintains that this is only partly explained by variations in the students' entry qualifications.

Ethnicity, gender and degree attainment are also examined in a report that provides a sector-wide picture of perceptions, policies and practices (ECU and HEA, 2008). It concludes that the reasons for differential attainment are difficult to identify due to the complexity of causal factors. However, it maintains that even after controlling for the majority of contributory factors, being from a minority ethnic group (except the 'Other Black', 'Mixed' and 'Other' census groups) still has a statistically significant negative effect on degree attainment. The research also shows that women are more likely to obtain a higher degree classification than men, except when attaining a first. The report points to the need for making the sector demonstrably inclusive and free of discriminatory processes and practices. Key recommendations are made to the institutions in areas of: analysis and use of institutional data; learning, teaching, assessment and student support; infrastructure and governance; and policies and practices.

Hockings et al. (2007) argue that academic engagement of higher education students within diverse classrooms is difficult, as learning environments may impact differently on students on entry to higher education. They look at these students' conceptions about teaching and learning that might affect their engagement with, and benefit from, higher education. David (2007) points to the diversity of forms of knowledge and learning, and notes that these diverse forms lead to inequities and injustices in the distribution of possibilities and privileges. She acknowledges that while ethnicity is on the higher education agenda with regard to students and staff, the diverse types of higher education maintain inequalities and injustices within and between local and global contexts. Archer (2007) argues that a diversity of students in higher education cannot be taken as an indicator of greater equality. She draws attention to ways in which diversity may operate as a moral discourse to override competing and critical accounts of widening participation. After all, the role of universities and higher education should be to contribute significantly to developing and sustaining democratic societies by effectively educating students to become democratic, creative, caring and constructive citizens (Harkavy, 2006).

Social inclusion and widening participation

Widening participation is an issue of social justice; succeeding at it contributes to social cohesion (Watson, 2006, p 2). The British government's policy on widening participation and social inclusion in higher education, critiqued from an historical perspective in Chapter Two in this volume, was implemented with ambition and enthusiasm. It aimed to involve working-class, minority ethnic and mature students, among others, in higher education. It has undoubtedly encouraged such 'non-traditional' students to access higher education, although the majority of these students are concentrated in the newer universities as these have lower entry requirements and are local to the students who usually have employment and/or caring responsibilities, may not have funds to afford accommodation close to another university and therefore find it easier to attend these universities. Nevertheless, widening participation and social inclusion is confined to recruitment and filling spaces on courses, and is not necessarily extended to retention, progression and success in degree attainment unless tutors and students make concerted efforts in these areas. According to a report by the National Audit Office (2007) on student retention in higher education, on average, the Russell Group universities have the highest continuation rate, and the post–1992 universities, which are the most successful in widening participation, have the highest withdrawal rate. These variations mainly reflect the type of students enrolled and their pre-entry qualifications. Reay et al. (2002) contend that 'non-traditional' students' access to, and involvement in, higher education remains a grand design and an inadequate realisation, despite the dedication and commitment of students and tutors. Also, the experience of those who get into higher education in Britain can be very different depending on the students' social class, gender, ethnic group, age, mode of study and so forth.

If a range of higher education institutions are seemingly operationalising widening participation and social inclusion, then why do disproportionate numbers of minority ethnic students still fail to succeed in education despite high ambitions? By and large, it appears that the young people who succeed do so with the support of their families, as noted in the discussion earlier. However, not all families can provide a similar degree of support. Educated and middle-class parents possess cultural and social capitals which seamlessly facilitate their children's transition to higher education and the professions. On the other hand, working-class parents with little or no tradition of education can also provide support through verbal encouragement, which is a form of capital too, although it requires considerable enterprise and struggle on the part of the children to obtain the same outcomes that middle-class children, brought up with social and cultural capitals, effortlessly do.

The different forms of capital have been thoroughly discussed by Pierre Bourdieu, James Coleman and Robert Putnam, among others. Bourdieu (1986, 1997) forwards the idea of cultural capital to explain the unequal educational achievement of children from different social classes by arguing that academic success is linked to the distribution of cultural capital, which is gained within the family milieu, with cultural practices of the family facilitating children's success in education. He argues that to a varying extent, and depending on the period, society and social class, cultural capital can be attained quite unconsciously, and is recognised and guaranteed by academic qualifications. He views cultural capital as the best hidden form of hereditary transmission of capital and therefore receiving greater weight in the system of reproduction strategies. On the other hand, he conceptualises social capital as the combination of actual and potential resources that are linked to having a stable network of relationships that provide support to its members (Bourdieu, 1986, 1997). Coleman (1994) utilises the notion of social capital largely to understand the connection between social inequality and educational achievement. Putnam (2000) further distinguishes between bonding social capital, which is exclusive, and bridging social capital, which is inclusive, with the former leading to reciprocity and solidarity by providing support to deprived family and community members, specifically among minority ethnic groups, and the latter helping community members to access external assets and networks. (For a more in-depth critique of cultural and social capitals, see Chapter One in this volume by Tariq Modood.)

Contemplating or experiencing higher education

Thus, cultural and social capitals motivate minority ethnic young people of working-class backgrounds to aspire to higher education. Yet these capitals are not illustrated in the same way in working-class families as they are in middle-class families, but manifest themselves as 'aspirational capital' (see Basit, forthcoming). Those who lack the conventional forms of social and cultural capitals, and yet are encouraged by their parents in the form of aspirational capital, may enter higher education with different emotions. While they may be excited about going to university, they may view higher education with trepidation and not feel confident about making a success of it. Christie (2009) writes about the experiences of 12 'non-traditional' students from disadvantaged backgrounds, aged 25 or under when they entered university, in two old elite universities in Scotland. These students had come into higher education through the access route. She notes the integral role of emotions in young people's pathways to higher education, and their implications for the choice of university, and understanding class relations. She points to negative emotions such as fear, resentment and guilt, as well as positive emotions such as enthusiasm, excitement and pride. Emotions played a decisive part in these students' desire to select prestigious universities as they were perceived as capable of delivering economic benefits, as opposed to the fear of opting for a university that may be the wrong choice. This resonates with what other researchers have found. For many working-class and minority ethnic students, who do not have the tradition of education in their families, their degree is a means to an end (Bhatti, 2003; Crozier et al., 2008). They do not have the luxury to spend a minimum of three years to study for a degree and not reap economic benefits when they graduate. This is also noted by Lehmann (2009) in his research on first-generation working-class students at a Canadian university who approach higher education with an ethos of vocational education and utilitarian concerns of employability, income and social mobility.

In this chapter, I draw on data collected during a research project that investigated young minority ethnic citizens' transition to adulthood. It includes the perceptions of 20 young people, comprising not only those who were in higher education, but also those who were at an earlier stage of education and were contemplating higher education, those who had completed higher education and were employed, and those who could not experience it and were currently not in education, employment or training (NEET). The chapter focuses on the qualitative component of the research based on individual face-to-face, in-depth interviews with 20 young minority ethnic citizens. These participants were chosen through stratified sampling from the questionnaire respondents in an earlier survey – which was part of a mixed-method study – who had expressed their willingness to be interviewed. Interview participants included young British people of African-Caribbean, Bangladeshi, Indian and Pakistani heritage. Some of them were from a working-class background with no tradition of higher education in their family, whereas others were from educated middle-class families. Some were attending or had attended an old university, while the others' experience was related to a new post-1992 university. Although they were all of a minority ethnic heritage, and shared common experiences in important ways, they were by no means a homogeneous group, as there were significant class, ethnic as well as gender differences between them. The study therefore makes no claims of generalisability. Nevertheless, a qualitative study of this kind is not meant to be generalisable, as the intention is to highlight the quality of perceptions, not the quantity of matching responses. The latter would lead to the assumption that since more participants had similar views about certain issues, their response was in some way more significant than that of a participant who made a profound observation, but was in the minority.

In awe of higher education

Denise, a young woman of African-Caribbean origin, who was currently in the final year of compulsory schooling, wanted to go to university and train to be a nurse. However, on visiting a few universities, she got the impression that her working-class background and her minority ethnic status would prove to be a hindrance in enrolling onto a higher education course:

> "I don't know if I'll ever get to be a nurse, because you have to go to university and people like me don't really go to university. I've never known someone like me go to university … I've been to those, them, things, where you look around the school, and stuff like that, and everyone seems and talks really posh, and they're just so different to me."

This lack of confidence as a result of the absence of cultural and social capitals is not unusual for someone of Denise's background. Similar feelings were expressed by Anish, a university student of Indian origin, who believed attending a poorly resourced inner city school did not prepare young people like him for higher education:

> "When you get to university, you see the other cultures, the other people, and their academic ability was far better than ours…. On one course, we were doing networking in computing, and those that had done it before in secondary school, were well advanced in things that we had no experience of whatsoever."

Anish's comment shows that young people who lack social and cultural capitals and attend schools that are not properly resourced may face problems at entering university. This may lead to difficulties in academic engagement, and may result in failure or withdrawal.

Aspiring to higher education

Regardless of the life stage they were at, all the young people who were interviewed attached a considerable value to higher education. Those who had not experienced it wanted to pursue it. However, it was evident that for some of these young people, such a desire was more realistic and attainable as compared with some others. Nusrat, a university student of East African Indian origin, who belonged to an educated middle-class family, was brought up with the cultural and social capitals that are hallmarks of such families. She therefore had the confidence as well as the motivation and desire to pursue higher education:

> "I always knew that I had to study further. It wasn't like I'll do my GCSEs and that was it, that's all I'll ever be able to do; there was never that choice. It was actually something that I wanted to do, probably because all my brothers and sisters had done it; and my parents, their brothers and sisters. It's always been in my family to go on and study further."

Because of such precedents in the immediate and extended family, young people were able to get sufficient guidance to make informed choices about the higher education courses that they should undertake, as reported by Chitra, a university student of Indian origin: "Because of my family, I think I made an informed decision about where I want to be and what I want to do". Nevertheless, Chitra also narrated her frustrated attempts at getting information from other sources prior to her family's advice:

> "When I was at college, choosing universities, I didn't even want to go. And I don't think I had enough information; I don't think I was well informed of university – not from the system anyway. I didn't feel like I could approach teachers … I didn't feel confident in my own questions. I didn't know what to ask; I didn't know where to look. I was completely ignorant of what I was supposed to do."

In addition to parental advice and guidance, some young people had the acumen to consider their own aptitudes and limitations, as noted by Nusrat: "My parents did give me their opinion on what areas they thought I should go into. Then I combined that with my own strengths and weaknesses, and decided to go into the sciences".

Other considerations included enjoyment of a subject and whether it led to a career, as noted by Rashid, a university student of Pakistani origin:

> "I want to be a research chemist … I was crap at chemistry in secondary school; I was better at physics, but when I started doing chemistry in college, that's when I started feeling I am actually good at this … I did not like physics, but I enjoyed chemistry … I looked at my grades and saw what I was actually getting good at. Chemistry seemed to be the good thing. That's when I thought it could be fun."

Some young people who did not have the tradition of education in their families still got verbal encouragement and motivation from their parents, and were persuaded to contemplate higher education, as recounted by Imran, a young man of Pakistani origin in further education:

> "I think education is very important because my parents have stressed that since I was a kid: 'You should always get an education; go to university.' It's just a part of me, because I've been taught that. You need to be someone.... My parents are lower working class and they don't want me to be that; they want me to be successful and achieve goals."

As this comment shows, despite, or rather because of, their own working-class status and lack of education, Imran's parents motivated him to consider higher education. This illustrates that educational and occupational aspirations and the desire for their children's upward social mobility are not confined to educated, middle-class parents. Minority ethnic parents with no formal education and limited knowledge about educational procedures can transmit similar ambitions to their children.

Exploiting the chance or wasting the opportunity

As noted earlier, parental support and guidance enabled the young people to choose trajectories that led to, or would ultimately direct them to, higher education. However, some young people in the NEET group, who had negative experiences in education, and did not have cultural and social capital, or aspirational capital, in their family to support them, lamented the wasted opportunity, as narrated by Ayub, a young man of Pakistani origin:

> "Dropped out of GCSEs; I went to college, but I dropped out of that. When I left after GCSEs and all that, I just messed about to be honest ... I should have stayed in education. I could have got a better job."

Yet, some of those who were currently in the NEET group were considering further and higher education and availing themselves of the opportunities open to them, thus anticipating better life chances than their ancestors, as noted by Shireen, a young woman of Bangladeshi origin:

> "My parents and my grandparents have not had the choice of whether they want to study further or not, so they are either unemployed or got basic jobs ... I have been given the privilege to study further and to make something of my life."

Interestingly, the young people in the NEET group did not seem to be familiar with the term, or being labelled as NEET. We categorised them as such because they were currently not in education, employment or training, although we recognise that this rhetorical and managerial discourse is not for the benefit of the young people labelled as such, and they may find it insulting if they become aware that they are being pigeonholed as NEETs. What was even more intriguing was the fact that they did not appear to view it as a permanent situation, which cautions against stereotyping young people as NEET and renouncing them as perennially disadvantaged. When asked where she saw herself in 10 years' time, Shireen said, "I would like to see myself with a job, with a degree, hopefully with a husband, and a couple of kids", thus showing hope and optimism for her personal and professional life in the future. Hayward et al. (2008) observe that NEETs are not a homogeneous group, and that these young people drop in and out of courses, training and low-level jobs. They may also temporarily hold the status of NEET if they are planning to go into further or higher education.

The young people who had completed higher education and were currently in employment also highlighted the role of family support, as noted by Kavita, a young woman of Indian origin:

> "I mean direction, I mean guidance ... to have that support, or to have somebody there. Preferably, I think it would come from the family, to be able to say that well, you've gone through that route, it didn't work out, but try this route, you know. And I think that's quite important and that will help you whether you're in employment, whether you go into education."

They were critical of the dearth of information available from educational sources that could have guided them. Vanessa, another young woman in employment, who was of African-Caribbean origin, commented on the limited resources available in this area:

"I think the one I found helpful was called Career Point or something.… It basically just gave a breakdown of what you needed in order to do this job, or if you wanted to get there what would be the best move. Not enough people know where to get information from … I don't think there was enough done about careers, about how to get there and that kind of thing, when I was at school … I've sort of been doing it by myself.… Go on the internet, or if I couldn't find anything, I would simply apply for a job to find out what it was about."

Similarly, Faraz, a young man of Pakistani origin, currently in employment, noted the lack of expectations the educational institutions he had attended had of him, and emphasised the role of self-motivation and the encouragement received from his parents:

"When I was going through the education system there were a lot of expectations from my parents. From the education system, not really, I don't know.… I didn't really feel any pressure or anything from the education system itself. A lot was about pleasing my parents, pleasing myself. Making sure that I could benefit my parents once I've done my education, so that I can go out and work, and earn enough money to support my family and people around me."

Faraz appeared to be aware of the low expectations that the education system had of working-class minority ethnic young people and was determined to prove them wrong. This is consistent with research conducted by Byfield (2008) who sampled black boys from families with little cultural capital who not only managed to survive the school system, but succeeded in it despite negative experiences.

Discussion and conclusion

The research shows evidence of an emphasis on the utilitarian purpose of higher education. Most parents encourage their children to pursue higher education, and the young people follow their advice in order to attain education and develop knowledge and skills leading to a career. The young people from educated middle-class families who are brought up in an environment of cultural and social capital effortlessly follow these routes. Nevertheless, those who belong to families with no tradition of education encourage their young people to pursue higher education and career options too, mainly through verbal encouragement. This kind of support, which is a kind of capital too, can be described as 'aspirational capital', which is prevalent in many minority ethnic families of working-class backgrounds, when parents have high aspirations for their children. The minority ethnic status of members of such families compels them to work harder as they believe they have to do better than the majority ethnic group to achieve the same goals (Basit et al., 2007), and their working-class status means that they have a more precarious investment and a much bigger stake in entering higher education. They cannot afford to waste valuable time and money in pursuit of a degree that may turn out to be unattainable for a variety of reasons, or may not lead to a career commensurate with their qualifications. However, they are cognisant of the rewards that higher education can bring. Beck (1992, pp 93–4) maintains that educated individuals become the creators of their own labour situation, and thus the producers of their own social biography. He further argues that education is related with selection and therefore assumes a person's anticipation of upward social mobility. These expectations continue to be effective even when upward social mobility through education is merely an illusion, as education is little more than a protection against downward mobility.

Nevertheless, the aspiration of upward social mobility may be harder to realise for working-class minority ethnic young people. This is particularly poignant, as the introduction of university fees, which requires students to pay for tuition albeit after graduation, may dissuade potential students from disadvantaged backgrounds from seeking upward social mobility through higher education. The Dearing Report (Dearing, 1997) recommended that graduates contribute around 25% of the cost of higher education tuition through an income-contingent mechanism. This was implemented through the Teaching and Higher Education Act 1998 with higher education costing £1,000 annually and £3,000 for a three-year degree course. Maintenance grants were also abolished. While at university, students' tuition was funded through loans, which they repaid once in employment and earning a certain amount. A few years later, the Higher Education Act 2004, which was passed by Parliament by a narrow margin, allowed universities to raise fees, and most universities chose to charge £3,000 per year. It is difficult to surmise how many young people from disadvantaged backgrounds were deterred from contemplating higher education because of the thought of having to pay £9,000 at the end of their degree. More recently, the Browne Review (Browne, 2010) of higher education funding and student finance made a number of recommendations to the government. Consequently, the cap on tuition fees has now been removed. The UK Coalition government has given permission to universities to charge students fees of up to £9,000 a year. The justification given is that it would enable universities to offer world-class education fit for the 21st century, and that it would encourage students from poor families to attain higher education. However, finance available to students will be linked to their aptitude. It will, therefore, become harder for young people from working-class minority ethnic backgrounds to contemplate higher education as these students are likely to have attended inner-city schools, many with dismal resources, overcrowded classes and poor examination results.

Education and career are the major priorities of young people (Basit, 2009). Yet, it is manifest that the young people who lack social and cultural capitals are not adequately supported by the education system and may encounter failure and disappointment when approaching higher education even if they possess aspirational capital. I would wish to argue that the pursuit of higher education be put on the agenda of every young person in compulsory education regardless of their social background and ethnic origin. While a proportion of young people from diverse backgrounds may not pursue further and higher education, and choose to go into an occupation after leaving school, they should all be given the opportunity, guidance and advice to consider it. The government's widening participation agenda will only be meaningful if those young people who have never imagined themselves as university students are able to enter higher education and make a success of it. This means starting much earlier than at the point of entry to higher education. While universities arrange visits for secondary school students and explain what different higher education courses entail, disproportionate numbers of young people fail to benefit from these schemes. Their schools either do not bother with such visits, or the young people are not able to learn from them because the information provided is not sufficiently simplified to match the young people's level of understanding, or because of their lack of confidence to ask questions about university procedures and relating them to their own prior experience.

What is therefore required is targeted support for working-class minority ethnic groups and other marginalised young people, as early as the point of choosing their GCSE options, through guidance and mentoring for the next three years and then into further education. University representatives do visit colleges of further education to recruit students. An extension of this can be to make such visits to young people at earlier stages of education to explain, support, advise and engage with them at a time when this kind of guidance will perhaps change the life course of a potential school dropout or failing student. This level of support will also help to identify the gaps in knowledge and skills that may hinder entrance and success in higher education. Students with such shortcomings should then be supported through apposite pedagogical strategies and focused programmes to enhance their skills both by their schools and by the university they hope to enter. As Lehmann (2009) points out, universities need to make commitments to diversity in academic needs and forms of engagement beyond the lip service paid to young people in glossy brochures and strategic plans. This means we need to extend the concept of widening participation in higher education to embed within it support mechanisms that go beyond recruitment, to incorporate retention and progression through higher education, ultimately resulting in successful minority ethnic students from working-class families who are an asset to their country and society.

Notes

[1] I am grateful to Leicestershire Centre for Integrated Living for funding the research project on which this chapter is based. I am also thankful to other members of the project team, Iris Lightfoote and Chino Cabon, for their support during the course of the project.

[2] Post-1992, or 'new', universities refer to polytechnics and colleges of higher education that were given degree-awarding status in 1992. A hierarchy of institutions quickly developed in the UK with 20 of the most research-intensive universities calling themselves 'the Russell Group'. The Russell Group universities take significantly fewer minority ethnic students than other institutions; the new universities take significantly more.

[3] The term 'majority ethnic' is used in this chapter to denote the white majority population of Britain. 'Minority ethnic' here refers to minority ethnic groups of Asian or African heritage. I acknowledge that the terms are reductionist and can be viewed as insulting. Some white people of Scottish, Welsh or Irish heritage may not consider themselves as majority ethnic, and minority ethnic people born and brought up in Britain may not see themselves as minority ethnic.

References

Abbas, T. (2007) 'British South Asians and pathways into selective schooling: social class, culture and ethnicity', *British Educational Research Journal*, vol 33, pp 75–90.

Ahmad, F. (2001) 'Modern traditions? British Muslim women and academic achievement', *Gender and Education*, vol 13, pp 137–52.

Ahmad, N., Watt, P., Lyle, C. and Dhami, R. (2006) 'Approaches, resources and barriers to embedding equal opportunities in the curriculum', Final Report, Policy Research Institute, University of Wolverhampton.

Archer, L. (2007) 'Diversity, equality and higher education: a critical reflection on the ab/uses of equity discourse within widening participation', *Teaching in Higher Education*, vol 12, pp 635–53.

Basit, T.N. (1997) *Eastern Values; Western Milieu: Identities and Aspirations of British Muslim Girls*, Aldershot: Ashgate.

Basit, T.N. (2009) 'White British; dual heritage; British Muslim: young Britons' conceptualisation of identity and citizenship', *British Educational Research Journal*, vol 35, pp 723–43.

Basit, T.N. (forthcoming) '"My parents have stressed that since I was a kid": young minority ethnic British citizens and the phenomenon of aspirational capital', *Education Citizenship and Social Justice*.

Basit, T.N., McNamara, O., Roberts, L., Carrington, B., Maguire, M. and Woodrow, D. (2007) 'The bar is slightly higher: the perception of racism in teacher education', *Cambridge Journal of Education*, vol 37, pp 279–98.

Beck, U. (1992) *Risk Society: Towards a New Modernity*, trans Mark Ritter, London: Sage.

Beck, U. (2000) *The Brave New World of Work*, trans Patrick Camiller, Cambridge: Polity.

Bhattachariya, G., Ison, L. and Blair, M. (2003) 'Minority ethnic attainment and participation in education and training', DfES Research Topic Paper, Department for Education and Skills.

Bhatti, G. (2003) 'Social justice and non-traditional participants in higher education: a tale of border-crossing, instrumentalism and drift', in C. Vincent (ed) *Social Justice, Education and Identity*, London: Routledge-Falmer.

Bourdieu, P. (1986) *Distinction: a Social Critique of the Judgement of Taste*, trans Richard Nice, London: Routledge and Kegan Paul.

Bourdieu, P. (1997) 'The forms of capital', in A.H. Halsey, H. Lauder, P. Brown and A.S. Wells (eds) *Education: Culture, Economy and Society*, New York: Oxford University Press.

Broecke, S. and Hamed, J. (2008) 'Gender gaps in higher education participation: an analysis of the relationship between prior attainment and young participation by gender, socioeconomic class and ethnicity', DIUS Research Report 08 14, Department for Innovation, Universities and Skills.

Broecke, S. and Nicholls, T. (2007) 'Ethnicity and degree attainment', DfES Research Report RW92, Department for Education and Skills.

Brookes, R. (2003) 'Young people's higher education choices: the role of family and friends', *British Journal of Sociology of Education*, vol 24, pp 283–97.

Browne, J. (2010) 'Securing a sustainable future for higher education: an independent review of higher education funding and student finance', 12 October. Available at: www.independent.gov.uk/browne-report (accessed 15 October 2010).

Byfield, C. (2008) *Black Boys Can Make It: How They Overcome the Obstacles to University in the UK and USA*, Stoke-on-Trent: Trentham.

Christie, H. (2009) 'Emotional journeys: young people and transitions to university', *British Journal of Sociology of Education*, vol 30, pp 123–36.

Coleman, J.S. (1994) *Foundations of Social Theory*, Cambridge, MA: Belknap Press.

Connor, H., Tyers, C., Modood, T. and Hillage, J. (2004) 'Why the difference? A closer look at higher education minority ethnic students and graduates', DfES Research Report no 552, Department for Education and Skills.

Crozier, G., Reay, D., Clayton, J., Colliander, L. and Grinstead, J. (2008) 'Different strokes for different folks: diverse students in diverse institutions – experiences of higher education', *Research Papers in Education*, vol 23, pp 167–77.

David, M. (2007) 'Equity and diversity: towards a sociology of higher education for the twenty-first century?', *British Journal of Sociology of Education*, vol 28, pp 675–90.

David, M., Ball, S., Davies, J. and Reay, D. (2003) 'Gender issues in parental involvement in student choices of higher education', *Gender and Education*, vol 15, pp 21–36.

Dearing, R. (1997) 'The national committee of inquiry into higher education: summary report' (The Dearing Report). Available at: http://www.leeds.ac.uk/educol/ncihe/sumrep.htm (accessed 23 August 2010).

ECU (Equality Challenge Unit) and HEA (The Higher Education Academy) (2008) 'Ethnicity, gender and degree attainment', final report, Equality Challenge Unit/The Higher Education Academy.

Harkavy, I. (2006) 'The role of universities in advancing citizenship and social justice in the 21st century', *Education, Citizenship and Social Justice*, vol 1, pp 5–37.

Hayward, G., Wilde, S. and Williams, R. (2008) *Engaging Youth Enquiry: A Report for Consultation*, Oxford: Nuffield Review/Rathbone.

Hockings, C., Cooke, S. and Bowl, M. (2007) '"Academic engagement" within a widening participation context: a 3D analysis', *Teaching in Higher Education*, vol 12, pp 721–33.

Howieson, C. and Iannelli, C. (2008) 'The effects of low attainment on young people's outcomes at age 22–23 in Scotland', *British Educational Research Journal*, vol 34, pp 269–90.

Ijaz, A. and Abbas, T. (2010) 'The impact of intergenerational change on the attitudes of working class South Asian Muslim parents on the education of their daughters', *Gender and Education*, vol 22, pp 313–26.

Lehmann, W. (2009) 'University as vocational education: working-class students' expectations for university', *British Journal of Sociology of Education*, vol 30, pp 137–49.

Mirza, H.S. (1992) *Young Female and Black*, London: Routledge.

Modood, T. (1998) 'Ethnic minorities' drive for qualifications', in T. Modood and T. Acland (eds) *Race and Higher Education*, London: Policy Studies Institute.

Modood, T. (2006) 'Ethnicity, Muslims and higher education in Britain', *Teaching in Higher Education*, vol 11, pp 247–50.

Modood, T. and Shiner, M. (1994) *Ethnic Minorities and Higher Education: Why Are There Differential Rates of Entry?*, London: Policy Studies Institute.

National Audit Office (2007) 'Staying the course: the retention of students in higher education', Report by the Comptroller and Auditor General, July. Available at: www.nao.org.uk/publications/nao_reports/06/07/0607616es.htm (accessed 19 August 2010).

Osler, A. (1999) 'The educational experiences and career aspirations of black and ethnic minority undergraduates', *Race, Ethnicity and Education*, vol 2, pp 39–58.

Pathak, S. (2000) 'Race research for the future: ethnicity in education, training and the labour market', DfEE Research Topic Paper 1, Department of Education and Employment.

Pinnock, K., Watt, P., Ahmad, N., Thandi, K. and Morgan, A. (2008) 'Embedding equality and diversity in the curriculum: developing and disseminating effective practice', final report, Policy Research Institute, University of Wolverhampton.

Putnam, R.D. (2000) *Bowling Alone*, New York: Simon and Schuster.

Reay, D., Ball, S. and David, M. (2002) 'It's taking me a long time but I'll get there in the end: mature students on access courses and higher education choice', *British Educational Research Journal*, vol 28, pp 5–19.

Richardson, J.T.E. (2008) 'The attainment of ethnic minority students in UK higher education', *Studies in Higher Education*, vol 33, pp 33–48.

Shiner, M. and Modood, T. (2002) 'Help or hindrance? Higher education and the route to ethnic equality', *British Journal of Sociology of Education*, vol 23, pp 209–32.

Tomlinson, S. (2008) *Race and Education: Policy and Politics in Britain*, Maidenhead: Open University Press/McGraw Hill.

TTA (Teacher Training Agency) (2000) *Raising the Attainment of Minority Ethnic Pupils: Guidance and Resource Materials for Providers of Initial Teacher Training*, London: TTA.

Watson, D. (2006) 'How to think about widening participation in UK higher education', discussion paper for HEFCE by Institute of Education, University of London. Available at: http://www.tlrp.org (accessed 15 October 2010).

NINE

Widening participation in the higher education quasi-market: diversity, learning and literacy

Rob Smith

Introduction

A starting point for this chapter is an understanding that the demands of global competition and the development of a 'knowledge economy' in the late 20th and early 21st centuries have led to the inception of a new 'mass' higher education (HE) service. Alongside this, within all sectors of education in England, there has been a strengthening of quasi-marketisation as a mechanism for improving 'standards'. Among the pieces of legislation underpinning these policies, the Further and Higher Education Act 1992 laid the foundations for a distinct stratification of universities: new universities entered the newly formed 'market' to compete with more established (so-called 'red brick') universities; with Oxford and Cambridge forming the crust of 'excellence'. But, while the new massification of HE might suggest increased social mobility and the expansion of middle-class privilege and general prosperity, instead, particularly since New Labour took office in 1997, social divisions appear to have widened and social mobility has stalled (Nunn et al., 2007). Issues of great concern have been expressed in a Cabinet Office report, *Unleashing Aspiration: The Final Report on the Panel on Fair Access to the Professions*, which sees improving access to 'professional' jobs as a key policy driver in the coming years (Cabinet Office, 2009).

Alongside an entrenchment of social division and privilege, cultural strands of late modernity have emphasised individual/group identities. Theory has opened up new perspectives and brought positive political benefits, but the kind of solidarity that was connected to social class in the first part of the 20th century has fragmented. So, while a sense of who we are and to which social groups we belong has strengthened (in terms of 'race', gender, disability, social class origins, etc), this radical awareness has not led to coordinated and collective challenges to policies and structures. Instead, these identities seem to have interacted with the market context in ways that have served to deepen structural problems of social injustice.

In 2009, the crisis in policies of market fundamentalism resulting from the collapse of trust in the global and local banking system signalled the possibility of a historic shift. However, the Comprehensive Spending Review (HM Treasury, 2010) that followed heralded significant cuts in public spending and contained no indication of any retreat from the market fundamentalism that led up to the crisis. So what does this mean for HE and teachers in HE? And how is the legacy of 20 years of marketisation manifested within classrooms in HE?

This chapter draws on my experience of teaching in a specific post-1992 HE setting and, after outlining the context of the Post Graduate Certificate in Education (PGCE) course, develops a discussion of two critical incidents (Tripp, 1994) involving a single class to explore these questions. Two vignettes are developed and the analysis that follows is used to flesh out how critical pedagogy can proceed and tackle the issues arising within a 'diverse' classroom.

The Post Graduate Certificate in Education and the post-compulsory education context

The group of students that this chapter centres on was a cohort of 20 would-be Literacy teachers. People recruited to this course are not required to have experience of teaching – but many are mature students bringing with them a wealth of experience from previous work and careers. The PGCE course is for students wishing to teach in post-compulsory education (PCE) contexts. For Literacy teachers, many of these contexts fall under the loose banner of Skills for Life provision; they can range from adult and ex-offender education, to Key Skills and Communications classes attached to vocational courses for 14–19 year olds. This 'integrated' PGCE course differs from the 'generic' PGCE in its inclusion of the assessment of subject specialist knowledge. What this means in practice is that students come from a variety of disciplines at degree level. Many may have studied humanities subjects, but they are required to develop their knowledge base to embrace the Literacy subject specialism in addition to learning pedagogical skills. The course makes use of critical reflection (Brookfield, 1995; Moon, 2002; Bolton, 2005) as a primary learning tool. It actively suggests to students that the teaching 'self' that will emerge during the course is deeply rooted in who they already are.

Students on the PGCE study a number of complementary modules. Alongside those modules that focus on students' development of a teacher's identity and those that focus on Literacy subject specialist knowledge, other modules look at the policy context of further education (FE) and curriculum issues. The quasi-market that FE was plunged into following the Further and Higher Education Act (see Smith, 2007) appears to have made it more vulnerable to instrumentalist and economised policy perspectives than schools, and the 'market-led' curriculum is a key feature of this vulnerability. Critiques of this policyscape have been many (eg Ainley and Bailey, 1997; Shain and Gleeson, 1999; Coffield, 2008). In 2001, in what appears to have been an attempt to reinforce the localism of instrumentalist policy, the Further Education Funding Council was replaced by another quango: the Learning and Skills Council (LSC). What has emerged after more than 15 years of experimentation with quasi-marketisation is a sector in which, year on year, provision and employment within colleges is increasingly unstable. Because colleges have to respond to incentives provided by their local LSC (and these sometimes change within the academic year (see BBC News, 2009), and shift provision to courses that draw down more money, this means that the FE curriculum is inherently unstable, 'restructuring' is a regular activity and employment consequently is secure only on a year-by-year basis.

The recent proposed reforms to the funding of HE appear to be steering it towards a quasi-marketisation and a funding-centredness not dissimilar from that experienced by the FE sector. Within the instrumentalist hegemony that currently grips the English education policy agenda, it might be assumed that a teacher education course for students aspiring to teach in the FE sector would see its task as churning out teacher-technicians perfectly equipped to administer 'the hand maiden of British industry' (Ainley and Bailey, 1997, p 14). However, as most of the staff teaching on the course in question are themselves refugees from the FE sector, a more challenging route has been plotted, one which involves confronting 'lost innocence' (Brookfield, 1995, p 239) and the unpalatable truth of a sector in which the thrust of economised policy militates against a set of deeply (teacherly?) held principles that see education primarily in humanistic and developmental terms.

All FE student-teachers have to come to terms with a managerialist hegemony engendered by this policyscape that sees assessment primarily in terms of outputs and performance. For Literacy teachers, there are particular pressures that can be summarised as follows: funding imperatives necessitate 'outputs' that are measured by online assessment tools; these are centrally assessed and prescriptive multiple choice assessments that test reading comprehension and technical accuracy; these have led to reductive approaches in which holistic Literacy Education has been displaced by the necessity of 'teaching to the test' in order to draw down funding (for a fuller discussion, see Literacy Study Group, 2008). The view of Literacy that underpins this is a decontextualised and 'autonomous' one (Street, 2003) that views students as defective repositories of skills who require 'upskilling' to make them employable.

The challenges for teacher educators in these circumstances are considerable. While the exigencies of supporting students as they learn to teach are demanding enough, familiarising students with the ideological and funding context of the sector almost makes the job impossible. The course seeks to open up these contradictions to the critical gaze of the students; but at times it does feel as though we are encouraging them to cultivate, providing them with seeds and trowels and then pushing them out on to a concrete slab.

Despite the continual emergence of policy initiatives targeted at areas connected to Literacy provision (eg Train to Gain launched in 2006/07), the naked instrumentalism of many of these presents an increasingly unattractive and alienating picture to would-be Literacy teachers: their target-led funding often seeming to reduce students to 'bums on seats' and to reduce education to spoon-feeding. In this context, the role of teacher educators is to walk the fine line between enabling students to access an accurate and realistic overview of the workplaces they are seeking to enter and offering support and encouragement to them in the face of a hostile environment that militates against the effective practice of many pedagogical principles.

The tutor group

Year on year, the profile of students recruited to the PGCE PCE tends to be very diverse. Typically, only around a third are in their early twenties, having just completed a degree. Students are much more likely to have returned to study after a number of years working and to be mature students whose route into higher education was through Access to HE classes or (distance) learning with the Open University. The cohort of the 20 Literacy students who provide the focus for this chapter was no exception to the rule.

As the university where the course is based is located within a large conurbation that includes Birmingham and the Black Country, the student population is diverse in terms of ethnicity or 'race' and the Literacy tutor group reflected this. Rather than going down a methodological route that would seek to categorise the complex diversity of the group in a technicist way, I prefer to suggest that in terms of diverse identities (that draw on categories of social class, 'race', sexual orientation, life experience/age, notions of dis/ability and educational background) any group of students in a 'new', post-1992 university context is likely to warrant the label 'diverse' and indeed this probably extends to *any* group of HE students – the *degree* of diversity probably being the more significant distinction.

The Literacy PGCE connects with this diversity inasmuch as students' identities are invoked as a starting point for reflective writing and then become a focus for reflexive study as students research their own language and literacy histories. This, coupled with the critical reflection that provides the spine of the course, invariably leads to intense teaching and learning encounters and as a teacher educator this has sometimes prompted me to ask the question: is the course *too* personal? And, if it does demand labour of such a personal kind, how does it encourage students to actively apply this self-knowledge in teaching and learning situations?

The rest of this chapter will explore the challenges of teaching a diverse student group and how that can be theorised through the concept of a 'community of practice' (Lave and Wenger, 1991). Lave and Wenger's concept has been much applied in educational settings (see eg Kimble and Hildreth, 2008). Particularly relevant in this case would be the work by the Literacy Study group (2010), which explores the different applications of the concept and relates it to PGCE students as they move towards qualification as FE teachers. In this study, the tutor group becomes the 'community of practice' through a sense of shared purpose and experience. This challenges the perspectives of others (eg Avis et al., 2002) who used the term to theorise the entrance of students into the community of practice of FE teaching.

In this case, the difference is that the concept is actively used and reflexively applied in a constructivist way. At its most basic, the community of practice concept 'impl[ies] participation in an activity system about which participants share understandings concerning what they are doing and what this means in their lives and for their communities' (Lave and Wenger, 1991, pp 97–8). But, while the concept is most often used to explore the entry of 'apprentices' into an established 'activity system' as they learn to become full members of that system, this piece of writing pulls the focus tighter and conceptualises the tutor group itself as the community. This innovation came about for two main reasons: first, because the notion of 'community' could only be used in a hopelessly generalised way when applied to the huge range of roles described by the term 'teaching in PCE'; and, second, and more pragmatically, the concept served a practical purpose in helping the students in the tutor group to construct a sense of group identity.

Having provided some background about the PGCE course and outlined the context of Literacy as a subject specialism, this chapter will now move on to look at two critical incidents (as experienced by me, the teacher) involving the case study cohort.

Two narrative moments from the course

This section will look at two distinct yet interrelated critical incidents drawn from my experience of being the tutor to this specific tutor group of Literacy specialists. I have presented these as two vignettes or brief descriptive narratives. On the other hand, though, it is attractive to see each as a link in a larger, unfolding narrative. After each vignette, I will present some analysis before offering some concluding remarks.

Vignette 1: Literacy Theories and Frameworks and cultural capital

This first vignette centres on one module of the programme, a module called Literacy Theories and Frameworks. This module is the primary vehicle for introducing students to the technical and grammatical features of English. This aspect of the content relates directly to the Adult Literacy Core Curriculum (ALCC), a matrix of knowledge about language that quickly assumed a prescriptive orthodoxy when it was launched in 2001, and which was underpinned by the *Subject Specifications for Teachers of Adult Literacy and Numeracy* (DES, 2002).[1] To that extent, some of the more esoteric, linguistic and grammatical concepts were familiar to only a small number of students in the group, notably those who had studied modern foreign languages or had recently undertaken A level English.[2] The students within the group all came to the course with diverse prior educational experience. This extended from students who had educational parabola that followed the more 'traditional' route of GCSEs to A levels through to degree level in a virtually unbroken progression to students whose experience of compulsory education ended at 16 and who had then returned to education, some via an Access to HE route, some years later.

What this meant in practice was that some students were encountering technical terms and concepts for the first time, while others (a much smaller number) were already confident and familiar with them. Many students felt diffident in this module. This diffidence arose from their lack of familiarity with grammatical terms and from their concern that this knowledge constituted the knowledge base of what was to become their subject specialism in their college placements. This anxiety was compounded by the fact that many of the students had joined the course seeking to specialise in their degree subject but, due to a limited number of placements in these subjects, had been steered towards Literacy Education. As the module progressed, it became apparent to me as tutor that while there were some students (those already familiar with the content) who were very vocal and keen to share their knowledge and push ahead, many of the others were confused and anxious because they were struggling to understand the technical content. The anxiety increased as we prepared to move on to looking at theoretical models of Literacy pedagogy.

It was at this point that I decided to call a halt and revisit the areas of knowledge that some students were still uncertain about. I ran the first part of the following session as a revision session, with games and practice activities designed to increase students' confidence. Significantly, I informed the class as a whole that students who felt comfortable did not need to attend. The result of this was that the already knowledgeable, vocal students stayed away. The students who attended openly expressed their fear at not being able to understand and how they felt their confidence eroded further when sitting alongside students who already seemed to know it all. The extra session and support seemed to go some way to resolving the situation.

Discussion: cultural capital and Critical Literacy Education

It could be argued that the problems I encountered in these sessions originated in a failure to differentiate adequately. There might be some truth in this. Certainly, the extent of the dichotomy in prior knowledge and understanding that became apparent among the students was unexpected. But more unexpected for me was how students invested great cultural significance in the understanding of grammar. From my perspective, this aspect of the module was much less important than the sessions that covered Literacy pedagogy and encouraged them to apply it to their own practice. I viewed dealing with word classes, cohesion and morphology – though enjoyable from a crossword enthusiast's perspective – as a largely redundant aspect of the module because although the knowledge, acquired across a teaching career, might enrich their experience as practitioners, many aspects of it would rarely feature in a useful way in any Literacy class. The students, however, felt differently. The anxiety they felt about grasping the concepts seemed to me to be out of all proportion to their real significance until I started to reflect on the situation.

The introduction of the ALCC following the Moser Report of 1999 was designed to assist in the assessment and understanding of students' existing literacy levels. This matrix became a tool for standardising and underpinning a reductive view of what constituted Literacy – a model that understood Literacy as the acquisition of a body of knowledge rooted in a monolithic (rather than historically contextual and contingent) view of standard English. Unfortunately, the ALCC has led in some cases to a very mechanistic application in which Literacy educators teach students through a whole set of technical terms that probably, in themselves, constitute an additional barrier to progress (see Literacy Study Group, 2008). It is not difficult to see the Literacy PGCE as potentially propping up this ideological prescription, mainly because of a set of learning outcomes for this particular module that (being prescribed by the overseeing UK Standards and Verification Agency) enshrine this valorisation of standard forms of English and associated knowledge. This inevitably ends up privileging some students over others.

Critical analysis of this issue can usefully draw on Bourdieu's notion of 'cultural capital' (Bourdieu, 2000), which can be described as the accumulated skills and knowledge of an individual acquired through family, educational and other social experiences and then strategically deployed – potentially to the advantage of the individual. The grammatical component of the module was invested symbolically with the cultural capital that some students brought with them to the course and others did not. In other words, there appeared to be a correlation between social class background and/or the prior educational experiences of students and the extent to which they already had a grasp of the grammatical frameworks of standard English.

Within the classroom, then, we had a playing out of what the impact of cultural capital can have in a diverse learning setting. What that meant was that certain students were vociferous and eager to contribute, to relate the knowledge they already had to the content of the sessions. The selfhood *they* brought to the classroom was affirmed. For others, who did not have this prior knowledge, these vocal contributions had a dispiriting effect. Their deficit of the cultural capital that is privileged within educational settings according to Bourdieu (and the ALCC) was highlighted. The power that ownership of this capital confers carries an aura that can disable those excluded before they even engage – if it is allowed to. The classroom, then, became an arena in which the social order was uncritically replicated rather than challenged.

My rearguard action, in which additional support and extra time was offered, went some way to undoing the harm and the sense of resentment and/or helpless incomprehension that had developed among this group of students. The purpose of these complementary sessions was as much to build students' confidence that they *did* have the ability to grasp the concepts as it was to practise applying the knowledge. In addition to this, the sessions on Literacy pedagogy came to my aid. It happened through an attempt to apply the theories of Critical Literacy Education (see Spener, 1992; Van Duzer and Florez, 1999) to the group. This involved me making transparent some of the forces at work and articulating an acknowledgement of the 'diversity' of the prior educational experiences of the group. There was a broad range of starting points, and an understanding of this needed to form part of the background consciousness of all group members as the 'new' knowledge was accessed. From there, an explicit insistence on a mutually supportive and safe environment, in which the pace of learning took account of everyone's needs was re-established.

Drawing again on Bourdieu, we can make sense of what happened through the concept of *habitus* (Bourdieu, 1990). *Habitus* is a complex concept that can be interpreted as ways of living and thinking and the influence these have on the actions of an individual in different situations. *Habitus* links back to the collective historical background of an individual and encompasses the values, behaviour and expectations of that individual, highlighting how these shape the choices they make in social situations. The extent to which students within the group were 'comfortable' with the material being studied is the issue here, but, beyond that, there is the disparate range of historical and familial experiences of operating and belonging in *educational* settings: some students belonged to the first generation to feel 'comfortable' in any educational setting.

Comfort, familiarity, confidence – for the classroom to work effectively, these needed to become the explicit aims of all members of the group through interactive collective consciousness – not the preserve of just a handful. Directing the attention of the group to the tacit operation of conflicting *habituses* might be the first step to addressing its negative impact within the classroom. Reay et al. (2005, p 28) highlight how critical reflection provides inroads into what might seem an overly deterministic concept: 'Implicit in the concept is that *habitus* operates at an unconscious level unless individuals confront events which cause self-questioning, whereupon *habitus* begins to operate at the level of consciousness and the person develops new facets of the self'.

The acknowledgement and making transparent the subtext of conflict within the classroom enabled reflection and communicative action. The experiences of disjuncture, discomfort and diffidence were acknowledged and transformed via reflective practice.

It would be wrong of me to claim that by the end of the module everyone felt equally at home with the technical content of the module, but the demystification of standard English as a dialect that through historical contingency and struggle has assumed pre-eminence over other dialects dispelled some of the aura and advantage of ownership that some students brought with them. Or, to flip it over, this approach dispelled some of the constraints of *habitus*, since some students had insisted that this knowledge could not belong to them.

Sociolinguistics makes use of the notion of idiolect (Hudson, 1991, p 185). This is the linguistic fingerprint of an individual. The idea is that we each of us carry inscribed within the language we use evidence of our social class background, our family history, our geographical origins (through dialect words and phrases), our cultural dispositions and capital. This is not conceived of as a monolithic repository. Instead, it is shaped by the different social networks we belong to – different language resources are called upon in different settings (Holmes, 2001, p 184).

There is a powerful argument for conceiving of the existing knowledge HE students bring with them to the classroom in a similar way. The important point behind this is that an acknowledgement of the individual and idiosyncratic knowledge base of each student is a prerequisite for engagement with new knowledge. The knowledge fingerprint or *idio-episteme* of each student provides the starting point for any educational enterprise. A shared understanding of the different knowledge bases students bring with them needs to form an early part in the unfolding of any HE experience.

This connects to another key theoretical tool that sits at the centre of my understanding of these incidents: that of the community of practice. Although the course was only in its early stages, already the need for some work to be done on the group-as-a-group was becoming apparent. The next critical incident, which followed soon after, made this imperative.

Vignette 2: Self and Identity: the collaborative seminar and the nascent community of practice

The second narrative moment I want to present arose in the spinal module of the PGCE programme called Self and Identity. This module initially focuses on practical considerations and the development of reflective practice before opening up a much broader vista of theoretical concepts and encouraging students to apply these to their ongoing teaching experience. One of the early components of the module requires the students to work in groups of three or four, to research a concept linked to their development as practitioners (eg professionalism, Literacy pedagogy, planning teaching and learning) and to deliver a seminar to the rest of the group. I allowed the groups to be self-selecting and I encouraged them to agree on a topic that seemed most relevant and interesting to group members. One student was away and, as placements were on half-term break the following week, I encouraged groups to plan ahead and set up meetings in which they could discuss and put together their seminar.

While the self-selection of groups was under way, I became aware that there were some strong feelings at work in terms of who was working with whom. One or two students started with one group and then switched, ostensibly to a preferred topic or because no group could have more than five members. This period of swapping round seemed to resolve itself and I reassured myself that this exercise in working together as mutually supportive peers was an important aspect of their professional development. I assigned the absent student to one group that had been left with only two members at the end of this process. My intervention in this brought together three students from different backgrounds and with different life experiences. My assumption was that together they would be able to make the group work as although there was diversity in the groups, these were adults whom I assumed had the intellectual and emotional resources to meet the challenges of the task.

As the date of the seminar approached, the group that was constructed at my direction seemed to be having problems meeting and communicating. I was copied into various emailed exchanges and feelings were seemingly running high. Then, on the evening before the seminars were due to be delivered, one member of that group asked to speak to me and described how there had been a heated argument between two group members. Accusations had been made about levels of participation, effort and commitment. Both students were hurt and angry about what had been said and it was being suggested that the group could not work together.

Before the session the next morning, I spoke to another member of the class who had witnessed the argument to ensure I had a rounded picture of the issues and what had happened. The disagreement stemmed from the different backgrounds, expectations and life histories of the group members. One student was totally focused on the course, the other had a young family and had a busy family life outside her studies. My complacent position that the diversity issue would take care of itself as these were all adults had hit a huge iceberg. This ship was sinking. Intervention was required and I decided on a course of action. But I felt nervous about proceeding as – although I had spent 20 years teaching in settings in which student groups were diverse and had taught about diversity and dealt with a multitude of incidents – these felt like uncharted waters for me because my plan was to tackle the incident more or less head on.

Following on from the last critical incident, I wanted to make transparent the tensions that had been bubbling under with the idea that making them visible would give all of us some purchase on how they were shaping relationships within the group as a whole. One reason for this was that I felt that the argument between the two individuals was in reality an expression of a much bigger group dynamic and perhaps also a mirroring of wider social tensions.

I was helped by being able to reach for the concept of the 'community of practice' (Lave and Wenger, 1991; Literacy Study Group, 2010), which figured as an important theoretical tenet in the model of reflective practice that the course championed – although this was usually introduced much later. For the first 45 minutes of that morning's session I talked to the whole group about where we were. In many ways, this diverse group of people would not join together in a shared enterprise in any other circumstances. The common goal to become Literacy educators was the unifying factor; that and a willingness to engage with the considerable challenges presented by the course. But the process of 'becoming' a Literacy teacher was difficult: it necessitated centring their emergent teacher's identity on who they were while also relating that to the different backgrounds and needs of 20 other individuals. I declared that I as tutor was another cohesive force as I was committed to using my agency to support everyone in the room to complete the course successfully. Coming together as a tutor group, as a nascent community of practice, required nuanced and sensitive interactions; but these relationships were a micro-politics, a playing out of principles and values that required *work* on their part.

That is more or less what I said. Despite the theoretical framework I invoked, it felt emotional. All the class knew that something was up. It was early days on placement and people were stressed. I do not know what they expected, but they sat and listened. Some contributed their own insights. Some of these contributions brought cheers and clapping from the group as a whole. It felt like I had achieved my aim: to make the unspoken visible and to try to tease out the knotty and seemingly intractable warp and weft of a complex group dynamic and make it an object for reflection. That was the first step. The real work had to be undertaken by the class members themselves. Having done the coordination, I knew that it was up to the individuals involved to resolve the conflict. I was relieved to see that the group caught up in the dispute had come together and was busy reconnecting and sorting the situation out in a separate room. After a quarter of an hour they reappeared and the seminars began. They delivered their seminar the following week.

Discussion: theorising the diverse community of practice

This episode saw the group reach a critical point in their understanding of themselves as individuals belonging within a cohesive 'community'. The conflict at the heart of the incident stemmed from one student believing the other was not actively enough taking responsibility for the group seminar. On the other student's part, there was a perception that the first student had an existing knowledge base and cultural capital that provided considerable comparative advantage. Once again, the diversity of the group was highlighting issues of knowledge and its 'ownership' as a source of potential conflict.

Reflection and communal communicative action

There is something inherently courageous and even extraordinary about expecting students to work on and develop a new identity as an integral aspect of an HE course. This is what underpins the PGCE course: the notion that a teaching identity can be consciously constructed. But while critical reflection through journal writing might provide the primary tool for achieving this, that suggests solitary endeavour. This critical incident highlights the importance of a collective dimension in reflective practice. Critical reflection involves individuals reaching beyond and outside the boundaries of their own experience and has the potential to challenge, but also extend and contribute to, their knowledge base. Brookfield asserts:

> Critical reflection is an irreducibly social process. It happens best when we enlist colleagues to help us see our practice in new ways. For many teachers, the best chance they have to learn critical reflection is through conversation with peers. (Brookfield, 1995, p 141)

As the PGCE course is founded on students constructing their identity as a teacher, in order to undertake this, they need to draw on the resource of existing experience. To that extent, identity is approached as 'already–in–place', as historically produced and, therefore, at the beginning of the course, essentialist. But the course moves beyond this in several ways. To start with, an important aspect of the learning process involves student teachers engaging with the idea of differentiation – which at its broadest means recognising the different origins and needs of the students in a group and accommodating these within the learning environment. With the group of student teachers that this chapter focuses on, in true reflexive style, it became necessary to materialise this notion of differentiation within the class because the different identities, encouraged to assert themselves, did not 'automatically' achieve harmonious relations. In other words, while an important aspect of the course was the exploration and articulation of identity (*What makes me who I am?*), another and equally important aspect became: *how do I manage myself-among-others in order to nurture and sustain a learning environment?* One way of conceptualising this journey is to see it as starting with an exploration of identity as essentialist and then shifting the focus to identity as *also* relational.

Gilroy (2000) is one of many writers on identity to explore the implications of the cultural identities that have emerged since the 1960s in the developed world. Developing a critique of 'race' and 'raciology', while acknowledging the importance of 'the magic of identity', Gilroy (2000, p 101) stresses the need to move beyond these formulations. His perspective is future–oriented and one that privileges a 'cosmopolitan' outlook that acknowledges the past but is motivated by a political imagining of the future. In this practical pedagogical context, within the diverse HE classroom setting, the unmediated 'magic of identity' led to unproductive and entrenching conflict. Given that, an educational environment had to be imagined that moved beyond a mere replication of social division and inequality.

The work the group then did was more than heuristic as it involved a much deeper level of engagement and reflection to facilitate 'communicative action'. Robinson (1999, p 2) defines communicative action – a concept drawn from the German critical theorist Jurgen Habermas – like this:

> Communicative action can be understood as a circular process in which the actor is two things in one: (i) an initiator, who masters situations through actions for which he is accountable and (ii) a product of the transitions

> surrounding him, of groups whose cohesion is based
> on solidarity to which he belongs, and of processes of
> socialisation in which he is reared.

Habermas uses the idea of communicative action to describe how human beings can bring about rational change in the world. There is an inherently social aspect to the concept that Robinson does not quite capture. Communicative action takes place when acts of communication are 'coordinated not through egocentric calculations of success but through acts of reaching understanding' (Habermas, 1986, p 286). Taken together, these definitions suggest that communicative action brings together some of the concepts already visited. Communicative action could stand in for collective reflective practice. In this case, it was also the meeting point for multiple diverse understandings of the world – of conflicting *habituses* – and their interleaving within some kind of sustainable fellowship.

In the tutor group environment, the difference that people felt constituted their identities and their different cultural experience was supported, but there was also an insistence on the 'decentred background consciousness of the relativity of one's own standpoint' (Habermas, 2002, p 150) that both facilitated and was affirmed by an emerging cohesion. This did not involve a suppression of self, but an adaptation to accommodate others' difference. The diversity of the classroom meant that we were not able automatically to rely upon a shared set of understandings and cultural reference points and this became an issue that needed to be made transparent. The confrontation between the two students presented an opportunity for the working out of what the group identity meant. From it, a particular kind of space could be established, a discursive, critical, mutually supportive learning environment – a consciousness that sustained them in their placement practice.[3]

Different knowledge types

Another way of viewing the operation of a community of practice of this kind is through an epistemological lens. In those terms, the community of practice can be seen as a locus of interaction between empirical and informal knowledge and official, 'legitimised' knowledge (Housee, 2006) as students move into and out of different social domains. Each domain has an associated bundle of appropriate knowledge, language and behaviour. The individual has their home space – associated with informal knowledge, the language of friends and family, behaviour associated with home-making and leisure. The learning space of their placement invokes different knowledge, primarily their subject specialism, but also, as the course progresses, the student should be able to apply and experiment with theory; appropriate language and behaviour may feel more formal as the student encounters different models of teacher identity (i.e. teachers) and strives to actualise their own preferred approach. For Literacy teachers, a personal awareness of their everyday use of non-dialect as opposed to standard forms of English may become a significant issue. Finally, there is the learning space in the university. If the community of practice model is used, this space should be able to create a bridge of understanding between the two other domains.

The progress made in establishing a teaching group as a community of practice might follow a trajectory of gradually mapping congruence between the *idio-epistemes* of different group members and thereby shaping a shared understanding that enables solidarity. To bring this about, knowledge has to be demystified and uncoupled from its associations with cultural capital. While students may be coming in with different levels of knowledge, for some, perceptions of the 'superior' knowledge of others can become a barrier to them making progress and stall the process by which they claim ownership of the new knowledge. This suggests the importance of the relational, communal self when we are talking about critical interactions with knowledge and critical education.

Table 9.1: The interaction of different domains and different types of knowledge

Domain	Home	University	Placement
Actants	**Family, friends**	*Peers, university tutors*	*Placement teachers, students at placement colleges*
Knowledge	**Informal, empirical**	*Informal, empirical and legitimised*	*Legitimised/sanctioned knowledge*
Language	**Informal**	*Dialect forms in discussion but including formal and 'theoretical' diction*	*Standard as opposed to dialect forms*
Behaviour	**Domestic activities but also reflecting, reading and writing**	*Discussion, reflection, sharing experience, reading*	*Observing teaching, teaching*

There is an obvious epistemological position underpinning the learning experience within a community of practice: that is, one in which knowledge is conceptualised as disinterested, as a tool for human use, as belonging (in absolute and exclusive terms) to *no one* and therefore as claimable by *anyone*. This way of thinking about knowledge was crucial in dealing with the issue of standard English and the technical frameworks associated with grammar. Once stated, it neutralised the aura that, for some students, activated and electrified *habitus* boundaries.

That said, it is unhelpful to talk about knowledge as inert. Knowledge production in a critical community of practice is not via transmission, but has to be reached through reflection facilitated by the teacher; this is assisted through the development of a sense of shared purpose. The project of critical educational practice is to recognise and acknowledge the *idio-episteme* of each student as the proper starting point for any educational process. The interaction that occurs in the classroom should involve the exploration of how those *idio-epistemes* relate to each other and then to the new, sanctioned, curricular knowledge.

I have not as yet in this chapter talked about conceptualisations of power. The way power operated through knowledge as an aspect of cultural capital (about grammar and language in this case) within the classroom needs to form part of the discussion on learning in HE settings characterised by diversity. Foucault (1982, p 779) talks usefully about the interrelationships between power and 'the subject' and how these take the form of 'struggles' that go beyond simply being 'anti-authority'. One category of such struggles he links to knowledge and sees as 'in opposition to the effects of power that are linked with knowledge, competence and qualification' – this category he calls 'the regime du savoir' (Foucault, 1982, p 779). This connects cogently with the tutor group's troubled engagement with the language knowledge at the heart of the ALCC. Foucault also suggests that power operates in such a way as to make subjects 'an effect of power': 'This form of power applies itself to immediate everyday life which categorises the individual, marks him by his own individuality, attaches him to his own identity' (Foucault, 1982, p 780).

In this context, the classroom became a place in which different existing subjects – those brought into the room that reflected inequalities in terms of 'racial' and social (and educational) class backgrounds – could be affirmed or challenged. A lack of intervention on my part was leading towards a simple replication of these subjects. But, by promoting and scaffolding the community of practice model, the classroom instead became a place in which subjects could be reformed to acknowledge the other and the until-then unspoken conflict and inequality within the group. This power was then channelled into critical group reflection in order to (echo Foucault and) ask the question of the group: 'Who are we?' (Foucault, 1982, p 781).

In some ways, this chapter has focused simply on my attempts to model consistency: *to walk the talk* as it were. How could I teach about Literacy Education – many of whose principles I believe in – without putting those principles into practice? I have been privileged to have spent my entire career as a teacher working in 'diverse' classrooms; but prior to this particular cohort, I had never felt it so totally necessary to make visible the way knowledge and cultural capital operate through people as an aspect of power. It felt to me that the students' sense of themselves as individuals was highly developed, but that this created conflict; that the benefits of being a member of a diverse group and the work on these selves that membership required was unfamiliar to them. I have carried it forward as an integral aspect of my practice since. The use of the 'communities of practice' concept has helped. In retrospect, though, this was a special group. They made me learn.

The model of pedagogy being used here may relate to hooks' notion of critical, engaged pedagogy (hooks, 1994) inasmuch as the way education takes place – the interactions of students and teaching staff with knowledge in learning environments – is conceived as political in and of itself. As such, the notion of a neutral and neutered education that involves some kind of 'transmission' of knowledge (as reified and enshrined in the term 'lecturer' and the practice it implies) is problematised.

Conclusions

So, after 20 years of an English education system that has strengthened the use of the quasi-market as a tool of organisation and improving quality, what are the challenges that face HE teachers and how can we organise to meet with them? Through the discussion of these vignettes, I hope the extent to which the tutor's role is necessarily political has become clear. For teacher educators, the community of practice becomes an organising principle; it facilitates a development and articulation of student teachers' identities rather than shoehorning them into a prescribed and hegemonic mould.

Within this, it is my contention that diversity cannot be skirted around, but, rather, needs to sit at the centre of the educational experience. Dealing with diversity is not about achieving a consensus in terms of everyone's views being ironed flat to fit a normative template. Instead, it is more about creating an equilibrium in which different views (and values) are held in creative tension. If one of the stated aims of education is to promote equality within diversity (a recommendation of the Macpherson Report of 1999), then the classroom has to become a meeting point of diversity that is unlike any other and that contains the seeds of the just society that contrasts with the society (and world) we now inhabit. That means the micro-politics of the classroom, the interrelationships of individuals and how their different levels of social and cultural capital meet in the classroom, need to be explicitly addressed.

What we come back to is the idea that the diverse community of practice is a locus in which students have to consciously adapt, represent and mediate their individuality as one feature of a whole. Being oneself with an awareness of the selves of others and being oneself as part of the group becomes the focus. But the selves brought from outside (after 20 years of entrepreneurial, individualistic and market triumphalism) are likely to carry marks of the current cultural context. So the classroom becomes a place in which the social world as *it is* and as *it can be* is made visible. This demands work around identity and how the personal connects with knowledge in an educational space that seeks to be democratic. The issue of diversity can be mobilised as a part of this.

This may be a materialisation of 'pragmatic universalism' (Gilroy, 2000, p 356) that moves human thinking beyond 'petty differences' within our classrooms. Because, whether we like it or not, while the current crisis of market fundamentalism is likely to be messy and drawn out, this small-scale, local context has become the front line in the struggle against the divisive forces of a marketised educational and global 'lifeworld' (Habermas, 1986, p 82).

Notes

[1] As an example, these specifications include a section on 'grammatical frameworks' which requires Literacy teachers to: 'Demonstrate knowledge and understanding of the terminology related to: sub-lexical features (Content guidance: graphemes, digraph, trigraph, phoneme, blend onset, rime, syllable, morpheme, word roots and stems, diphthong)' (DES, 2002, p 12).

[2] It is tempting to see the overly prescribed grammar focus of the ALCC as being a late manifestation of the 'back to basics' content that originated in the so-called Black Papers of 1969 and that has become a feature of English across the national curriculum. Certainly, grammar and a similarly reductive

and technicist approach has been imposed on English as a subject at A level – as if in response to the charge that standards are slipping that resurfaces regularly in the tabloid media.

[3] I would not want to suggest that this was a completed project. We made a start. I have no doubt that if the course had been longer, other differences (around age and experience perhaps, or possibly around religious beliefs) might have become a focus for more communicative work.

References

Ainley, P. and Bailey, B. (1997) *The Business of Learning*, London: Cassell.

Avis, J., Bathmaker, A. and Parsons, J. (2002) 'Communities of practice and the construction of learners in post-compulsory education and training', *Journal of Vocational Education and Training*, vol 54, pp 27–49.

BBC News (2009) 'Fears over college training fund', 14 June. Available at: http://news.bbc.co.uk/1/hi/education/8101019.stm (accessed 21 July 2009).

Bolton, G. (2005) *Reflective Writing. Writing and Professional Development*, London: Paul Chapman.

Bourdieu, P. (1990) *The Logic of Practice*, Palo Alto: Stanford University Press.

Bourdieu, P. (2000) *Reproduction in Education, Society and Culture*, London: Sage.

Brookfield, S. (1995) *Becoming a Critically Reflective Teacher*, San Francisco: Jossey Bass.

Cabinet Office (2009) *Unleashing Aspiration: The Final Report on the Panel on Fair Access to the Professions*, London: HMSO. Available at: www.cabinetoffice.gov.uk/media/227102/fair-access.pdf (accessed 22 July 2009).

Coffield, F. (2008) *Just Suppose Teaching and Learning Became the First Priority*, London: LSN.

DES (Department for Education and Skills) (2002) *Subject Specifications for Teachers of Adult Literacy and Numeracy*, Available at: http://waes-elearn.waes.ac.uk/moodle-resources/Basic%20Skills/Delivery%20Skills/02_FENTO'S%20Sub_spec.pdf (accessed 30 September 2011).

Foucault, M. (1982) 'The subject and power', *Critical Inquiry*, vol 8, no 4, pp 777–95. Available at: http://www.jstor.org/stable/1343197 (accessed 13 May 2011).

Gilroy, P. (2000) *Between Camps*, Harmondsworth: Penguin Books.

Habermas, J. (1986) *The Theory of Communicative Action, Vol 1*, Cambridge: Polity Press.

Habermas, J. (2002) *Religion and Rationality*, Cambridge, MA: MIT.

HM Treasury (2010) 'Spending review 2010'. Available at: http://cdn.hm-treasury.gov.uk/sr2010_completereport.pdf (accessed 5 November 2010).

Holmes, J. (2001) *An Introduction to Social Linguistics*, Harlow: Pearson Education Limited.

hooks, b. (1994) *Teaching to Transgress: Education as the Practice of Freedom*, Routledge: London.

Housee, S. (2006) 'Battlefields of knowing: facilitating controversial classroom debates', in S. Spencer and M.J. Todd (eds) *Reflections on Practice: Teaching Race and Ethnicity in Further and Higher Education*, Birmingham: C-SAP, pp 54–70.

Hudson, R.A. (1991) *Sociolinguistics*, Cambridge: CUP.

Kimble, C. and Hildreth, P. (eds) (2008) *Communities of Practice: Creating Learning Environments for Educators*, Charlotte, NC: Information Age Publishing.

Lave, E. and Wenger, J. (1991) *Situated Learning: Legitimate Peripheral Participation*, Cambridge: CUP.

Literacy Study Group (2008) "Sometimes no amount of reflection or theory helps' – thoughts on the 'quality' of literacy provision across a range of Black Country providers', *Journal of Vocational Education and Training*, vol 60, pp 441–54.

Literacy Study Group (2010) 'The allegiance and experience of student literacy teachers in the post compulsory education context: competing communities of practice', *Journal of Education for Teaching*, vol 36, pp 5–19.

Macpherson of Cluny, W. (1999) *The Stephen Lawrence Inquiry*, HMSO: London.

Moon, J. (2002) *Reflection in Learning and Professional Development*, London: Kogan Page.

Nunn, A., Johnson, S., Monro, S., Bickerstaffe, T. and Kelsey, S. (2007) 'Factors influencing social mobility', Research Report No 450, Department for Work and Pensions. Available at: http://research.dwp.gov.uk/asd/asd5/rports2007-2008/rrep450.pdf (accessed 13 May 2011).

Reay, D., David, M.E. and Ball, S. (2005) *Degrees of Choice: Class, Race and Gender in Higher Education,* Stoke-on-Trent: Trentham Books.

Robinson, S. (1999) 'The Jurgen Habermas web resource'. Available at: http://www.msu.edu/user/robins11/habermas (accessed 22 July 2009).

Shain, F. and Gleeson, D. (1999) 'Teachers' work and professionalism in the post-incorporated further education sector', *Education and Social Justice*, vol 1, pp 55–63.

Smith, R. (2007) 'Work, identity and the quasi-market: the FE experience', *Journal of Educational Administration and History*, vol 39, pp 33–47.

Spener, D. (1992) 'The Freirean approach to adult literacy education', Center for Applied Linguistics. Available at: http://www.cal.org/caela/printer.php?printRefURL=http%3A//www.cal.org/caela/esl_resources/digests/FREIREQA.html (accessed 22 July 2009).

Street, B. (2003) 'What's "new" in New Literacy Studies? Critical approaches to literacy in theory and practice', *Current Issues in Comparative Education*, vol 5, pp 77–91, available at: www.tc.edu/cice/Archives/5.2/52street.pdf (accessed on 29 September 2001).

Tripp, D. (1994) 'Teachers' lives, critical incidents and professional practice', *Qualitative Studies in Education*, vol 7, pp 65–76.

Van Duzer, C. and Florez, M.A.C. (1999) 'Critical literacy for adult English language learners', CAELA. Available at: www.cal.org/caela/esl_resources/digests/critlit.html (accessed 3 March 2008).

TEN

Para crecer[1]: successful higher education strategies used by Latina[2] students

Pamela Hernandez and Diane M. Dunlap

Introduction

Many Latinas succeed in graduating from colleges and universities every year, in spite of statistics that tell them and us that they are unlikely to succeed. What can we learn from successful students? What can their successes say to others about how to succeed, and to colleges and universities that want them to succeed?

At the university where this study was conducted, Latino students had the lowest retention rate when compared to other ethnic groups or to the white majority (OUS, 2006). The numbers of Latinos and other minority ethnic groups graduating were no better. For instance, only 41% of white students, 37% of Asian students, 28% of Latino students, 22% of African-American students and 16% of Native American students graduated from this university within the designated four-year start-to-finish undergraduate programmes (OUS, 2006).

Unfortunately, these statistics of failure to thrive in a university are reflected across the US. In the 2000 US Census Bureau survey, 35.3 million Latinos were found to live in the US, indicating that Latinos had surpassed African-Americans as the largest minority ethnic group in the US (US Census, 2000a, 2000b). Yet this growth in population is not as evident when reviewing participation rates of Latinos in higher education (Campaign for College Opportunity, 2010). In 2005, white students represented 72% of enrolees at all four-year colleges and universities nationally, while black students represented 11% and Latino/as represented just over 6% (Horn, 2006). Only 11% of Latinos over the age of 25 hold a bachelor's degree, while 29% of white people and 25% of other non-Hispanics hold bachelor's degrees (Santiago et al., 2004). Nationally, Latinos graduate from colleges at a rate lower than any other group except Native Americans, who attend in even lower numbers than Latinos (Shore, 2005). Only 13% of Latinos got a college degree in California in 2003 (the largest Latino population in the US resides in California). This was compared to 15% for African-Americans, 31% for white people and 62% for Asian-Americans (Shore, 2005; Kelly et al, 2010). The gap increases when women's enrolment for each ethnic group is compared. In 2004, Latinas comprised only 11.6% of the female undergraduate enrolment in all colleges and universities, compared to 14.6% black women and 64.7% white women (NCES, 2006). Thus, Latinas consistently graduate at a lower than statistically proportionate rate (Arbona and Nora, 2007).

Latina students' educational experiences

While these numbers are helpful in evaluating general participation rates, interpreting specific data for Latinos is difficult. Many data sources do not distinguish native-born from immigrant Latinos and many different countries of origin are clumped together in the 'Latino' definition. Also, racial and ethnic categories include all socio-economic levels. In other words, the categories themselves include a wide range of variability. Identity issues, due to a person's identification with multiple cultures, ethnicities or ancestries, make it difficult to compartmentalise a single 'Latino' experience. In research studies, that means the variability within the sample population is likely to wash out any commonalities in experience.

On the other hand, the number of Latinas who attend college, stay in college, graduate from college and attend graduate school escalated during 1990–2010, surpassing gains made by any other historically under-represented group of students in higher education. When researchers asked about how increased rates of attendance could be accompanied by lower completion rates, they found culturally related issues. They reported that Latina achievements often come at great personal cost and challenge. For example, Gonzalez et al. (2004) related the challenge of meeting the family and cultural expectation to live at home while they attend college and the sacrifice of leaving home for college from the Latina students' perspective. Women felt guilty and happy when they were expected to live at home, but they also felt a sense of independence from the home in conjunction with family tensions because of the move away from home (see also Melendez and Melendez, 2010). The simple fact of pursuing higher education was fraught with cultural and personal tension, even before issues of academic performance came into play.

Particularly interesting in the Gonzales et al. and Melendez and Melendez studies are two consistent findings. Parents often expressed feelings of *need* for their daughter to stay at home because of their concern about 'who was going to take care of her'. This is a value and belief system Latinas have to confront; women are 'unable to take care of themselves' and can only be taken care of by parents, family and a spouse. Second, the sacrifice of leaving home for college was reported by the students to be less difficult than staying away from family. Junior and senior Latina women in this study continued to report being 'in turmoil' because they wanted to continue on to graduate school but not neglect family expectations.

What actually constitutes the day-to-day lived experience of Latinas in higher education is not well documented. Of previous research studies that provided some insights to us, most authors approached the academic success of Latinas primarily from a 'barriers and challenges' point of view. These studies used Latinos as a comparison group and focused on such predictors of failure as low motivation and academic unpreparedness (Kenny and Stryker, 1996; Rodriquez et al., 2000; Bordes et al., 2006). Other research studies focused on factors that might contribute to success, but more often acted as barriers to success (Phinney et al., 2005; Sy and Romero, 2008). Cultural factors included a strong sense of family interdependence and obligation to the family (Martin, 2010; Perrakis and Hagedorn, 2010). Individual factors comprised the multiple cultural identities Latino students had, the individual's 'motivation level' and individual career aspirations. In summary, researchers identified that there were barriers, mostly not overcome due to low motivation and career expectations, and less use of adequate social networks. In other words, the combined findings of the studies explained failure, but did not document strategies for success.

A few researchers looked at success strategies (Bonner, 2010). For example, Gloria et al. (2005) assessed the coping responses to stress by Mexican-heritage college women in relation to their reported sense of well-being. These researchers briefly described the conflict between the traditional stay-at-home, quiet roles expected of Catholicised Latinas, and the behaviours expected of a more assertive and aggressive successful student. The authors concluded that the most frequently reported coping strategy was a Latina student's conversation with others about her problem, and the second most frequently reported was actively finding out more about a particular situation, and then taking some positive, planned approach to the situation.

While valid conclusions can be drawn from this research, the scattered findings pointed us in the direction of a deeper exploration of how Latinas make sense of their lived worlds within the academic context: how they use their sense-making skills, negotiation skills and critical thinking skills to assist them in navigating higher education and graduating when many others were not able to persist.

Theoretical framework

We used the ecological theory of social development as developed and adapted by Urie Bronfenbrenner (1979, 1986, 1989; Bronfenbrenner and Morris, 1998) as the primary theoretical framework for this study and as the organiser for review of prior research findings. Bronfenbrenner's theory consists of five interconnected systems that range from the individual within close interpersonal interactions to the broader influences of institutions and culture. He called the five systems the macrosystem, exosystem, mesosystem, microsystem and chronosystem.

Figure 10.1 is a graphic representation of Bronfenbrenner's model as applied to the study of Latina college students. The macrosystem is made up of the dominant paradigm of the society, the culture and social values and norms. Values and norms around race and gender are critical to interpretation of the findings of this study, as cultural values and norms are being enacted by the participants in this study and by those with whom they come into contact. In this case, women may receive mixed messages from the macrosystem about whether they can be a 'good Latina', a good US woman and a 'good student' all at the same time. The exosystem is where society's values and norms are codified into policies, laws and rules. What policies and practices might successful Latina students identify as barriers to their success, and how do they overcome those barriers? The mesosystem is where linkages between the microsystems of home, school, Church, community and so on are negotiated.

We used Sedikides and Brewer's (2001) extension of Bronfenbrenner's original definition of the individual within the microsystem to include three primary aspects of identity formation and negotiation: individual, relational and collective. This is a primary focus of this study: how do these successful Latinas successfully navigate the sometimes conflicting values and expectations in the microsystems of their lives? How do they succeed at being Latina, being proud of being Latina and being successful in a predominantly white culture and institution all at the same time?

Figure 10.1: Bronfenbrenner's ecological theory

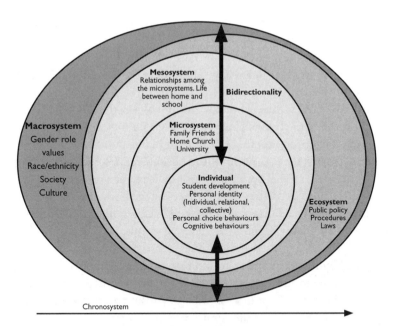

Source: Adapted from Sedikides and Brewer (2001) and model format from Dunlap (2008).

Methodology

The overall methodological design used was an embedded exploratory case study of Latinas in one US Research I-category university setting during the winter term of 2008. A survey, interviews and focus groups were used to explore behaviours and perceptions of this population of students. Surveys were distributed to the whole population of 83 Latina women in the predominantly white institution as identified through the campus office of institutional research ($N = 83$; from OUS, 2006). The survey included demographic questions such as age, gender, class standing, grade point average, ethnic identity, on/off campus involvement. It also included questions about students' perceptions of success, identification of expectations and barriers, as well as recommendations for improvement in the experience of Latinas within the university system. The initial and follow-up survey inquiries were sent by campus email. We pursued additional measures to reach out to this population. The research team members identified individual Latina students through person-to-person connections and contacted individuals through friends and colleagues. The lead researcher is Latina herself and was actively involved in the Latino community in this north-western university, thus allowing her access to both Latino- and Latina-based organisations.

Due to the low response rate of the survey, the primary data sources became an individual interview where that was the method chosen by the individual (N = 3) and data from three focus groups where individuals chose to meet in small groups (N = 8; thus, N = 11 for the data reported here). Informal interactions via phone conversations with other researchers conducting research on Latina populations indicated to us that reluctance to respond to research requests was a common problem. Further email communications with Latina groups and Latina researchers prompted the use of a free list in both the focus group and interviews, in addition to field-tested general questions. A free list process is useful for identifying items in a cultural domain (Denzin and Lincoln, 2000). Researchers interpreted the frequency of words produced by the participants to indicate the items' importance to the group, and the group's ability to define for themselves a 'Latina' group identity. The survey questions and partial answer results were used to inform the questions for the semi-structured interview protocol and for the subsequent focus group questions. This proved to be a highly successful method to open discussions and to encourage the women to talk about their experiences when asked the original survey questions in this new context.

The interview and focus group participants included women who did and did not complete the original survey. Women included in the final interview and focus group sample were 11 seniors who had been continuously enrolled in the same institution for the four- or five-year span leading to their senior year and who had accumulated 150 hours or more towards graduation by the end of the fall term. The women were chosen because of their willingness to participate in the research study. These women were from a variety of countries of origin and ancestry, were first- or second-generation native citizens, and were 'traditional' or 'non-traditional' students by age and family status. All the women's families resided in the Pacific Northwest of the US, specifically the states of Oregon or California.

All survey, interview and focus group data was transcribed and separately coded by three independent coders. Codes were discussed and modified through agreed-upon definitions until a high level of inter-rater reliability was obtained. The privacy of participants was protected by assignment of pseudonyms at the time of transcription.

Findings

The first finding of this study was a surprise to us. When we first did not receive a strong response to our survey request, we assumed that it must be because it was a busy time of the term, or we had not used a good title and students were deleting the initial email erroneously, or some other hypothesis, unrelated to any particular fact related to this particular student population. However, when subsequent email contacts were also unsuccessful and we moved to an individual, person-to-person identification process, we began to understand that there was a reluctance within this population to work with us, for several reasons. Many of these women said that they thought that their own participation would not make a big difference in our study. They were busy and thought someone else could take care of our needs. Some of the women went on to tell us that they did not think that they represented this population because of their perceptions of an 'ethnic' Latina identity, or that they did not have unique experiences that would be of interest to 'researchers'. These women were quick to open up and talk about their experiences, once the interview or focus group began, but were not easy to convince that they might have knowledge that would be useful to us as researchers or to other students.

This was not the only study where we experienced reluctance to participate based on individual assumptions about their ability to contribute. While we were conducting this study, we were simultaneously attempting to conduct a study of Latina freshmen and encountered a similar problem (Garrison et al., 2008). Another student colleague who was in the early stages of her counselling dissertation research at the same time with the same population also had the same issue. We found this ability to 'disappear' into the milieu of the campus and to resist being drawn out as a representative of any particular group a common enough experience to call it a 'finding'. Perhaps one of the best coping mechanisms for these successful Latinas is the ability to resist taking on any additional work that is not directly in their path to graduation!

We experienced what we finally decided was a similar issue when we attempted to convene the focus groups. Almost all of the women said they felt uncomfortable in a group setting. In response to this concern being expressed over and over again to us by different students, we decided to reduce the typical number in a focus group of 6–10, to pairs and trios. These women were more comfortable with meeting in smaller groups. We also adjusted our researcher strategy so that only one researcher was present at any given time, so as to not overwhelm the women in the setting with unnecessary deference to the researcher or to a non-Latina.

In the initial moments of both the interviews and the focus groups, many of the women said they were hesitant to meet individually or in a group because they did not feel they represented the 'greater female Hispanic' population. Here again, in the small groups, was the hesitation about identity that we had repeatedly experienced in attempting individual personal and telephone contacts. As we compared our experiences with each other, we refocused the opening activity of the interviews and focus groups on the issue of group identity for Latinas. We began to develop the free word list that was subsequently used in the focus groups to further explore this phenomenon.

The following topics were emphasised by the 11 Latina seniors who participated in our study. Six types of expectations from actors or aspects were identified by most of the women: family, friends, partner/boyfriend, academic, religious and gender expectations. We examine the campus environment these Latinas experienced and the way these Latinas managed the expectations and behaviours within the campus environment in order of the six topical areas.

Family expectations

The women were asked who they considered to be their 'family'. Most mentioned that their immediate, biological or adopted family would be considered family. One student, Sarah, said she did not have a family. She felt that she was alone in her entire educational venture due to her parents' disagreement with her pursuit of higher education. Sarah was a 'non-traditional' student, who began her college experience at a later age, and was a divorced mother of two children. The other 10 women related that their families consisted of parents, siblings and extended family.

The Latinas reported that parents and some extended family members had both overt and covert expectations for most of these women. When asked what expectations and obligations their families had of them, the women were able to clearly state the expectations. One expectation was to graduate, a second was to maintain a connection with family while in college and a third was to be a role model for the family. Although some parents were reluctant to hear about their daughter's decision to attend college, particularly when attendance would be away from home, they were anxious to see them graduate. Many were the first in their families to attend and graduate from college. There was only one woman, JoAnne, whose parents already expected her to attend college, and also expected her to do very well academically. They even ensured she transitioned successfully by not making her responsible for paying for the first year of college.

A second expectation for these Latinas was to remain connected to family by visiting home on a consistent basis, with the exception of Sarah. Many expressed how parents would want them to visit home on weekends or to set out time during summer or spring breaks to be with family or work in the family trade. Rosario stated:

> "We've talked about that and now I'm going to study abroad this summer and it's the first time since I turned 15 that I'm not going to work over the summer. I'm just really excited about realising that that was an obligation but that I was not being held to that."

Rosario perceived that it was an obligation for her to go back home and work as a firefighter, but once she spoke to her parents about the possibility of going abroad, she was relieved that she was not obligated or expected to provide for the family every summer, which allowed her to explore other opportunities and study abroad.

A third expectation was for these women to be role models for their family and siblings. The behaviour of a role model varied for most women, and some were more direct than others. For instance, the mere fact that these women were in college illustrated to their parents and siblings that they were doing something positive that their siblings should emulate. Two females said they directly became a role model to a sister and cousin who were also undergraduate students. Isabel mentioned how her parents expected her to help her sister figure out what were better methods of learning due to her sister's difficulty with academic work: "So it's really important to my mom and my dad to check in with her and figure out what kind of things I've learned over the course of my four years to really help".

Erica related how her cousin looked up to her for information about college, such as what courses to take and what to get involved in. Erica at first was met with antagonism from her cousin regarding her pursuit of higher education to gain status within the family, but later reflected on the things Erica was doing. She had prepared herself in similar ways to attend the same university as Erica.

Friends' expectations

Friendships played an integral role in the lives of all of these Latinas. Friends were acquired through residential halls, organisation/club membership, work or in classes. For all women, their friends were their 'second family'. Friends were established for a certain purpose, such as socialisation, a connection to the Latino and Latina culture, an academic resource, or as an intellectual outlet. The pressures to meet expectations were most often not as strong among friends as reported for immediate family. However, for a few of these women, the expectations were set high. For example, Lizbeth's relationships with her friends in the organisation in which she was a leader were difficult. They expected her to be a voice for other under-represented students and the Latino community in general. She claimed they would say "No, you don't get a good corporate job and a big mansion. You need to cure poverty and provide health care for all Latinos". She went on to say:

> "There's all that pressure, and that will be with me forever
> even if I move on and I might not see these people anymore.
> That will always stick with me, I can't let those people down,
> even those people I have yet to meet in my community."

Another role Lizbeth's friends played was to challenge her academically by making her critically think about the knowledge she was gaining in and out of the classroom. These women reported that their friends created a space of familiarity for women, particularly familiarity with the Latino and Latina culture. Five of the 11 participants sought out a Latino organisation and Latina group to find people who 'looked like them' and with whom they could share the higher education experience. Anahie mentioned the student union in which she was involved:

> "We've been through everything together, from protesting
> to marches to like, you name it, we've done it. And I live
> with two women that I met through [the unions], and
> they're like my sisters.... Things you share – like personal
> experiences."

Isabel confessed to having tried other social groups, such as student government, but really felt she needed to find a Latino- and Latina-specific group with which she could identify. While Isabel learned and experienced many things in student government, she lacked that familiar connection of language, culture and history that was in Latino-based organisations.

Of the 11 women interviewed or who participated in a focus group, only five women identified a Latina group as an important friends network for them. Not only did they interact within this group, they formed an additional network of women into an informal sorority to create an even greater connection. Karla describes this group of 'Alpha Beta Brownies (ABB)' most accurately:

> "It's just like this group of girls who became really good friends and have somehow managed to stay really close together. So it's like my sisters, my mom. Like it started out with a few of the upper classmen when I was a freshman, and we would hear about it all the time.... It's just a bunch of strong, independent, very intelligent women getting together and calling each other ABB."

Latinas also found friends in the classroom. For Sarah, the classroom was the only venue in which she found friends, and a positive connection to the university:

> "Usually when I meet people in classes we start talking and I figure out that 'oh, that person has kids too', or that person is also a non-traditional student or she's older like me.... One time I found one of my schoolmates had a child at the day care my children went to."

While all of these women named social groups as important to them in some way, and while five women named a Latina group as very important to them, the majority of these women did not name a cultural or Latina-specific group as important to them. The other women who did not seek a Latino- or Latina-related group sought other clubs such as ballroom dancing, the Christian ministry on campus or focused on doing things on an individual basis. For instance, JoAnne enjoyed photography and related how she enjoyed doing things on her own. All of the women worked either in a work-study position and/or an off-campus job. Erica stated that she did not have time for extracurricular activities because she worked as a waitress. For JoAnne, her work-study position in the International Centre was her method of interacting with various students.

Partner/boyfriend expectations

Four out of the 11 women mentioned that they had or were currently in a relationship while in college. There were not that many references to partners or boyfriends, but the few women who did mention a partner as part of a social network also mentioned that they had expectations to meet with them too. To illustrate the partner or boyfriend expectation, Rosario said: "I was in a relationship that really took a lot of time. It was a great relationship but my grades suffered because of the time away from my studies". Anahie resonated the same observation: "I do spend a lot of time with my partner, and I should be hanging out a little bit more with my family and my homework".

A second expectation were gender-based behaviours, such as Lizbeth's partner who expected her to be a caretaker and submissive at times. She stated:

> "I just can't be your partner, I have to be your caretaker when you need it, your supporter when you need it, and at the same time be submissive when you need it and that's really hard to juggle while also trying to be a leader through Mecha."

These expectations conflicted with Lisbeth's role as a leader in the Latino organisation on campus: "I think my roles in Mecha have really butt heads and conflicted. Cause I'm not that type of mujer to be very submissive; and sometimes I feel like … I don't have to be a part of my relationship".

Academic expectations

As mentioned earlier, family members had expectations for their daughters to achieve academically. Erica's parents expected her to have a 3.0 grade point average. This expectation did not seem to be taken literally by Erica, but it was something that she kept in mind and said she tried to achieve most terms because her parents expected it of her. Furthermore, the parents of Isabel and Lizbeth were displeased with their daughters' choice of major (Ethnic Studies). They expected Isabel and Lizbeth to choose the sciences or political sciences in order for them to find a job or profession that would pay well. Isabel's parents aspired for her to be a doctor, but she realised early on in her education that she was unable to understand science and mathematics. Lizbeth, on a similar note, related how her parents wanted her to find a job that would pay well, but that this would be unlikely as she was interested in political or community organising and non-profit work.

Another expectation that Sarah discovered was that her professors had underlying expectations for their students:

> "And also working around professors, being a worker here, I've learned that there's certain things that they expect but they don't say they expect … they'll assign a paper that's three to four pages long but they really want four to five pages long … they give a better grade to the student who does more. I've learned that and I do that and I've noticed I get better grades."

Religious expectations

Religious expectations consisted of the practice of a particular religion, thus abiding by the social values and mores of that religion. From the 11 participants, nine of them did not see religion as a support system, but related how they were either spiritual or believed in God, but did not practise a particular religion. Religion was negated for a couple of the participants because of their support for the homosexual community. Only one Latina, Mrs Depp, mentioned that she was Christian, and tried to follow the practices of Christianity. Also, only Sarah loudly renounced the Jehovah's Witness religion due to her parents' constant pressures to abide by the behaviours and values of the religion. She clearly states why the religion is not helpful to her:

> "When I was doing that [religious practices] I was in a bad situation, getting married and domestic violence and then homelessness and then hunger. When I left the religion I started to see change in my life and for now I'm in a better situation and it has happened because I have left. I have decided that it's okay if I don't fulfil those requirements as they [parents] think I should."

Because many Hispanic cultures are heavily influenced by the Catholic Church, we expected religion to play a larger role in these women's lives. However, these women had made their own deliberate choices about religion and most of them did not see it as helpful to them in their lives. They questioned the gender roles expected of them from traditional religion and rejected any attempts to define them into a space where they could not use their minds as they saw fit.

Gender expectations

The participants expressed various gender expectations that related to a woman's physical appearance and behaviour. They believed they were expected by males to be presentable all the time, 'looking physically appealing'. Also resonating in many of the Latinas were parental expectations of them to not get pregnant. Rosario illustrated how the expectation of not getting pregnant is connected to an issue of trust:

> "I just want to echo that 'don't get pregnant' was like the first and foremost thing I received from home as I was leaving my home and like moving to pursue my education. You know, 'we are giving you our trust, don't break it'. So I think there's definitely this trust issue and code of like what's going to be acceptable and what isn't."

Additionally, when asked the expectations of female college students, they described a difference in behaviours among white European women and women of colour. Behavioural expectations of Latinas consisted of being docile, but being leaders in their communities, being intelligent to a certain level, and being on 'good behaviour' on campus. Isabel noted: "Like the typical expectation for women is to be the ones studying but still fun, and smart but not too smart, and informed but not overbearing on their opinions".

White women, on the other hand, were described as usually ones who were involved on campus, worked out in the athletic facility, had leisure time and no family responsibilities. Isabel elaborated: "The typical white girl, the typical college student, is a white woman like involved in something because it's going to help her résumé later". She explained that she thought most Latinas focused on their academic work and their complex family responsibilities, and "did not think that much about doing things to build a résumé for later".

Also, a salient discussion about the gender expectations of Latinas needing to 'be pure, virgin-like', due to the cultural and religious link to the Virgin Mary, was conflicting to these Latinas. Mercedes explained this symbolic figure:

> "Things like in cultures like in the Latino culture like the Virgin Mary, like who could be like her, like nobody. It's just too hard. It's so much pressure, whether they say it or not, it is. They do hold you, that is like a model for a lot of

Latinas I feel like. And that purity and that sanctity. Who can have that? Only this religious figure can have that."

Anahie, Mercedes, Mrs Depp and Sarahie mentioned that this religious figure or symbol is difficult to emulate because of the many life pressures and circumstances they are surrounded with, and also because the image itself is one that denies any sexuality and perpetuates a patriarchal system within the Latino community.

The campus environment

Eight out of the 11 women felt the lack of a presence of Latinas on campus, and thus related feelings of isolation. Also, four out of the eight women expressed what they thought of as the campus perception about them as 'token' minority students, who are only in college to meet a quota or a diversity requirement. The women who were involved in a Latino organisation on campus were more vocal about the need for institutional change to increase recruitment, retention, access and graduation rates of Latino students and other under-represented students. The other women who were not involved in a Latino organisation expressed a double standard for female college students compared to male college students in regards to academic expectations. In the workplace, only Sarah stressed the feeling of inferiority due to her Latina identity and immigrant status.

Classroom dynamics were reported to be very different for each woman. A positive or negative experience was related to the type of course. For those courses in the social sciences, such as Ethnic Studies or Spanish, the women felt a freedom to say what they thought and 'be who they were', as well as being validated by students and professors. On the other hand, in the sciences or mathematics courses, students reported that they did not feel such freedom. Specifically, Mercedes was critical of the Journalism Department, her major, because it was a classroom in which she had to behave and interact differently than in her Spanish class. Sarah also responded to Mercedes' interactions by stating that she had to continuously participate in class in order for her professor to recognise her and believe that she had done the reading for the class discussion.

Although the campus environment provided some challenges, there were 'safe spaces' women were able to find, such as the office of multicultural academic services and the corridor hall in which the student unions/organisations were located. The multicultural office provided academic services and advice for multi-ethnic students at this north-west university. In such spaces, six out of the 11 women felt they could be themselves, share particular experiences that only multi-ethnic students could understand and have no need to explain to people what they mean when they are speaking about a certain situation or incident on campus. On the contrary, they also defined unsafe spaces on campus. Lizbeth described her work as a driver for the campus' designated driver shuttle service, a student-run programme with a mission to see to it that students do not put themselves at risk by driving while they are under the influence of alcohol or any other illegal substance. This work space and the process of picking up students was not a safe space because the students who were providing the service did not know about campus diversity-related topics and did not know how to react to prejudicial comments by students towards multi-ethnic or international students.

Methods of managing the mesosphere

Latinas in this study were able to find venues of support and use language skills and behaviours in different situations and settings in order to navigate the college environment and also manage the various expectations described earlier. In relation to Sy and Romero (2008), Latinas were able to use their language brokering in different situations, which made them able to deal with different expectations. Validation in experiences and opinions was an important aspect of their interactions with individuals and allowed them to discover supporters, allies or safe spaces in the college campus.

Experiences with religion were usually not pleasant and not supportive of success in the college or university. Most of these women reported withdrawing from active religious participation but also reported being 'spiritual' and 'moral'. The topic of religious expectations correlated with the perceived gender expectations of many of the women by their family, extended family and overall community values. These expectations did not include attendance at, or success at, a college or university. Thus, many of these women have had to redefine personal Latina female roles and behaviours to fit their values system in order to accommodate success in an academic setting.

Discussion

These successful Latina students deliberately used sorting and diagnostic strategies to balance between conflicting familial expectations, among social and personal relationships, and in managing academic expectations, religious behaviours and gender expectations, in order to create an educational experience and space in which they could succeed academically. They reported feeling isolated because they were often the only Latinas in their classrooms or place of employment, or just one of the few walking around campus. To alleviate the feeling of isolation, a few resorted to the safe spaces such as student organisations and multicultural spaces such as the multicultural centre and corridor.

They were constantly redefining their role and value systems, and altering their own expectations of themselves and of other Latinas. They sought academic opportunities such as research, study abroad and academic support programmes to achieve academically. They talked explicitly about using communication strategies, such as language code switching and visual 'shape-shifting' to gain more cultural congruity between their own values and that of the surrounding, mostly white, middle-class campus values context. The changes in value systems of many occurred when religion or the religious beliefs of family, friends or partners began to interfere with their growing sense of who they were becoming. Religious beliefs many times set gender roles they did not feel they should or would follow, which caused tension in relationships with family members. Also, the gender expectations from family and partners were challenged when the women got involved in organising, extracurricular activities or work, which required them to take a leading role and be a voice for others.

We identified a process Latinas used to manage these various expectations and perceived feedback loops. First, they confronted or identified the expectation. They observed the behaviours of professors and classmates and noted how those behaviours differed from what they might have experienced in the past. Through their own feelings of guilt or pressure, they realised that what others were asking of them, or seemed to be asking of them, was an expectation that they might or might not choose to acknowledge and validate in their own actions. Then, they reported what they were observing and talked through the issue with family or friends in the form of asking for advice or by expressing their concerns about the expectations. Gloria et al.'s (2005) psychological coping mechanisms were confirmed by this study: conversations with others, researching the issue and then taking action. In the end, the women began to redefine themselves by testing the limits of expectations and obligations and by refocusing on what was important to them and what they most valued, that is, education and personal growth.

Conclusion

This research study focused on the experiences of Latinas within a predominantly white institution, a campus where the population of white European students is an estimated 15,000 students in a total population of 20,000 students. For these Latinas, success in higher education is not merely graduating from the university, but also being able to do so while managing successfully their various roles as women, daughters, mothers, role models, academics, scholars and leaders.

Within the study, these women experienced a wide range of campus environments from student services, extracurricular activities, various majors and workplaces. In the sense of the ecological theory model, these individuals were constantly collecting observational data in all settings, balancing and comparing that data with their prior experiences and their own expectations, and then initiating seeking of advice and counsel from trusted friends in a 'safe place' in order to decide for themselves what choices they needed to make between conflicting demands. Most of these women reported every stage of this process, but did not seem to be consciously aware of the process they used, or that what they were doing might differ from what other students might experience.

While these students found some help from institutional sources when they initiated the contact, they mostly relied on themselves and their trusted friends to negotiate successful strategies. Unlike the findings of previous studies, these women's friends and friendships played a major role in the intellectual, personal, social and political development of the Latina students. Friends were used for both assistance-related functions and non-assistance functions, such as providing tangible resources and information, as well as emotional support. Many times, friends were the impetus for change and action; change in value sets or gender roles and action to empower the community.

We found the modified Bronfenbrenner theoretical model useful both in framing our research questions, and then in sorting and interpreting the data. As might be expected when researchers attempt to focus on a particular ethnic/cultural identity, most of the conflicts appeared between the individual and elements of the microsystem, such as family, friends, Church and the university itself. However, unlike the findings from prior research studies, it was apparent to us that each individual's understanding of her individual behaviours and skills, her relational needs and expectations, and her sense of collectively falling into a 'Latina' category was greatly influenced by personal choice behaviours and then reflection upon the consequences of choices. Thus, we found Sedikides and Brewer's (2001) extension of Bronfenbrenner's original definition of the individual within the microsystem particularly useful. We conclude that the individual's ability to test new actions, and modify subsequent behaviours, is essential to success.

For these successful Latina students, their personal journeys were fraught with conflicts between personal and cultural expectations, and also because of attending college in a cultural setting predominantly different from their own home culture. They were able to grow as individuals, and to succeed academically, but always with tensions between individual, cultural and community expectations. There were commonalities in how these women experienced campus environments and in the ways these Latinas successfully managed confusing and challenging expectations coming from others and from within themselves.

While it is not our intent to address critical race, oppression or feminist theoretical perspectives in this study, we conclude that the reactions of these successful students probably represent pervasive embedded conflicts between success at defining their individual Latina identity, but always at the expense of relational and collective identities. Further, the extraordinary skills of these successful women at negotiating conflicts in an often apparently hostile and alien environment appear to us to be undervalued by the women themselves and unnoticed by their institution. Those who succeed against great odds have skills and knowledge that can be helpful to other students and to their institutions.

Notes

[1] '*Para crecer*' is Spanish for growing as a person; a personal journey; to explore possibilities for one's life.

[2] The young women in this study were a diverse group including first- and second-generation women of Cuban, Mexican, Puerto Rican and South or Central American descent. 'Latina' in this context refers to any female student of Hispanic origins where Spanish may be the first language in the home in which they were raised.

References

Arbona, C. and Nora, A. (2007) 'The influence of academic and environmental factors on Hispanic college degree attainment', *Review of Higher Education*, vol 30, pp 247–69.

Bonner, F. (2010) 'An empirical investigation of the success factors influencing academically gifted (high-achieving) Latino student success in engineering', Paper presented at the Mexican American/Latino Research Centre, Texas A&M University, 18 October.

Bordes, V., Sand, J., Arredondo, P., Kurpius, S. and Rayle, A. (2006) 'Validation of four measures of social support with Latina/o and non-hispanic white undergraduates', *Hispanic Journal of Behavioral Sciences*, vol 28, no 1, pp 65–83.

Bronfenbrenner, U. (1979) *The Ecology of Human Development*, Cambridge: Harvard University Press.

Bronfenbrenner, U. (1986) 'Ecology of the family as a context for human development: research perspective', *Development Psychology*, vol 22, pp 723–42.

Bronfenbrenner, U. (1989) 'Ecological systems theory', *Annals of Child Development*, vol 6, pp 187–249.

Bronfenbrenner, U. and Morris, P. (1998) 'The ecology of development process', in W. Damon and R. Lerner (eds) *Handbook of Child Psychology. Vol 1 Theoretical Model of Human Development* (5th edn), New York: Wiley, pp 993–1028.

Campaign for College Opportunity (2010) *Divided We Fail: Improving Completion and Closing Racial Gaps in California's Community Colleges*, Sacramento, CA: Institute for Higher Education Leadership and Policy.

Denzin, N. and Lincoln, Y. (2000) *Handbook of Qualitative Research* (2nd edn), Thousand Oaks, CA: Sage Publications.

Dunlap, D. (2008) 'A theoretical model for focusing research questions and design', Paper presented at the American Educational Research Association Conference, New York.

Garrison, A., Hernandez, P., Dunlap, D. and Clott, A. (2008) 'Impacto familiar: Latina students in transition', Paper presented at the American Educational Research Association Conference, New York.

Gloria, A., Castellanos, J. and Orozco, V. (2005) 'Undergraduates' perceived educational barriers, cultural fit, coping responses, and psychological well-being of Latina', *Hispanic Journal of Behavioral Sciences*, vol 27, p 161.

Gonzales, K., Jovel, J. and Stoner, C. (2004) 'Latinas: the new Latino majority in college', *New Directions for Student Services*, vol 105, pp 17–27.

Horn, L. (2006) *Placing College Graduation Rates in Context: How 4-Year College Graduation Rates Vary with Selectivity and the Size of Low-Income Enrollment (NCES 2007-161)*, Washington, DC: US Department of Education, National Center for Educational Statistics.

Kelly, A.,Schneider, M. and Carey, K. (2010) *Rising to the Challenge: Hispanic College Graduation Rates as a National Priority*, Washington, DC: American Enterprise Institute.

Kenny, M. and Stryker, S. (1996) 'Social network characteristics and college adjustment among racially and ethnically diverse first-year students', *Journal of College Student Development*, vol 37, pp 649–58.

Martin, I.R. (2010) 'Insights into the complexities of identity in persisting Latina college students', unpublished dissertation, University of Massachusetts at Amherst.

Melendez, M.C. and Melendez, N.B. (2010) 'The influence of parental attachment on the college adjustment of white, black and Latina/ Hispanic women: a cross-cultural investigation', *Journal of College Student Development*, vol 51, no 4, July/August, pp 419–35.

NCES (National Center for Education Statistics) (2006) *Digest of Education Statistics, 2005 (NCES 2006-030)*, Washington, DC: US Department of Education. Available at: http://nces.ed.gov/programs/digest/d05/tables/dt05_205.asp (accessed 29 October 2006).

OUS (Oregon University System Office of Institutional Research) (2006) 'Enrollment by ethnicity, fee status, and student level: University of Oregon, fall 2006 fourth week'. Available at http://former.ous.edu/dept/ir/reports/er2006/erdd 03-06f4wk_uo.htm (accessed 1 October 2011).

Perrakis, A. and Hagedorn, L.S. (2010) 'Latino/a student success in community colleges and Hispanic-serving institution status', *Community College Journal of Research and Practice*, vol 34, no 10, pp 797–813.

Phinney, J.S., Dennis, J.M. and Gutierrez, D.M. (2005) 'College orientation profiles of Latino students from low socioeconomic backgrounds: a cluster analytic approach', *Hispanic Journal of Behavioral Sciences*, vol 27, pp 387–408.

Rodriquez, A., Guido-DiBrito, F., Torres, V. and Talbot, D. (2000) 'Latina college students: issues and challenges for the 21st century', *NASPA Journal*, vol 37, pp 511–27.

Santiago, D., Santiago, D. and Brown, S. (2004) *Federal Policy and Latinos in Higher Education: a Guide for Policymakers and Grant Makers*, Washington, DC: Pew Hispanic Center. Available at: http://pewhispanic.org/reports/report.php?ReportID=32 (accessed 29 October 2006).

Sedikides, C. and Brewer, M. (eds) (2001) *Individual Self, Relational Self, Collective Self*, Philadelphia: Psychology Press.

Shore, E. (2005) 'Are Latino children missing out on preschool? Why Latino families are reluctant to send their kids', *New California Media*, 21 April. Available at: http://news.newamericamedia.org/news/view_article_id=a649930e279c7c5a94a3644268eda909 (accessed 1 October 2011).

Sy, S. and Romero, J. (2008) 'Family responsibilities among Latina college students from immigrant families', *Journal of Hispanic Higher Education*, vol 7, pp 212–27.

US Census Bureau (2000a) 'Profile of general demographic characteristics: 2000'. Available at: http://factfinder.census.gov/servlet/QTTable?_bm=yand-geo_id=01000USand-qr_name=DEC_2000_SF1_U_DP1&ds.name=DEC=2000_SF1_U&geo_id=01000US. (accessed 1 October 2011).

US Census Bureau (2000b) 'Census 2000 demographic profile highlights'. Available at: http://factfinder.census.gov/servlet/SAFFFacts?_event=andgeo_id=01000USand_geoContext=01000US%7C04000US41and_street=and_county=and_cityTown=and_state=04000US41and_zip=and_lang=enand_sse=onandActiveGeoDiv=and_useEV=andpctxt=fphandpgsl=010and_submenuId=factsheet_1andds_name=DEC_2000_SAFFand_ci_nbr=400andqr_name=DEC_2000_SAFF_R1040andreg=DEC_2000_SAFF_R1040%3A400and_keyword=and_industry= (accessed 20 April 2007).

ELEVEN

Empowering 'non-traditional' students in the UK: feedback and the hidden curriculum

Andy Cramp

Introduction

This chapter considers the importance of feedback to students in higher education (HE). It discusses the notion of the hidden curriculum as a context for critiquing how feedback to students can work in a complex and unstable UK HE sector. The chapter then looks at an intervention to help (particularly first-generation) students develop their understandings of feedback and work towards supporting their confidence, self-esteem and academic development.

Written feedback to students is often a private 'exchange' constructed by lecturers working their way through hundreds of scripts as quickly as possible. There is evidence of a growing and significant degree of student dissatisfaction with feedback as a meaningful and supportive learning process in HE, to which I will return later. Because it is often assumed that feedback is a straightforward 'common-sense' transmission process, the complexity of feedback as a vital part of learning and teaching has been undermined by other institutional discourses. This is where the notion of the hidden curriculum becomes useful, and some historical context helps to develop the significance of the phrase to feedback discourses.

The hidden curriculum is a well-used but highly ambiguous phrase, subject to a range of uses and interpretations. Most writers agree that the term was first used in the context of compulsory schooling by Philip Jackson (1990 [1968]) who seems to have introduced the phrase in his important text, *Life in Classrooms*; although John Dewey's (1963 [1938]) notion of 'collateral learning' also came close to this idea. Jackson identifies three key characteristics of school life that are 'not immediately visible' but are as 'important as those that are' (Jackson, 1990 [1968], p 10). He chooses 'crowds', 'praise' and 'power' (Jackson,

1990 [1968], pp 10–11) and after analysing these as key aspects of the hidden curriculum he comments:

> the crowds, the praise, and the power that combine to give a distinctive flavour to classroom life collectively form a hidden curriculum which each student (and teacher) must master if he is to make his way satisfactorily through the school. The demands created by these features of classroom life may be contrasted with the 'academic' demands – the official curriculum so to speak – to which educators traditionally have paid the most attention. (pp 33–4)

Jackson's functionalist approach focuses on what was, at that time, the relatively unexplored idea of schooling as social practice. Jackson's key issues of 'crowds', 'praise' and 'power' can clearly be applied to a UK HE context. As Martin (1976, p 155) comments, the hidden curriculum can often 'lurk in other habitats'. But it was not until 1971 that the idea of the hidden curriculum was directly applied to HE; and then in a quite different way to Jackson's work. Benson Snyder's *The Hidden Curriculum* (1970) considers the 'dissonance' between student and university values during the US public crises of the late 1960s and early 1970s. Snyder comments that the shifting nature of student agendas in that period came into conflict with a decaying and conservative university order. Snyder focuses particularly on the increasing gap between student goals and university curricula. For students, the 'old rewards were becoming the object of suspicion of attack or ridicule' (Snyder, 1970, p 179). Snyder refers to the increasing gap between formally stated requirements for academic success and what students could actually get away with and still succeed in HE. Snyder argues that the failure to engage students in any intrinsic self-motivated process of personal development comes out of cynicism towards moribund conservative university values clearly at odds with students' lived experiences in the US public world. It is worth bearing in mind that the Kent State University shootings took place just two months before Snyder wrote the Foreword to his text.

Snyder's 'hidden curriculum', then, refers to the tacit understanding among students that HE success was about credentials and not growth and that universities were unable to acknowledge or act on the gap between students and university values. Similarly, Henry Giroux uses the notion of the hidden curriculum to identify a gap or deficit, but for Giroux (2007) this is a gap between the crucial role of the university as a public resource for democracy and civic life on the one hand,

and, on the other, the aim of neoliberal policies to commodify and corporatise the academy. Snyder and Giroux both explore the ways universities engage (or not) with the 'outside' world, but whereas Snyder looks at dissonance between universities and students, Giroux discusses tensions between universities and government policy. Giroux's version of the hidden curriculum, then, identifies commodification and vocationalisation as the growing and largely unheeded threats to university curricula. Where Snyder sees a moribund academy unable to change, Giroux identifies reckless and irresponsible changes induced by neoliberal political pressures instead. Giroux (2006, p 69) comments that the notion of the hidden curriculum was now redundant: 'What was once part of the hidden curriculum of higher education – the creeping vocationalisation and subordination of learning to the dictates of the market – has become an open, and defining principle of education at all levels of learning'.

Giroux (2008) attacks universities for not just allowing but encouraging and embracing the corporatisation of higher education to the extent that this change is now part of conventional thinking about the purpose of a university and not hidden or covert any more. He develops this argument further by scrutinising the growing militarisation of US universities as, similarly, no longer requiring covert status. He also identifies the open pressures on academics to accept or remain silent about militarisation or face 'retaliatory accusations that equate their views to treason' (Giroux, 2006, p 67).

Giroux's use of the hidden curriculum in HE, then, identifies the increasing influences of the New Right and the undermining of the role of universities in democratic public spheres for the sake of activity justified only in terms of commercial or national security value. It is interesting to note that although Giroux refers mainly to the US, there is some evidence of Giroux's thesis in the UK too. Consider, for example, the Labour Party's decision in 2009 to include universities in a government department for 'Business, Innovation and Skills', and, more recently, Lord Browne's (2010) review of UK HE recommending zero government funding for undergraduate arts and humanities programmes.

The hidden curriculum in HE is further developed in a text edited by Eric Margolis (2001). Various perspectives of HE are considered with the notion of the hidden curriculum as the context. The process of mentoring graduates for example and dissertation advising are critiqued as conventional processes hiding tacit, rarely questioned, assumptions about power and identity.

This short review of the hidden curriculum makes clear how open to interpretation the phrase is and constant re-examination is necessary in response to changing sets of power relations in the public world. However, the phrase is still useful because it serves to make visible and explicit what is sometimes covert and this is where the phrase becomes pertinent to feedback processes. The phrase can be useful in the context of feedback to identify gaps, deficits and inadequately critiqued 'common-sense' understandings, which often disguise powerful hegemonic relationships between students and the academy. This can be particularly true for 'non-traditional' students, whose hidden curriculum can be framed by, on the outside, glossy prospectuses with successful case studies and, on the inside, the struggle to find enough contact with academic staff to be successful (Leathwood and O'Connell, 2003).

The significance of written feedback and the hidden curriculum

Over the past two years, the HE sector has been publicly criticised for the poor quality of its feedback to students (see eg Quality Assurance Agency, 2008; also, for the *Times Higher Education* reports on the National Student Survey, see Tahir, 2008; Newman, 2009; Ramsden, 2009). There are two reasons why this criticism has occurred. The first is that feedback on students' summative assessment performance is often regarded as a straightforward operational process separate from and not as important as 'teaching'. Nicol and Macfarlane-Dick (2006, p 200) note that feedback 'is still generally conceptualised as a transmission process', while Askew and Lodge (2000, p 1) suggest feedback is often 'embedded in a common sense and simplistic dominant discourse'. There is some evidence to suggest that because feedback is regarded as a simple transaction, it does not therefore require further enquiry. Sastry and Bekhradnia (2007), for example, reported on the 'academic experience' of students in English universities for the Higher Education Policy Institute (HEPI), but feedback experience was not part of the data collection. The HEPI report of the same name in 2006 (Bekhradnia et al.) did not collect data on feedback either. Furthermore, in a useful literature review of the first-year higher education experience, Harvey et al. (2006) were unable to find any research about feedback in the first year when it might be assumed that feedback to new students would be particularly worthy of investigation and innovation.

Such an unquestioned operational view of feedback, coupled with the notion that it requires no further investigation, has been challenged by writers committed to establishing the hidden importance and complexities of feedback in higher education. For example, feedback plays a part in reproducing institutional values and beliefs, principally the nature of relationships between lecturers and students. Carless (2006, p 221) suggests that the characteristics of 'authoritative academics' are valorised by an approach to assessment based just on the 'correcting and judging of scripts', where encouragement to engage in debate with learners driven by a set of agreed values has been lost. Furthermore, Nicol and Macfarlane-Dick (2006) refer to research establishing the complexity and significance of effective feedback. They cite Sadler's (1989) work on the importance of dialogue and negotiation and Black and Wiliam's (1998) study in the compulsory sector about assessment for learning where feedback plays a crucial role. Askew and Lodge (2000) rightly situate the notion of feedback within broader discourses of learning and point out the 'need to explore feedback alongside associated beliefs about learning to consider how feedback can be most effective in promoting learning' (2000, p 1). These are important points, but although they establish feedback as an influential component of a whole approach to learning, that influence is often hidden by other institutional discourses around 'delivery' and 'efficiency'.

The second explanation for the public criticism of feedback is directly linked to the first. With an increasing emphasis in UK higher education on 'processing' large numbers of students with increasingly diverse backgrounds, there is little time to reflect on the complexities of feedback and it becomes hidden by a transmission discourse that suits the current policy direction and financial pressures. In an interview with *Times Higher Education*, Nicol (2008) reflects on how dialogue and individuality in feedback is compromised in many contemporary HE settings by an increase in student numbers without a commensurate increase in funding:

> In a previous era, students would get feedback, discuss it with their tutor, revise their work and have further discussions and feedback in an ongoing dialogue. But in a mass higher education system, written feedback, which is essentially a monologue, is being asked to do the work of dialogue.

Nicol's point here about 'monologue' and 'massification' emphasises how the complexities of feedback are being ignored or hidden with even greater consequences as the student body becomes more diverse. Furthermore, Knight and Trowler (2000, p 71) outline how the 'changing nature of higher education' militates against 'improving practice in learning and teaching'. They mention longer work hours, 'hard' managerialism, loss of collegiality, greedy institutions (more for less without caring sufficiently for the humans who work in it) and reduced self-confidence as the changes affecting learning and teaching. Preece (2009, p 26) also mentions how 'the dominance of economic discourses masks continuing inequalities in the sector'. Love (2008, p 21) refers to an HE environment demanding constant change and rapid response and reflects on the outcomes of these changes:

> Education is divested of its heritage and revalued; it is deemed useful only in as much as it can respond to the business needs of the moment.... It brings out of its past only what is of use for the moment and blindly wanders toward a future it has no power to inform but to which it must simply respond.

These comments explain how a 'common-sense' interpretation of feedback as a process simply involving grades and comments in an apparently neutral exchange between lecturer and student serves the managerialist agenda of performativity and standardisation very well, denying and disguising in the process the need for complex changes necessary in HE learning structures to respond equitably to the increasing 'non-traditional' diversity of the student body. Understandings of the value of ethical, dialogic feedback to students for example are relegated and hidden by the powerful discourses of efficiency gains and the pressure to do more work with fewer resources. This is why feedback receives public criticism, particularly from students.

An interesting turnaround can now be discussed within the concept of the hidden curriculum. Historically, the hidden curriculum has been used to expose covert undesirable or unethical practices. But, in HE today, it is vital pedagogical discussions in the light of greater diversity that have become hidden or ignored. They have become the threat to the establishment and to the speedy 'processing' of students. Reflections on how the complexities of feedback can be unpicked to improve the process for learners are often pushed aside in favour of the requirements of a fast-moving business. As a result, this drive towards efficiency 'simplifies' pedagogies to 'best practice' and 'teaching tips'. So, if we return to Giroux's comment that what was once hidden is now overt, we find that this idea has taken another step. The reversal in the notion of the hidden curriculum is that it is now the positive debate and dialogue around learning and teaching that has become 'hidden' and consigned to a kind of 'dark art' status, covered on the surface by a dumbed-down set of ideas about 'delivery' to a business plan.

Establishing feedback dialogue – an intervention

It may be that the only way to develop dialogic feedback in the current HE environment is to find space in the broader curriculum where innovative practices might flourish. The rest of this chapter will consider a feedback intervention designed to engage 'non-traditional' students in particular in discussions around the complexity, importance and power of feedback. It discusses a compulsory meeting in the first year to support the development of new academic identities at a time when all students may be feeling most vulnerable to low self-esteem and isolation (Murphy and Roopchand, 2003). Research in this field suggests that working with students as individuals after an assessment judgement has taken place can encourage a sense of belonging that is significant to students' continued successful learning (Read et al., 2003; Yorke and Thomas, 2003). Yorke and Thomas (2003) focus on the importance of making students feel at home, especially those from lower socio-economic groups. Furthermore, the conclusions of the UCU (2008) stress survey suggests larger class sizes can compromise dialogic feedback and reduce the staff–student interaction that some writers refer to as being so important (Higgins et al., 2001; Rust et al., 2003). Carless (2006, p 220) has focused on feedback as conversation and collaboration and puts forward an argument for 'assessment dialogues'. Finally, Lillis (2001) discusses these issues too and frames feedback in terms not of 'one-off exchanges' (2001, p 10), but 'shared strands of meaning' where the provisional nature of writing is considered alongside the notion of writing as social practice.

These contextual comments help justify an intervention that developed out of a lack of engagement between students and feedback. The intervention takes place in a post-1992 university in the West Midlands which 'has one of the highest percentages of students from the lowest social class backgrounds, from "low participation neighbourhoods", and from families with no previous background of higher education' (Gipps, 2011). The student body is therefore complex and diverse. The intervention has been in place for two years and applies to all first-year full-time students on Early Childhood Studies, Education Studies and Special Needs and Inclusion Studies courses, totalling around 200 students. The intervention was designed to shift away from the notion of student self-referral for tutorial contact and move instead towards informal dialogue to support students' first summative feedback in their university lives. Leathwood and O'Connell (2003) and Read et al. (2003) found that 'non-traditional' students felt that they were expected to be independent learners too early and with little support. The dialogue initiated by this intervention is based on the written feedback students receive and the intention is to reduce the impact of the judgemental aspects of feedback and move beyond this to a dialogue based on the feelings students have and a plan for future assessments.

The intervention uses the tutorial system because this is a common structure to most post-1992 UK universities. Tutorial systems have survived corporatisation and often have lecturer hours attached, but, like feedback, personal tutoring across the HE sector in the UK suffers from a lack of research (Thomas and Hixenbaugh, 2006). This lack of research may be because of the 'taken-for granted nature of personal tutoring' to which Stephen et al. (2008, p 449) refer. Again, as with feedback, this comment suggests personal tutoring is also generally accepted as a straightforward transmission process and therefore not worthy of further investigation. Yorke and Thomas (2003) refer to the tutorial system as being capable of providing a stable point in the face of other changes to student–institution interaction, but if that personal tutor system is inappropriate or poorly developed, students may have little personal support to fall back on, especially during their first formal assessments when identities and self-esteem are particularly challenged. This dialogue intervention, then, tries not only to reveal the hidden importance of feedback, but also to revitalise the tutorial system and position its activity firmly in the area of academic development.

The review meeting

The dialogue process begins in January when all first-year students are sent a simple self-assessment pro forma to complete after semester one assignments are assessed and returned. This pro forma asks them to look carefully at the written feedback they have received from the three or four assignments completed in semester one. The pro forma is in two parts. The first encourages them to look for feedback points common to two or more of the assignments and start to identify what they feel are the patterns and trends in their written feedback. The second part asks students to think about these patterns and trends and suggest actions they can take to improve their assessed work for semester two. The next step for students is to make an appointment in February with their personal tutor. To this review meeting, students bring their completed pro forma and their summative assignments with written feedback. What students bring to this meeting is an important aspect of the intervention. It ensures students have already collected assignments and not just accessed grades online; this has been reported as an issue by Mutch (2003) and Duncan (2007) and has certainly been an issue for the students in this study. Using the students' completed pro formas, the assignments and the written feedback, personal tutors can initiate a face-to-face dialogue with their tutees ranging across their feelings and perceptions of their first experience of HE assessment. This can help new learners to think more about the learning potential of the feedback and less about the emotional response to grades, which can threaten their self-esteem (Young, 2000; Carless, 2006).

The outcomes of these meetings varied according to student needs. Some came away from the meeting with a negotiated plan designed to maintain enthusiasm and commitment after achieving high grades. For others, the outcome was based on vital changes to academic practice to prevent failure. Whatever the range of positive outcomes were, it became clear to us that working dialogically with students to create more effective use of feedback can help to support students vulnerable to feelings of isolation and distance from the HE community. Reay et al. (2010) refer to Bourdieu and Passeron's (1979) notion of working-class students as 'fish out of water' and in the same paper comment that first-generation students can have 'learner identities that are more fragile and unconfident' (p 11) than middle-class counterparts. These comments provide a useful context for our attempts to develop our support practices.

Evaluating the review meeting

We wanted to ensure that students had the opportunity to tell us if the review meetings were worthwhile, so after the first year of the process we organised an evaluation. This took place through one-to-one in-depth interviews with 15 students. Participants were between 18 and 25 years old and all female, reflecting the gender balance of the degree programmes involved. Twelve were first-generation students. Only four had followed a pure 'A' level route into HE. The other 10 had followed a 'vocational' qualification (eg a BTEC National qualification) or a mix of A level and vocational qualifications. None of the participants had followed an Access to Higher Education programme. Discussions were also undertaken with five personal tutors involved with the February reviews. These discussions took place during the course of award meetings and the review process of our personal tutor strategies.

However, the focus of this exercise was primarily to listen to the voices of the students.

During early planning, there were rightly some concerns from personal tutors about the demands the review meetings would make on their time. To some extent, these concerns were realised; 25 review meetings over a period of about three weeks did impact significantly on colleagues' workloads. Nevertheless, personal tutors were still generally very positive about the outcomes of the review meetings. Some said they welcomed the opportunity to catch up with a few personal tutees they had not seen since 'welcome week'. Some personal tutors also felt that the meetings saved time later in the year because assessment challenges could be supported before the start of semester two. The majority of meetings were conducted positively and personal tutors agreed with the benefits students mentioned (see later). Some personal tutors enjoyed seeing the variety of styles of feedback from colleagues and module teams; this was an unexpected spin-off in terms of professional development and shifted feedback from a 'private' to a more 'public' forum.

General benefits of the review meetings

First, students felt the review meeting extended their understandings around how to be more successful in summative assessments. Students felt they understood more clearly that many important assessment challenges are generic to many modules, despite any variations in types of assessment. For example, students felt the review meeting confirmed for them that wider reading and written accuracy were issues vital for success across many module assessment formats from traditional essays to poster presentations. This goes some way to challenge the idea that summative feedback at the end of a module is of limited use to subsequent assessments, as suggested by Lea and Street (2000, p 44). The review meeting became an opportunity to retrieve as much from summative feedback as possible to create a type of generic formative to go forward and build on in the next round of summative assessment the student would encounter. This benefit makes assumptions about how closely students will work with the outcomes of the review meeting; this depends on the development of their organisation and time-management skills. However, students also reported that they understood more about the importance of these types of skills after the review meeting. Angela, for example, made the point that the action plan evolving from her review meeting was on her desk "next to the work I'm doing at the moment". Ravinder also stated that her planning skills were better after the review meeting.

The second general issue was that many of the assessment challenges students wished to discuss during the review meetings were either new to them or they felt too inexperienced to achieve their potential in those particular challenges. They mentioned, for example, assessments through virtual learning environments (VLEs), the necessity for wider reading and the emphasis on accurate referencing as issues that did not form a significant part of their earlier education experiences. This seemed to be more significant for those students who had completed 'vocational' courses at The National Qualifications Framework level 3. Penny and Naomi compared their 'vocational' college courses with university and both felt that there were significant differences. Penny commented: "It's similar in the way that you had to do a lot of things for yourself at college, but there is a difference in the academic side in higher education". Ravinder was more outspoken about her HE experiences and said she was "shocked" by differences between school and university assessment; she felt she really needed to focus on these new demands to even survive, let alone thrive. Angela also felt the difference, particularly in terms of her worries about referencing. When she read a relevant point on a web site, she was reluctant to include it because she was not sure how to reference it accurately and did not want to 'look stupid'. Angela was therefore carrying out some useful wider reading, but not feeling confident about using that reading to enhance her summative assessment.

The review meetings therefore provided opportunities for students to take risks and comment about their perceived shortcomings in a safe environment away from the arena of module assessment. Personal tutors were able to share tacit knowledge with students about some of the spaces between stated assessment intentions and the messages students receive about what they should be learning. Despite studying at university for five months, students' first summative assessments remain an early testing ground of their academic preparedness. Most participants in the evaluation felt they had fallen short of their potential because they lacked some of the previously hidden understandings about assessment at university. The review meetings therefore helped to fill the space between earlier education experiences and some of the mysteries of their current challenges. As a result, most participants felt more positive after the review meeting about their next assessment opportunity in semester two.

The third general point from students was that the meeting raised their awareness of how other study skills support services in the university could help them achieve greater assessment success. During the review meeting, students appreciated the direct opportunity to clarify issues such as referencing, the importance of wider reading, finding journal articles and the possible dangers of drifting into plagiarism. However, where personal tutors felt it necessary, they referred students directly to cross-university services. First-year students had often not yet accessed university support services such as one-to-one study support, online support from learning centres, the Student Union, careers advice and counselling services. So the review meeting provided some direct support for these general study issues, but also acted as a broker for broader university services. This is the kind of role that tutorial systems are conventionally expected to carry out, but with a self-referral system, new students do not always feel confident in making contact with personal tutors. The review meeting, as a compulsory part of the first-year experience, provides the opportunity to raise student awareness of services outside their department and school at a time when and in a context where relevance to assessment success will be high.

More specific benefits of the review meetings

A smaller number of participants made a range of comments that resonate with published debates on assessment feedback. The first of these raises the issue of making clear links between one module and another. Like most students, Kath, for example, had read her feedback at different times because it is common for students to receive different assignments back at staggered intervals. As a result, she did not make immediate connections between feedback comments from one module to another as effectively as she did subsequently in and after the review meeting. She commented: "I could see more clearly after the review meeting what was going on from one assessment to another". Mary made a similar point about the value of this particular aspect of the review meetings: "You can do individual modules and they seem to have no relevance to each other but then in the meeting you can just see them altogether like how they link in with each other".

Kath and Mary both found it difficult to see the links between feedback and subject from one module to the next. But, by talking about the feedback from different modules at the same time, some of the spaces between modules can be identified and connections made more visible to students.

The second particular issue raised by Penny, Ravinder and Kath was how the meeting helped them to understand written feedback, which they had previously found difficult to read or 'interpret'. Interpretation of feedback is a complex area considered in more detail by other writers (Ivanic et al., 2000; Lea and Street, 2000; Hounsell, 2004), but it is worth considering here the variety of styles and types of feedback students experience. For example, the written feedback to Kath's three pieces of work from semester one was, as she says, "a bit of everything". Her feedback came in three different formats: around the text itself, a pro forma tick sheet and a feedback form with space for narrative comments only. Since this study, we could now include e-submission and assessment.

There is of course an argument for differentiation in feedback methods and styles, but consideration must be given to student perceptions and interpretations of this patchwork of feedback formats. This study suggests that variety conveys some confusing messages to students, fuelled by powerful hierarchical and subordinating relationships between lecturers and students sometimes hidden by the rhetoric of a transmission interpretation of feedback. Confusing feedback messages is raised by the Quality Assurance Agency (2008) report, referred to earlier. Modular systems are to some extent responsible for making student feedback experiences complex and challenging to interpret. The point here is that in situations where variety of feedback types and formats exists, the review meetings can go some way to help clarify differences and begin to reveal and resolve what may be perceived by students as confusing variations and contradictions within feedback processes.

Another important aspect of the intervention relates to the discussion earlier in this chapter about 'belonging'. Linda, for example, was asked if she thought the review should continue and she responded: "Yes I do because it is helpful. You also feel as if you belong". This echoes the findings of other writers (Leathwood and O'Connell, 2003; Read et al., 2003) who refer to the culture of academia as potentially alien and unsettling. This can be true for those from lower socio-economic backgrounds or holders of different cultural capital, and becomes another aspect of the feedback 'moment' that remains hidden in an HE system encouraged to move quickly by administrative structures and financial imperatives.

Ravinder also referred to an issue linked to 'belonging' but combined this with a comment about self-esteem. Her point raised the tendency for students to feel insecure about what they think they do not know. Ravinder's written feedback formed a pattern around a shortage of evidence of wider reading. In response, her personal tutor helped her to search for journal articles and Ravinder says:

> "My tutor showed me how to research through journals, which was something I did not know how to do myself. I missed the tour of the learning centre so I didn't know how to do that and I was reluctant to ask for help."

Ravinder agreed that she felt insecure revealing what she thought she did not know and it is not unusual for students seeking help to label themselves, and be labelled by others, as 'low-ability' students (Blumenfield, 1992). This feeling is linked to the accepted status of students as 'independent learners'. Unquestioned acceptance of this notion can put pressure on students not to seek support when they need it because they have absorbed the message that HE is about 'independent learning'. Self-referral tutorial systems can work to endorse the idea that 'bothering' your personal tutor is a sign of 'weakness'. This is especially the case for 'non-traditional' students (Leathwood and O'Connell, 2003). For Ravinder, the review meeting provided the first 'safe' space for her to take part in a compulsory but more open discussion about these kinds of insecurities. As a result of the review meeting, Ravinder felt more confident about using the Learning Centre and accessing what she needed to improve her wider reading. Ravinder's experiences identify a general finding from the evaluation that where the meeting was successful, there was a general improvement in relationships between student and personal tutor. This is a crucial but less tangible aspect of the review meeting, as noted by Linda: "She [her personal tutor] helped me all round really because I was doubting what I wanted to do and she helped me get things into perspective". Leslie made a similar statement: "My tutor said that I could go and see her about anything, which I thought was really nice because I never would have been able to do that at school".

These comments suggest that the review meetings help address the emotion and power relationships involved with lecturers' feedback to which both Boud (1995) and Carless (2006) refer. Students' relationships with academic staff are an important part of integration into academic life, particularly for working-class students (Leathwood and O'Connell, 2003).

In general, the evaluation suggested that most students felt they understood more about academic practices after the review meeting than before. However, two students in the evaluation had negative comments to make about the review. These focused generally on a lack of detail, time and 'friendly' dialogue. Clearly, the intervention relies on the skills and commitment of the personal tutor and how effectively the review meeting is carried out. This in turn rests on the extent of any personal tutor's willingness to commit to a dialogic co-constructivist approach. Simpson et al. (2005, p 120) point to John Dewey's comment that students easily identify teachers who work out of obligation, not out of interest in them, although the pressures of day-to-day HE working practices can compromise the principles of the most committed lecturers. Unsurprisingly, the best meetings were those that involved time to endorse strengths and support areas for development. The least effective were those that took place in pairs, without very much individual time and therefore lacking detail. This professional development issue is crucial to the future success of this type of dialogic review.

Conclusion

This chapter has argued that assessment feedback is not a simple transmission process, but a complex aspect of social practice that requires more attention in the light of public criticism. It is argued that a dialogic approach to supporting students' use of written feedback can be of significant benefit to first-year students, particularly those without a lifetime's access to middle-class cultural capital. The post-1992 student body is more complex and diverse than is often acknowledged and it is suggested that universities prioritise delivery and efficiency rather than pedagogical issues relevant to diversity in the student body and the complexity of feedback and personal tutoring. These issues have been interpreted through the shifting notion of the hidden curriculum, which provides a useful context for debate around unchallenged assumptions and covert practices. The feedback review meetings can support students in an increasingly unstable HE environment by providing a space for open and supportive dialogue. Students found that this opportunity extended their understandings of unfamiliar assessment practices and assisted the process of inclusion into the HE community. Most importantly, the meeting helped to nurture the renegotiation of 'non-traditional' student identities at a time when they are most vulnerable to low confidence and self-esteem. Whatever form feedback interventions might take, this chapter endorses the position that feedback is: first, a crucial part of a whole approach to learning; and. second, a complex social practice requiring dialogue and mutual respect.

References

Askew, S. and Lodge C. (2000) 'Gifts, ping-pong and loops – linking feedback and learning', in S. Askew (ed) *Assessment for Learning*, London: RoutledgeFalmer.

Bekhradnia, B., Whitnall, C., and Sastry, T. (2006) *The Academic Experience of Students in English Universities*, Oxford: Higher Education Policy Institute.

Black, P. and Wiliam, D. (1998) 'Assessment and classroom learning', *Assessment in Education: Principles, Policy and Practice*, vol 5, pp 1–54.

Blumenfeld, P.C. (1992) 'Classroom learning and motivation: clarifying and expanding goal theory', *Journal of Educational Psychology*, vol 84, no 3, pp 272–81.

Boud, D. (1995) *Enhancing Learning through Self-Assessment*, London: Kogan Page.

Bourdieu, P. and Passeron, J. (1979) *The Inheritors; French Students and Their Relation to Culture*, Chicago, IL: University of Chicago Press.

Browne, J. (2010) 'Securing a sustainable future for higher education. An independent review of higher education funding and finance'. Available at: www.independent.gov.uk/browne-report (accessed October 2010).

Carless, D. (2006) 'Differing perceptions in the feedback process', *Studies in Higher Education*, vol 31, pp 219–33.

Dewey, J. (1963 [1938]) *Experience and Education*, Collier-Macmillan.

Duncan, N. (2007) '"Feed-forward": improving students' use of tutors', *Assessment & Evaluation in Higher Education*, vol 32, pp 271–83.

Gipps, C. (2011) *Who Goes to University? And Why it Matters*, p 14. Available at: www.wlv.ac.uk/PDF/vc_publiclecture_june2011.pdf (accessed 4 October 2011).

Giroux, H. (2006) 'Higher education under siege: implications for public intellectuals', *Thought and Action*, Fall, pp 63–78.

Giroux, H. (2007) 'Academic repression in the first person: the attack on higher education and the necessity of critical pedagogy', CUNY Graduate Center Advocat, February. Available at: http://gcadvocate.org/index.php?action=view&id=124 (accessed June 2009).

Giroux, H. (2008) 'The militarization of US higher education after 9/11', *Theory, Culture and Society*, vol 25, pp 56–82.

Harvey, L. and Drew, S., with Smith, M. (2006) *The First Year Experience: A Review of Literature*, York: Higher Education Academy.

Higgins, R., Hartley, P. and Skelton, A. (2001) 'Getting the message across: the problem of communicating assessment feedback', *Teaching in Higher Education*, vol 6, pp 269–74.

Hounsell, D. (2004) *Improving Feedback to Students. Scottish Quality Enhancement Workshop on Assessment*, Glasgow: University of Glasgow.

Ivanic, R., Clark, R. and Rimmershaw, R. (2000) 'What am I supposed to make of this? The messages conveyed to students by tutors' written comments', in M.R. Lea and B. Stierer (eds) *Student Writing in Higher Education*, Buckingham: Open University Press.

Jackson, P.W. (1990 [1968]) *Life in Classrooms*, New York: Teachers College Press.

Knight, P.T. and Trowler, P.R. (2000) 'Department-level cultures and the improvement of learning and teaching', *Studies in Higher Education*, vol 25, pp 69–83.

Lea, M.R. and Street, B.V. (2000) 'Staff feedback: an academic literacies approach', in M.R. Lea and B. Stierer (eds) *Student Writing in Higher Education*, Buckingham: Open University Press.

Leathwood, C. and O'Connell, P. (2003) '"It's a struggle": the construction of the "new student" in higher education', *Journal of Education Policy*, vol 18, pp 597–615.

Lillis, T.M. (2001) *Student Writing: Access, Regulation, Desire*, London: Routledge.

Love, K. (2008) 'Higher education, pedagogy and the "customerisation" of teaching and learning', *Journal of Philosophy of Education*, vol 42, pp 15–34.

Margolis, E. (ed) (2001) *The Hidden Curriculum in Higher Education*, New York: Routledge.

Martin, J.R. (1976) 'What should we do with a hidden curriculum when we find one?', *Curriculum Inquiry*, vol 6, pp 135–51.

Murphy, H. and Roopchand, N. (2003) 'Intrinsic motivation and self-esteem in traditional and mature students at a post-1992 university in the north-east of England', *Educational Studies*, vol 29, pp 243–59.

Mutch, A. (2003) 'Exploring the practice of feedback to students', *Active Learning in Higher Education*, vol 4, pp 24–38.

Newman, M. (2009) 'Students' campaigns take some ugly turns', *Times Higher Education*, 4–10 June.

Nicol, D. (2008) 'Lecturers' feedback efforts "misguided"', *Times Higher Education*, 31 July. Available at: www.timeshighereducation.co.uk/story.asp?storycode=403012 (accessed June 2009).

Nicol, D. and Macfarlane-Dick, D.J. (2006) 'Formative assessment and self-regulated learning: a model and seven principles of good feedback practice', *Studies in Higher Education*, vol 31, pp 199–218.

Preece, S. (2009) *Posh Talk: Language and Identity in Higher Education*, London: Palgrave Macmillan.

Quality Assurance Agency (2008) 'Outcomes from institutional audit. Assessment of students', Second series: Sharing good practice, QAA 178 03/08.

Ramsden, P. (2009) *The Future of Higher Education Teaching and the Student Experience*, London: Department for Innovation, Universities and Skills.

Read, B., Archer, L. and Leathwood, C. (2003) 'Challenging cultures? Student conceptions of "belonging" and "isolation" at a post-1992 university', *Studies in Higher Education*, vol 28, pp 261–77.

Reay, D., Crozier, G. and Clayton, J. (2010) '"Fitting" in or "standing out": working class students in UK higher education', *British Educational Research Journal*, vol 36, pp 107–24.

Rust, C., Price, M. and O'Donovan, B. (2003) 'Improving students' understanding of assessment criteria and processes', *Assessment and Evaluation in Higher Education*, vol 28, pp 147–64.

Sadler, D.R. (1989) 'Formative assessment and the design of instructional systems', *Instructional Science*, vol 18, pp 119–44.

Sastry, T. and Bekhradnia, B. (2007) *The Academic Experience of Students in English Universities*, Oxford: Higher Education Policy Institute.

Simpson, D., Jackson, M. and Aycock, J. (2005) *John Dewey and the Art of Teaching. Toward Reflective and Imaginative Practice*, California: Sage.

Snyder, B. (1970) *The Hidden Curriculum*, New York: Alfred A. Knopf.

Stephen, D.E., O'Connell, P. and Hall, M. (2008) 'Going the extra mile, fire-fighting or laissez-faire? Re-evaluating personal tutoring relationships within mass higher education', *Teaching in Higher Education*, vol 13, pp 449–60.

Tahir, T. (2008) 'Feedback must be top priority', *Times Higher Education*, 4 January. Available at: www.timeshighereducation.co.uk/story.asp?sectioncode=26&storycode=400008 (accessed July 2009).

Thomas, L. and Hixenbaugh, P. (2006) *Personal Tutoring in Higher Education*, Stoke-on-Trent: Trentham Books.

UCU (2008) 'Stress survey', press release, 28 May. Available at: http://www.ucu.org.uk/index.cfm?articleid=3316 (accessed October 2009).

Yorke, M. and Thomas, L. (2003) 'Improving the retention of students from lower socio-economic groups', *Journal of Higher Education Policy and Management*, vol 25, pp 63–74.

Young, P. (2000) 'I might as well give up: self-esteem and mature students' feelings about feedback on assignments', *Journal of Further and Higher Education*, vol 24, pp 409–18.

TWELVE

Teaching Indigenous teachers: valuing diverse perspectives

Ninetta Santoro, Jo-Anne Reid, Laurie Crawford and Lee Simpson

Introduction

In Australia, education is failing Indigenous people, who remain the most disadvantaged group in the nation (ABS, 2007; Doyle and Hill, 2008). Indigenous students' school participation rates are lower than their non-Indigenous peers, they leave school earlier and are less likely to complete secondary schooling (James and Devlin, 2005; Doyle and Hill, 2008). Barnhardt and Kawagley, drawing on the work of Battiste, assert that:

> Students in Indigenous societies around the world have, for the most part, demonstrated a distinct lack of enthusiasm for the experience of schooling in its conventional form – an aversion that is most often attributable to an alien institutional culture rather than any lack of innate intelligence, ingenuity, or problem-solving skills on the part of the students. (2005, p 10)

In Australia, Indigenous students are under-represented in universities and other tertiary education institutions. Only 26% of those aged 25–64 have obtained a non-school qualification and 5% have obtained a bachelor's degree and above. This compares unfavourably with the non-Indigenous population, where 53% have a non-school qualification and 21% have a bachelor's degree (ABS, 2008). Similar results are evident in other First Nations communities such as those in Canada (Freeman, 2008) and the US (Locke, 2004).

As a means to improve Indigenous students' participation in schooling, there have been ongoing calls for many years in Canada, North America, New Zealand and Australia to increase the number of Indigenous teachers so that students can be taught by those who best understand their needs and cultural backgrounds (Locke, 2004; Reid, 2004; White et al., 2007). In Australia, Paul Hughes' famously optimistic goal of '1000 teachers by 1990' (Hughes and Willmot, 1982) was aimed primarily at retraining Aboriginal Education Assistants (AEAs) already working in schools.[1] However, this target was not achieved. Nearly 20 years on, and even acknowledging the number of successful enclave and support programmes that were subsequently established for Indigenous teachers, the numbers of Indigenous teaching staff as a proportion of all teaching staff in government schools has remained at less than 1% over this time, while in the Catholic system, the proportion is far smaller at 0.23% (DEEWR, 2008). While most Indigenous students in higher education are likely to be studying Teacher Education, they still only comprise 2% of Teacher Education students overall (DEEWR, 2008, p 119).

In the US, White et al. (2007, p 72) report on some of the factors that affect the overall numbers of Hopi and Navajo people in teacher education:

> The pattern of under-representation of Indian educators replicates the national pattern of other cultural groups. Many students of color are attracted to fields outside of education where recruiting is more effective, and where monetary rewards and prestige are higher. High student attrition rates, students' difficulties with standardized tests and college admission requirements, and the unresponsiveness of colleges and universities to the needs, abilities, and expectations of students of color are formidable obstacles.

We suggest that similar issues are true in Australia, where universities struggle to provide the pastoral and academic support required to recruit and retain Indigenous student-teachers (see Reid et al., 2009).

Theoretical frameworks

We have drawn on post-structuralist theories of identity and subjectivity (Foucault, 1980; Henriques et al., 1984; Davies, 1993; Venn, 2006; Wetherell, 2008) to inform our work. Clarke, commenting on the 'postmodern turn' suggests:

> If modernism emphasized universality, generalization, simplification, permanence, stability, wholeness, rationality, regularity, homogeneity, and sufficiency, then

> postmodernism has shifted emphases to partialities, positionalities, complications, tenuousness, instabilities, irregularities, contradictions, heterogeneities, situatedness, and fragmentation – complexities. (2005, p xxiv)

Identity is taken up and performed by the self, in and through the body, as well as through discursive practices. According to Venn, identity 'refers to the relational aspects that qualify subjects in terms of categories such as race, gender, class, nation, sexuality, work and occupation, and thus in terms of acknowledged social relations and affiliations to groups – teachers, miners, parents, and so on' (2006, p 79). The participants in the study reported here are teachers – they are also Indigenous. As we argue, an 'Indigenous teacher' identity can be, and is often, ascribed by others, and understood as fixed and singular. The ascription of an essentialised identity disregards the complexities within and between the category 'Indigenous', as well as the category 'teacher'. There are multiple ways of being both Indigenous and teacher that are shaped by social and discursive practices, as well as factors such as gender and social class. Furthermore, such factors are inextricably intertwined and intersect in complex ways. Indigenous teachers, for example, are also gendered, and they are positioned and take up positionings within social classes. Some scholars use the term intersectionality to describe the 'multiple positioning that constitutes everyday life and the power relations that are central to it' (Phoenix, 2006, cited in Flintoff et al., 2008, p 74). Others are critical of the term because it implies that there are 'fixed, observable realities and homogenized social categories that are added together in some way, which can, at some later stage, still be separated' (Flintoff et al., 2008, p 75). Youdell (2006, p 29) prefers to consider identity categories as 'constellations', and states:

> This is not to suggest that each category that is embroiled in such a constellation is discreet or sealed. Rather, it is to ask how these categories might come to be meaningful through their relationships to other categories within particular constellations and whether constellations might be necessary for apparently singular categories to be meaningful ... each marker is informed by its intersections and interactions with further markers to form a 'constellation' that comes to 'be' the apparently 'whole' person.

Identities are always being produced, in a state of becoming, changing and shifting in response to different social contexts and dynamics.

Indigenous teachers 'become' who they are, as they construct and perform themselves in the range of social situations in which they participate. According to Nakata, the formation of Indigenous identities in postcolonial contexts always takes place in the 'cultural interface':

> the place where we live and learn, the place that conditions our lives, the place that shapes our futures and more to the point the place where we are active agents in our own lives – where we make decisions – our lifeworld. For Indigenous peoples our context, remote or urban, is already circumscribed by the discursive space of the Cultural Interface. We don't go to work or school, enter another domain, interact and leave it there when we come home again. The boundaries are simply not that clear. (2004, p 27)

This chapter draws upon a selection of data from a study that investigated the teaching experiences and career pathways of current and former Indigenous teachers in Australian schools and some of the reasons for their under-representation in the teaching profession. Here, we report on just one aspect of the findings of the study: Indigenous students' experiences of teacher education in relation to their positioning as Indigenous by teacher education curricula and practices. We suggest that such practices do not take into account the diverse nature of Indigenous identities and cultures, nor do they build upon the diverse experiences Indigenous people bring with them to teacher education.

The study

The study brought together, in partnership, a team of Indigenous and non-Indigenous researchers[2] during a four-year period to produce a set of qualitative case studies. Data collection comprised semi-structured interviews with 50 former and current teachers who ranged in age from 25 through to 61; there were 14 males; 30 of the teachers began their teaching degrees as mature-age students rather than as school leavers and 22 completed enclave or separate programmes for Indigenous teacher trainees. Of the total participant numbers, 12 were former teachers who had left teaching either to take on administrative roles in schools or other education systems, become teacher educators or taken up other occupations entirely. The 38 current teachers have taught for periods of time ranging from one to 17 years in primary and secondary school contexts located in small rural communities or in larger regional and metropolitan areas of the Australian states of Victoria and New South Wales (NSW).

The interviewees were selected from networks of Indigenous teachers to which the project's Aboriginal[3] co-researchers were connected. This led to a snowballing method of recruitment whereby the teachers recommended other potential participants. Because there are few Indigenous teachers in Australia and demographic information about them is not readily available, this method of recruitment was deemed to be the most viable. The interviews lasted between one and two hours, were conducted by individual members of the research team, and were recorded. The transcriptions were returned to interviewees for member checking and verification. This chapter draws specifically on interview data obtained from interviews with five teachers who had completed either mainstream or separate Indigenous teacher education courses between two and 18 years prior to the interviews.

As a research team, we are culturally diverse with a range of cultural, historical and institutional relationships of power. We have all worked as teachers and teacher educators, but are differently positioned in terms of Indigenous and Aboriginal knowledge. While we actively seek to construct knowledge about Indigenous teacher education, we do this from our own histories and experiences. Our practice therefore requires us to acknowledge and accept Nakata's claim that 'all knowledge systems are culturally embedded, dynamic, respond to changing circumstances and constantly evolve' (2004, p 28). Thus, we have needed to interrogate and debate the data together, drawing on our different interpretive perspectives and our collective personal and professional experience, which includes a complex range of insider/ outsider perspectives or standpoints (Merriam et al., 2001; Clancy and Simpson, 2002; Shah, 2004). This collaborative approach ensures that our interpretations resonate with and have meaning for a number of groups, including people in Indigenous communities who might want to become teachers.

A thematic analytic approach was used to highlight the complexities of the teachers' lived experiences as recounted in the interviews. For example, data were organised and clustered around themes and sub-themes such as 'reasons for becoming a teacher', 'nature of experiences during teacher education' and 'teaching relationships' – with colleagues, students and parents. The analysis also attended to the silences, what was not said and the discursive practices that shaped identities in implied, but not explicit, ways. We understand the interviews with our participants as sites of contestable and contested meanings. Furthermore, stories of 'experience' are never complete in themselves when they are told – we need to understand the meanings available from different positions at the cultural interface, and then to interrogate the social structures that have worked to produce some of these meanings as more powerful, more 'telling', than others. In this way, we have attempted to highlight the complexities of the student-teachers' lived experiences, and the complex effects of these experiences on the construction of their different subject positions as Aboriginal teachers. In analysing the transcription texts, we have focused on *what* participants have told us about their experiences as well as *how* they have talked about them.

Such a methodological position has effects for us as researchers, too, in that we are forced to acknowledge that rather than being able to identify truth statements or knowledge about Indigenous teachers that pre-exist our inquiry and lie 'hidden' in the transcripts for us to 'discover', we actively *produce* knowledge through our interaction and interpretation of the words of our participants.

We do not seek to generalise from our findings and the data presented here are not intended to represent the perspectives of *all* Indigenous pre-service teachers. Nevertheless, the data provide valuable insights into the discursive practices that shaped how the pre-service teachers were positioned as Indigenous within discourses of Australian teacher education.

Understandings of Indigenous culture as fixed and mono-dimensional

Indigenous student-teachers, like any group of people, are not homogeneous. No culture is homogeneous – cultures change, are fluid, multiple, mediated by individuals' social class and gender, and understood differently at different times by individuals who cross cultural boundaries and belong to, and identify with, different aspects of particular cultures at different times. In Australia, Indigenous groups are characterised by over 200 diverse traditional cultural practices that mark their tribal association and links to 'country' (Droste, 2001; Stuurman, 2003). The knowledge and traditional cultural practices of people from each of these groups is very different. Such diversity is reflected in our sample of interviewees, who were only drawn from a relatively small area of the country, that is, the states of Victoria and NSW, yet were representative of seven tribal groups: Bundjalung, Gamilaroi, Wirudjeri, Wirundjeri, Dharug, Dharawal and Gureng.

Indigenous identities are also complicated by the effects of past assimilation practices in which Aboriginal people were removed from their land onto missions and reserves and forced to abandon their language and traditional cultural practices in favour of the values and practices of white Australia. Between the 1880s and the early 1970s, with a strong movement in the 1930s, several generations of fair-skinned Aboriginal children were forcibly removed from families by government authorities and brought up as wards of the state, adopted or fostered by white families (Clark, 2000). These practices occurred most frequently in areas of Australia where there was a significant settled white population, rather than in remote areas of the country. Such assimilation practices resulted in a loss of language and cultural practices. Fredericks (2002) argues that, for many Indigenous people, the process of identification as 'Aboriginal', with just one particular social group, is complicated inexorably by history:

> Aboriginal people live in the contemporary world and weave in and out of two, three and even more cultural domains. We are part of colonisation, just as it is part of us. Aboriginal culture has needed to adapt, adjust and modify itself in order to survive within the contemporary world. This does not mean that our cultures are not, and that we are not, Aboriginal. You might have to look and listen more closely, but culture is always there in some form, always was and always will be. (Fredericks, 2002)

The degree to which Indigenous people are in touch with traditional cultures depends on whether they have had cultural knowledge passed down to them through successive generations. A history of colonisation and assimilation has fragmented families, making cultural learning almost impossible for some Indigenous people. As Colleen,[4] one of our interviewees, says, "We're still finding out who we are. And it wasn't our choice that some of us know nothing about being Aboriginal. We had to learn it later in life". Grant, when asked whether his knowledge of Aboriginal culture was passed on to him from his parents, says:

> "No, it wasn't passed down from my family. My mother was taught as a kid that being Aboriginal was not a good thing to be and she still, to this day, doesn't claim Aboriginality. But my grandfather made sure that all the grandkids knew that they were Aboriginal, he was proud of it. I've always claimed to be Aboriginal. I've been proud of it too, but all the learning and the finding out about the Aboriginal culture is something I've had to actually go and do."

Most of our interviewees do not speak an Aboriginal language and their understanding of Aboriginal culture is varied. Some are urban Aboriginals, through relocation policies of the past; many are not living in their traditional country; some are fair-skinned, others are dark-skinned. This diversity, however, does not mean that they are not Indigenous – they simply understand Aboriginal culture and their Aboriginality in a range of ways: 'It must be recognized that Indigenous people do not require particular phenotypical traits, certain forms of cultural alterity, specific ethico-moral beliefs/actions or a certain level of social disadvantage in order to be Indigenous' (Paradies, 2006, p 363). Paradies goes on to suggest that there is a need to 'recognize that although the poor and the rich Indigene, the cultural reviver and the quintessential cosmopolitan, the fair, dark, good, bad and disinterested may have little in common, they are nonetheless all equally but variously Indigenous' (2006, p 363).

Although there are multiple ways of being Indigenous, pre-service teachers are frequently positioned by the discourses of teacher education as homogeneous. Such positionings and associated 'identity borders … constructed around primitivist, romantic and colonial discourses' (Paradies, 2006, p 362) do not recognise that 'Indigenous people who, by adapting and changing, have survived colonialism while unavoidably shedding their pristine primeval identity' (Paradies, 2006, p 361). Kirsten, referring to how she was positioned by some of her fellow students and lecturers, says:

> "You know you always have to prove yourself as an Aboriginal person in their eyes. They want you to act in a certain way because that's what they deem Aboriginal people to be and it's just like, you know, we don't have those mission farms anymore so don't try and farm me because I won't do it!"

Most of our interviewees, reflecting on their pre-service teacher education experiences, reported feeling marginalised during their study because the construction of Indigenous identity, via teacher education curricula, was at odds with how they understood themselves and their own Indigeneity. This was particularly so in the case of curricula that aimed to prepare the student-teachers to teach Indigenous students. Shirley, a Dharawal[5] woman who grew up in a coastal NSW town and completed her teacher education 16 years before our interview, reflects on the appropriateness of the advice given to her and other pre-service teachers about addressing the needs of Aboriginal school students:

> "We weren't happy with what the lecturer was saying because they were talking about cultural practices that might be relevant to the mob up the Northern Territory, but not here! And so we found it quite foreign.... Like I mean, some of the stuff we saw in schools too, they were sort of reinforcing stereotypes. It doesn't have to be the Aboriginal man with his leg up on his knee holding a spear ... that's a stereotype. But there's a lot of that out there.... It needs to be put more strongly to the kids that this is the past ... this is not what happens necessarily now."

There appears to have been no acknowledgement by the lecturer of the complexities of Indigenous cultures and that there are many Indigenous cultures. The portrayal of this particular Indigenous culture as *the* Indigenous culture also serves to alienate those Indigenous pre-service teachers who are unable to identify with cultural practices belonging to "the mob up the Northern Territory", many thousands of kilometres away. Shirley's concern about the stereotypical representation in school curricula of an "Aboriginal man with his leg up on his knee holding a spear" is the type of image Paradies calls 'the pernicious fantasy of the "Indigenous look"' (2006, p 359). Such an 'Indigenous look' is also a dark-skinned look, an essentialised identity that for fair-skinned Aboriginal people leads to feelings of 'ambivalence, and doubts about themselves as "real" [Indigenous] people' (Boladeras, 2002, cited in Paradies, 2006, p 359).

Alicia, a Gulidjan woman who completed her teacher education 12 years before her interview, also talks about the stereotypes of Aboriginal people that informed much of the curriculum she encountered as a pre-service teacher:

> "It was like, I didn't grow up like that! There was a lot of stereotyping that they were telling us about Aboriginal children. They sniff petrol, and they do this and they do that, and you think well no ... that doesn't happen everywhere. But the white fellas came out [of the class] believing that *all* Aboriginal children sniff petrol when they're this age, and they *all* do this when they're that age, and they *all* can't read when they're this age.... So, yeah, it was very negative. I was thinking yes, that does happen, but not everywhere.... Anyway, I had problems with that and didn't end up going to a lot of the classes, and that was one of the reasons I failed, I stopped going.... Yeah."

The construction of Aboriginal children as universally deficit not only alienated Alicia to the point where she gave up going to classes, but is also problematic in terms of preparing pre-service teachers to adequately address the educational needs of Aboriginal students. Such a construction works to position the children as the problem without due acknowledgement and recognition being given to the systemic injustices that limit their choices and marginalise them.

Indigenous Studies has recently become a mandatory component of all teacher education courses in NSW. Prior to 2004, it was an optional aspect of pre-service teacher education, aimed at developing non-Indigenous students' understandings of Indigenous histories and cultures. Many of the institutions where our interviewees studied included Indigenous Studies as part of their course. For some, it facilitated deeper and different understandings of their own identities. For many, however, it was troubling because it often presented just one version of Indigeneity. Kirsten, a Gamilaroi woman who completed her teacher education eight years prior to our study, reflected on a lecture that was part of Indigenous Studies in her course. Her frustration is clear:

> "They had a guest speaker come in and she was talking about Aboriginal culture and stuff … and I was up the back of the room thinking, 'you don't know me! How dare you tell me what I'm like'. And that's when I got up and shouted, 'What a lot of crap!' and walked out."

Alicia claimed that the non-Indigenous students accepted the subject content of Indigenous Studies more readily than she did. This may have been because, in most cases, they began with little knowledge, or the subject may simply have reinforced the stereotypes they already held about Aboriginal people. She says about her own experiences:

> "I failed Aboriginal Studies in my first year, and when I went to see the lecturer because I failed it he said, 'You'll have to do it again' … and then I said, 'But I'm Aboriginal!' I said, 'I find it quite irrelevant, I didn't enjoy it and I thought a lot of it was stereotyping'. But I got nowhere. I just had to do it again."

While the lecturer's perspectives about why Alicia failed Indigenous Studies are unknown, from Alicia's perspective, there appears to be a disjuncture between her personal experiences of Aboriginal cultures and identities and those portrayed through the subject content.

Overall, the pre-service teachers felt powerless to do anything but tolerate what they considered to be misrepresentations of Aboriginal people occurring within teacher education curricula, or the curriculum they were required to teach in schools during their practicum. Kirsten, however, saw her written assignments as an opportunity to express her cultural knowledge even though she was not sure that doing so would be of 'much use' anyway. Her concern about being misunderstood by her lecturers only led to more work because she felt compelled to annotate what she had written:

> "Sometimes I'd draw on my Aboriginal identity in my assignments but I often wondered how much use it would be anyway … yeah, I was really worried that they wouldn't understand what I was trying to get across so I would write up accompanying notes so they could actually understand what it was I was actually getting at."

Clare, a Gamilaroi woman who had completed her teacher education only three years earlier, said:

> "I just thought a lot of it was crap … I brought in a lot of knowledge and previous experience, like when I was growing up, my experience in education and my work experience. But they didn't take any notice of it and they didn't sort of teach me much. At times it did make you want to give up, you know, tell them where to shove the course because you felt that you didn't fit in. I felt very isolated at university. It was almost like you were invisible."

Brayboy and Maughan, whose research focused on teacher education for Native Americans, also found the hegemony of mainstream teacher education problematic. As they assert: 'The teacher education program that we worked with, like many programs, could be rigid, narrow, and unforgiving to different ways of engaging the world' (Brayboy and Maughan, 2009, p 4). Like the programmes our interviewees experienced, it also failed to take into account diverse Indigenous perspectives.

Colleen, a Wiradjuri woman who had been teaching for 18 years, reflects on her experiences on practicum. Her supervising teacher used the opportunity to assess Colleen's performance as satisfactory but also to report: "I think she'll only be able to teach Aboriginal kids." This assessment of Colleen is worrying for two main reasons. First, if Indigenous teachers deal exclusively with Indigenous students and Indigenous education issues, they run the risk of being assigned an identity as 'the Indigenous teacher' and being caught up in a multitude of concerns including initiating new policies around Indigenous education, sitting on committees internal and external to the school, acting in an advisory capacity for the non-Indigenous teachers in regards to Indigenous pedagogies, and establishing home–school relationships and partnerships with parents and families. Although most Indigenous teachers report that they became teachers to help Indigenous students achieve better educational outcomes and access a better life (Santoro, 2010), the all-consuming responsibilities of being 'the Indigenous teacher' can mean that the same opportunities for professional development as their non-Indigenous peers are not available to them. In previous work, we have claimed that for many, if not for all, Indigenous teachers, 'this identity, once ascribed, becomes a means of identification, or a label, behind and beneath which individual difference and affiliation is systematically obscured' (Santoro and Reid, 2006, p 298).

Second, the supervising teacher's assessment of Colleen as only able to teach Aboriginal kids is worrying because it implies that there are two categories of teacher: those who are able to teach non-Indigenous students and those who are able to only teach Indigenous students. We argue elsewhere (Reid and Santoro, 2006, p 153) that '"The Indigenous Teacher" remains marked, and signified as inferior to that of "the teacher", who is understood as "normally" a non-Indigenous person'. Indigenous teachers are frequently positioned 'in their professional field as less knowledgeable and less well-trained than their non-Indigenous colleagues' (Reid and Santoro, 2006, p 154).

Conclusion

The research findings reported here have some significant implications for teacher education. First, curricula that do not take into account and acknowledge the diverse nature of Indigenous identities and cultures can work to alienate Indigenous pre-service teachers. Many of our interviewees failed subjects or stopped attending lectures because they felt marginalised. While they ultimately managed to negotiate the discourses of teacher education curricula in order to complete teaching degrees, many did so at some personal cost – the ways they understood themselves in their home, family and community often rubbed up against the identities constructed by and through discourses of teacher education. What is not clear from our research is the degree to which other Indigenous people who begin teacher education courses discontinue because of such marginalisation. Locke, speaking from a North American perspective, suggests that often courses simply 'perpetuate[d] the status quo by forcing Native Americans to examine their culture through a Euro-American perspective, which has worked to oppress them in the first place' (2004, p 21). Similar concerns are valid in the case of Australian teacher education whereby curricula either simplified or homogenised Indigenous cultures and identities, forcing students to engage with their own cultures through a foreign lens.

Furthermore, on the basis of the experiences of the participants reported here, it would seem that Australian teacher education does not adequately acknowledge or build upon the diverse experiences of Indigenous pre-service teachers. It is they who have experienced first hand the schooling practices that frequently perpetuate white middle-class privilege and it is they, collectively, who best understand the complex nature of Indigenous cultures and identities. However, Indigenous pre-service teachers are often positioned as complete novices with little to add to the discussion of Indigenous education. According to Moreton-Robinson: 'Aborigines have often been represented as objects – as the "known". Rarely are they represented as subjects, as "knowers"' (2004, p 75).

There is a need for teacher education to reposition Indigenous pre-service teachers as 'knowers'. This will mean acknowledging the value of their life-experience and its potential to enhance all pre-service teachers' understandings of the complexities of Indigenous identities. As Brayboy and Maughan claim:

> It is not enough for teacher education programs to simply claim commitment to the training of Indigenous educators. They must also be able to see that the construction of knowledge is socially mediated and that Indigenous students may bring other conceptions of what knowledge is and how it is produced with them to their teaching. (2009, p 19)

It is essential that teacher educators engage in systematic and ongoing critique of what goes on 'naturally' and 'normally' in teacher education practice. What are the assumptions about Indigeneity that underpin teacher education pedagogy and how might teacher education value the experiences and knowledge of Indigenous pre-service teachers and draw on such knowledge in productive ways? Without such critique there is the potential for Indigenous pre-service teachers to continue to see, feel and speak of themselves as different, and, often, as less successful than non-Indigenous people, in the subject position of teacher.

Notes

[1] AEAs do not have teaching qualifications. They are employed to perform para-professional tasks and home–school liaison.

[2] This research is funded by the Australian Research Council Discovery Program (Santoro, Reid and McConaghy, 2004–07) and includes Indigenous researchers Laurie Crawford and Lee Simpson.

[3] There is debate in Australia about the terminology used to name and classify Indigenous people. Throughout this chapter, we use 'Indigenous' as a general, formal, institutional and policy term to refer to the range of people who might identify themselves as Aboriginal, Torres Strait Islander, Nunga, Wongai, Yolgnu, Wiradjuri Koori, Murri, and so on, depending on their own history and allegiances. Whenever we refer to individuals and their experiences or quote from their interviews, we use the terminology they use themselves. In this way, we are able to make a distinction in the discussion between particular Aboriginal people with whom we have worked, and the larger group of Indigenous teachers who work around Australia.

[4] Pseudonyms are used for all participants' names and place names in order to preserve anonymity.

[5] All of our participants identified themselves as belonging to particular tribal areas. We foreground this information when referring to them for the first time.

References

ABS (Australian Bureau of Statistics) (2007) ABS directions in Aboriginal and Torres Strait Islander statistics, catalogue no. 4700.00'. Available at: www.abs.gov.au/ausstats/abs@.nsf/Latestproducts/4700.0Main%20 Features1Jun%202007?opendocument&tabname=Summary&prodn o=4700.0&issue=Jun%202007&num=&view= (accessed 2 October 2011)

ABS (2008) 'The health and welfare of Australia's Aboriginal and Torres Strait Islander peoples, 2008, catalogue no. 4704.0'. Available at: www.abs.gov.au/ausstats/abs@.nsf/mf/4704.0/ (accessed 19 December 2008).

Barnhardt, R. and Kawagley, A.O. (2005) 'Indigenous knowledge systems and Alaska Native ways of knowing', *Anthropology and Education Quarterly*, vol 36, no 1, pp 8–23.

Brayboy, B.M.J. and Maughan, E. (2009) 'Indigenous knowledge and the story of the bean', *Harvard Educational Review*, vol 79, no 1, pp 1–21.

Clancy, S. and Simpson, L. (2002) 'Literacy learning for indigenous students: setting a research agenda', *Australian Journal of Language and Literacy*, vol 25, no 2, pp 47–63.

Clark, Y. (2000) 'The construction of aboriginal identity in people separated from their families, community, and culture: pieces of a jigsaw', *Australian Psychologist*, vol 23, no 2, pp 150–7.

Clarke, A. (2005) *Situational Analysis: Grounded Theory after the Postmodern Turn*, Thousand Oaks, CA: Sage.

Davies, B. (1993) *Shards of Glass: Children Reading and Writing Beyond Gendered Identities*, St Leonards, NSW: Allen and Unwin.

DEEWR (Department of Education, Employment and Workplace Relations) (2008) *National Report to Parliament on Indigenous Education and Training 2007*, Canberra, ACT: Commonwealth of Australia.

Doyle, L. and Hill, R. (2008) 'Our children, our future: achieving improved primary and secondary education outcomes for Indigenous students', report published by the AMP foundation. Available at: www.socialventures.com.au/wp-content/uploads/2010/09/Our_Children_Our_Future.pdf (accessed 2 October 2011).

Droste, M. (2001) 'A discussion paper on the issue of Aboriginal identity in contemporary Australia', *Aboriginal and Islander Health Worker Journal*, vol 24, no 6, pp 11-13.

Flintoff, A., Fitzgerald, H. and Scraton, S. (2008) 'The challenges of intersectionality: researching difference in physical education', *International Studies in Sociology of Education*, vol 18, no 2, pp 73–85.

Foucault, M. (1980) 'Truth and power', in C. Gordon (ed) *Power Knowledge: Selected Interviews and Other Writings, 1972–1977*, Brighton: Harvester Press, pp 109–33.

Fredericks, B. (2002) 'Urban identity', *Eureka Street: a Magazine of Public Affairs, the Arts and Theology*. Available at: http://www.eurekastreet.com.au/articles/0412fredericks.html (accessed 31 March 2005).

Freeman, K. (2008) '"To remain working for the people": Ojibwe women in an Indigenous Teacher Education program', *Encounters on Education*, vol 9, Fall, pp 121–43.

Henriques, J., Hollway, W., Urwin, C., Venn, C. and Walkerdine, V. (1984) *Changing the Subject: Psychology, Social Regulation and Subjectivity*, London: Methuen.

Hughes, P. and Willmot, E. (1982) 'A thousand Aboriginal teachers by 1990', in E. Sherwood (ed) *Aboriginal Education: Issues and Innovations*, Perth: Creative Research.

James, R. and Devlin, M. (2005) 'Towards a new policy environment for Indigenous people, culture and knowledge in Australian higher education', Paper presented at Education-Led Recovery of Indigenous Capacity: Reshaping the Policy Agenda, Canberra.

Locke, S. (2004) 'Reflections of Native American teacher education on Bear Ridge', *The Rural Educator*, vol 26, no 1, pp 15–23.

Merriam, S.B., Johnson-Bailey, J., Lee, M., Kee, Y., Ntseans, G. and Muhamad, M. (2001) 'Power and positionality: negotiating insider/outsider status within and across cultures', *International Journal of Lifelong Education*, vol 20, no 5, pp 405–16.

Moreton-Robinson, A. (2004) *Whitening Race*, Canberra: Aboriginal Studies Press.

Nakata, M. (2004) 'Indigenous knowledge and the cultural interface: underlying issues at the intersection of knowledge and information systems', in A. Hickling Hudson, J. Matthews and A. Woods (eds) *Disrupting Preconceptions: Postcolonialism and Education*, Flaxton, QLD: Post Pressed, pp 19–38.

Paradies, Y.C. (2006) 'Beyond black and white: essentialism, hybridity and indigeneity', *Journal of Sociology*, vol 42, no 4, pp 355–67.

Reid, C. (2004) *Negotiating Racialised Identities: Indigenous Teacher Education in Australia and Canada*, Melbourne: Common Ground.

Reid, J. and Santoro, N. (2006) 'Cinders in snow? Indigenous teacher identities in formation', *Asia Pacific Journal of Teacher Education*, vol 34, no 2, pp 143–60.

Reid, J., Santoro, N., Crawford, L. and Simpson, L. (2009) 'Talking teacher education: factors impacting on teacher education for Indigenous people', *Australian Journal of Indigenous Education*, vol 38, pp 42–54.

Santoro, N. (2010) '"If it weren't for my mum ...": the influence of Australian Indigenous mothers on their children's aspirations to teach', *Gender and Education*, vol 22, no 4, pp 419–29.

Santoro, N. and Reid, J. (2006) '"All things to all people": Indigenous teachers in the Australian teaching profession', *European Journal of Teacher Education*, vol 29, no 3, pp 287–303.

Shah, S. (2004) 'The researcher/interviewer in intercultural context: a social intruder!', *British Educational Research Journal*, vol 30, no 4, pp 405–16.

Stuurman, R.J. (2003) 'Aboriginal identity in contemporary society', in Access to Indigenous Records National Forum, 19–20 June 2003, State Library Queensland, Brisbane.

Venn, C. (2006) *The Postcolonial Challenge: Towards Alternative Worlds*, London: Sage.

Wetherell, M. (2008) 'Subjectivity or psycho-discursive practices? Investigating complex intersectional identities', *Subjectivity*, vol 22, pp 73–81.

White, C., Bedonie, C., de Groat, J., Lockard, L. and Honani, S. (2007) 'A bridge for our children: tribal/university partnerships to prepare indigenous teachers', *Teacher Education Quarterly*, Fall, pp 71–86.

Youdell, D. (2006) *Impossible Bodies, Impossible Selves: Exclusions and Student Subjectivities*, New York: Springer.

THIRTEEN

Widening access to higher education through partnership working

Jaswinder K. Dhillon

Introduction

This chapter considers the policy and practice of partnership working among educational organisations and related service providers as a means of promoting social inclusion in higher education (HE). It draws on an empirical study of partnership working in an area of England that has low levels of participation in HE, consistently performs poorly in national measures of educational achievement and contains pockets of severe economic and social deprivation. The empirical research focuses on the work of senior managers from 17 organisations who formed a sub-regional partnership as a strategy to raise aspirations, widen participation in HE and promote social inclusion.

During the five-year research, these senior managers expanded the influence and reach of the partnership to include 103 individuals and 30 organisations in their collaborative activities, which involved developing progression routes into HE for 'non-traditional' learners. The study was undertaken during New Labour's period in office during which both partnership working and social inclusion were key policy priorities vigorously promoted through initiatives and financial incentives. The chapter, therefore, also reflects on the policy context and the agency of individuals and organisations in working towards the goal of social inclusion. It begins by considering the broader context of collaboration and partnership working as a means for increasing participation and social inclusion in HE, and then presents data from the case study to illuminate the practice on the ground.

Collaboration and partnership working between further and higher education

Collaborative working arrangements between different sectors of education, for example, compacts between schools and colleges, and franchising between further education colleges and universities, have existed from the 1980s (Bird, 1996). Such arrangements have been a means for opening up opportunities for individuals and groups who may not have aspired to further and higher education, or as routes for adults without traditional entry qualifications, and hence linked to strategies for promoting social inclusion, as noted in Chapter One of this volume. Paczuska (1999) dates links and partnerships between further education (FE) and HE to the 1960s, although the main growth was in the 1980s and 1990s. The increase is linked to a 'growing emphasis on widening access to further and higher education [that] emerged in the second half of the 1980s' (Gallacher and Thompson, 1999, p 14) as the government became interested in attracting more students to return to education to improve their qualifications and skills. During the 1980s, 'Access' courses developed to provide special routes and a second chance for those who had missed out on the opportunity to enter HE (Jary and Jones, 2004). The provision of Access courses was located in FE colleges with progression routes linked to HE institutions and, according to Stuart (2002), it was mainly women, who had been denied education earlier in their lives, who participated in such programmes.

In the 1990s, the marketisation of FE (Ainley and Bailey, 1997) and the ending of the binary divide between polytechnics and universities, through the Further and Higher Education Act 1992, enabled more joint working between the sectors (Bocock and Scott, 1994) and diversification of both educational provision and the links between institutions. The labels that emerged to describe these closer working relationships between the FE and HE sectors included associate college arrangements, validation and accreditation arrangements, franchising, subcontracting, joint provision, and preferred partnerships. The categories attempt to capture the nature of the relationship between an HE institution and FE colleges, which are often located in the same geographical region. They also reflect the attempt to formalise and simplify regional progression arrangements designed to benefit those traditionally under-represented in HE and hence to promote social inclusion. However, they also carry the risk of creating a two-tier system of HE where new or post-1992 universities produce graduates for second-tier, lower-status occupations in the labour market, while old and elite universities provide a different kind of HE experience for standard age and background students. Jary and Jones (2004, p 1) argue that recent HE policy 'has a Janus-face' as the government endeavours to create fair access and social justice in a much expanded system while at the same time setting out to maintain a minority of institutions as 'world-class universities'.

The university that is a key partner in the case study reported in this chapter is a post-1992 university with a strong mission for widening participation in higher education and a deep commitment to promoting social inclusion. It also has a long history of working collaboratively with FE colleges and other stakeholders across the region in developing a range of courses and establishing collaborative links with other institutions through franchising, accreditation and validation activities. The case study illustrates how both the national policy context, in particular during Tony Blair's period as Prime Minister from 1997 to 2007, and the individual agency of a key number of senior managers of educational organisations drove the formation and development of a partnership to promote social inclusion in HE through partnership working at a local and sub-regional level.

New Labour, partnership working and social inclusion

The election of the Labour government in 1997 brought a vigorous impetus to the development of collaborative working arrangements between HE and FE institutions, in particular through initiatives that promoted partnership working as a strategy for achieving social inclusion in higher education. The Labour government, which had rebranded itself as New Labour, placed partnership working at the centre of its reform of public-sector services including education, health and social services. In their edited collection of partnership working in policy and practice published in 2001, Balloch and Taylor affirm that New Labour 'firmly tied its colours to the partnership mast' by announcing 'its intention to move from a contract culture to a partnership culture' (Balloch and Taylor, 2001, p 3). Powell and Glendinning (2002) analyse the variety of terms used by New Labour in its collaborative discourse, including compacts, inter-agency working and seamless services, and confirm that partnership is the most widely used term in policy documents. This is reflected in key policy documents, such as the White Paper *Learning to Succeed*, which states that the 'new framework for post-16 learning' aims to 'create a framework based on partnership and co-operation between individuals, businesses and communities, as well as institutions' (DfEE, 1999, p 4). The nuances between different terms such as co-operation, collaboration and partnership are not made explicit in this discourse, but the policy thrust on working together rather than in competition is very clear and can be seen in the analysis of data presented later in this chapter.

The emphasis placed on 'partnership' as a new way of working between different government departments, voluntary and statutory agencies, and the private sector underpins notions of 'joined-up' government, another key term in New Labour's policy discourse. This reflects wider debate about types of governance structures (Field, 2000) and New Labour's third way (Giddens, 1998) approach to policy development and implementation in the drive to improve education and other public-sector services. In this approach, partnership is also seen as a strategy for tackling deep-rooted problems, such as social exclusion, by producing 'joined-up solutions to joined-up problems' (SEU, 2004, p 1). The rhetoric of 'joined-up' working permeates New Labour's education policy, and partnership is presented as a 'new' way of working despite the history of collaboration and partnership working in the field of education discussed earlier in this chapter. The promotion of partnership as a new way of working has prompted researchers to assess the impact of New Labour on the practice of partnership working through empirical studies of partnerships in a range of settings, including education, health, social policy, regeneration and community development (eg Clegg and McNulty, 2002; Glendinning et al., 2002; Cardini, 2006).

The prominence of partnership in New Labour's education and social policy is matched by other priorities that are relevant to the context of this chapter, including lifelong learning, social inclusion and active citizenship. In one of its major policy documents for post-16 learning, *The Learning Age*, it is stated that 'learning is essential to a strong economy and an inclusive society' and that 'learning contributes to social cohesion and fosters a sense of belonging, responsibility and identity' (DfEE, 1998, p 11). In New Labour's education policy, lifelong learning is presented as a 'magic bullet' (Coffield, 1999) and the route for achieving both economic competiveness and social inclusion in globalised capitalism, although it was a highly contested concept both in theory and in practice during Tony Blair's period in office. These themes are reflected in the empirical study discussed in the remainder of this chapter and form the landscape for the work of the case study, which illustrates how partnership working contributed to social inclusion by increasing and widening participation in learning.

Midlands Urban Partnership: a case of partnership working to promote social inclusion in higher education

Midlands Urban Partnership (MUP) started in 1997 as a small grouping of providers of post-16 education and training and grew over the next three years to become a complex partnership of all the key stakeholders involved in the planning and provision of post-16 learning in the Black Country[1] sub-region of the Midlands in England. This included six further education colleges, one sixth-form college, a regional university, four Training and Enterprise Councils (TECs) and representatives of Employment Services, Private Training Providers, Adult Education Services, the Prospects Careers Service, the Open College Network of the West Midlands and the Workers Educational Association. A combination of policy, serendipity and individual and organisational commitment to the aims of the partnership contributed to its formation and growth and the individual agency of a small number of senior managers sustained the partnership through peaks and troughs of development. The aims of the partnership were underpinned by a set of shared values, in particular, a passion for widening participation in post-16 learning, including participation in further, higher and adult education, which held the partners together through 'thick and thin'. During the research, MUP progressed through four stages of development, which are shown visually in Figure 13.1. The figure also indicates the methods of data gathering used in the fieldwork and significant activities and events during these stages in the life course of the partnership.

Methods used for data gathering

The study took a grounded approach and the fieldwork gathered mainly qualitative data through: observations of MUP meetings; analysis of documentary evidence of partnership working, such as minutes of meetings, reports, newsletters, action plans and bids prepared for collaborative projects; and semi-structured interviews with the members of the partnership. The data from all sources was synthesised to construct the framework of the four stages in the life course of MUP to explain the development and progress of the partnership and is presented in the next section of this chapter with the documentary evidence referenced as MUP documents.

Figure 13.1: The four stages in the life course of MUP

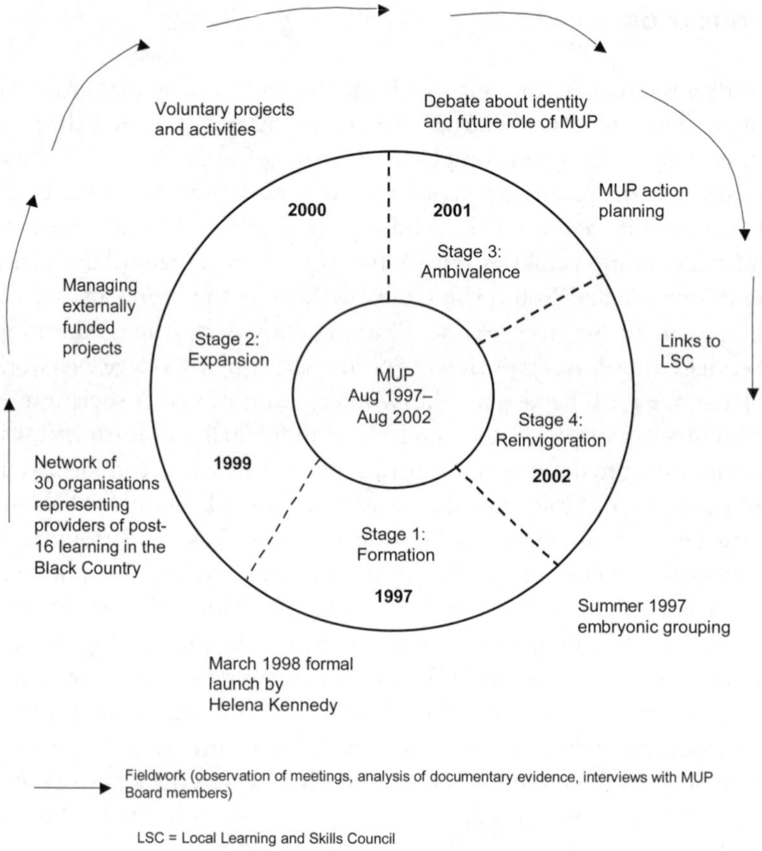

Voluntary projects
and activities

Debate about identity
and future role of MUP

MUP action
planning

2000 | 2001

Stage 3:
Ambivalence

Managing
externally
funded
projects

Stage 2:
Expansion

MUP
Aug 1997–
Aug 2002

Links to
LSC

Stage 4:
Reinvigoration

Network of
30 organisations
representing
providers of post-
16 learning in the
Black Country

1999

2002

Stage 1:
Formation

1997

Summer 1997
embryonic grouping

March 1998 formal
launch by
Helena Kennedy

Fieldwork (observation of meetings, analysis of documentary evidence, interviews with MUP
Board members)

LSC = Local Learning and Skills Council

Stage 1: Formation and early development

MUP grew out of a network of individuals prompted by a series of events during the summer of 1997. The major catalyst for bringing the key actors together was a request to colleges from the Further Education Funding Council (FEFC), set out in FEFC Circular 97/23, to form a partnership to develop collaborative widening participation strategies (MUP, 1997a). This was in response to one of the recommendations of the committee on widening participation in further education chaired by Helena Kennedy QC, which had suggested the promotion of partnership approaches to stimulate demand for learning at the local level (Kennedy, 1997). One of the key individuals that initiated the formation of MUP described the Kennedy report as "an absolutely seminal work" in the development of the further education sector

(Gillian, principal of a college). The individuals who instigated the formation of the partnership already had existing links with each other's organisations, but the opportunity to bid for funding focused their attention and prompted them into action. Principals from two FE colleges contacted a senior manager at a university seeking assistance with the establishment of a partnership:

> "It [MUP] started when Stephen phoned Margaret as he had been sent a circular by FEFC. Margaret is also a governor at [name of institution] and was contacted by Gillian, who said 'we can't start it ... we need some form of mediation ... an independent without a vested interest' and so approached Margaret." (Kelly, administrator for MUP)

A Chair who was trusted and perceived by the various actors as a neutral broker was to be crucial in the formation and successful operation of MUP. The individual needed to facilitate the shift from competition to cooperation in the local education and training environment where the legacy of competition was still evident. As Wylie observed 'having undergone a period of intense competition after incorporation the FE colleges did not trust each other sufficiently to let any one take the lead' (Wylie, 1999, p 2). The challenges of moving towards collaboration did not deter the key actors in MUP, however, as "for the first time, it [MUP] had Black Country providers working together instead of at each other's throats" (Andrew, principal of a college).

The embryonic grouping of three key individuals drew in representatives of other education and training organisations in the Black Country to form the core of MUP (MUP, 1997b). The frantic pace of activity that led to the formation of the partnership and an indication of the challenges to partnership working are revealed by the administrator, who was heavily involved in the first year of the partnership's development:

> "It was a hellish meeting to organise ... I was sitting here in July ringing up all these college principals during the summer when no one is around ... academics are on holiday and we had to get the bid in ... we had to achieve a quick turnaround and overcome two major barriers ... one the barrier of talking to each other [colleges] and the other that nobody trusted their neighbour." (Kelly, administrator for MUP)

The first meeting, an exploratory meeting hosted by the university, was mainly attended by college principals and was held on 14 July 1997 (MUP, 1997b). Within two weeks, other organisations and agencies were invited to the second meeting and by 19 August, only a month since the initial call for action, a full consortium with representation from all the appropriate agencies was formed (MUP, 1997c). Kelly reflected how they "moved quickly ... within a month launching a recognised partnership in order to get funding".

The developing grouping gave itself a name (not MUP at this stage), and the pace and shape of activity was driven by the FEFC's requirements for funding widening participation projects. The catalyst for all this activity was the need to write a bid (MUP, 1997a) and at this point in its development the actors came together specifically for bidding purposes, but this was not the sole reason for the formation or subsequent expansion of MUP. The application for funding submitted to FEFC in September 1997 stated: 'The purpose of the Consortium is to establish and facilitate collaboration between its members and other agencies in order to widen participation in education and training within the Boroughs' (BCC, 1997, p 2).

The focus of the bid was three action research projects to be located in different Black Country boroughs and the development of a strategic plan aimed at increasing participation in post-16 education and training by under-represented groups (BCC, 1997). The Black Country is culturally and ethnically diverse with minority ethnic groups constituting between 5% (Dudley) and 25% (Sandwell) of the population (BCC, 2000, Annex 1) and the projects aimed to work with African-Caribbean males, Bangladeshi women and white adults from social classes IV and V[2]. They were identified as the most disadvantaged and socially excluded groups in the four boroughs with individuals from these backgrounds most likely to be non-participants in education and training (BCC, 1997; CIHE, 1997; Woodrow, 1998; for a more detailed discussion of levels of participation in education and achievement by minority ethnic groups, see also Chapter 8 in this volume).

The process of writing the bid had brought the group of senior managers together in a very productive collaborative relationship, in the words of one of the participants:

> This was the honeymoon period. There was a genuinely positive commitment to working together and early in the process it was agreed that the partnership would stay together whatever the outcome of the bid because there

was such a need to address the common problems of the sub-region with common solutions. (Wylie, 1999, p 2)

The bid from MUP to FEFC for funding as a partnership was unsuccessful, but for various reasons the actors decided to stay together. The synergy that marked the first few months of the life of MUP was driven by national government policy (MUP, 1997a), but other reasons for collaboration were evident even at the early stages and became much more explicit as MUP expanded into a strong and active sub-regional voice.

Stage 2: Expansion

In 1998, the partners (the word they chose to describe themselves) organised a high-profile launch using their social connections to attract a national figure, Helena Kennedy QC, to formally launch MUP (MUP, 1998a). The level of activity was recalled vividly:

> "It was frantic at times ... government changes to national policy meant we had to move quickly ... Helena Kennedy, an old mate of Paul Smith,[3] came to launch the partnership in 1998 ... it was a huge bash at the Science Park ... a conference was held ... we used the word 'partners' rather than members and they all signed a memorandum of cooperation." (Kelly, administrator for MUP)

At the formal launch on 23 March 1998, Helen, the FE college principal who delivered the welcome speech, proclaimed:

> We are very proud to have Baroness Kennedy here with us today to witness our signatures of this partnership agreement ... today, we are also pledging ourselves to work to bring about the 'Renaissance in Learning' which is the Government's vision for a new Britain. This partnership is not a 'virtual one' it is very real. It is also an over arching one. (MUP, 1998b, p 1)

She concluded that by working together, the partners could translate the vision of a self-perpetuating learning society into reality (MUP, 1998b). At national and international levels this was a period of intense policy interest in notions of lifelong learning and the learning society. The British government's vision had been articulated in the publication of *The Learning Age* (DfEE, 1998) and it had started a research programme, the ESRC-funded *Learning Society Programme*, to investigate lifelong learning in the UK (Coffield, 1997, 1999, 2000). The launch of MUP indicated how the vision espoused in national policy fired the imagination of individuals in the local landscape of the Black Country and brought them together to take action to widen participation in learning. The formal launch of MUP was attended by 41 senior managers representing educational institutions, training organisations and other stakeholders in post-16 learning in the Black Country together with nine students representing different member institutions (MUP, 1998c).

The partners set about working towards this vision with energy and enthusiasm. Key people saw partnership working as an opportunity to work in new ways with other organisations and individuals and there was an element of hope in this aspiration, as indicated by another FE college principal:

> "Many of us who'd worked in further education for many years prior to incorporation in 1992 remembered, with a mix of positives and negatives, other ways of going about things and ways of regarding other educational institutions, not merely as hostile competitors … and it was very much like a breath of fresh air after the early atmosphere of the '90s…. We wanted to try a different way of doing things … and the other thing about the Helena Kennedy thinking … was reminding us that at the heart of the FE mission was something very specific about tackling disadvantage and promoting social inclusion and those aspirations were not part of the government prior to '97, they were not part of the previous government's priorities." (Gillian, principal of a college)

This optimism was surprising given the tensions arising from the marketisation of education and the challenges of partnership working, which a university senior manager articulated as: "I think there's a rhetoric about partnership you know talking about partnership is easy, making it happen is much, much harder … and I think MUP has struggled to get beyond the rhetoric but I think all partnerships do" (Mark, senior manager at a university).

Despite the challenges and tensions, the energy and activity that marked this stage of the partnership's development is captured as:

"By August 1999, the partnership had expanded beyond belief ... HEFCE and FEFC had approved MUP and given money for projects ... I was impressed with the commitment shown ... MUP is a provider voice, a forum ... a lobbying forum to LSC and has a future tied to funding requirements ... the three-year HEFCE project ... Ufi for two years ... Ufi is a big driver for colleges." (Kelly, administrator for MUP)

During this period of rapid expansion, the members of MUP created organisational structures to manage the work of the partnership. They formed a partnership Board, MUP Board, which included representatives from all stakeholders, and a smaller MUP Executive Group consisting of seven people drawn from representatives of the full partnership Board (MUP, 2000a). The Executive Group was formed to act on the decisions made by the partnership, as the MUP Board had become a large and unwieldy group with 17–30 representatives attending meetings (MUP, 1999a). Other subgroups were formed to manage projects and other collaborative activities as shown in Figure 13.2.

Figure 13.2: Organisational structures in MUP

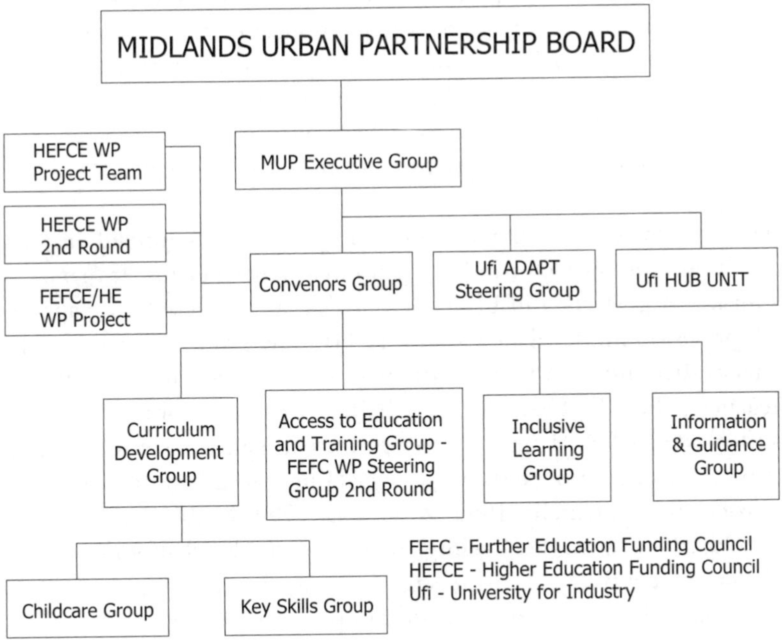

Source: MUP (2000b, p 1).

Figure 13.2 shows the range of organisational structures developed by the partnership to manage its activities during this stage in its life course. The individuals and organisations that were key to MUP's growth were involved in a variety of groups and subgroups, including the MUP Board, MUP Executive Group, convenors' group and steering groups for externally funded projects, for example, FEFC, HEFCE and University for Industry's (Ufi).[4] The convenors' group organised and participated in practitioner groups for curriculum development, access to education, inclusive learning and information and guidance.

MUP was by now a complex network of individuals and organisations that had firmly established itself in the post-16 education and training landscape in the Black Country. It managed a number of externally funded projects for widening participation in further and higher education and successfully bid to become a Learndirect hub as part of the Ufi's strategy for widening participation in post-16 learning (Ufi, 1999, 2004). The summary of MUP's constitution and commitments drawn up in July 2000 states:

> MUP has a remit for widening participation and its activities have reflected this focus. Broadly it has two key areas of work. The first is the practitioner group activity in curriculum development, inclusive learning, information and guidance, and access, which has enabled staff to come together in conferences and workshops to undertake various development projects. The second is the area of funded projects, where the Partnership has been singularly successful and has continuing responsibilities. (MUP, 2000a, p 1)

MUP's success in bidding for and securing externally funded projects was an important factor in its expansion as a partnership. It managed four major projects: a FEFC-funded project that focused on mapping FE provision in the Black Country; a HEFCE-funded project (Right Track) that aimed to widen participation in HE for 'non-traditional' learners; the Ufi Learndirect hub in the Black Country; and an Ufi-funded ADAPT project to produce learning resources. These projects were all funded through special funding streams for widening participation (HEFCE, 1999, 2000; Ufi, 1999; MUP, 1999b, 1999c, 1999d, 2000c) and reflected implementation of New Labour's policies, through incentives for partnership working and funding for projects that claimed to widen participation in post-16 learning.

The role of externally funded projects in the extension and expansion of MUP activity is highlighted by a Chair of the MUP Board:

> "It [MUP] was driven by projects ... and so it became a
> partnership, erm, which owned a number of projects ...
> because we were successful in bidding it developed a kind
> of momentum around that and, erm, a set of responsibilities
> which meant we had to keep going and people found some
> benefit in keeping going, if only on the basis of information
> exchange and being involved in something which as it were
> was leading edge." (Margaret, senior manager at a university)

However, the synergy, organisational structures and networks that
characterised MUP's expansion were not sustained, and for about a
year the partnership experienced a rapid decline in its activities as it
went through a period of ambivalence.

Stage 3: Ambivalence

The period from September 2000 to July 2001 marked a deep trough
in MUP's life course as a partnership. During this stage of ambivalence,
tensions, ambiguity and challenges to collaboration disrupted the
process of partnership working and dissipated the partnership.

In terms of process, two meetings were cancelled and only a handful
of members attended the other two held during this period. This was
partly due to a breakdown in communication, as some representatives
had not received sufficient notice of the dates of the meetings, while
a few had to prioritise other commitments over attending an MUP
meeting. Both these aspects are well illustrated by Andrew, a founder
member, who identified some of the problems that MUP was currently
experiencing and the issues that he as a college principal had to take
into consideration when resolving clashes of meetings:

> Andrew:"Erm there's a problem and of course I don't know
> if you're going to the meeting on Friday ..."

> JD:"Mmmm."

> Andrew:"But a number of people including me didn't know
> about it; now that will be the fault of some of the individuals
> concerned ... I think whoever is now secretary to the
> partnership [MUP] should be more pushful in checking
> that people have got dates in diaries I think that is an issue,
> erm ... the clash that we have is that the Black Country

Learning and Skills Council wants to have a meeting of principals ..."

JD: "Yes."

Andrew: "And, erm, any principal that does not respond to that wants his head looking at!"

JD: "Yes, right."

Andrew: "Erm, and I understand that they're trying to ensure that the LSC meeting finishes at around 10.30 so that people can go to the MUP meeting but you see there is yet another clash that one or two of us are going to a consult ... a DfEE consultation event at Bristol after that so ... and so one of the things I have to do this morning is making sure that this college is represented."

Andrew decided to send his assistant principal to the next MUP meeting (MUP, 2001b) rather than attending personally. In his interview, he commented that although MUP was still engaging in important work, for him and his organisation, other priorities had emerged that needed more urgent attention. This included the formation of the LSC and the growing importance of borough-based partnerships, in contrast to MUP, which had a sub-regional focus. Other founder members confirmed that during this period, though, they ensured that they were represented at MUP meetings and they "delegated tasks to other people to keep the relationship going more or less" (Helen, assistant principal at a college).

During the ambivalence stage, MUP was not involved in any new initiatives, projects or major developments, while three of the four existing externally funded projects came to an end (MUP, 2001b). Other collaborative activities lost momentum and petered out. There was a breakdown in communication and information flows as Jenny, the partnership administrator, left in June 2000 when the funding for her post came to an end. She had taken a key role in establishing and maintaining functioning networks, which had been the conduit for information flows and underpinned the effectiveness of the partnership during its expansion.

Furthermore, the members engaged in an introspective debate about the future, identity and role of MUP. In May 2000, a subgroup produced a discussion paper entitled 'MUP: the next generation' (MUP, 2000a).

This paper began by stating:'MUP has for the last year been concerned about its future role.This paper lays out the framework for a change of role in the context of the emerging subregional relationships around the provision of education and training' (MUP, 2000a, p 1).

It then outlined the current commitments of the partnership (in terms of its role in managing funded projects and collaborative activities), the changes to the subregional context and, finally, posed the question: 'Whither the MUP?' (MUP, 2000a, p 2). This question was debated at three MUP Board meetings held during 2000–01 (observations 2–4) and it was finally agreed that MUP should promote itself as a 'sub-regional provider forum' (MUP, 2001a).The rationale for this was that as learners travelled across the boundaries of the four boroughs for education and training, the members of MUP could address issues around learner needs and quality of training across the Black Country through the forum of the MUP Board.This debate, though challenging, did actively engage all members of the MUP Board, but it also exposed another source of tension in the partnership. This was in relation to resourcing the costs of partnership working, as illustrated in an extract from observation 3:

> Chair: "On the item of resources … the university has resourced the partnership [for over three years] and for the future MUP has to determine what resources it's going to put in to support the partnership."

> [Silence. People avoiding eye contact, staring at the floor, shuffling uncomfortably as the Chair continued.]

> Chair: "The practitioner groups need to be reinvigorated … we need some admin support … the university is happy to contribute but the partners need to recognise their responsibilities … resourcing needs to be a *shared* responsibility."

These tensions and the lack of clarity about the purpose and goals of the partnership were in sharp contrast to the clear articulation of reasons for collaboration and declarations of working to realise the vision of a Learning Society in Stages 1 and 2 of the life course of MUP. My observations of partnership working led to the conclusion that MUP would fizzle out and die. However, it turned out to be a much more resilient partnership than my observations suggested.

In June 2001, key individuals who were founder members of MUP held an action-planning day, which served to reinvigorate the partnership and pull it out of the deep trough it had reached (MUP, 2001a). The event was instigated by one founder member and hosted by another and the aim was to produce a two-year plan of MUP activities to articulate with LSC objectives to encourage participation in learning and raise skill levels among post-16 learners (observation 6). The 21 participants, representing 16 organisations, were enthused by the agenda, and, by the end of the day, had generated concrete actions to form the basis of a draft action plan.

MUP seemed to have found its focus again and sought to reinvent itself as a provider forum that would establish relationships with the local LSC, which now had responsibility for funding post-16 learning. Despite this, it took another six months of behind-the-scenes work by key individuals for the partnership to join-up, reinvigorate itself and re-emerge as a subregional voice with some presence.

Stage 4: Reinvigoration

After the hive of activity in June and July 2001, MUP quietened down again as key individuals were pulled back to responsibilities within their own organisations. Each organisation had to manage the implementation of the new funding framework brought in by the LSC (DfES, 2001), which was placing additional demands on staff time. In interviews, many principals complained about LSC staff coming into their college "to find out what they did" (Helen). They were exasperated by having to talk to so many LSC staff, but realised that they had to cooperate with the representatives of the new funding body for post-16 learning.

By March 2002, MUP had established firm links with the Black Country LSC and become a subscription-based partnership with a dedicated administrator (MUP, 2002a) posed to bid for new projects, including partnerships for progression, a jointly funded initiative by the LSC and HEFCE (HEFCE, 2001) to widen participation and meet the target of 50% participation of 18–30 year olds in HE by 2010. The synergy evident during its expansion in 1998–2000 was again re-emerging and the MUP Executive Group proposed using some funding to reinvigorate MUP by holding a policy forum involving all Board members, learning providers and LSC representatives in October 2002 (MUP, 2002b). The marked improvement in attendance at the MUP Board meeting held in July provided visible evidence of the much more active role that members were now taking in partnership activities. The key actors had successfully rekindled interest in the partnership and it was re-emerging as a significant voice in the subregion. One of the actors pinpointed two vital aspects of MUP's work as a partnership:

> "Well, it is the only pan-Black Country organisation in town ... erm, in the subregion ... there ain't nothing like it ... so I think it's value is that it does provide that forum as a regular set of meetings and now with the attempt to work with the LSC ... its other value has been that it has involved a much wider range of organisations than anything else that I've known ... I think that sort of heterogeneity of membership is really important." (Roger, senior manager at a university)

Another member of MUP Board said:

> "Over the past number of years I think there's been a clear benefit in terms of having a subregional focus rather than a parochial focus when I was involved just in [name of borough] so I think that was helpful and also it gave the opportunity to meet people from outside [name of borough] in the wider education lifelong learning field and share good practice." (Ian, director of a training and enterprise council)

The subregional focus of the partnership, its attempt to be inclusive in terms of membership and its aspiration to spread good practice in the field of lifelong learning, which at this time was widely interpreted as post-16 learning, held the actors together despite high and low points in its life course. Partnership working in MUP was supported by layers of collaboration among the groups and subgroups that were drawn into the partnership and underpinned by social networks based on trust and shared norms and values, which sustained the partnership (for a discussion of these aspects of partnership working, see Dhillon, 2009).

Conclusion

By working in partnership, the members of MUP made a significant contribution towards social inclusion in post-16 learning in the Black Country. They created learning opportunities and progression routes into HE for learners from economically, socially and educationally disadvantaged areas and promoted the concept of lifelong learning in all fields of post-16 learning. The life course of MUP also demonstrates how partnership working was effectively used to capitalise on government priorities, policy imperatives and targeted funding streams to progress projects and collaborative work, which was based on the shared values of the individuals and organisations that participated in the partnership. Although the trigger for the formation of MUP was a policy imperative, representing the government's 'carrots and sticks' (Powell and Glendinning, 2002) approach to widening participation in learning, the members of MUP were able to develop the partnership so that it became an internally driven entity in which they determined aims and priorities based on their individual and organisational commitment to social inclusion in higher education and lifelong learning. MUP *felt* like a partnership that was driven by members who collectively agreed the goals they were going to pursue, although in reality the power and personalities of a few key individuals actually steered the agenda and actions. However, this feeling of ownership, self-determination and individual agency contributed to keeping the partnership alive, and today MUP continues to function as a partnership with a voice in the subregion in which it is situated.

The four stages in the life course of MUP show how shifting national policy priorities, government initiatives and financial incentives to increase and widen participation in learning through partnership working affected the work of educational organisations and the individuals who led and managed these organisations during New Labour's period in office. The case study reveals how policy as espoused was implemented and experienced in a subregion with low levels of educational achievement, areas of economic and social disadvantage, and pockets of severe deprivation. It also shows how the individual agency of managers and practitioners can shape the implementation of policy imperatives and enable the achievement of shared goals, which were determined by the participants in a partnership rather than externally imposed by a government department or funding agency. This individual agency meant that members were able to, and did, focus on longer-term strategies to widen participation in learning than was possible in New Labour's 'initiatives and incentives' approach (Hodgson and Spoors, 2000), which focused on short-term projects. For example, MUP developed one of the first accredited routes for experienced childcare workers studying in FE to progress into HE to undertake a part-time degree in Early Childhood Studies, thus enabling 'non-traditional' students to gain a degree qualification. After 2002, the partnership obtained charitable status and although the membership changed over the course of the next eight years, MUP continued to work in the field of post-16 education and training to influence and inform initiatives and strategies to widen and increase participation in learning. At the present time, it is a forum for exchanging ideas and policies in relation to the provision of post-16 education and training in the Black Country.

Notes

[1] The Black Country consists of the four boroughs of Dudley, Sandwell, Walsall and Wolverhampton.

[2] Social class IV refers to partly skilled and social class V to unskilled.

[3] Paul Smith is a fictitious name.

[4] FEFC, HEFCE and Ufi are funding councils for further, higher and post-16 education and training in England.

References

Ainley, P. and Bailey, B. (1997) *The Business of Learning: Staff and Student Experiences of Further Education in the 1990s*, London: Cassell.

Balloch, S. and Taylor, M. (eds) (2001) *Partnership Working: Policy and Practice*, Bristol: The Policy Press.

BCC (Black Country Consortium) (1997) 'The Black Country Strategic Partnership for Widening Participation application for funding, circular 97/23, Sept 1997', The Black Country Consortium.

BCC (2000) 'Connexions in The Black Country', outline partnership proposal, Black Country Consortium for Regeneration, June 2000.

Bird, J. (1996) 'Further and higher education partnerships: the evolution of a national policy framework', in M. Abramson, J. Bird and A. Stennett (eds) *Further and Higher Education Partnerships: The Future for Collaboration*, Buckingham: SRHE and OUP.

Bocock, J. and Scott, P. (1994) 'HE/FE partnerships: redrawing the boundaries', in S. Brownlow (ed) *Equal Outcomes – Equal Experiences?* Bristol: The Staff College, Coombe Lodge.

Cardini, A. (2006) 'An analysis of the rhetoric and practice of educational partnerships in the UK: an arena of complexities, tensions and power', *Journal of Education Policy*, vol 21, pp 393–415.

CIHE (Council for Industry and Higher Education) (1997) *Widening Participation in Lifelong Learning: A Progress Report*, London: The Council for Industry and Higher Education.

Clegg, S. and McNulty, K. (2002) 'Partnership working in delivering social inclusion: organizational and gender dynamics', *Journal of Education Policy*, vol 17, pp 587–601.

Coffield, F. (1997) 'Can the UK become a learning society?', Kings College London, Annual Education Lecture, June 1997.

Coffield, F. (1999) 'Breaking the consensus: lifelong learning as social control', *British Educational Research Journal*, vol 25, pp 79–99.

Coffield, F. (ed) (2000) *Differing Visions of a Learning Society*, Bristol: The Policy Press.

DfEE (Department for Education and Employment) (1998) *The Learning Age: A Renaissance for a New Britain*, London: The Stationery Office.

DfEE (1999) *Learning to Succeed*, London: The Stationery Office.

DfES (Department for Education and Science) (2001) 'Learning partnerships funding announcement'. Available at: www.lifelonglearning.co.uk/iip/archive/htm (accessed 18 April 2003).

Dhillon, J.K. (2009) 'The role of social capital in sustaining partnership', *British Educational Research Journal*, vol 35, pp 687–704.

Field, J. (2000) 'Governing the ungovernable: why lifelong polices promise so much yet deliver so little', *Educational Management and Administration*, vol 28, pp 249–61.

Gallacher, J. and Thompson, C. (1999) 'Further education: overlapping or overstepping', *Scottish Journal of Adult and Continuing Education*, vol 5, pp 9–24.

Giddens, A. (1998) *The Third Way: The Renewal of Social Democracy*, Cambridge: Polity Press.

Glendinning, C., Powell, M. and Rummery, K. (eds) (2002) *Partnerships, New Labour and the Governance of Welfare*, Bristol: The Policy Press.

HEFCE (Higher Ediucation Funding Council for England) (1999) 'Widening participation in higher education: invitation to bid for special funds', HEFCE 99/33.

HEFCE (2000) 'Funding for widening participation in higher education. New Proposals 2000–01 to 2003–04', Consultation 00/50.

HEFCE (2001) *Partnerships for Progression: Proposals by the HEFCE and the Learning and Skills Council HEFCE 01/73 December 2001 Consultation*, Bristol: HEFCE.

Hodgson, A. and Spours, K. (2000) 'Building a lifelong learning system for the future', in A. Hodgson (ed) *Policies, Politics and the Future of Lifelong Learning*, London: Kogan Page, pp 191–205.

Jary, D. and Jones, R. (2004) 'Widening participation: overview and commentary'. Available at: www.heacademy.ac.uk/assets/York/documents/resources/wpoverview_and_commentary_WDP044.pdf (accessed 23 August 2010).

Kennedy, H. (1997) *Learning Works: Widening Participation in Further Education*, Coventry: FEFC.

MUP (Midlands Urban Partnership) (1997a) 'Circular 97/23, invitation to bid for funding', Sept 1997.

MUP (1997b) 'Minutes of meeting held 14/7/97'.

MUP (1997c) 'Minutes of meeting held 19/8/97'.

MUP (1998a) 'Itinerary of Helena Kennedy's visit 23/3/98'.

MUP (1998b) 'Welcome speech given at launch of MUP 23/3/98'.

MUP (1998c) 'List of people who attended the launch of MUP on 23/3/1998'.

MUP (1999a) 'MUP: organisational involvement', document distributed at MUP board meeting held 1 October 1999.

MUP (1999b) 'Further education students in the Black Country – survey of existing provision', June 1999.

MUP (1999c) 'Ufi report on preliminary visit to MUP', September 1999.

MUP (1999d) 'Proposal for funding for widening participation special funding programme 1999–2000 to 2001–02', Paper discussed at meeting held 1 October 1999.

MUP (2000a) 'MUP: the next generation', Paper discussed at meeting held 7 July 2000.

MUP (2000c) 'Black Country Learndirect update', Document distributed at meeting held 7 July 2000.

MUP (2001a) 'Programme for planning day', 8 June 2001.

MUP (2001b) 'Minutes of meeting held 29/6/01'.

MUP (2002a) 'Minutes of meeting held 3/3/02'.

MUP (2002b) 'Minutes of meeting held 14/6/02'.

Paczuska, A. (1999) 'Further education and higher education: the changing boundary', in A. Green and N. Lucas (eds) *FE and Lifelong Learning: Realigning the Sector for the Twenty-first Century*, London: Institute of Education, University of London.

Powell, M. and Glendinning, C. (2002) 'Introduction', in C. Glendinning et al. (eds) *Partnerships, New Labour and the Governance of Welfare*, Bristol: The Policy Press, pp 1–14.

SEU (Social Exclusion Unit) (2004) 'Social Exclusion Unit, What is the SEU?'. Available at: www.socialexclusionunit.gov.uk (accessed 27 May 2004).

Stuart, M. (2002) *Collaborating for Change? Managing Widening Participation in Further and Higher Education*, Leicester: NIACE.

Ufi (University for Industry) (1999) 'A new way of learning: the Ufi network – developing the University for Industry concept', Ufi network.

Ufi (2004) 'Learndirect – a new way of learning'. Available at: www. ufi.com (accessed 04 June 2004).

Woodrow, M., with Lee, M.F., McGrane, J., Osbourne, B., Pudner, H., and Trotman, C. (1998) *From Elitism to Inclusion*: *Good Practice in Widening Access to Higher Education*, London: CVCP.

Wylie, V. (1999) 'Black Country Partnerships: coping with policy initiatives', Keynote speech given at Conference of Journal of Vocational Education and Training, GMB National College, Manchester ,14–16 July.

FOURTEEN

Higher education, human rights and inclusive citizenship

Audrey H. Osler

Two interlinked stories

In 1888, the first ever woman to study law at a British university arrived in Oxford to take up a place at the newly founded Somerville Hall (now Somerville College). She was Cornelia Sorabji, an imperial British subject from a privileged Indian family. Like other Somerville women, Sorabji was not subjected to any religious tests or obligations. Nevertheless, at that time, women were excluded from the University of Oxford, for it was not until 1920 that they were eligible to become full members and be awarded degrees. Despite this restriction, Cornelia Sorabji successfully struggled to persuade the authorities to allow her to sit the examinations in law alongside men. Since the bar was not open to women, she was at first denied the right to become a barrister, although she eventually took up this career in India.

Somerville remains proud of its early tradition of religious inclusion and its respect and recognition of cultural diversity, which set it apart from its Anglican counterpart, Lady Margaret College. It is, then, curious that Somerville has been slow to acknowledge or celebrate Sorabji's achievements. Although she is now mentioned on the college website, this is a recent development. In 2010, open-day visitors to Somerville using the College's self-guided tour had their attention drawn to alumnae and ground-breaking achievers such as the Nobel prize-winning British chemist Dorothy Hodgkin, Indian Prime Minister Indira Gandhi and British Prime Minister Margaret Thatcher. These alumnae are celebrated prominently within the college buildings and grounds for students and visitors alike. Cornelia Sorabji remains invisible and her story untold. This reflects perhaps a wider tendency to overlook people of colour in the narrative of British history as it is presented at the beginning of the 21st century (Osler, 2006). The achievements of women of colour in particular remain largely invisible.

Although Somerville boasts a tradition of cultural diversity, Oxbridge colleges and other prestigious British universities have a long tradition of exclusion, on which the widening participation agendas of various political parties in relation to higher education appears to have had limited impact. Official data, released under the Freedom of Information Act as a result of requests made by David Lammy MP, confirm continuing patterns of exclusion by gender, ethnicity and social class. A total of 21 Oxbridge colleges made no offers to black British candidates for undergraduate courses in 2009 and one Oxford college has not admitted a single black student in five years. Just one black Briton of Caribbean descent was accepted for undergraduate study at Oxford in 2009. At Oxford, 89% of undergraduates are drawn from the top three socio-economic groups, while at Cambridge 87.6% come from these same groups. While black candidates with top A level grades are more likely to apply to both institutions than their white counterparts, data show that white students were more likely to be successful than black applicants at every Cambridge college except one. The only explanation that the universities put forward is that black candidates apply for the most competitive subjects. Interestingly, the college with the worst record at Cambridge was the all-women Newnham, where black women applicants had a 13% success rate compared with 67% for white women (Vasagar, 2010).

Both Oxford and Cambridge enjoy public funding and both have special schemes designed to attract applications from publicly funded schools and from minority ethnic students, in line with the widening participation agenda. My own interest in the situation of minority ethnic students in British universities stems from my experiences of working in three different UK institutions, all of which rate quite highly in the league tables and two of which are members of the prestigious Russell Group. In the 1990s, I began to work as a university lecturer and to study for a PhD, having previously followed a career as a teacher and advisor in a number of local authorities. As I collected data on the lives and careers of teachers from minority ethnic backgrounds (Osler, 1997), I decided to include in my sample of interviewees, black British undergraduates who did not want to be teachers. Finding it difficult to locate such students in my own Russell Group university, I enquired of the administration how many existed and in which departments. They gave me the total figure for undergraduates and postgraduates. Once I had discounted PhD students and trainee teachers in the School of Education, the rest, across the whole university, could be counted on the fingers of one hand. No wonder they were proving so difficult to locate.

In 1998, I was appointed to a Chair in Education at another university. The London-based black British newspaper *The Voice* reported that I was the first black woman to be appointed to a Professorship in Education in Britain. This was picked up by a Leicester student serving an internship on the university's newspaper, and she, in turn, wrote a piece about me. On my first day in post, I received a visit from the dean who was very concerned and deeply apologetic about this article. When I explained to him that as someone of mixed descent, I was not troubled by the descriptor 'black' his face lit up. He left the room congratulating himself on his unwitting achievement as a member of my appointment panel. Yet it was not until I was invited to my first senate dinner as a new member of the professoriate that I realised the extent to which I did not conform to the university community's common understanding of how a professor should look. A couple of colleagues came up to introduce themselves and congratulate my escort on his appointment. He had to explain it was me, not him, who was the new professor. Attending my first meeting of senate some weeks later, armed with what was clearly a bundle of senate papers, a well-meaning man pointed out that I was in the wrong place. He explained: "This, my dear, is senate".

The widening participation agenda is directed at students, yet the processes of exclusion, by race, gender and social class, continue in the early years of the 21st century and impact on academic staff as well as students. My own area of study includes the examination of citizenship, human rights and learning. My experiences have encouraged me to study not only those who have been judged out-of-place or rendered invisible through the processes of history, as is the case with Cornelia Sorabji and countless other women, particularly women of colour, but also to explore the complexities of exclusion and the ways in which issues of race, class and gender, including sexual and gender identities, are inextricably interlinked and overlapping. This can be identified both in the discourse and in the practices of institutions of higher education, with some identities remaining invisible today.

Looking through a human rights lens

The editors explain in the introduction that they focus in this book on class, ethnicity and gender because they are 'more significant mainly because they affect a very large proportion of the student population'. I argue that a human rights lens is a particularly helpful tool that can be used to examine the ways in which multiple factors work together to exclude individuals and groups. In other words, a human rights framework supports an understanding of intersectionality in the ways individuals experience inclusion or exclusion. Mechanisms and processes of exclusion are complex and changing, sometimes making it difficult to isolate factors such as class, ethnicity, gender or a combination of these in the processes. Other factors such as religious identity or tradition may be inseparable from ethnicity, or may play a key role in individuals' explanations of their own resources in achieving success, despite encountering discrimination and exclusion (Tomlinson, 1983; Osler, 1997).

Equally importantly, human rights provide a framework for a critical reading of the world (Freire, 2004) and for working for greater justice by encouraging diverse individuals and groups to work together to understand their shared interests and develop solidarity across the ethnic, religious and cultural divides that exist in many different social contexts. Human rights apply to us all and if used to analyse issues of inclusion and exclusion, they may aid our understanding, as both teachers and students, of how inclusion in higher education is the concern of all regardless of whether we teach (or are) the relatively privileged or are working with (and/or belong to) groups that experience various forms of exclusion. Viewed in this way, human rights provide a tool that can be used to assess our own complicity, as members of the academy, in the processes of exclusion.

Political efforts to develop higher education to include 'non-traditional' students have focused largely on dismantling the barriers faced by such students in entering a previously elitist system and some of the obstacles to success that they encounter during their studies. This chapter focuses on the *processes of teaching and learning* about human rights and equality, drawing specifically on my experience of teaching graduate students in a US university. In particular, it examines how both teachers and learners in higher education can enable participation or exclude students, either wittingly or unwittingly.

Education in human rights is critical, for we cannot claim our rights unless we know about them. It is impossible for individuals or groups to claim rights without a basic knowledge of these rights. This is a first step. In practice, human rights are secured through processes of struggle. For this reason, part of human rights education needs to engage with such struggles. The development of learners' individual and collective narratives about rights can be empowering, since it enables learners to see themselves and others not as the victims of exclusion, discrimination and abuse, but as actors engaged in struggles for justice. In this sense, students are also 'writing the world' (Freire, 2004), a process that he argued must necessarily proceed from reading the world. From this standpoint, learners are in a stronger position to see both themselves and others as political actors with agency, and not view others merely as the objects of compassion or charity. Human rights provide a universal framework in which people from different ethical, religious and cultural backgrounds can work together to realise social justice. They depend on human solidarity across national, religious, ethical and cultural borders. They are recognised in principle by the nation states across the globe as well as by non-governmental organisations (NGOs), as was confirmed at the Vienna World Conference (UNHCHR, 1993), when, significantly, representatives of 171 states adopted a common plan for the strengthening of human rights around the world and some 7,000 participants, including academics, treaty bodies, national institutions and representatives of more than 800 NGOs, two thirds of them at the grass-roots level, renewed the international community's commitment both to the promotion and protection of human rights and to the principle of the universality of rights.

Despite this, some individuals have legitimate concerns about the ways in which a human rights discourse may be co-opted by the powerful in an attempt to universalise the experiences of the vulnerable or excluded, effectively denying their legitimate voices in the debate. It was for this reason that from the 1980s, women had to assert their human rights using the slogan: 'women's rights are human rights'. Although human rights instruments acknowledged women's equal status as holders of human rights, in practice, they found it difficult to use human rights mechanisms and structures to claim these same rights. From the 1980s, women from different cultures and contexts began to work together, using the human rights framework to develop the analytical and political tools that we recognise today as the concepts of women's human rights (Mertus and Flowers, 2008; Osler and Starkey, 2010). For this reason, the concept of recognition (embodied in human rights texts) needs to be stressed within the universal framework of human rights.

Some authoritarian states and leaders have challenged the universality of human rights, citing cultural specificities or concepts such as 'Asian values'. In fact, this stance tends to work against the interests of women and of various vulnerable minorities (Osler and Starkey, 2010). In practice, human rights can be enacted in different cultural contexts and universal human rights standards maintained in these different contexts. It is important to remember that no culture is static. In culturally plural societies, it is generally possible to 'agree about *what* to do even when we don't agree *why*' (Appiah, 2006, p 67, original emphasis). Different traditions arrive at a common acceptance of human rights, but on different philosophical grounds. A cross-cultural dialogue is likely to strengthen human rights.

In the subsequent parts of this chapter, I explore the potential of human rights as procedural principles for debate and consider ways in which contentious social, political and religious differences can be explored in an atmosphere of trust. Effectively, the aim is to examine the potential of human rights to provide a framework for enabling greater inclusion in contexts of diversity. What follows is a study of the complexity and intersectionality of various factors relating to nationality, transnationality, citizenship, gender, sexuality, ethnicity and religious diversity as they were enacted in one graduate classroom.

The graduate seminar, entitled 'Learning to live together', took place in Utah in the US in 2010 and comprised 10 sessions. It was designed for PhD students and carried credit towards their final award. The seven students who took part in this programme were all female and a number were mature returners to study. They included US nationals, a long-term resident without US nationality and an international student. The international student was studying full time; all the others had a professional background of teaching in publicly funded schools. Two were working full time in schools; two were teaching and supervising students on teacher training programmes; some had two paid jobs; and two were mothers of school-aged children, with all the additional responsibilities of parenthood. The small town in which the university was situated was somewhat remote, and Utah is quite sparsely populated. The majority religion, Mormonism – more commonly referred to locally as LDS (Latter Day Saints) – is strongly patriarchal.

Although the university offered a range of distance learning options and modules for graduate students in education, for the 'Learning to live together' class there was no distance option. One student was in fact undertaking a round trip of over three hours to attend. These seven well-motivated students had signed up to a programme that explained:

> We will consider human rights as principles for living together and focus on human rights education as a possible means to working towards the cosmopolitan ideals of justice and peace. We will examine a number of issues, including:
>
> • Why do teachers need to be familiar with human rights?
> • In multicultural societies, whose values take precedence?
> • How might schools resolve tensions between children's rights and teachers' rights?

- What difference can young people's perspectives make to contemporary debates on schooling?
- What impact do children's human rights have on educational research ethics?

> By the end of the course, you will be familiar with the Universal Declaration of Human Rights and the UN Convention on the Rights of the Child. The tutor is from the UK. It is expected that there will be a genuine cultural exchange between participants and tutor as well as mutual learning.... As part of the preparation for the various classes, you will reflect on your own positioning in relation to various human rights and justice issues.

In preparing for the class, I aimed to create a secure yet challenging environment wherein students could explore human rights as principles for everyday living. From day one, I was aware that this might in itself be challenging. The point was reinforced when a woman working in the university's international office asked if she might audit the class. I explained that we would be looking at human rights specifically in the local and national contexts, rather than focusing on distant places. Her response: "I hope you don't think I'm being presumptuous, but don't you think there are other parts of the world where there are more serious human rights problems?". Of course, she is in many senses right. Her response is not peculiar to the US; it might just as easily be articulated in any Western European country. The difference is that there is a growing awareness in many contexts of the need to create a culture of human rights and for human rights education, which I would argue is not yet commonplace in the US. In the US, human rights are more likely to be associated with distant places. Specific civil rights campaigns such as women's rights and more recently gay rights have used human rights as a campaigning slogan. It is widely assumed that the US constitution offers full protection for citizens (if not for non-citizens) and that the project for civil rights is complete. The notion that civil rights may need to be supported by social and economic rights, and vice versa, is generally not high on the public agenda.

Early in the programme, I asked my students to identify and write a commentary on a human rights news story. Among the stories chosen were a case of child workers in Kenya; the case of Sakineh Mohammad Ashtiani, sentenced to stoning in Iran for her alleged adultery; and children engaged in the sex industry in Thailand. The concept of human rights was seen as 'over there' rather than 'right here'. I kept repeating to my students the mantra: 'right here, right now'. Yet, from the beginning, some were willing to apply human rights to alternative cases, which had some local resonance. One student selected the story of former National Basketball Association star, John Amaechi, who was reportedly refused entry to a gay bar in Manchester, UK, because he was 'big, black and could be trouble' (BBC News, 2010). Diverse examples allowed us to apply universal principles to different social contexts; to study the principles themselves and become familiar with the concepts of universality, reciprocity and solidarity embedded in human rights.

If the further implementation of the widening participation agenda is to be successful, then university teachers will need to be ready to address questions of conflicting values and work with their students in culturally diverse classrooms to identify peaceful ways of resolving these. It is for this reason, among others, that it is critical in multicultural nation states such as the US and the UK that we embrace an understanding of human rights as applying right here and right now.

Rethinking citizenship and multiculturalism

One of the central purposes of the programme was to consider the relationship between human rights and values and the contribution that a human rights framework can make to the processes of living in contexts of cultural pluralism. Whereas in the UK and in a number of European nation states the concept of multiculturalism as a policy approach has come under attack, in countries such as the US such attacks may not be understood. The term 'multicultural' is more commonly understood in the US as a descriptor of society rather than a policy approach.

In October 2010, German Chancellor Angela Merkel, addressing a conference of the youth wing of her Christian Democratic Union (CDU) Party, claimed that multiculturalism in Germany has 'failed utterly' (Weaver, 2010). She asserted that that Germans and foreign workers could not 'live happily side by side'. Senior political figures in Britain have criticised multiculturalism and stressed the importance of developing a stronger sense of national identity. Such calls gained a degree of momentum following the 2005 London suicide bombings. After the bombings, ethnic diversity was given a new emphasis within the programme of study for citizenship education in schools, in response to fears about terrorism. Unfortunately, little attention was attached to barriers to democratic participation, such as inequalities and racism (Osler, 2008).

Although in December 2006 Prime Minister Tony Blair asserted the importance of multiculturalism, his perspective was not reflected among other leading Labour politicians. In 2008, the future Conservative Prime Minister David Cameron claimed that: 'State multiculturalism is a wrong-headed doctrine that has had disastrous results. It has fostered difference between communities.' Cameron asserted that 'people today don't worry that criticising multiculturalism is coded racism' (Sparrow, 2008). In attacking 'state multiculturalism', Cameron is making a point about social and education policies that support and value diversity. Such policies might relate to formal education, and a range of informal and non-formal activities and events covering anything from museums, to sport and music. He equates diversity with 'difference' and implies that difference itself is undesirable. Yet diversity enhances democracy. If we were all to share the same outlook, there would be no need for democratic structures and procedures.

When Angela Merkel claims that multiculturalism has failed, she is referring to ethnic diversity. One response to the claim that multiculturalism has failed is that what has not been tried cannot be said to have failed. For decades, Germany denied citizenship to its 'guest-workers' on the premise that German citizenship could only be acquired through bloodlines. Britain has never had an out-and-out policy of multiculturalism. Instead, it has had piecemeal multicultural policies, for example, in education, depending on local authorities' degree of commitment (Figueroa, 2004; Tomlinson, 2009; Osler, 2011). There has not been a comprehensive nationwide policy of 'multicultural citizenship' (Kymlicka, 1996).

Today, in the US, multicultural education encompasses a broad range of concepts and issues that extend far beyond race and ethnicity. Multicultural education has been described as:

> an educational reform movement, and a process whose major goal is to change the structure of educational institutions so that male and female students, exceptional students, and students who are members of diverse racial, ethnic, language and cultural groups will have an equal chance to achieve academically. (Banks and Banks, 2010, p 1)

In keeping with current thinking, Banks and Banks (2010) include chapters on the intersection of race and gender in classrooms and on sexual and gender minorities in their most recent edited volume addressing multicultural education. While US academics advocating multicultural education make explicit the links between multicultural education and education for democracy, many advocates of democratic education have been slow to espouse a multicultural perspective or acknowledge that democratic education implies addressing the barriers to full participation, including those of racism and sexism. A similar criticism can be made of initiatives to promote education for democratic citizenship in the UK (Osler, 2000; Osler and Starkey, 2002). I would argue that democratic education that fails to examine such barriers is flawed, as is any form of anti-racist initiative that is premised solely on recognition of cultural diversity, but which neglects to discuss racism as a barrier to full social, economic and political participation.

Education for democratic citizenship is likely to look different in a nation state that views itself as a multicultural democracy compared with one that does not. In considering citizenship education, it is helpful to conceive of citizenship as status, feeling and practice (Osler and Starkey, 2005). Inclusive institutions of higher education are likely to need, as a prerequisite, inclusive understandings of citizenship and belonging. If citizenship is understood as status, being a national of a particular country, then it is necessarily exclusive. An individual is either a British citizen or s/he is not. While citizenship, as nationality, is necessarily exclusive, the status of human rights-holder is inclusive. All are holders of human rights. Citizenship as feeling is not tied absolutely to nationality. A person can feel a sense of belonging according to how society treats that individual. A sense of belonging depends on a sense of security and on the absence of discrimination. A resident non-national can feel a sense of belonging, for example, if these conditions are met. The practice of citizenship relates to an individual's engagement in the community and to 'acts of citizenship' (Isin and Neilsen, 2008). Citizenship as practice is not dependent on status, but may be influenced by citizenship as feeling. Many non-nationals may be actively engaged in acts of citizenship within communities. If an individual does not feel a sense of belonging within the political and social spheres, that person is less likely to engage in acts of citizenship. Status, feeling and practice are interrelated. If a person feels included, the practice of citizenship is likely to follow. A sense of belonging cannot be a prerequisite for naturalisation. Processes of naturalisation and the adoption of the formal status of citizenship may support a sense of belonging.

Developing an inclusive sense of citizenship does not simply have implications for citizenship education policies within higher education, often conceived of as voluntary community work or service learning. The development of universities as inclusive communities implies policies relating to fee structures and access arrangements, for example, which do not privilege nationals over resident non-nationals. In order to meet their obligations under international human rights legal frameworks, children in publicly funded schools are generally treated on a basis of equality regardless of their nationality status, with access determined primarily by residence. This does not necessarily apply within higher education. Resident non-nationals may be treated in different ways within different institutions of higher education. In further education colleges in England, they are required to pay fees for courses for which nationals are exempt. In universities in England, they are generally treated in the same way as nationals, subject to their fulfilment of a qualifying period of residence. The situation of resident but undocumented students is often problematic. In the US, where in a number of states there are significant numbers of undocumented workers and children, such children have access to publicly funded schools, with a no-questions-asked policy. But when such students graduate from high school and wish to progress to higher education their undocumented status is frequently a bar to enrolment.

The framework that I offered my students encouraged them to develop their own human rights narratives, both individually and collectively, thereby developing a human rights discourse to address issues of justice and injustice in their own lives. This approach was informed by Delanty's (2003) study of citizenship as a learning process. Effective political education for citizenship and human rights, from this perspective, should necessarily include opportunities to explore and reflect upon various identities and cultural attributes, and create personal narratives.

Human rights and an inclusive dialogue

My original aim was to encourage my students (many of whom were teachers) to look through a human rights lens to enable greater inclusion in their own professional practice. What developed from this was a deeper process of reflection on what makes for effective practice in education for human rights and social justice in the higher education seminar room.

The challenge was to permit an open dialogue on contentious issues; to explore opportunities for listening to alternative viewpoints; and, if possible, work collectively towards consensus and shared understandings of these issues while at the same time respecting minority viewpoints and religious and political freedom. As an outsider to this socially conservative and strongly patriarchal context, I hoped that my outsider status might allow for the presentation of alternative perspectives that might otherwise have been given little consideration.

Political debate in the US in the autumn of 2010 in the build-up to the mid-term elections was in many ways toxic, both in content and in tone. The attempted assassination of a congresswoman in Arizona in January 2011 and the commentary that followed drew the attention of the wider world to this phenomenon. Within Utah, the broader issue of political intolerance was complicated by local factors when, in September 2010, a leader in the LDS Church chose to speak out against same-sex relationships and in defence of the traditional family. The student body was deeply divided on this issue and the students in my class were eager to discuss the question within the framework of human rights.

I contend that human rights provide us with principles that can be used to establish procedural guidelines when addressing contentious issues. Based on equal dignity and recognition for all, human rights demand mutual respect for all persons in the debate, regardless of their identities. Freedom of speech is an important principle, but it is set in tension with others' right to human dignity and to feel secure and not threatened. Freedom of speech is not a limitless freedom to insult or abuse another.

I also contend that human rights provide a framework for living together in communities and for living and working together within the community of the university. My contentions were put to the test by my students on a number of occasions, but were placed under particular scrutiny when discussing the rights of lesbian, gay, transgender and bisexual (LGTB) citizens. The issue was also raised when I gave a public lecture on human rights as principles for living together.

The class had studied the Universal Declaration of Human Rights (UDHR) and had applied it to a range of personal and professional contexts. What follows is an application of the UDHR to a specific set of events, in a case raised by a student, concerning vandalism against an LDS church in Los Angeles in 2008.

The vandalism took place following the Mormon Church's funding of Proposition 8, a ballot passed in the 2008 California state elections that removed the right of same-sex couples to marry. Proposition 8 asserted that 'only marriage between a man and a woman is valid or recognized in California'. An examination of the Los Angeles vandalism case and its context allowed us to examine the rights of various parties and interests through a human rights lens, using the UDHR.

We began with the members of the Mormon Church and a consideration of their rights. Article 1 of the UDHR states that: 'All human beings are born free and equal in dignity and rights'. This, of course, applies to all parties in this case regardless of religious beliefs or sexual orientation, as does Article 2, which asserts the principle of non-discrimination. Article 18 states that: 'Everyone has the right to freedom of thought, conscience and religion; this right includes freedom to change his religion or belief, and freedom, either alone or in community with others and in public or private, to manifest his religion or belief in teaching, practice, worship and observance'. Importantly, Article 19 adds that: 'Everyone has the right to freedom of opinion and expression'. So an act of vandalism on a church in Los Angeles amounts to an attack on the freedom of worshippers to practise their religion. By extension, it may undermine the physical security of worshippers within that congregation (in contravention of Article 3) and effectively serve to limit the freedom of religion and public worship of other members of the faith in other locations.

There is, however, nothing in the UDHR that equates freedom of thought, conscience and religion with an entitlement to impose moral standards deriving from one's religion on a wider public. So the Church leadership's support for Proposition 8 cannot be justified as a right. The leaders are entitled to their belief that same-sex relationships are wrong or even sinful, but cannot impose this moral stance on others who do not share it.

Are Mormon leaders justified in speaking out against same-sex relationships? Article 18 suggests they have a right to manifest their beliefs in teaching, but this right must be tempered by a consideration of the impact of such teaching. If the direct or indirect outcome of their proclaimed beliefs undermines the 'right to life, liberty and security' (Article 3) of gays (and there is a documented history of homophobic murders and of the increased risk of bullying, self-harm and suicide among gay teens), then there is no right to condemn others or place their security at risk. The rights within the UDHR are a package; freedom of belief and religion cannot be privileged in a way that undermines the rights of others. As Article 30 confirms:

> Nothing in this Declaration may be interpreted as implying for any State, group or person any right to engage in any activity or to perform any act aimed at the destruction of any of the rights and freedoms set forth herein.

Does Proposition 8 undermine the rights of gay and lesbian citizens in banning same-sex marriage? We have noted the principles of equal dignity, equality of rights and non-discrimination. Article 6 asserts that 'Everyone has the right to recognition everywhere as a person before the law', and Article 7 states that 'All are equal before the law and are entitled without any discrimination to equal protection of the law'. Marriage is a legal contract that brings with it many privileges, including: shared health care benefits; inheritance and other next-of-kin rights; pension entitlements; and, in the US, tax benefits. Article 16 neither anticipated nor ruled out same-sex marriage in the formula: 'Men and women of full age, without any limitation due to race, nationality or religion, have the right to marry and to found a family'. Those who drafted the UDHR aimed to be inclusive of different family arrangements cross-culturally. The principles of equal recognition before the law and equal protection of the law apply regardless of sexual orientation. So, all couples wishing to form a marriage contract, opposite-sex or same-sex, should be accorded this equal protection and recognition, according to the standards of the UDHR.

In debating the questions, it is critical that we do not essentialise any of the parties. It is important to remember that neither all Mormons nor all LGBT persons share the same beliefs and political opinions. Nor do all Mormons or all gays think and act alike. Neither grouping is homogeneous. Spokespersons for either community cannot be taken to represent the opinions of all. Some Mormons are gay (either openly or not) and some gays are Mormon. Not all gays want same-sex marriage and not all Mormons are against it. Equally, the experience of being Mormon in Utah, for example, is likely to be very different from other locations where the LDS Church is not the dominant religion. This was brought home to me in Madison, Wisconsin, when a young graduate student confided in me that she was Mormon, but that she did not want her advisor or fellow students to discover this for fear of prejudicial and inaccurate judgements about her social and political perspectives.

Applying human rights and inclusive citizenship in universities

By analysing a contentious case through close study of the various articles of the UDHR, it is possible to apply legal reasoning and to avoid an immediate emotional or intuitive reaction about what is just or unjust. In the example above, universal principles are applied to the various parties: the worshippers, the Church leadership, LGTB citizens, those who commited the acts of vandalism, and so on. Students can apply the legal logic, without necessarily feeling threatened by having to make a case based on their own feelings or prejudices. All parties are subject to the same scrutiny and the same standards.

It does not necessarily mean anyone will change their position on the issue, but that option remains open. What is permitted is a dialogue, rather than a reinforcement of existing positions. Both teacher and students are subject to the same processes of reasoning. Moreover, the approach encourages a procedural process based on respect for the dignity of all parties, including the learners. At a later stage in the learning process, it might be reasonable to engage the emotions: for example, learners might listen to the accounts of those whose church was vandalised or those to whom a marriage contract was denied.

The example of same-sex marriage and freedom of conscience and religion was one that these particular students raised and that we examined as a human rights case. The approach adopted might be reapplied in different social or cultural contexts to examine other contentious issues through a human rights lens, when there is no clear consensus. Other human rights issues raised by these students, such as domestic violence and legally condoned violence towards women, were not contentious within the group, but condemned by all. In another social or cultural context where there was any ambivalence about such violence, it might have been appropriate to explore the issue in a similar fashion, using the UDHR as a framework.

This example, addressing the processes of teaching and learning, focused on an issue pertinent to the lives of graduate students living, teaching and studying in a specific location. The approach adopted is one that might be used to address a range of questions of inclusion, exclusion and social justice that are contentious in other contexts. In the UK, there is often a degree of intolerance for religious perspectives and beliefs, both within the academy and beyond. Yet, as has been argued, all have the right of freedom of religion. Human rights require that we defend the rights of all, even those with whom we disagree.

Figueroa reminds us that:

> Pluralism does not assume that all people are contingently the same ... or that *de facto* they enjoy equal power, status or resources. Rather pluralism sets equity – not simply sameness – as a social ideal. It assumes that people *qua* people are equal, and that as human beings they are fundamentally comparable to each other and are basically of equal worth. (2000, p 54)

In the culturally plural society, and a culturally plural university, a human rights framework provides both recognition of our equal dignity as human beings and a starting point for realising equity as a social ideal.

From this framework, universities can work towards the development of analytical and practical tools for the social change that is essential if the goal of widening participation is to be fully realised. Those in universities need to address the implications of working with students from different backgrounds, with different access to power, status and resources. By explicitly adopting a commitment to universal human rights, anxieties about alienating or excluding students on the grounds of religious or ethical beliefs might be reduced.

The founders of Somerville College, who insisted that lack of commitment to a specific religious tradition should be no bar to participation in higher education in the 1880s, adopted an inclusive approach compatible with contemporary human rights standards from which many universities might learn today. It is, of course, possible to exclude indirectly, for example, by failing to provide students with the facilities to fulfil their religious commitments or simply by making assumptions about them from a position of power. Yet, in leaving invisible to 21st-century students the past achievements of pioneers such as Cornelia Sorabji, the very same college may be at risk of compounding exclusive practices that persist today, and which are experienced by both students and academic staff. My own experience and that of observing my students and colleagues leads me to believe that the practice persists of assuming, for example, that a woman from a particular cultural tradition or family background is unlikely to excel in a particular academic field or as a leader in the academy.

This chapter has explored the potential of human rights as a framework to create an inclusive classroom context in which contentious issues can be addressed without alienating or excluding particular groups of students because of their religious or ethical beliefs. In contexts of cultural pluralism, human rights provide a starting point for establishing common ground and shared understandings, whereby diversity can be recognised as an asset to democracy, rather than a deficit. Human rights offer a framework from which an inclusive sense of belonging and a genuinely inclusive citizenship can be developed, appropriate to the needs of a multicultural democracy.

Changes in global migration patterns, together with the internationalisation of higher education, means that, at the beginning of the 21st century, many universities that previously recruited from apparently homogeneous local communities find they need to respond to increasingly diverse student populations, with multiple worldviews and perspectives. Across the European Union, the European Commission supports the mobility of millions of European students who elect to spend part of their studies in another member state.

The challenge is to enable academic freedom while at the same time respecting minority viewpoints and religious and political freedom. Human rights provide a starting point for enabling students to write the world and read the world. The challenge is, first, to acknowledge long-standing diversity and retell our history in inclusive ways, as illustrated by the story of Cornelia Sorabji. At the same time, it is critical that new ways are found to enable students to begin a fruitful dialogue that will lead to the creation of more inclusive collective narratives for a cosmopolitan citizenship based on shared human rights.

References

Appiah, K.A. (2006) *Cosmopolitanism: Ethics in a World of Strangers*, London: Allen Lane.

Banks, J.A. and Banks, C.A.M. (eds) (2010) *Multicultural Education: Issues and Perspectives* (7th edn), Hoboken, NJ: John Wiley.

BBC News (2010) 'NBA star John Amaechi in bar access row', 13 September. Available at: http://www.bbc.co.uk/news/uk-england-manchester-11287865

Delanty, G. (2003) 'Citizenship as a learning process: disciplinary citizenship versus cultural citizenship', *International Journal of Lifelong Education*, vol 22, no 5, pp 597–605.

Figueroa, P. (2000) 'Citizenship education for a plural society', in A. Osler (ed) *Citizenship and Democracy in Schools: Diversity, Identity, Equality*, Stoke-on-Trent: Trentham Books.

Figueroa, P. (2004) 'Diversity and citizenship education in England', in J.A. Banks (ed) *Diversity and Citizenship Education: Global Perspectives*, San Francisco, CA: Jossey-Bass.

Freire, P. (2004) *Pedagogy of Indignation*, Boulder, CO: Paradigm.

Isin, E. and Neilsen, G. (2008) *Acts of Citizenship*, London: Zed Books.

Kymlicka, W. (1996) *Multicultural Citizenship: A Liberal Theory of Minority Rights*, Oxford: Oxford University Press.

Mertus, J. and Flowers, N. (2008) *Local Action, Global Change: A Handbook on Women's Human Rights*, Boulder, CO and London: Paradigm.

Osler, A. (1997) *The Education and Careers of Black Teachers; Changing Identities, Changing Lives*, Buckingham: Open University Press.

Osler, A. (2000) 'The Crick Report: difference, equality and racial justice', *Curriculum Journal*, vol 11, no 1, pp 25–37.

Osler, A. (2006) 'Changing leadership in contexts of diversity: visibility, invisibility and democratic ideals', *Policy Futures in Education*, vol 4, no 2, pp 128–44.

Osler, A. (2008) 'Citizenship education and the Ajegbo report: re-imagining a cosmopolitan nation', *London Review of Education*, vol 6, no 1, pp 11–25.

Osler, A. (2011) 'Education policy, social cohesion and citizenship', in P. Ratcliffe and I. Newman (eds) *Promoting Social Cohesion: Implications for Policy and Frameworks for Evaluation*, Bristol, UK, and Portland, OR: The Policy Press.

Osler, A. and Starkey, H. (2002) 'Education for citizenship: mainstreaming the fight against racism?', *European Journal of Education*, vol 37, no 2, pp 143–59.

Osler, A. and Starkey, H. (2005) *Changing Citizenship: Democracy and Inclusion in Education*, Buckingham: Open University Press.

Osler, A. and Starkey, H. (2010) *Teachers and Human Rights Education*, Stoke-on-Trent: Trentham Books.

Sparrow, A. (2008) 'Cameron attacks "state multiculturalism"', *The Guardian*, 26 February. Available at: http://www.guardian.co.uk/politics/2008/feb/26/conservatives.race

Tomlinson, S. (1983) 'Black women in higher education. Case studies of university women in Britain', in L. Barton and S. Walker (eds) *Race, Class and Education*, London: Croom Helm, pp 66–80.

Tomlinson, S. (2009) 'Multicultural education in the United Kingdom', in J.A. Banks (ed) *The Routledge International Companion to Multicultural Education*, New York, NY: Routledge.

UNHCHR (United Nations High Commissioner for Human Rights) (1993) 'Vienna Declaration and Programme of Action', adopted by the World Conference on Human Rights in Vienna on 25 June. Available at: www2.ohchr.org/english/law/vienna.htm

Vasagar, J. (2010) 'Twenty-one Oxbridge colleges took no black students last year', *The Guardian*, 6 December. Available at: www.guardian.co.uk/education/2010/dec/06/oxford-colleges-no-black-students

Weaver, M. (2010) 'Angela Merkel: German multiculturalism has "utterly failed"', *The Guardian*, 17 October. Available at: www.guardian.co.uk/world/2010/oct/17/angela-merkel-german-multiculturalism-failed

Index of authors

A

Abbas, T. 175
ABS 255
ACT 68
Adelman, C.
Ahmad, F. 26, 175
Ahmad, N. 75
Ainley, P. 195, 274
Allen, M. 52
Allen, W.R. 87
American Association of
    Community Colleges
    110, 113
American Council on
    Education 67
Anaya, G. 76
Anderson, D.S. 150, 156
Anderson, R.D. 47, 53,
    59, 60
Andrews, L. 161
Appiah, K.A. 299
Arbona, C. 216
Archer, L. 177
Archer, M.S. 2, 3
Archer, S. 42, 44, 58
Askew, S. 240, 241
Astin, A.W. 87–8
Aungles, P. 161

B

Ball, S.J. 42
Ballard, R. 18, 23
Balloch, S. 275
Banks, J.A. 303
Bankston, C.L. 30, 31, 32
Barnes, S.V. 50
Barnett, R. 3, 5, 42
Barnhardt, R. 255
Basit, T.N. 26, 174, 175,
    179, 186, 187
Baty, P. 57
BCC 280
Beck, U. 173–4, 186
Bekhradnia, B. 240
Berger, J. 151-2
Bergeran, D.M. 66
Betz, N.E. 66
Bhattachariya, G.
Bhatti, G. 179
Bird, J. 274
Black, P. 241
Blackledge, D. 59, 60

Blumenfield, P.C. 250
Bocock, J. 274
Bok, D. 122
Bolton, G. 194
Bonner, F. 217
Bordes, V. 217
Boud, D. 250
Bourdieu, P. 4–5, 17,
    28–9, 178, 200, 245
Boursicot, K. 138–9
Bowen, W.G. 110, 111,
    116
Boyer, E. 119
Bradley, D. 4, 151, 153,
    154, 159, 163, 166
Bradley, S. 23
Brayboy, B.M.J. 265, 267
Broecke, S. 20, 175, 176
Bronfenbrenner, U. 218
Brookes, R. 175
Brookfield, S. 194, 195,
    205
Brown, A. 140
Brown, R. 42
Browne, J. 4, 132, 186–7,
    239
Burgess, S. 26
Byars-Winston 69
Byfield, C. 185

C

Cabinet Office 193
Cairncross, S. 71
Campaign for College
    Opportunity 215
Cardak, B.A. 161
Cardini, A. 276
Carless, D. 241, 243, 245,
    250
Carnevale, A.P. 111, 112
Carroll, J.B. 68
Chapman, B. 161
Charles, D.R. 6
Christie, H. 179
Chubin, D.E. 72
CIHE 280
Clancy, S. 259
Clark, S.M. 67
Clark, Y. 261
Clarke, A. 256–7
Clegg, S. 276
Coates, H. 89

Coffield, F. 42, 195, 276,
    282
Cole, D. 69, 75
Coleman, J. 30, 31, 179
Connor, H. 20, 21, 27, 35
Crozier, G. 142, 179
CSHE 103

D

Daempfle, P.A. 69
Darity, W., Jr. 67
David, M. 130, 131, 132,
    138, 140, 141-4, 175,
    177
Davies, B. 256
Davies, J. 88
Dawkins, J.S. 157–8, 159
Dearing, R. 42, 190
DEET 159
DEEWR 103–4, 151,
    269
Delanty, G. 305
Denzin, N. 220
Department for
    Education and Skills
    59, 198, 211, 288
DEST 93, 97
Devine, F. 17
Dewey, J. 237
DfEE 275, 282
Dhillon, J.K. 289
Diez, M.E. 122–3
Dobson, I. 89
Douglass, J. 87
Doyle, L. 255
Droste, M. 260
Duncan, N. 245

E

ECU 176
Ehrlich, T. 117, 118, 119

F

Fairclough, N. 46, 51, 57
Fekjaer, S. 37
Fenton, S. 17
Field, J. 53, 276
Fieldhouse, R. 42, 50, 51
Figueroa, P. 303, 309
Finkelstein, M.J. 116
Finnie, R. 161
Finson, K.D. 69
Fitzclarence, L. 165

Flintoff, A. 257
Foskett, N. 161
Foucault, M. 209–10, 256
Fredericks, B. 261
Freeman, K. 255
Freire, P. 298
Friedman, T.L. 115
Fryer, B. 42, 59
Fuller, A. 142

G

Gale, T. 149
Gallacher, J. 274
Garrison, A. 221
GEA 129, 139
Giddens, A. 163, 276
Gillard, J. 163, 164, 165
Gillborn, D. 25
Gilroy, P. 206, 211
Gipps, C. 243
Giroux, H. 238–9
Gittoes, M. 36
Glendinning, C. 276
Gloria, A. 217, 231
Godden, N. 161
Golden, D. 86
Goldthorpe, J. 22
Gonzales, K. 216, 217
Gorard, S. 4
Grandy, J. 69
Granovetter, M.S. 32
Green, A. 2
Greenbank, P. 59
Greig, A. 152
Guardian 57

H

Habermas, J. 207, 211
Hagell, A. 26
Hall, R.M. 67
Hall, S. 35
Halsey, A.H. 3
Hansen, E. 74
Harkavy, I. 177
Harmston, M.T. 68
Harper, S.R. 120
Harvey, L. 240
Hayward, G. 184
HEFCE 36, 88, 151–2, 288
Heffer, S. 56
Henriques, J. 256
Higgins, R. 243
HM Treasury 193
Hoachlander, G. 114
Hobsbawm, E. 47
Hockings, C. 142, 177
Hodgson, A. 290

Holmes, J. 202
hooks, b. 210
Horn, L. 215
Hounsell, D. 249
Housee, S. 207
Howieson, C. 175
Hudson, R.A. 202
Hughes, P. 256
Hurtado, S. 73

I

Ijaz, A. 175
Isin, E. 304
Ivanic, R. 249

J

Jackson, P. 237–8
James, R. 83, 89, 91, 92, 162, 255
Jary, D. 274, 275
Jessop, B. 3
Johns, A.M. 120
Johnson, D. 69
Jones, S.A. 73
Jones, V. 119

K

Kellogg Commission 117
Kelly, A 216
Kennedy, H. 42, 278
Kenny, M. 217
Kim, S. 67
Kimble, C. 197
King, R. 6
King, T. 114–15
Kirp, D. 4
Kitchener, K. 76
Knight, P.T. 241–2
Kolb, D. 75
Kymlicka, W. 303

L

Langa-Rosado, D. 131
Laughlo, J. 37
Lave, E. 197, 204
Layer, G. 86
Lea, M.R. 246, 249
Leathwood, C. 55, 144–5, 240, 244, 249, 250
Lehmann, W. 180, 188
Leslie, L.L. 69
Lillis, T.M. 243
Literary Study Group 197, 204
Locke, S. 255, 256, 267
Loury, G. 30–1
Love, K. 242
Lovett, T. 53, 55

Lowe, R. 42, 46, 48, 49, 50
Lubinski, D. 68
Lugg, R. 137–8

M

Macintyre, S. 156
Macpherson, W. 211
Maki, P. 122, 123
Marginson, S. 1, 2, 6, 122, 151, 154, 155, 158, 161, 165
Margolis, E. 239
Marsh, G. 50
Martin, I.R. 217
Martin, J.R. 238
Martin, L. 105, 155, 159, 161
Martin, Y.M. 151
Maton, K.I. 69, 72
May, S. 17
Mayo, M. 53, 54
McGivney, V. 42
McNicol, S. 55
Melendez, M.C. 216, 217
Merriam, S.B. 259
Mertus, J. 299
Metzger, W.P. 110
Mills, R. 155
Mirza, H.S. 175
Modood, T. 23. 24. 25, 34, 35, 174
Mohan, S. 71
Moon, J. 194
Moreton-Robinson, A. 267
Morley, L. 136–8, 145
Mukhopadhyay, C. 120
Mullen, R. 123
Murphy, H. 243
Murray, K. 155
Mutch, A. 245

N

Naidoo, R. 103
Nakata, M. 258, 259
National Audit Office 178
National Science Board 67
National Science Foundation 114
NBEET 84, 105, 159, 160
NCES 216
NEP 25, 35
Nelson, B. 161
Newman, M. 240

Nicol, D. 240, 241
Nixon, J. 5
NSF 66
Nunn, A. 193

O

Oakes, J. 67, 68
Oakley, A. 131
OECD 6–7, 86, 88, 151
Ogbu, J.U. 29
Ong, A. 6
Orr, D. 56
Oseguera, L. 87
Osler, A. 174, 295, 296, 299, 302, 303, 304
OUS 215, 219
Owen, D. 25

P

Paczuska, A. 274
Paradies, Y.C. 262, 263
Pascarella, E.T. 74
Pathak, S. 174
Perrakis, A. 217
Phinney, J.S. 217
Pinnock, K. 176
Portes, A. 31
Powell, M. 275, 290
Preece, J. 42
Preece, S. 242
Putnam, R. 29–30, 179

Q

Quality Assurance Agency 240, 249

R

Ramsay, E. 158, 160–1
Ramsden, P. 240
Rawls, J. 84, 166
Read, B. 243, 249
Reay, D. 17, 42, 43, 55, 178, 201, 245
Reid, C. 256
Reid, J. 256, 266
Richardson, J.T.E. 176
Robinson, S. 206–7
Rodriquez, A. 217
Romero, J. 230
Rose, J. 43
Rust, C. 243
Rustin, M. 47, 49, 50, 52

S

Sadler, D.R. 241
Santiago, D. 215
Santoro, N. 266
Sastry, T. 240

Saunders, P. 152
Savage, M. 17, 24
Sax, L. 70, 75
Schnitzer, K. 86
Schuller, T. 7
Scott, P. 42
Sedikides, C. 218, 219
Sefa Dei, G.J. 165
Sen, A. 84
SEU 276
Seymour, E. 68–9
Shah, B. 35, 36
Shah, S. 259
Shain, F. 195
Shavit, Y. 137
Shiner, M. 20–1, 36–7, 174
Shore, E. 216
Simon, B. 42, 44, 45, 47, 49, 51, 52–3
Simpson, D. 251
Sirianni, C. 117, 118, 122
Slaughter, S. 131, 140
Smith, D.E. 131
Smith, D.G. 119, 122
Smith, R. 195
Snyder, B. 238, 239
Snyder, T.D. 114
Sparrow, A. 303
Spelke, E.S. 66
Spener, D. 201
Stanley, J.C. 68
Stephen, D.E. 244
Stevens, F.I. 67
Stevenson, S. 153
Storen, L.A. 37
Strayhorn, T.L. 72–3
Street, B.V. 196
Stuart, M. 274
Stuurman, R.J. 260
Sullivan, A. 4
Supiano, B. 67
Suskie, L. 122
Swail, W.S. 69
Sy, S. 217, 230

T

Tahir, T. 240
Tapper, T. 1, 4
Tate, W.F. 67, 68, 71
Tawney, R.H. 50–1
Taylor, J. 53
Thelin, J.R. 116
THES 57–8
Thomas, E.A.M. 42, 54
Thomas, L. 244
Thompson, D.W. 59
Tierney, W.G. 120

Tight, M. 42
Tomlinson, S. 174, 298, 303
Tonkin, H. 117
Torres, V. 120
Tripp, D. 194
Trow, M. 98, 151, 154
TTA 174

U

Ufi 284
University of California Riverside 112
University of Melbourne 150
US Census Bureau 215
US Department of Education 65, 114

V

Van Duzer, C. 256, 257
Vasagar, J. 296
Venn, C. 256, 257
Vinson, T. 152

W

Wallman, S. 18
Washington, P. 119
Watson, D. 42, 177
Watson, L.W. 69
Weaver, M. 302
WEA 49, 52
Weiler, K. 134, 135–6
Wells, J. 152
Werbner, P. 18
West, R. 161
Westwood, S. 53, 54–5
Wetherall, M. 256
White, C. 256
Wicks, J. 152
Williams, B. 157
Williams, J. 1, 142, 143–4
Wilson, R. 113
Winfeld, L.F. 67, 68
Wolf, A. 89
Woodrow, M. 280
Wylie, V. 279, 280–1

Y

Yates, L. 134–5
Yorke, M. 243, 244
Youdell, D. 257
Young, P. 245
Young, R.L. 119

Z

Zhou, M. 30, 31, 32, 34

Index of subjects

The letter f following a page number indicates a figure, n an endnote and t a table.

A

A level examinations 36n3
AUT *see* Association of University Teachers
academic merit 84, 89, 98, 101
access
  Australia 158
  barriers to 96–7
  United Kingdom 86
  widening 273–91
  see also social inclusion
Access courses 54–5, 274
access movement 53
adult education
  extension movement 49
  Freire and 53
  Thatcher government and 53–4
  Workers Education Association (WEA) 51–2
  working class 42, 46–7, 60
Adult Literacy Core Curriculum (ALCC) 198, 200
African-Caribbeans
  aspirations 180–1, 184–5
  cultural capital 35
  GCSE performance 23
  higher education 19t, 20, 21t, 27t, 35–6, 174
  Oxbridge 296
  school careers 25
  social class 24t
AIDS 51
aristocracy: and educational reform 45–6
arts 132
Asians
  cultural capital 35
  identity 33
  racism 25
  social mobility 30, 36
  United States 32, 112, 114, 215, 216
  see also Bangladeshis; Chinese; Indians; Pakistanis
Association of University Teachers (AUT) 53
Association to Promote the Higher Education of Working Class Men 4
Australia

Backing Australia's Future (Nelson) 161
binary system of higher education 155, 157
Centre for the Study of Higher Education (CSHE) 96, 103
Commonwealth Learning Scholarships 162
Crossroads review (Nelson) 161
disadvantage 99, 152, 157
equal opportunities 89, 153–6, 157–60, 162
equity 83–5, 89–90, 94–103, 162
Equivalent National Tertiary Entrance Rank (ENTER) 98
expansion of higher education 150–2, 164
A Fair Chance for All (DEET) 84, 159, 160
fairness 152–3
Fraser government 157
Future of Tertiary Education in Australia 155
Higher Education Contribution Scheme (HECS) 89
Higher Education Equity Program (HEEP) 100, 157, 164
Howard coalition government 160, 161
Indigenous peoples 90, 97
  Aboriginal Participation Initiative (API) 157
  teacher training 255–68
Labor Party 157
low socio-economic status students 90–4, 150, 152, 153, 155–6, 162, 163, 165
participation 163–4
Participation and Equity Program 157
poverty 152, 154
privatisation 160–2
rationalisation 156–7
Review of Australian Higher Education (Bradley) 103–4, 153, 163
Rudd government 163
scholarships 162
social inclusion 83–5, 89–105, 163–4
  equity advancement 98–103
  equity of access myths 94–8
social justice 149–65

socio-economic status 99–100, 103
Technical and Further Education
    (TAFE) 157
universities 103, 150, 158
    Group of Eight (Go8) 92, 98, 100,
        101
    hierarchies 6
    Whitlam government 155, 156–7
    women 89–90
    feminist educational scholars 135
Australian Tertiary Admissions Rank
    (ATAR) 98
autodidacticism 43

B

Bangladeshis 19t, 20, 21t, 27t, 183–4
Bentham, Jeremy 44
Black Africans 19t, 20, 21t, 24t, 27t
Blair, Tony 88, 89, 163, 303
Board of Education 51–2
Boursicot, Dr Kathy 138–9
Bradley, Professor Denise 103, 163
Bristol University 56
British empire 4
Brougham, Henry 44
Browne, Lord 239
Browne Review of higher education
    funding and student finance 186–7
bullying 25

C

Cabinet Office: *Unleashing Aspiration:
    The Final Report on the Panel on Fair
    Access to the Professions* 193
Cambridge University 3–4, 44, 48, 49,
    50, 297
Cameron, David 303
capitals
    aspirational 179, 186
    cultural 17–18
        Bourdieu and 28–9, 34
        and Critical Literacy Education
            199–202
        families 178–9
        minority ethnic groups 35, 181–2
    social 18
        families 178, 179
        minority ethnic groups and 181–2
        Putnam and 29–30
        United States 30–4
career guidance 185
'The challenges for democracy and
    fairness in higher education'
    (symposium) 136–9
childcare studies 290
Chinese students 19t, 21, 22, 27t
citizenship
    and human rights 308–11

and multiculturalism 302–5
    and sense of belonging 304
civil rights 301
Coalition government vii, 187
Cole, Margaret 49
communicative action 205–7
Communist Party 51, 52
community development 53
community of practice 197–8, 204–5,
    208, 209, 210, 211
community organisations 34
competition 94, 102
Comprehensive Spending Review 194
'connectionist' pedagogies 143–4
Critical Literacy Education 201
cultures
    academic 249
    and ethnicity 18
    and human rights 299
    Indigenous Australians 260–6
    of inquiry 124
    Latina students 224, 228, 233
    middle class (19th century) 47
    Native Americans 267
    outcomes 124
curriculum 101–2, 143, 165
    and diversity 175–6
    further education 195
    hidden 237–43, 251
    teacher training
        Indigenous Australians 262–3, 266,
            267

D

Dawkins, John 157–8
Dearing Report 186
degrees
    Australia 90, 91, 104, 151
    United Kingdom 44
        Cambridge University 3, 132
        childcare studies 290
        course applicants 21t
        Foundation Degree programme 53
        minority ethnic groups 174, 177–8
        Oxford University 132, 295
    United States 8, 65, 66, 67, 68, 72, 110,
        112, 115
    value of 6
democracy
    social and cultural capitals 4
    United States 109, 116, 117, 118, 119,
        120
Department for Education and Skills
    (DfES) 174
Dewey, John 237, 251
differentiation 206
discourse, social theory of 46

Discourse: Studies in the Cultural Politics of Education (journal) 134
discrimination
  institutional 22
  racial 23, 87, 174 *see also* segregation
  sexual 67
diversity 175–6
  civic universities 48, 174–7
  and democracy 303
  Indigenous peoples 261, 263
  PGCE students 197, 201, 210–11
  social 139–40
  United States 74, 120

E

Economic and Social Research Council
  (ESRC) Teaching and Learning
  Research Programme (TLRP) 140,
  141
Edinburgh Review 44
education
  citizenship 302
  democratic 304
  Literacy Education 193–212
  reform (19th century) 47
  research 139–40
  and social justice 41–60
    access 43–52, 241–2
    barriers 51, 56–60
    expansion 52–5
    see also further education; higher
    education
Education at a Glance (OECD) 86
educational research 139–40
*Effective Learning and Teaching in UK
  Higher Education* (David) 140
elitism 53, 55, 86, 94, 132, 150
engineering
  minority ethnic students 72, 73–4,
    77
  women 65, 66, 67
  see also STEM
English language 198–200, 202
  grammar 199, 209, 211nn1, 2
equal opportunities
  Australia 89, 153–6, 157–60, 162
  local education authorities 54
equity
  Australia 83–5, 89–90, 94–103, 162
  and participation 95, 141–4
  and pluralism 309
  social 144–5
  United Kingdom 88–9
ethnic diversity *see* multiculturalism
ethnicity: and culture 18 *see also*
  minority ethnic groups
examinations 22–3, 36n3, 67
exclusion *see* social exclusion

Exeter University Extension College 50
extension movement 49–50

F

FEFC *see* Further Education Funding
  Council
families
  cultural capital 28
  minority ethnic 26–8, 175
    Latino 217, 222–3, 226–7, 228
  parent–child relationships 33
  and STEM 77
  social capital 31–2
  support from 178–9, 181–2, 183, 184,
    185
feminism
  and higher education research 136–9,
    141–2
  pedagogies 145
  second-wave 130, 134–6
  and social inclusion 130–1, 144–5
  and social research 133–6
Finland 88
Foundation Degree programme 53
freedom of speech 306
Freire, Paulo 53
Further and Higher Education Act 1992
  (UK) 193, 274
further education (FE)
  access 274–5
  partnerships 273–91
  quasi-marketisation 195
Further Education Funding Council
  (FEFC) 195, 278

G

GCSE examinations 22–3
gender
  education policies 139
  equity 20, 65, 69, 137, 145, 162, 306,
    see also discrimination: sexual
  Latina students 228–9
  stereotyping 310
gender studies 53
Germany 86, 302, 303
ghettos 34
Giddy, Davies 45–6
Gillard, Julia 163, 164
graduates
  outcomes measurement 102
  unemployment 6

H

HEFCE *see* Higher Education Funding
  Council for England
HEPI *see* Higher Education Policy
  Institute
habitus 201–2, 209

Halstead, Robert 49
Heffer, Simon 56
The Hidden Curriculum (Snyder) 238
hierarchies 53
  and social class 57
  United States 87
  universities 6, 48, 94
higher education
  contemplating/experiencing 179–85
  cost of 96
  expansion 2–3, 48, 52–5, 131–2,
    150–2
  feminist research perspectives 133–6
  participation 85–9, 141–4
  partnerships 273–91
  purpose 124, 185
  White Paper (2003) 55, 59
  see also polytechnics; universities
Higher Education Act 2004 (UK) 186
Higher Education Contribution
  Scheme (HECS) 157–8
Higher Education Funding Council for
  England (HEFCE) 56, 88
Higher Education Policy (journal) 136–7
Higher Education Policy Institute
  (HEPI) 240
Higher Skills Development at Work
  (Brown) 140
human rights 297–302
  and civil rights 301
  and exclusion 299
  'Learning to live together' seminar
    (Utah, 2010) 300–2
  Universal Declaration of Human
    Rights (UDHR) 306–8
  universities 308–11
  women 299
humanities 132
Hume, Joseph 44

I

identity 33, 193–4, 211, 257–8
  Indigenous peoples 258, 261, 265–6
  Latina students 216, 218, 220, 221,
    222, 229–30, 233
  PGCE students 194–5, 206, 207
  and self 202–3
  social 43
idiolect 202
immigrants 173 *see also* migrants;
  minority ethnic groups
Indians
  aspirations 180–2, 184
  GCSE performance 23
  higher education 19–20, 21t, 27t
  identity 33
  racism 25
  social class 24t

Indigenous peoples 255–6
  Australia 90, 97, 157
    culture 260–6
    identity 258, 261, 265–6
    teacher training 255–68
industrial revolutions 43, 47
Institute of Education 89
intelligence 57
International Federation of Workers'
  Educational Associations 59
Ireland 88

J

Johnson, President Lyndon B. 86–7

K

Kennedy, Dame Helena 278–9, 281

L

Labour Party (UK) 239 *see also* New
  Labour government
leadership 120–1, 122, 123, 125
The Learning Age (DfEE) 276, 282
Learning and Skills Council (LSC) 195
Learning Society Programme (ESRC) 282
Learning to Succeed (DfEE) 276
Life in Classrooms (Jackson) 237–8
Literacy Education 193–212
  community of practice 202–5
  and cultural capital 199–202
  knowledge types 207–10
  Literacy Theories and Frameworks
    module 198–9
  PGCE course 194–8
  reflection and communal
    communicative action 205–7
Literacy Study group 197
local education authorities 54

M

Macpherson Report 211
majority ethnic groups 176 *see also*
  whites
Mansbridge, Albert 50
market fundamentalism 194
mathematics
  and STEM 132, 143, 144
  United States 65, 67–8, 115
medicine 138–9, 144
Merkel, Chancellor Angela 302, 303
middle class
  19th century 44–5, 47, 48
  20th century 48–9
  and advantage 60
  and university admissions policies 56
Midlands Urban Partnership 277–91
  ambivalence 285–8
  data gathering 277

expansion 281–5
formation and early development
  278–81
life course 278f
organisational structures 283f, 284
reinvigoration 288–9
migrants 18, 23–4 *see also* immigrants;
  minority ethnic groups
Mill, James 44–5
Millar, J.P.M. 51
minority ethnic groups 19–28, 85
Australia 90, 97, 157, 255–68
barriers to 4, 17–18
and civic engagement 119
and cultural capital 35
and majority ethnic groups compared
  176
motivation of 26–8
and racism 25–8
and social class 22–4
United Kingdom 29, 173–88
  diversity 174–7
  experience 179–85
  Oxbridge 296
  social inclusion 177–9
United States 29, 112, 114, 121 *see also*
  United States: African Americans;
  Asian Americans;
  Asian-Pacific American students;
  Latina students; Native Americans
see also immigrants; migrants
Morley, Louise 136–7
Moser Report (1999) 200
multiculturalism 302–5
Muslims 20, 25, 175

N

National Audit Office 178
National Council of Labour Colleges
  (NCLC) 51
NEETs (young people not in education,
  employment or training) 183–4
Nelson, Brendan 161–2
neo-liberalism 133–4
New Labour government 43, 56, 141,
  275–6
New Right 54
Newby, Howard 56
norms enforcement 31, 32, 33

O

Obama, President Barack 110, 121
Organisation for Economic Co-
  operation and Development
  (OECD) 6–7, 151
  Education at a Glance 86
  Thematic Review of Tertiary Education 88
outcomes culture 124

*Oxford and Working-Class Education
  Report* (1908) 55
Oxford University
19th century 44, 47, 48, 295, 310
exclusion 297
female students 296, 297
Ruskin College 4
Somerville College 295, 310

P

PGCE *see* Post Graduate Certificate in
  Education
PSI Fourth Survey 25
Pakistanis
aspirations 182–3, 185
cultural capital 28
GCSE performance 23
higher education 18, 21t, 23, 27t, 175
NEET (not in education, employment
  or training) 183
racism 25
social capital 30
social class 24t
parents *see* families
participation, expanding 95–6, 97,
  177–9, 187–8
partnerships 273–91
  Midlands Urban Partnership 277–91
  New Labour and 275–6
  United States 121–2
pedagogies 144, 210
  Literacy 199, 201
Percy, Lord Eustace 51–2, 58
Place, Francis 46
pluralism 309
Pollard, Professor Andrew 140
polytechnics 53, 54
Portugal 86
Post Graduate Certificate in Education
  (PGCE) 194–8
critical reflection in 194, 197
Self and Identity module 203
students' knowledge 194, 199, 200,
  201, 202, 205, 207–10
and teacher identity 206
postmodernism 256–7
power 209
The Price of Admission (Golden) 86

Q

Quality Assurance Agency 249

R

racial discrimination 23, 87, 174 *see also*
  segregation, ethnic
racism 25, 69, 174
rationalisation 156–7
reactionaries 56–8

Reading University College 50
recession 6
relationships 32 *see also* families
religion
   Latina students 227, 230
   Mormonism 300, 306, 307, 308
   universities 44, 45, 310
   see also Muslims
Robbins Report 52
Roberts, Professor Trudie 138–9
role models
   Australia 90
   United States 10, 29, 66, 67, 69, 70, 71,
      72, 74, 223
Ruskin College, Oxford 4
Russell Group universities 6, 53, 178,
   188n2, 296

S

Scholarship Reconsidered (Boyer) 119
scholarships 50, 162
schools
   Australia 100, 101, 151
   Germany 86
   United Kingdom 20–1, 181, 187–8
science
   civic universities 48
   minority ethnic students 67, 68, 72
   women 66
   see also STEM
segregation, ethnic 34, 117
Select Committee on Education and
   Skills 56
Skills for Life 194
Smith, Sidney 44
social class 17
   and educational outcomes 22–4
   and English grammar 200
   and hierarchies 57, 60
   and higher education 4, 50–1, 55, 85
      Australia 90–4, 95, 151–2, 153,
         155–6, 161, 163, 164, 165
      United Kingdom 173, 174, 183, 186
   and participation 95, 137–8, 178,
      179–85
   and social identity 43, 99
   see also aristocracy; middle class;
      working class
social development: ecological theory of
   218, 219f
social engineering 56, 58
social equity: feminist perspective 144–5
social exclusion 4, 5, 34, 55
   and cultural capital 200
   and human rights 297–8
   middle class (19th century) 45
   and partnership working 276
   and racism 22, 25, 174

universities 132, 158–9, 295, 296, 310
social identity 43
social inclusion
   Australia 83–4, 89–105, 163–4
   feminist perspectives 130–1, 144–5
   and widening participation 131–3,
      177–9, 275–6
social justice
   Australia 149–65
   and cultural capital 3–5
   definition 149
   distributive 149
   and higher education 41–60
   recognitive 149
   retributive 149, 150, 165
social mobility 186, 193
   Asians 30, 36, 183
   Australia 150
   community organisations and 34
   Goldthorpe's theory of 22
   and racial discrimination 23
social sciences 132
   feminists and 130–1, 133–6, 141–2
Somerville College, Oxford 295, 310
Sorabji, Cornelia 295
STEM (science, technology, engineering
   and maths) 132, 133, 139, 142, 145
   mathematics and 143
   United States 65–78, 114–16
      funding 76, 77–8
      minority racial/ethnic students
         67–70, 71–4
      policy and practice
         recommendations 76–8
      research limitations/implications
         75–6
      women 66–7, 70–1
Stephenson, the Reverend Nash 46
stereotyping
   gender 66–7, 74, 310
   NEETs (not in education,
      employment or training) 184
   racial 25
      Australia 262, 263–4, 266
      United Kingdom 297, 302
      United States 69, 74–5
students
   assessments 122, 246–8
   belonging, sense of 249
   employment 114–15
   engagement 124
   feedback 237–51, 243–4
      criticism 240–3
      review meetings 244–51
      written 240–4
   grants 121
   international 102–3, 305, 310
   learning 113, 115, 118–21

mature 53
Australia 101, 104, 163
Literacy Education 194–6
United States 110, 111, 113
'non-traditional', definition 12n1
selection 100, 101
social mix 54
Subject Specifications for Teachers of Adult Literacy and Numeracy (DES) 198
subjects 131, 132 *see also* STEM

T

TLRP *see* Economic and Social Research Council (ESRC) Teaching and Learning Research Programme
TUC (Trades Union Congress) 52
targets 20, 89, 100, 103–4
Tawney, R.H. 50–1
teachers
Indigenous 255, 266–7
Australia 255–6, 258–66, 267
United States 256, 267
Literacy 194
and Robbins Report 52
see also tutors
Teaching and Higher Education Act 1998 (UK) 186
Teaching and Learning Research Programme (TLRP) 132
technology-based instruction 113, 115
tests *see* examinations
Thatcher government 53–4
Transactions of the National Association for the Promotion of Social Science 46
tuition fees 5, 161, 186, 187
tutorial system: Literacy students 196–8, 199, 204, 207
tutors
and assessment 247
and feedback 244, 245, 246
role of 210, 249–51
and widening participation 177–8
see also teachers

U

unemployment 6, 53 *see also* NEETs
United Kingdom Standards and Verification Agency 200
United Nations: Vienna World Conference (1993) 299
United States
access 86–8
accountability 122–3
African Americans 68–9, 75, 112, 215
Agricultural Extension Office 117
Alliance for Graduate Education and the Professoriate (AGEP) Program 72, 76
Alverno College, Milwaukee 122
American College Test (ACT) 68
American Educational Research Association (AERA) 134–6
Asian Americans 32, 215, 216
Asian-Pacific American students 112, 114
California public higher education system 116
City University of New York: City College 110
communication 121–2
community-building partnerships 120–1
community colleges 110, 112, 114, 116, 124
Dartmouth College 'Engineering Workshops' 73–4
democracy 109, 116, 117, 118, 119, 120
differentiation 113–14
diversity 109–25
engaged campus movement 117–22
expansion 110–11
feminism 135
G.I. Bill 110
Hispanic students *see* Latina students
immigrants 32, 110–11
K-16 pipelines 123–4
Kellogg Commission 117
Lafayette College POSSE programme 73, 75, 76
Laser Academy, New York 70, 75
Latina students 112, 215–33, 222–9
barriers 217
educational experiences 216–18
expectations 217, 222–7, 228
identity 222, 229–30, 233
mesosphere management 230
STEM (science, technology, engineering and maths) 68–9, 75
learning outcomes 122–3, 124
'Learning to live together' seminar 300–2
majority education 116–18
minority ethnic students 29, 112, 114
see also: African Americans; Asian Americans; Asian-Pacific American students; Latina students; Native Americans
Mormons 300, 306, 307, 308
Morrill Land Grant Act (1862) 116–17
multicultural education 303–4

Napier University student support forum for females (SSF4F) programme 71

National Centre for Education Statistics 115

National Science Foundation (NSF) 66

National Survey of Student Engagement 122

Native Americans 215–16, 256, 267

older students 110, 111, 113

opportunities to learn (OTL) 67–8

racial discrimination 87

racial mix 111–12

Rose-Hulman Institute of Technology 70–1

social capital 30–4

social justice 4

STEM (science, technology, engineering and maths) 65–78, 114–16

student diversity 109–25
  challenges 116–18
  resources 121

universities 6, 113–14, 117

University of California, Riverside 70

University of Maryland, Baltimore County (UMBC): Meyerhoff Scholars Program 71–2, 75, 76

University of Wisconsin-Madison: Women in Science and Engineering (WISE) programme 70, 76

Vietnamese migrants 32

Universal Declaration of Human Rights (UDHR) 306–8

universities
  access to 44, 274, 304
  Australia 6, 103, 150, 158
  Group of Eight (Go8) 92, 98, 100, 101
  civic 48–9, 50
  corporatisation 239
  economic performance 89
  extension courses 4
  funding 3, 54, 160, 162, 186–7, 239 *see also* tuition fees
  future 145
  and globalisation 5–7
  hierarchies 6, 48, 94
  human rights 308–11
  idea of 5
  militarisation 239
  new 193, 274
    benefits 1, 6–7
    definition 188n2
    dropout rates 57
    Million+ group 6
    minority ethnic students 20, 21
    student retention 178

old 21, 274–5 *see also* Cambridge University; Oxford University

Russell Group 6, 53, 178, 188n2, 296

stratification 193

Sullivan Commission 69

support services 248

women 3–4, 150, 295

see also Bristol University; Cambridge University; higher education; Oxford University

University of Birmingham 48

University of London 45

University of Wolverhampton 1

Unleashing Aspiration: The Final Report on the Panel on Fair Access to the Professions (Cabinet Office) 193

V

vocational courses 247

W

WEA *see* Workers Education Association

WETUC *see* Workers Educational Trade Union Committee

The Westminster Review 44–5

whites
  higher education 19t, 20, 21t, 27t
  social class 24t
  see also majority ethnic groups

Willetts, David 129–30, 139

women
  access 274
  Australia 89–90, 135, 150
  courses 53
  feedback 245–51
  higher education 85, 133, 145
  human rights 299
  Latina 215–33
  medicine 138–9
  motivation 26
    STEM (science, technology, engineering and maths) 65, 66–7, 70–1, 74, 75, 76, 77–8, 114
  stereotyping 310
  university entrance
    19th century 295
    Australia 150
    early 20th century 3–4
    ethnic minority 19, 20, 175
  white 228
  see also feminism

Woodhead, Chris 57

Workers Education Association (WEA) 4, 49, 51–2 *see also* International Federation of Workers' Educational Associations

Workers Educational Trade Union
    Committee (WETUC) 51
working class
  education 4, 42–3, 59–60
    19th century 45, 46
    Australia 90–4, 135
    further 280
    higher 49–50, 53, 94, 178, 179–81,
      183, 185
    United States 110, 111, 116, 123
  minority ethnic 173, 174, 180–1, 183,
    185–6, 186
  opportunities 130
  participation 186